T5-AFM-133

General Washington's Correspondence

concerning

The Society of the Cincinnati

HIS EXCELLENCY

GENERAL GEORGE WASHINGTON

Commander-in-Chief of the Continental Army

President General of the Society of the Cincinnati from its institution until his death
Portrait by Gilbert Stuart in Cincinnati Memorial Hall, Exeter, New Hampshire

Published by permission of the
Society of the Cincinnati in the State of New Hampshire

General Washington's Correspondence concerning The Society of the Cincinnati

EDITED BY

LIEUTENANT-COLONEL

EDGAR ERSKINE HUME

President of the Society of the Cincinnati in the State of Virginia and Assistant Secretary General

BALTIMORE

THE JOHNS HOPKINS PRESS

1941

PRINTED IN THE UNITED STATES OF AMERICA
BY J. H. FURST COMPANY, BALTIMORE, MARYLAND

TO

CAPTAIN FRANCIS HUME

OF THE VIRGINIA STATE LINE

ORIGINAL MEMBER OF THE CINCINNATI

AND HIS THRICE-GREAT-GRANDSON,

EDGAR ERSKINE HUME, JR.,

WHO IS MY SON

INTRODUCTION

EVERYONE acquainted with the Society of the Cincinnati knows that General Washington was its first President. That he was a very active head of this, the oldest military society in America, is less well appreciated. He did not consider that office a nominal one. He felt it his duty to carry on correspondence with European and other officers seeking admission, with the heads of the branches in the several States and in France, and, most important of all, with political and military leaders of this country and France. When the Cincinnati was attacked by politicians he defended it and at the same time sought to have its Institution so modified that criticism would be obviated. All of these objectives are reflected in the letters he wrote and those that he received.

Never before have all these letters been published, not excepting during the Washington Bicentennial of 1932 nor in the monumental *Writings of Washington,* edited by the late Dr. John Clement Fitzpatrick. All of the earlier compilations of Washington's letters and other writings embrace only what he himself wrote. The letters that he received are not included. The completion of Fitzpatrick's work is delayed through lack of Congressional appropriation and the volumes for 1783-1799, the years of Washington's connection with the Cincinnati, remain in the proof stage only. But even when they ultimately appear they will, like the works of Jared Sparks, President of Harvard College (twelve volumes, 1834-1837) and Worthington Chauncey Ford, Chief of the Division of Manuscripts of the Library of Congress (fourteen volumes, 1889-1893), embrace only half of the General's correspondence—the half that he wrote himself.

The archives of the Society of the Cincinnati are rich in Washingtoniana. Treasured jealously through the hundred and fifty-eight years of the Cincinnati's existence, they are a valuable and almost untouched source of data on an important phase of early American history. Since 1930 these documents have been deposited in the Division of Manuscripts, Library of Congress, under an agreement by which they may be used only with the Society's permission. But few students have had the privilege of examining these muniments. The present work is the first that the Society itself has published, with its archives as a basis.

The other sources are, first the *Washington Papers,* the letters received by General Washington, the *Washington Letter Books,* the retained copies of the letters that he wrote. Both of these series are in the Division of Manuscripts of the Library of Congress. Secondly, the archives of each of the State Societies of the Cincinnati and the branch in France. Lastly, there are in various libraries throughout the country and in a few private collections, a small number of letters written by or to General Washington. An earnest effort has been made to secure copies of all such material.

The arrangement is chronological, footnotes being used to link a letter and its reply, and to show other connections. Introductory paragraphs give the reader the background of some of the letters.

The Supplement consists of brief biographies of those with whom General Washington corresponded about the Society of Cincinnati. To the Secretary General, Mr. Francis Apthorp Foster, the editor is indebted for great help in the preparation of such biographies, particularly those of French officers, some of whom could not have been identified otherwise. He has devoted himself for years to a study of the French volunteers and other French officers who served in the American War of Independence.

The editor is grateful to Dr. St. George Leakin Sioussat, Chief of the Division of Manuscripts, Library of Congress, for suggestions and for permission to use the material in his charge. Two members of his staff, Miss Vastine and Mr. Eaton, during their free hours made transcripts of numerous documents. The Rev. Jules A. Baisnée of Catholic University, Washington, has most kindly read the proof of the letters in French, which is usually as archaic as is the English of those written by Americans of that period. Contemporary translations, in many instances attached to the originals, have been reproduced without change. The editor has made translations of other French papers.

The book is published by the Johns Hopkins Press on behalf of the Society of the Cincinnati in the State of Virginia. It forms the official souvenir of the General Meeting of the Cincinnati, Richmond, Virginia, 15-17 May 1941.

EDGAR ERSKINE HUME

Carlisle Barracks, Pennsylvania
1 May 1941

SKETCH OF THE SOCIETY OF THE CINCINNATI

FROM the earliest there has been a tendency among men who have served together in war, to form associations, when such wars were over, for the purpose of continuing the bonds, which, in days of stress, had been cemented with their blood. The greater the hardships suffered in war, the more lasting have been such ties and the more marked the affection in which veterans have held their society.

During the Revolution the American officers of the Continental Line, forerunner of the present Regular Army, had seen their French Allies wearing the crosses of the Royal and Military of Saint-Louis, and of the Order of Military Merit, conferred for attainments.[1] British officers captured, or who were met by the Americans after the Peace, wore the Most Honourable Order of the Bath, and other decorations of military merit. It was but natural that Americans should desire something of the kind to mark their long service to their country.

It appears from an entry in Jefferson's diary, 16 March 1788, that Major-General Henry Knox, Washington's Chief of Artillery, in a conversation with Adams as early as 1776, expressed a "wish for some ribbon to wear in his hat or in his button-hole, to be transmitted to his descendants as a badge and proof that he had fought in defence of their liberties. He spoke in such precise terms as showed that he had revolved it in his mind before."

Proposals for the creation of "a society to be formed by the American officers and to be called the Cincinnati," were drawn up in Knox's handwriting and dated "Westpoint, 15 April 1783." These "proposals" having been communicated to the several regiments, each appointed an officer, who in conjunction with the general officers, met at the "Cantonment of the American Army on Hudson's River," on 10 May 1783, to consider them. This gathering was held in the "Temple," the large structure, officially known as the "Public Build-

[1] The Royal and Military Order of Saint-Louis was instituted in 1693 by Louis XIV, for military merit. It was conferred only on Catholic officers. In 1759, Louis XV founded the Order of Military Merit for Protestant officers. Otherwise eligibility for the two orders was identical. That of Saint-Louis was suspended from a red ribbon and that of Military Merit from a ribbon of dark blue. The latter was conferred on John Paul Jones. Later the Order of Military Merit was merged in that of Saint-Louis, and requirements as to religion removed.

ing," which had been built as a place of worship and other gatherings of the soldiers. On the 13th, the committee which had been appointed to revise the "proposals" met in the Verplanck Manson, General de Steuben's headquarters, at Fishkill and accepted the "Institution," as it was called.

The name of the society was taken from that of the illustrious Roman general, Lucius Quintus Cincinnatus, who at the call of country left his farm and led the armies of Rome to victory, and when that victory had been achieved, returned again to his plough, refusing the honors proferred him by a grateful Senate—the ideal of Roman simplicity and a model to his countrymen.

The Society of the Cincinnati thus came into being without reference to political questions, four years before the meeting of the Convention to frame the Constitution of the United States, and before political parties existed. At the meeting on May 13th it was unanimously resolved to ask General Washington to become the President General, and a committee consisting of Generals Heath, Steuben and Knox, was appointed formally to notify General Washington of his election. The Commander in Chief, who in his own conduct had so strikingly resembled Cincinnatus of old, immediately accepted the honor.

It was further voted to recognize members, the officers of the French Navy and Army who had served in America, giving them the right to organize a branch of the Society in France. All officers were required, upon signing its rolls, to contribute one month's pay to maintain the society and aid members in need. To be eligible for membership, one must have served for three years in the Continental Army or to have been in service to the end of the war. Later the officers of the Navy were also admitted.

The Eagle or Badge of the Cincinnati

The Institution thus describes the Eagle or badge of the Society of the Cincinnati:

"The Society shall have an Order, by which its members shall be known and distinguished, which shall be a medal of gold, of a proper size to receive the emblems, and suspended by a deep blue ribbon, two inches wide, edged with white, descriptive of the union of America and France, viz.: The principal figure *Cincinnatus*, three Senators presenting him with a sword and other military ensigns—on a field in the back-ground, his wife standing at the door of their cottage—near it a plough and implements of husbandry. Round the whole, *Omnia Reliquit Servare Rempublicam.* On the reverse, Sun rising—a city with open gates, and vessels entering the port—Fame crowning Cincinnatus with a wreath, inscribed *Virtutis Præmium.* Below, hands joined, supporting a heart, with the motto: *Esto Perpetua.* Round the whole, *Societas Cincinnatorum Instituta* A. D. 1783."

The design having been approved on 13 May, the meeting on 19 June 1783, charged Major Pierre-Charles L'Enfant, Continental Army, the French engineer who was later to plan the city of Washington, with the duty of their procurement. He was requested by General Washington to attend to the preparation of the Eagles in Paris. L'Enfant accepted the task, having on 10 June 1783 written to General de Steuben enclosing designs for the medal. He added, however, that medals in Europe were the rewards for artists, artisans or religious bodies. On the other hand the bald eagle, a bird peculiar to America might better be adopted as the Society's emblem, and he enclosed two designs, one of which was adopted. The Eagle bears on its breast a medallion on which, enameled in colors, are the emblems described in the Institution. Grasped in the Eagle's talons are golden olive branches, and above its head and olive wreath enameled green by which it is suspended from the ribbon. The ribbon is of watered silk, light blue edged with white.

L'Enfant had the Eagles made in France and returned with a supply of them in time for the first General Meeting of the Society in Philadelphia in May 1784. His account for his expenses form the basis of a number of General Washington's letters.

Benjamin Franklin, then in France, wrote to his daughter, Mrs. Sarah Bache, criticizing the Latin of the motto and objecting to the Eagle as looking too much like a turkey, adding:

"For my own part, I wish the bald eagle had not been chosen as the representative of our country; he is a bird of bad moral character; he does not get his living honestly; you may have seen him perched on some dead tree, where, too lazy to fish for himself, he watches the labor of the fishing-hawk; and, when that diligent bird has at length taken a fish, and is bearing it to his nest for the support of his mate and young ones, the bald eagle pursues him and takes it from him. . . . Besides he is a coward. . . . He is therefore by no means a proper emblem for the brave and honest Cincinnati of America, who have driven the king-birds from our country. . . . I am, on this account, not displeased that the figure is not known as a bald eagle, but looks more like a turkey. For, in truth, the turkey is in comparison a much more respectable bird, and with all a true original native of America. . . . He is besides (though a little vain and silly, it is true, but not the worst emblem for that), a bird of courage, and would not hesitate to attack a grenadier of the British Guard, who should presume to invade the farm-yard with a *red* coat on."

General Washington procured one of the Eagles for himself and six for his principal Aides-de-Camp, to which some of the letters refer. Of yet more interest is the Eagle set in diamonds that was presented to General Washington by the Count d'Estaing on behalf of the officers of the French Navy. This precious emblem was presented at General Washington's death, by his widow to Major-General Hamilton, his successor as President General. His heir gave it to the third President General, Major-General Charles Cotesworth Pinckney, now best remembered for his words, "Millions for defense, but not one cent for tribute." General Pinckney presented it to the Society and ever since it has served as the badge of office of the Presidents General.

The Eagle of the Order of the Cincinnati is one of the oldest decorations in the world, if we count only those which have remained unchanged. The British orders have all undergone revision, and often radical change. The orders of the Kings of France, Spain, Portugal, as well as those of the Holy Roman Empire, Russia, and the once independent German States, have all disappeared. Newer governments have created their orders since the Cincinnati was instituted. In Europe only the Order of the Elephant of Denmark is unchanged in statutes from a period anterior to the institution of the Cincinnati. No country outside Europe has an order anything like so old as the Cincinnati.

The Diploma of the Cincinnati

The Diploma of the Society of the Cincinnati was, like the Eagle, designed by Major L'Enfant. The Diploma is thus described in Lossing's "Pictorial Field-Book of the Revolution:"

"The design represents American Liberty as a strong man armed, bearing in one hand the Union Flag, and in the other a naked sword. Beneath his feet are British flags, and a broken spear, shield, and chain. Hovering by his side is the eagle, our national emblem, from whose talons the lightning of destruction is flashing upon the British lion. Britannia, with the crown falling from her head, is hastening toward a boat to escape to a fleet, which denoted the departure of British power from our shores. Upon a cloud, on the right, is an angel blowing a trumpet, from which flutters a loose scroll. Upon the scroll are the sentences: *Palam nuntiata libertatis A. D. 1776. Fœdus sociale cum Gallia, An. D. 1778. Pax: libertas parta, An. D. 1783.* "Independence declared, A. D. 1776. Treaty of Alliance with France declared A. D. 1778. Peace: independence obtained, A. D. 1783."

To the right and left are depicted the obverse and reverse of the medallion described in the Institution (see page 6).

The diploma, following L'Enfant's design, was drawn by Augustin-Louis La Belle (1757-1841), a member of a family of celebrated artists. The copperplate was engraved by Jean-Jacques-André Le Veau (1729-1786), one of the best known engravers of the day. The plate, which is in the Society's Archives, is still used.

The diplomas were signed by General Washington as President, and by General Knox as Secretary. The wording is given on page 164. It was customary for the diplomas to be signed in blank by these two officers and then sent to the State Secretaries for completion and issue to members. Several of the letters are reproduced in this collection.

There are in existence several provisional certificates of membership, signed by General Washington before the completion of the diplomas, see pages 20, 21, 30, 45 and 46.

Early Opposition to the Cincinnati

Hardly was the institution of the Society of the Cincinnati announced before there was published a pamphlet by an eccentric South Carolina Judge, Ædanus Burke, attacking it violently. Writing under the name " Cassius " he issued " Considerations on the Society or Order of Cincinnati; lately instituted by the Major-Generals, Brigadier-Generals, and other officers of the American Army. Proving that it creates a Race of Hereditary Patricians or Nobility. Interspersed with remarks on its Consequences to the Freedom and Happiness of the Republic. Addressed to the People of South Carolina, and other Representatives, by Cassius, Philadelphia, 1783." This lengthy title more or less sums up the grounds for Burke's fears. It formed the basis for a similar attack on the Cincinnati by the Count de Mirabeau in France, for all that his own brother, the Viscount de Mirabeau, was an Original Member. Mirabeau's book went through a French, a British, a German, and three American editions. He advanced few arguments of his own, and was strongly taken to task by Burke for having stolen his thunder.

Burke had served in the Continental Army, but his service was not long enough to qualify him for membership, which may have been a factor in his jealousy, though he stoutly denied this and indeed offered to fight a duel with anybody so stating.

Burke's pamphlet served to arouse a number of opponents in the Society in high places. In nearly every case these were themselves ineligible to membership. Statesmen who had rendered military service, even though not enough to qualify for membership, for instance John Marshall and Edmund Randolph, were not hostile to the Cincinnati. The chief enemies of the new Order were the Adamses, Jefferson, Jay and Gerry. LaFayette wrote from Paris to John Adams that he had heard with regret that the Cincinnati had been termed by Adams a "*French Blessing,*" against which Adams was said to be very violent. Adams replied that this was not true for he "was not a violent man." But he added that the new order "instituted by private gentlemen," is "against our confederation, against the constitutions of the several States, against the spirits of our governments and the genius of our people." To Charles Spencer he wrote that the Cincinnati "is the first step taken to deface the beauty of our temple of liberty." John Adams even tried to show that Cincinnatus himself had been over rated!

Sam Adams wrote to John that the Cincinnati was become very unpopular in Boston, while John Quincy Adams wrote in glee to his father, commenting on a recent election in that State: "Mr. Adams [meaning Samuel] has been much opposed to General Lincoln, and had sufficient influence to prevent his being chosen even a councilor, because he is a member of the Society of the Cincinnati." He added that the Society "is daily gaining strength, and will infallibly become a body dangerous, if not fatal to the Constitution." John Jay wrote to Gouverneur Morris that the Cincinnati "does not either do credit to those who formed and patronized it, or to those who suffered it." In another letter Jay said that if the Cincinnati "took well in the States, [he] would not care if the Revolutionary War had succeeded or not." Samuel Adams wrote to Elbridge Gerry that he was "happy in having adopted an opinion of the Cincinnati so similar to what I found yours to be."

Most influential of the Society's enemies was Thomas Jefferson. He wrote to Gates that there was opposition to the Cincinnati: "the division is precisely into civil and military." He felt, he said, that since the Congress had created no orders, that the members of the Cincinnati should not have created one. Jefferson's most lengthy objections were addressed to General Washington himself, as the letters show. To James Madison he wrote that he was opposed to orders in general, and particularly "the society of the Cincinnati, a *self-created* one, carving out for itself hereditary distinctions, lowering over Constitution eternally, meeting together in all parts of the Union, periodically, with closed doors, accumulating a capital in their separate treasury, corresponding secretly & regularly, & of which society the very persons denouncing the democrats are themselves the fathers, founders & high officers. Their sight must be perfectly dazzled by the glittering of crowns & coronets, not to see the extravagance of the proposition. . . . I have never heard, or heard of, a single expression or opinion which did not condemn it as an inexcusable aggression." He advised the members to "distribute their funds, renounce their existence," and "melt up their eagles."

All this opposition caused some of the State legislatures to consider action against the Cincinnati, though no such steps were ever taken. Charles William Janson, a British visitor, reported this criticism of the Cincinnati and told of a clergyman who held that the Eagle being the emblem of a heathen deity, Jupiter, it might properly be regarded as an idol. He further "shewed from the scripture that in the last times idoliters were to spring up, and concluded by an insinuation that this Order of the Cincinnati might be the Gog and Magog of the Apocalypse!"

Burke was not the only eccentric judge who attacked the Cincinnati. Judge Hugh Henry Brackenridge of Pennsylvania, had served in the Revolution, but did not render service adequate for membership in the Society. His book "Modern Chivalry," which though now forgotten was immensely popular in its day, was based on his poem "The Modern Chevalier." In it there is an attack in verse against the Cincinnati, covering some twenty-five printed pages. It is written in doggerel metre, forced rhyme, and is generally tedious in character, being a sort of imitation of the style of Butler's *Hudibras.*

General Washington was naturally troubled at all this opposition and his letters show his efforts to learn the opinions of the country's leaders as to possible dangers. He urged that the first general meeting of the Society, held in Philadelphia in May of 1784, be well attended so that the matter could be fully considered. That meeting was, in fact, a full one and, though the members did not feel that they had done anything unpatriotic in forming the Cincinnati, they preferred to change the Institution rather than suffer blame from any quarter. Accordingly they voted to delete the provisions concerning hereditary membership. This action was not ratified by the State Soiceties and so the Society, hereditary principle and all, has come down to us unchanged.

By the time of the adoption of the Constitution of the United States opposition had about ceased. It was impossible for the country long to fear a body of old soldiers headed by the Father of his Country himself. There was even a reaction in public feeling in favor of the Cincinnati. In 1798, when war again threatened, an ancient enemy of the Cincinnati, John Adams, was President of the United States. His letters to several State Societies of the Cincinnati express his gratitude for their patriotic sentiments, and his faith in them. To the Rhode Island Cincinnati he wrote, "I trust that, by the blessing of Heaven, and the valor of our citizens, under their ancient and glorious leader, you will be able to transmit your fairest inheritance to posterity." To the South Carolina Cincinnati he wrote: "When the Cincinnati of South Carolina pledge their lives, their fortunes, and their sacred honor, I believe no man will doubt their integrity." (*Cf.* E. E. Hume, Early Opposition to the Society of the Cincinnati, *Americana,* 1936, xxx, 597-638).

Historians have frequently stated that the *Tammany Society* or *Columbian Order* was founded for the purpose of opposing the Cincinnati. Quite the reverse is the case. The Tammany Society of New York, one of the many bodies of that name, was made up of patriotic men, most of them ineligible to membership in the Cincinnati, but inspired by laudible purposes. At the meetings of each Society in New York it was the custom to drink a toast to the other. In 1790 the *Sagamore,* or president, of the Tammany Society, sent to the Baron de Steuben, President of the Cincinnati, a peace-pipe which he had been directed by the Tammany braves to transmit "as a pledge of that friendship which they wish to cultivate with the New York Society of the Cincinnati." This was, of course, long before Tammany became interested in politics. General Washington, President General of the Cincinnati, was made Honorary Sagamore of the Tammany Society (*Cf.* E. E. Hume, The Society of the Cincinnati and the Tammany Society, *New York Genealogical and Biographical Record*, 1937, lxviii, 45-50).

In France opposition to the Cincinnati during the Terror took a more violent turn, as will be described presently.

The Society of the Cincinnati in France

The Society of the Cincinnati was immediately popular in France, where it was known as *L'Ordre de Cincinnatus.* Early letters of Washington to the French military and naval commanders express the Society's desire that they accept membership. It was decided that French officers of the grade of Colonel or higher would be eligible, this seemed to disregard the naval officers of corresponding rank, but all was soon put to rights by the Society. Several of Washington's letters bear on this apparent oversight. French officers who had served in the American Army were eligible on the same basis as American officers. (i. e. three years as officer, etc.). The Institution itself made seven senior French officers members, *viz* the Chevalier de La Luzerne, Minister Plenipotentiary; the Sieur Gérard, late Minister Plenipotentiary; the Count d'Estaing, the Count de Grasse, the Count de Barras, the Chevalier des Touches, and the Count de Rochambeau.

On 7 January 1784 two meetings of newly admitted French members were held in Paris simultaneously. The officers who had served in the French land and sea forces met at the house of the Count de Rochambeau in the rue Cherche-Midi. The officers who had served under commissions from the Continental Congress met at the house of the Marquis de LaFayette in the rue de Bourbon, and after considering the claims of a number of officers, proceeded in a body to the house of the Count de Rochambeau to unite with the other French Cincinnati there in session. In the bicentennial year of Washington's birth plaques were dedicated at the former residence of the Count de Rochambeau 40 rue du Cherche-Midi, to mark the birth of the French branch of the Cincinnati. On 8 January, 1784, LaFayette wrote from Paris to General Knox:

" Our Association meets with great success. On Thursday next a sufficient number of Eagles will be made to answer immediate purposes. I intend inviting all American officers to my house, and to conduct them in a body, with our regimentals to the Generals of the French Army, to whom we will present the marks of the Association. You will receive many applications relative to the brotherhood" (Archives of the General Society).

LaFayette was right. The Society's records contain a great number of letters of application, many from French officers whose services had not qualified them for admission to the Order. Many wrote directly to General Washington, as the Society's archives show.

The French members included, as the Baron de Contenson says, " the very *élite* of the French nobility." Among them were Marshal of France the Count de Rochambeau, Commander of the French Auxiliary Army in America; Admiral the Count de Grasse, naval commander without whom there could have been no victory at Yorktown; Lieutenant-General the Count d'Estaing, Commander of the French Coöperating Army in America, first President of the French Cincinnati, who perished on the guillotine; General the Count d'Aboville, commandant of artillery in the French Expeditionary Force, who died in the Restoration; Count d'Autichamp, father of one of the principal chiefs of the Vendée; Vice-Admiral Count de Bougainville, the celebrated navigator, for whom the flower *Bougainvillea* is named; Prince Victor de Broglie, Deputy of Alsace to the States General, who perished on the guillotine and whose descendant and representative, the Duke de Briglie, is now President of *La Société des Cincinnati de France*; the Duke de Castres, son of the Minister of Marine; Berthier, future Prince de Wagram and one of Napoleon's generals; the Marquis de Chastellux, one of the celebrated philosophers of the eighteenth century and an "Immortal" of the French Academy; the Marquis du Châtelet who during the Revolution poisoned himself in prison, as did also his friend Condorcet; the Count de Custine, General in Chief during the French Revolution, who died on the guillotine; the Duke de Damas; five members of the great Irish noble family of Dillon; General Aubert du Bayet, later Ambassador; the Count de Fersen of Sweden, who made such heroic efforts to rescue Queen Marie Antoinette; the navigator Fleuriot de Langle; the Duke de Lauzun, later Duke de Biron, General in Chief of the Armies of the Republic; the three brothers de Lameth; Colonel the Viscount de Mirabeau, brother of the arch enemy of the Cincinnati; Admiral the Count de Kersaint, Deputy to the Convention, who perished on the guillotine; the Duke de Montmorency, the future Academician and Minister of Foreign Affairs under the Restoration; the Marquis de la Tour du Pin, Prefect of the Empire; Captain the Viscount des Cars who was killed at the battle of Les Saintes; the Marquis de Mac Mahon; Lieutenant-General the Baron de Montesquieu, grandson of one of France's greatest thinkers; the great La Motte-Picquet; the Viscount de Noailles, brother-in-law of LaFayette and Deputy to the Assembly and later hero of a famous naval engagement; the Count de Ségur, later Ambassador and Grand Master of Ceremonies of Napoleon; the Bailli de Suffren, one of the greatest sailors of the eighteenth century, Admiral of the Fleets of the Sovereign Military Order of Malta and the Order's Ambassador to the French Court; the Marquis and the Count de Saint-Simon; Colonel the Marquis de Pange, who fell in Vendée; General the Count de Tallyrand-Périgord; Lieutenant-General the Marquis de Bouillé, Governor of the Antilles; the Count de Vioménil, Marshal of France under the Restoration; and many more. One of the first hereditary members admitted in France was the son of Major-General the Baron de Kalb, who was mortally wounded at the battle of Camden, 1780.

His Most Christian Majesty, Louis XVI, gave his officers permission for his officers to become members of the Cincinnati and wear the Eagle, though at that no foreign decoration, save the Order of the Golden Fleece, could be worn in France. Some of the applications for membership of French officers, now in the General Society's Archives, are accompanied by documents, bearing the King's sign manual, attesting their rank and services. (See page 111 *et seq.*).

The Revolution caused dispersion of the members of the *Ordre de Cincinnatus* in France. Although the National Assembly, by decree of 19 June 1790, suppressed all titles of nobility, orders, liveries, and armorial bearings, and thus prevented further bestowal of French orders of Knighthood, the Order of the Cincinnati seems to have been exempted from the provisions of the decree. As late as February, 1792, so great was the desire for membership, that the Standing Committee submitted to the King, through the Minister of War, the names of a selected list of applicants who had served with distinction during the American War and who had been promoted in recognition of such service. This list, personally indorsed by the King on 3 February 1792, was his last act in connection with the Cincinnati.

But amidst the whirlwind of the Revolution, in which so many members of the Cincinnati perished on the scaffold, there came a time when possession of the coveted Eagle became a great danger. Desmoulins in his attack on LaFayette cited his membership in the Cincinnati among his "crimes."

At the Restoration of 1814 membership in the Cincinnati was again authorized, and a great many applications were made for admission. Preliminary measures looking towards the complete revival of the Order in France were being made during the reign of Louis-Philippe, when the *coup d'état* of 2 December 1851 induced a postponement. From that time on there were efforts to restore the French branch, but only in 1923 was it fully revived as the fourteenth Society. It had, at the outbreak of the World War of 1939, one of the largest memberships of any constituent Society of the Cincinnati. (*Cf.* Baron de Contenson, *La Société des Cincinnati de France et la Guerre d'Amérique,* Paris, 1934; E. E. Hume, LaFayette and the Society of the Cincinnati, *Institut Français de Washington,* 1934).

Though LaFayette declined the Legion of Honor on Napoleon's offer, thirty-three original members of the French Society were decorated with that order. (*Cf.* E. E. Hume, The Order of the Cincinnati in France and Original Members who were Légionnaires, *Légion d'Honneur,* New York, October, 1930, i, 37-49).

The City of Cincinnati is Named

In 1787, Major-General Arthur St. Clair, President of the State Society of the Cincinnati of Pennsylvania, was appointed Governor of the Northwest Territory. He arrived at *Losantiville,* the chief city, on 2 January 1790. He named the county in which it was located *Hamilton County,* in honor of Major-General Alexander Hamilton, Secretary of the Treasury, and a few years later to become the second President General of the Cincinnati. In the following year the name of the town was changed from Losantiville to *Cincinnati* by General St. Clair in honor of the Society, for many of the original members had removed to what is now the Ohio metropolis. There was at first a question as to the form of the name which the city should bear. Judge John Cleves Symmes wrote to a member of the New Jersey Cincinnati, Captain Jonathan Dayton, for whom another Ohio city was named:

"Having mentioned Cincinnata, I beg you, sir, you will inquire of the literati in Jersey whether Cincinnat*a* or Cincinnat*i* be most proper. The design we had in giving that name to the place was in honor of the Order, and to denote the chief place of their residence; and so far as my little acquaintance with cases and genders extends, I think the name of a town should terminate in the feminine gender where it is not perfectly neuter. Cincinnati is the title of the order of knighthood, and can not, I think, be the place where the knights of the order dwell. I have frequent combats in this country on the subject, because most men spell it with *ti,* when I always do with *ta.*"

But "the i's had it" and the city bears, without change, the name of the Order, though sometimes the name is pronounced as though Symmes had had his way. (*Cf.* E. E. Hume, The Naming of the City of Cincinnati, *Ohio Archæoligical and Historical Quarterly,* January, 1935, xliv, no. 1, 81-91).

General Meetings of the Cincinnati

The meeting of the officers at which the Cincinnati was instituted, voted to have the first general meeting in 1784. President General Washington chose Philadelphia, the capital of the country, as the place of the meeting and presided at its sessions. Since that time General Meetings have been held triennially, being known in the Society as "Triennials." Except a meeting in Washington in 1802, the General Meetings were all held in Philadelphia until 1848, the dates being: 1784, 1787, 1788, 1790, 1791, 1793, 1796, 1799, 1800, 1805, 1811, 1812, 1825, 1829, 1832, 1835, 1838, 1839, 1844, and 1848. There after the meetings have been held as follows: New York, 1851; Baltimore, 1854; Charleston, 1855; Trenton, 1856; Philadelphia, 1860; New York, 1863; Trenton, 1866; Baltimore, 1869; Boston, 1872; New York, 1875; Philadelphia, 1878; Charleston, 1881; Princeton, 1884; Newport, 1887; Baltimore, 1890; Boston, 1893; Philadelphia, 1896; New York, 1899; Hartford, 1902; Richmond, 1905;

Charleston, 1908; Newport, 1911; Baltimore, 1914; Asheville, 1917; Exeter, 1920; Wilmington (Delaware), 1923; Princeton, 1926; Boston, 1929; Philadelphia, 1932; New York, 1935; Hartford, 1938; Richmond, 1941.

"The Rule of 1854"

The General Meeting of the Cincinnati held in Baltimore in 1854 adopted an important rule of eligibility. It was voted that officers of the army (Continental Line and State Line) and the navy of the Revolution who had been eligible to membership in the Society but who never exercised their privilege of joining, could nevertheless be represented by their heirs under the law of primogeniture. This rule was approved by all the State Societies and became immediately effective. Later the State Society of the Cincinnati of Pennsylvania rescinded this rule and has not since admitted descendants of officers who were not original members, with the exception of officers who died in service. The "Rule of 1854" is in effect in all other branch Societies of the Cincinnati.

Revival of Dormant State Societies

The Society of the Cincinnati in the States of Massachusetts, New York, New Jersey, Pennsylvania, Maryland and South Carolina have had a continuous existence. Those of the other original thirteen States and in France became dormant for one reason or another, some during the period of the opposition to the Cincinnati. All branch societies have been revived and now flourish. The dates of such revivals are: Rhode Island, 1881; Connecticut, 1888; Delaware, 1895; Virginia, 1886; North Carolina, 1896; Georgia, 1899; and France, 1925.

Work of the Society

The Society of the Cincinnati does not exist only for the purpose of preserving the friendships formed by the founders during the days of storm and stress of the Revolution. It seeks to transmit to posterity their ideals of service, of sacrifice and of Americanism. The funds of the Cincinnati have been generously expended for these purposes. The Pennsylvania Cincinnati erected a bronze statue of General Washington at the entrance to Fairmount Park, Philadelphia, at the expense of a quarter of a million dollars. It is perhaps the most effective equestrian statue of Washington in the country. The Virginia Cincinnati gave their entire fund, about twenty-five thousand dollars, to establish a chair of mathematics at Washington College (now Washington and Lee University). It has also given ten thousand dollars to the Virginia

Military Institute. The New Hampshire Society presents annually medals for academic attainment at the Phillips Exeter Academy. That Society also maintains as a public museum the historic Gilman House at Exeter, New Hampshire. Nearly all of the State Societies of the Cincinnati have contributed to the education of the descendants of Revolutionary soldiers. The Virginia Society presents medals and cash prizes at the Virginia Military Institute, the University of Virginia, and the College of William and Mary. The Society as a whole is sponsoring public addresses on patriotic topics, with radio broadcasts, etc. The Society's Headquarters, Anderson House, Washington, is open to visitors, particularly school-children, the museum feature being stressed. The French Society of the Cincinnati has been given two rooms in the Library at Versailles, formerly the Foreign Office, where the treaty of alliance between France and the United States was signed in 1778. There they maintain a museum of material pertaining to the American Revolution.

Privileges of the Society

The Society of the Cincinnati has been given precedence over other military and hereditary societies at the White House, and its representatives have taken official part in such events as the Yorktown Centennial, 1881; the Yorktown Sesquicentennial, 1931; the burial of Major L'Enfant in Arlington Cemetery; the dedication of the monuments to Washington and other American and foreign Revolutionary leaders in the national capital; the ceremonies in the House of Representatives marking the centenary of LaFayette's death, etc. The Regulations of the United States Army, Navy and Marine Corps all authorize the wearing of the Eagle of the Cincinnati on the uniform, all in accord with an Act of Congress.

Headquarters and Museum of the Society of the Cincinnati

For more than a century and a half the Society of the Cincinnati had no permanent place in which to keep its records and other valuable historical material. The Secretaries General, in succession, were charged with the care of the records. Finally the records were stored in a safety vault in New York until their deposit in the Library of Congress in 1930 on loan for safekeeping. The Society was unable to carry out the patriotic and historical work for which it came into being as desired by General Washington and the other founders. Finally, through the munificent legacy of a member an appropriate headquarters and museum was obtained.

Captain Larz Anderson (1866-1937) sometime United States Minister to Belgium and Ambassador to Japan, requested in his will that his beautiful home at 2118 Massachusetts Avenue, Northwest, Washington, D. C., be presented to the Society. Mrs. Anderson complied with his desire and the Society now has possession of the building, known as Anderson House. It serves as headquarters and museum. Already important gifts have been made, since there is now adequate space for safe keeping of such material. The Society is beginning an extensive educational campaign, by means of lectures and radio presentations, Anderson House serving as headquarters for research and presentation. The building is open without charge to the visiting public.

Famous Original Members

Besides Washington himself, some of the leaders of American independence who helped to institute the Cincinnati were: Hamilton, LaFayette, Greene, Steuben, Benjamin Lincoln, Knox, both Pinckneys, John Paul Jones, McDougall, Kościuszko, Mifflin, Gates, Putnam, Schuyler, "Lighthorse Harry" Lee, Monroe, Moultre, Sullivan, Anthony Wayne, St. Clair, Morgan, Muhlenberg, Weedon, Eustis, Huntington, Trumbull, Clinton, Dayton, Tilton, Smallwood, McIntosh, Habersham, Howard, Scott, Clark (of the Lewis and Clark Expedition), Bland, Barry, and McIntosh. There were about 2000 original members in all.

Distinguished Hereditary Members

It is not possible to give a lengthy list but the roster has included such statesmen as President Franklin Pierce; Secretaries of State Hamilton Fish and Edward Livngston; such soldiers as General March; such sailors as Admiral Hillary Jones; such churchmen as James DeWolf Perry, Presiding Bishop of the Episcopal Church; such engineers as General Lytle Brown, Chief of Engineers of the Army; such architects as Cass Gilbert, who built our Supreme Court Building and Charles A. Coolidge; such archæologists as Herbert Winlock, Director of the Metropolitan Museum; such jurists as Justice Oliver Wendell Holmes; and so on.

In all among members of the Society of the Cincinnati there have been fifteen Presidents of the United States, fourteen Secretaries of State; thirteen Secretaries of War; six Secretaries of the Treasury; four Attorneys General; four Postmasters General; six Secretaries of the Navy; twenty Generals-in-Chief or Chiefs of Staff of the Army; six Justices of the Supreme Court; three Speakers of the House of Representatives; seventy-eight American Ambassadors and Ministers, as well as numerous Senators, Governors and other important office bearers. Nine Signers of the Declaration of Independence and twenty-seven of the Framers of the Constitution of the United States were members of the Society.

Honorary Members

The Institution states:

" As there are, and will at all times be, men in their respective States, eminent for their abilities and patriotism, whose views may be directed to the same laudable objects as those of the Cincinnati, it shall be a rule to admit such characters as honorary members, for their own lives only: Provided always, that the number of Honorary Members, in each State, does not exceed a ratio of one to four of the officers or their descendants."

Under this provision some of the most noted men of this and other countries have been elected to honorary membership, including Franklin, Gouverneur Morris, Paca, Perry, Bainbridge, Winfield Scott, Decatur, Zachary Taylor (son of an original member), Webster, Grant, Sherman, Farragut, Cleveland, Dewey, Schofield, Benjamin Harrison, McKinley, Woodrow Wilson, Newton Baker, Leonard Wood, Pershing, both Roosevelts, Cordel Hull, General Marshall, Taft, and others. Of the fifteen Presidents of the United States who have been members of the Cincinnati, Washington and Monroe were original members, and Pierce who was an hereditary member. Among the foreign honorary members, besides distinguished French officers elected in the early days of the Society there have been: Marshals Joffre, Foch, and Pétain, President Loubet of France, the present Crown Prince of Sweden, French Ambassadors Jusserand, Daeschner, Claudel and Saint-Quentin, and British Ambassador, Sir Ronald Lindsay.

Presidents General of the Cincinnati.

1783-1941

1783 — General George Washington of Virginia.
1800 — Major-General Alexander Hamilton of New York.
1805 — Major-General Charles Cotesworth Pinckney of South Carolina.
1825 — Major-General Thomas Pinckney of South Carolina.
1829 — Major-General Aaron Ogden of New Jersey.
1839 — Major General Morgan Lewis of New York.
1844 — Brevet Major William Popham of New York (last surviving original member).

1848 — Brigadier-General Henry Alexander Scammel Dearborn of Massachusetts.
1834 — Hon. Hamilton Fish of New York, Secretary of State.
1896 — Hon. William Wayne of Pennsylvania.
1902 — Hon. Winslow Warren of Massachusetts.
1932 — Hon. John Collins Daves of North Carolina.
1939 — Lieutenant-Colonel Bryce Metcalf of Connecticut.

Vice-Presidents General.

1784 — Major-General Horatio Gates of Virginia.
1787 — Major-General Thomas Mifflin of Pennsylvania.
1799 — Major-General Alexander Hamilton of New York.
1800 — Major-General Charles Cotesworth Pinckney of South Carolina.
1805 — Major-General Henry Knox of Massachusetts.
1811 — Brigadier-General John Brooks of Massachusetts.
1825 — Major-General Aaron Ogden of New Jersey.
1829 — Major-General Morgan Lewis of New York.
1839 — Major William Shute of New Jersey (last Continental officer to hold the office).
1844 — Hon. Horace Binney of Pennsylvania.
1848 — Hon. Hamilton Fish of New York.
1854 — Hon. Charles Stewart Davies of Massachusetts.
1866 — Mr. James Warren Sever of Massachusetts.
1872 — Hon. James Simons of South Carolina.
1881 — Dr. William Armstrong Irvine of Pennsylvania.
1887 — Hon. Robert Milligan McLane of Maryland.
1896 — Hon. Winslow Warren of Massachusetts.
1902 — Colonel James Simons, Jr., C. S. A., of South Carolina.
1920 — Mr. Charles Beatty Alexander of Pennsylvania.
1929 — Hon. Francis Key Pendleton of New York.
1932 — Lieutenant-Colonel Bryce Metcalf of Connecticut.

Secretaries General.

1783 — Major-General Henry Knox of Massachusetts.
1799 — Major William Jackson of Pennsylvania (last Continental officer to hold the office).
1829 — Mr. Alexander Washington Johnston, of Pennsylvania.
1857 — Mr. Thomas McEuen of Pennsylvania.
1875 — Mr. George Washington Harris of Pennsylvania.
1884 — Lieutenant-Colonel Asa Bird Gardiner U. S. A., of Rhode Island.

1920 — Mr. John Collins Daves of North Carolina.
1932 — Mr. Francis Apthorp Foster of Georgia.

Assistant Secretaries General.

1784 — Brigadier-General Otho Holland Williams of Maryland.
1787 — Brevet Major George Turner of South Carolina.
1790 — Brigadier-General William MacPherson of Pennsylvania.
1799 — Surgeon Nathan Dorsey of Pennsylvania.
1802 — Colonel William Dent Beall of Maryland.
1825 — Brevet Captain John Markland of Pennsylvania (last Continental officer to hold the office.)
1829 — Mr. Thomas McEuen of Pennsylvania.
1857 — Mr. George Washington Harris of Pennsylvania.
1857 — Mr. Richard Irvine Manning of Maryland.
1890 — Mr. Thomas Pinckney Lowndes of South Carolina.
1896 — Hon. Nicholas Fish of New York.
1905 — Mr. John Cropper of Virginia.
1908 — Mr. John Collins Daves of North Carolina.
1920 — Mr. Francis Apthorp Foster of Georgia.
1932 — Lieutenant-Colonel Edgar Erskine Hume, U. S. A., of Virginia.

Treasurers General.

1783 — Major-General Alexander McDougall of New York.
1796 — Major William Jackson of Pennsylvania.
1799 — Brigadier-General William MacPherson of Pennsylvania.
1825 — Captain Allan McLane of Pennsylvania.
1832 — Brevet Captain John Markland of Pennsylvania (last Continental officer to hold the office.)
1838 — Hon. Joseph Warren Scott of New Jersey.
1872 — Hon. Tench Tilghman of Maryland.
1875 — Mr. Alexander Hamilton, Jr., of New York.
1881 — Mr. John Schuyler of New York.
1896 — Mr. Richard Meredith McSherry of Maryland.
1899 — Mr. Frederick Wolcott Jackson of New Jersey.
1905 — Mr. Francis Marinus Caldwell of Pennsylvania.
1911 — Mr. Charles Isham of Connecticut.
1920 — Mr. Henry Randall Webb of Maryland.
1935 — Major Horace Morison of New Hampshire.

Assistant Treasurers General.

1825 — Mr. Alexander Washington Johnston of Pennsylvania.
1829 — Brevet Captain John Markland of Pennsylvania (last Continental officer to hold the office.)
1832 — Hon. Joseph Warren Scott of New Jersey.
1838 — Hon. William Jackson, Jr., of Pennsylvania.
1851 — Mr. John Henry Markland of Pennsylvania.
1863 — Mr. John McDowell of New Jersey.
1872 — Mr. William Berrian Dayton of New Jersey.
1881 — Dr. Herman Burgin of New Jersey.
1893 — Mr. Henry Thayer Drowne of Rhode Island.
1899 — Mr. John Cropper of Virginia.
1905 — Mr. Charles Isham of Connecticut.
1911 — Mr. Henry Randall Webb of Maryland.
1920 — Mr. James Wall Schureman Campbell of New Jersey.
1929 — Mr. Francis King Wainwright of Delaware.
1932 — Major Horace Morison of New Hampshire.
1935 — Mr. Lawrence Monck Pinckney of South Carolina.

TABLE OF CONTENTS

GENERAL WASHINGTON'S CORRESPONDENCE

1783

1785

1786

1788

1789

1790

1791

SUPPLEMENT

ILLUSTRATIONS

The Society of the Cincinnati

The document on which the Society of the Cincinnati is based is known as the *Institution*. It sets forth the objects of the Cincinnati and something of the plan of organization. General Washington and all other original members signed it, or were supposed to do so (some could not because they removed to distant places before the Institution was ready). The paragraphs giving the purposes of the Cincinnati are read at every meeting of the Society.

THE INSTITUTION

CANTONMENT OF THE AMERICAN ARMY, ON HUDSON'S RIVER, 10TH MAY, 1783.

PROPOSALS for establishing a Society, upon principles therein mentioned, whose Members shall be officers of the American Army, having been communicated to the several regiments of the respective lines, they appointed an officer from each, who, in conjunction with the general officers, should take the same into consideration at their meeting this day, at which the Honorable MAJOR GENERAL BARON DE STEUBEN, the senior officer present, was pleased to preside.

The proposals being read, fully considered, paragraph by paragraph, and the amendments agreed to, MAJOR GENERAL KNOX, BRIGADIER GENERAL HAND, BRIGADIER GENERAL HUTINGTON and CAPTAIN SHAW, were chosen to revise the same, and prepare a copy to be laid before this assembly at their next meeting, to be holden at MAJOR GENERAL BARON DE STEUBEN'S quarters, on Tuesday, the 13th instant.

TUESDAY, 13TH MAY, 1783.

The representatives of the American Army being assembled agreeably to adjournment, the plan for establishing a Society, whereof the officers of the American Army are to be Members, is accepted, and is as follows, viz.:

"It having pleased the Supreme Governor of the Universe, in the disposition of human affairs, to cause the separation of the colonies of North America from the domination of Great Britain, and, after a bloody conflict of eight years, to establish them free, independent and sovereign States, connected, by alliances founded on reciprocal advantage, with some of the great princes and powers of the earth.

"To perpetuate, therefore, as well the remembrance of this vast event, as the mutual friendships which have been formed under the pressure of common danger, and, in many instances, cemented by the blood of the parties, the officers of the American Army do hereby, in the most solemn manner, associate, constitute and combine themselves into one SOCIETY OF FRIENDS, to endure as long as they shall endure, or any of their eldest male posterity, and, in failure thereof, the collateral branches who may be judged worthy of becoming its supporters and Members.

"The officers of the American Army having generally been taken from the citizens of America, possess high veneration for the character of that illustrious Roman, LUCIUS QUINTUS CINCINNATUS; and being resolved to follow his example, by returning to their citizenship, they think they may with propriety denominate themselves—

THE SOCIETY OF THE CINCINNATI

"*The following principles shall be immutable and form the basis of the Society of the Cincinnati*:

"AN INCESSANT ATTENTION TO PRESERVE INVIOLATE THOSE EXALTED RIGHTS AND LIBERTIES OF HUMAN NATURE, FOR WHICH THEY HAVE FOUGHT AND BLED, AND WITHOUT WHICH THE HIGH RANK OF A RATIONAL BEING IS A CURSE INSTEAD OF A BLESSING.

"AN UNALTERABLE DETERMINATION TO PROMOTE AND CHERISH, BETWEEN THE RESPECTIVE STATES, THAT UNION AND NATIONAL HONOR SO ESSENTIALLY NECESSARY TO THEIR HAPPINESS, AND THE FUTURE DIGNITY TO THE AMERICAN EMPIRE.

"TO RENDER PERMANENT THE CORDIAL AFFECTION SUBSISTING AMONG THE OFFICERS. THIS SPIRIT WILL DICTATE BROTHERLY KINDNESS IN ALL THINGS, AND PARTICULARLY, EXTEND TO THE MOST SUBSTANTIAL ACTS OF BENEFICENCE, ACCORDING TO THE ABILITY OF THE SOCIETY, TOWARDS THOSE OFFICERS AND THEIR FAMILIES, WHO UNFORTUNATELY MAY BE UNDER THE NECESSITY OF RECEIVING IT.

"The General Society will, for the sake of frequent communications, be divided into State Societies, and these again into such districts as shall be directed by the State Society.

"The Societies of the districts to meet as often as shall be agreed upon by the State Society, those of the State on the fourth day of July annually, or oftener, if they shall find it expedient, and the General Society on the first Monday in May, annually, so long as they shall deem it necessary, and afterwards, at least once in every three years.

"At each meeting, the principles of the Institution will be fully considered, and the best measures to promote them adopted.

"The State Societies will consist of all the members resident in each State respectively; and any member removing from one State to another, is to be considered, in all respects, as belonging to the Society of the State in which he shall actually reside.

"The State Societies to have a President, Vice-President, Secretary, Treasurer, and Assistant Treasurer, to be chosen annualy, by a majority of votes, at the State meeting.

"Each State meeting shall write annually, or oftener, if necessary, a circular letter, to the State Societies, noting whatever they may think worthy of observation, respecting the good of the Society, or the general union of the States, and giving information of the officers chosen for the current year: copies of these letters shall be regularly transmitted to the Secretary General of the Society, who will record them in a book to be assigned for that purpose.

"The State Society will regulate everything respecting itself and the Societies of its districts consistent with the general maxims of the Cincinnati, judge of the qualifications of the members who may be proposed, and expel any member who, by a conduct inconsistent with a gentleman and a man of honor, or by an opposition to the interest of the community in general, or the Society in particular, may render himself unworthy to continue a member.

"In order to form funds which may be respectable, and assist the unfortunate, each officer shall deliver to the Treasurer of the State Society one month's pay, which shall remain for ever to the use of the State Society; the interest only of which, if necessary, to be appropriated to the relief of the unfortunate.

"Donations may be made by persons not of the Society, and by members of the Society, for the express purpose of forming permanent funds for the use of the State Society, and the interests of these donations appropriated in the same manner as that of the month's pay.

"Moneys, at the pleasure of each member, may be subscribed in the Societies of the districts, or the State Societies, for the relief of the unfortunate members, or their widows and orphans, to be appropriated by the State Society only.

"The meeting of the General Society shall consist of its officers and a representation from each State Society, in number not exceeding five, whose expenses shall be borne by their respective State Societies.

"In the General meeting, the President, Vice-President, Secretary, Assistant Secretary, Treasurer, and Assistant Treasurer Generals, shall be chosen, to serve until the next meeting.

"The circular letters which have been written by the respective State Societies to each other, and their particular laws, shall be read and considered, and all measures concerted which may conduce to the general intendment of the Society.

"It is probable that some persons may make donations to the General Society, for the purpose of establishing funds for the further comfort of the unfortunate, in which case, such donations must be placed in the hands of the Treasurer General, the interest only of which to be disposed of, if necessary, by the general meeting.

"All the officers of the American army, as well as those who have resigned with honor, after three years' service in the capacity of officers, or who have been deranged by the resolution of

Congress upon the several reforms of the army, as those who shall have continued to the end of the war, have the right to become parties to this institution; provided that they subscribe one month's pay, and sign their names to the general rules, in their respective State Societies, those who are present with the Army immediately; and others within six months after the Army shall be disbanded, extraordinary cases expected; the rank, time of service, resolution of Congress by which any have been deranged, and place of residence must be added to each name—and as a testimony of affection to the memory and the offspring of such officers as have died in the service, their eldest male branches shall have the same right of becoming members, as the children of the actual members of the Society.

"Those officers who are foreigners, not resident in any of the States, will have their names enrolled by the Secretary General, and are to be considered as members in the Societies of any of the States in which they may happen to be.

"And as there are, and will at times be, men in the respective States eminent for their abilities and patriotism, whose views may be directed to the same laudable objects with those of the Cincinnati, it shall be a rule to admit such characters, as Honorary Members of the Society, for their own lives only; Provided always, That the number of Honorary Members, in each State, does not exceed a ratio of one to four of the officers or their descendants.

"Each State Society shall obtain a list of its members, and at the first annual meeting, the State Secretary shall have engrossed, on parchment, two copies of the Institution of the Society, which every member present shall sign, and the Secretary shall endeavor to procure the signature of every absent member; one of those lists to be transmitted to the Secretary General, to be kept in the archives of the Society, and the other to remain in the hands of the State Secretary. From the State lists, the Secretary General must make out, at the first general meeting, a complete list of the whole Society, with a copy of which he will furnish each State Society.

"The Society shall have an order, by which its members shall be known and distinguished, which shall be a medal of gold, of a proper size to receive the emblems, and suspended by a deep blue riband two inches wide, edged with white, descriptive of the union of France and America, viz.:

"The principal figure,

CINCINNATUS:

Three Senators presenting him with a sword and other military ensigns—on a field in the background, his wife standing at the door of their Cottage—near it

A PLOUGH AND INSTRUMENTS OF HUSBANDRY.

Round the whole.

OMNIA RELIQUIT SERVARE REMPUBLICAM.

On the reverse,

Sun rising—a city with open gates, and vessels entering the port—Fame crowning CINCINNATUS with a wreath, inscribed

VIRTUTIS PRÆMIUM.

Below,

HANDS JOINED, SUPPORTING A HEART.

With the motto,

ESTO PERPETUA.

Round the whole,

SOCIETAS CINCINNATORUM INSTITUTA.

A. D. 1783"

The Society, deeply impressed with a sense of the generous assistance this country has received from France, and desirous of perpetuating the friendships which have been formed, and so happily subsisted, between the officers of the allied forces in the prosecution of the war, direct that the President General transmit, as soon as may be, to each of the characters hereafter named, a medal containing the Order of the Society, viz.:

His Excellency the CHEVALIER DE LA LUZERNE, Minister Plenipotentiary,

His Excellency the SIEUR GERARD, late Minister Plenipotentiary.

Their Excellencies

The COUNT DE ESTAING,
The COUNT DE GRASSE,
The COUNT DE BARRAS,
The CHEVALIER DES TOUCHES,
Admirals and Commanders in the Navy,

His Excellency the COUNT DE ROCHAMBEAU, Commander in Chief,

And the Generals and Colonels of his army, and acquaint them, that the Society does itself the honor to consider them members.

Resolved, That a copy of the aforegoing Institution be given to the senior officer of each State line, and that the officers of the respective State lines sign their names to the same, in manner and form following, viz.:

"We the subscribers, officers of the American army, do hereby voluntarily become parties to the foregoing Institution, and do bind ourselves to observe, and be governed by, the principles therein contained. For the performance whereof we do solemnly pledge to each other our sacred honor.

"Done in the Cantonment, on Hudson's River, in the year 1783."

That the members of the Society, at the time of subscribing their names to the Institution, do also assign a draft on the Paymaster-General, in the following terms (the regiments to do it regimentally, and the generals and other officers not belonging to regiments, each for himself, individually), viz.:

"*To* JOHN PIERCE, *Esquire, Paymaster-General to the Army of the United States:*

"*Sir:* Please to pay to..........Treasurer for the.......... State association of the Cincinnati, or his order, one month's pay of our several grades respectively, and deduct the same from the balance which shall be found due to us on the final liquidation of our accounts; for which this shall be your warrant."

That the members of the several State Societies assemble as soon as may be, for the choice of their President and other officers; and that the Presidents correspond together, and appoint a meeting of the officers who may be chosen from each State, in order to pursue such further measures as may be judged necessary.

That the General officers, and the officers delegated to represent the several corps of the Army, subscribe to the Institution of the General Society, for themselves and their constituents, in the manner and form before prescribed.

That GENERAL HEATH, GENERAL BARON DE STEUBEN, and GENERAL KNOX, be a committee to wait on his Excellency the Commander-in-Chief, with a copy of the Institution, and request him to honor the Society by placing his name at the head of it.

That MAJOR GENERAL WILLIAM HEATH, second in command in this Army, be, and hereby is, desired to transmit copies of the Institution, with the proceedings thereon, to the commanding officer of the Southern Army, the senior officer in each State, from Pennsylvania to Georgia, inclusive, and to the commanding officer of the Rhode Island line, requesting them to communicate the same to the officers under their several commands, and to take such measures as may appeal to them necessary for expediting the establishment of their State Societies, and sending a delegation to represent them in the first general meeting, to be holden on the first Monday in May, 1784.

The meeting then adjourned without day.

MINUTES OF THE FIRST MEETING OF THE CINCINNATI.

At this meeting, at which Major-General de Steuben presided, the Society elected General Washington President General:

CANTONMENT

OF THE AMERICAN ARMY, 19TH OF JUNE, 1783.

At a meeting of the General officers, and the gentlemen delegated by their respective regiments, as a convention for establishing the Society of the Cincinnati, held by the request of the President, at which were present:

Major General BARON DE STEUBEN, Inspector General, President.

Major General ROBERT HOWE.

Major General HENRY KNOX, Chief Continental Corps of Artillery.

Brigadier General JOHN PATTERSON.

Brigadier General EDWARD HAND, Adjutant General.

Brigadier General JEDEDIAH HUNTINGTON.

Brigadier General RUFUS PUTNAM.

Colonel SAML. BLACHLEY WEBB, 3d Regiment Connecticut Continental Infantry.

Lieutenant Colonel EBENEZER HUNTINGTON, 1st Regiment Connecticut Continental Infantry.

Major JOSEPH PETTENGILL, 1st Regiment Massachusetts Continental Infantry.

Lieutenant JOHN WHITING, Adjutant 2d Regiment Massachusetts Continental Infantry.

Colonel HENRY JACKSON, 4th Regiment Massachusetts Continental Infantry.

Captain SAMUEL SHAW, 3d Regiment Continental Corps of Artillery.

Lieutenant Colonel WILLIAM HULL, 3d Regiment Massachusetts Continental Infantry.

Lieutenant Colonel HUGH MAXWELL, 8th Regiment Massachusetts Continental Infantry.

Colonel PHILIP VAN CORTLANDT, 2d Regiment New York Continental Infantry.

General BARON DE STEUBEN acquainted the Convention that he had, agreeably to their request, at the last meeting, transmitted to his Excellency the CHEVALIER DE LA LUZERNE, Minister Plenipotentiary from the Court of France, a copy of the Institution of the Society of the Cincinnati, with their vote respecting his Excellency, and the other characters therein mentioned; and that his Excellency had returned an answer, declaring his acceptance of the same, and expressing the grateful sense he entertains of the honor conferred on himself, and the other gentlemen of the French nation, by this act of the Convention.

Resolved, That the letter of the CHEVALIER DE LA LUZERNE be recorded in the proceedings of this day, and deposited in the archives of the Society, as a testimony of the high sense this Convention entertains of the honor done to the Society by his becoming a member therof.

The letter is as follows:

PHILADELPHIA, 3d June, 1783.

"*Monsieur le Baron:* I have received with much gratitude, the Institution of the respectable Order that the officers of the American army have founded. If courage, patience, and all the virtues that this brave army have so often displayed in the course of this war could ever be forgotten, this monument alone should recall them. I dare assure you, sir, that all the officers of my nation that you have been pleased to admit in your Society will be infinitely honored by it. I pray you to be fully persuaded I feel, for my part, in the most lively manner, the honor the officers of the army have done me in deigning to think of me upon this occasion.

"I expect to pay my respects to his excellency General WASHINGTON, as soon as the definite treaty shall be signed, and I shall have the honor of assuring them, personally, of my respectful acknowledgment.

"I seize, with great eagerness, this occasion of expressing to you the sentiments of the most perfect and most respectful attachment with which I have the honor to be, Monsieur le Baron, your very humble and very obedient servant.

LE CHEVALIER DE LA LUZERNE.

TO BARON DE STEUBEN, Major General in the
service of the United States Head Quarters."

The Baron having also communicated a letter from Major L'ENFANT, enclosing a design of the medal and order, containing the emblems of the Institution.

Resolved, That the bald eagle, carrying the emblems on its breast, be established as the order of the Society, and that the ideas of Major L'ENFANT, respecting it and the manner of its being worn by the members, be adopted. That the order be of the same size, and in every other respect conformable to the said design, which for that purpose is certified by the BARON DE STEUBEN, President of this Convention, and to be deposited in the archives of the Society, as the original, from which all copies are to be made. Also, that silver medals, not exceeding the size of a Spanish milled dollar, with the emblems, as designed by Major L'ENFANT, and certified by the President, be given to each and every member of the Society, *together with a diploma, on parchment, whereon shall be impressed the exact figures of the order and medal, as above mentioned*; *anything in the original Institution, respecting gold medals, to the contrary notwithstanding.*

Major L'Enfant's letter is as follows:

PHILADELPHIA, 10th June, 1783.

"*My General*: Immediately on receiving your letter of the 20th May, which I met by accident at the Post office, on the 7th inst., I set myself about the plan of the medal. I send you both faces of the design, which I have made large, so that you may better judge of them. In the execution they can be reduced to a convenient size, which on account of the precision required in the design, ought not to be less than a dollar, the subject being too complex to admit of its being properly detailed in a smaller compass.

"I have not made it oval, agreeably to your desire, as such a form is not proper for a medal; besides, it can be done in the execution, if the idea should be persisted in of having the order in that form, to which, however, I think any other preferable. I also believe and hope that you will be persuaded of this, and endeavor to convince the gentlemen of it who compose the committee for forming the Institution, and to whom I beg you to communicate the following observations:

"A medal, whether round or oval, is considered, in the different states of Europe, only as the reward of the laborer and the artist, or as a sign of a manufacturing community, or religious society; besides the abusive custom prevailing particularly in Germany and Italy, of sending to France mountebanks, dancers and musicians, ornamented in this manner, renders it necessary to distinguish this Order by a form which shall be peculiar to itself, and which will answer the two-fold purpose of honoring those invested with it, and making itself respected for its simplicity, by such as may be in a situation minutely to examine its different parts.

"Not that I suppose one form or another will change the opinion of a republican people accustomed to think; I only say, that in an Institution of this sort, the main design should be to render it respectable to everybody, and that it is only in appealing to the senses that you can engage the attention of the common people, who have certain habitual prejudices which cannot be destroyed. A gentleman already invested with any European Order would be unwilling to carry a medal, but if flattered by receiving a mark of distinction from a respectable society, he should do it, the manner of it would by no means increase the value of the Order. On the contrary, giving it a new and particular form will be adding a recommendation to its real value, and engage those invested with it to wear it in the same manner, as their other Military Order, which is the surest means of putting it at once upon a footing with them.

"The bald eagle, which is peculiar to this continent, and is distinguished from those of other climates by its white head and tail, appears to me to deserve attention.

"I send you two essays which I have made, and desire one of them may be adopted instead of the medal. In one, I make the eagle supporting a star with thirteen points in the centre of which is the figure of the medal, with its inscription, as well in front as on the reverse. A legend might be added in the claws and go round the neck of the eagle, with a particular inscription, or the contour of the medal transferred there. In the other, I have made simply the eagle, supporting on its breast the figure of the medal, with a legend in his claws and about the neck, which passes behind and sustains the reverse. I would prefer the latter, as it does not resemble any other Order, and bears a distinct character; nor will it be expensive in its execution. The first device, although more complex, would not be so dear as people might imagine, especially if the execution of it should be committed to skillful persons, which would not be the case any more than with the medal, but by sending it to Europe, where it would not take up a great deal of time, nor be so expensive as to trust the execution of it here to workmen not well acquainted with the business.

"A medal is a monument to be transmitted to posterity; and, consequently, it is necessary that it be executed to the highest degree of perfection possible in the age in which it is struck. Now, to strike a medal well, is a matter that requires practice and a good die; and as there is not here either a press proper for this work, nor people who can make a good die, I would willingly undertake to recommend the execution of the Medal, the Eagle, or the Order, to such persons in Paris as are capable of executing it to perfection.

"So far from proposing to change the oval medal into an eagle, on which should be impressed the medal, I do not pretent to say medals cannot be made. On the contrary, my idea of the subject is that silver medals should be struck, at the common expense of the Society, and distributed, one to each member, as an appendage to a diploma of parchment, whereon it would be proper to stamp the figure of the medal, the eagle, or the star, in its full dimensions, and properly colored, *enjoining on the Members to conform to it,* though leaving them the liberty, provided it be at their own expense, of having it made of such metal and as small as they please, without altering any of the emblems. It seems to me by no means proper that the Honorary Members should wear the Order in the same manner as the Original Members; it would be necessary that they should wear the Medal, the Star, or the Eagle, round their necks, and the Original Members at the third button-hole.

"These remarks, I beg you, my General, to have translated and submitted to the gentlemen concerned. I shall be obliged to you to let me know the issue of this letter, and their decision upon it.

"I have, etc., etc., etc.,

"L'ENFANT.

N. B. The head and tail of the eagle should be silver, or enamelled in white, the body and wings gold, the medal on its breast and back enamelled in the same color as the legend; sprigs of laurel and oak might be added in the wings enamelled in green; the star should be pointed in gold, or enamelled in blue and white; those who would be at the expense might, instead of white, have diamonds. The riband, as is customary in all orders, should be watered."

"*Resolved,* That the thanks of this Convention be transmitted, by the President, to Major L'ENFANT, for his care and ingenuity in preparing the aforementioned designs, and that he be acquainted that they cheerfully embrace his offer of assistance, and request a continuance of his attention in carrying the designs into execution, for which purpose the President is desired to correspond with him.

"*Resolved*, That his Excellency the Commander-in-Chief be requested to officiate as President General, until the first general meeting, to be held in May next."

That a Treasurer General and a Secretary General be balloted for, to officiate in like manner.

The ballots being taken, Major-General M'DOUGALL was elected Treasurer General, and Major-General KNOX, Secretary General, who are hereby requested to accept said appointments.

Resolved, That all the proceedings of this Convention, including the Institution of the Society, be recorded (from the original papers in his possession) by Captain SHAW, who at the first meeting was requested to act as Secretary, and that the same, signed by the President's Secretary, together with the original papers, be given into the hands of Major-General KNOX, Secretary-General to the Society; and that Captain NORTH aide-de-camp to the Baron DE STEUBEN, and acting secretary to him as President, sign the said records.

The dissolution of a very considerable part of the Army, since the last meeting of this Convention having rendered the attendance of some of its members impracticable, and the necessity of some temporary arrangements, previous to the first meeting of the General Society, being so strikingly obvious, the Convention found itself constrained to make those before mentioned, which they have done with the utmost diffidence of themselves, and relying entirely on the candor of their constituents to make allowance for the measure. The principal objects of its appointment being thus accomplished, the members of this Convention think fit to dissolve the same, and it is hereby dissolved accordingly.

STEUBEN, Major General,
President.

S. SHAW, Capt. of Art.,
Secretary to the Convention.

WILLIAM NORTH, A. D. C.,
and Secretary to the President.

SIGNATURES TO THE INSTITUTION.

Society of the Cincinnati. Done in the Cantonment on Hudson's River in the Year 1783.[1]

G°. Washington
W. Heath, M. G.
B. Lincoln, M. G.
Nath Greene, Maj Genl.
Robert Howe, M. G.
Alex McDougall, M. general
Steuben, M. G.
M. Gist, B. Genl.
H. Knox, M. G.
C. Armand, Mq de la Rouerie, B. G.
Duportail, M. G.
John Patterson, B. Genl.
Edw. Hand, Brig. & Adjt. Genl.
John Greaton, B. Genl.
Rufus Putnam, B. Genl.
Elias Dayton, Brig. Gel.
Jed. Huntington, B. Gen.
Timothy Pickering, Col & G. M. Gen.
H. Swift, Col 2d Conct Regiment
J. Cortlandt, Colo 2d New York Regt.
Henry Jackson, Col 4th Mass Reg.
Samuel Shaw, Captain Massachusetts Artillery
Wm. Hull, Lt. Colo. 6th Mass Regt.
Jos Pettingill, Majr. 1st A. Regt
Samuel Whitwell, Surgn 3d M. Regt
Moses Knap, Maj 5th M Regt.
John Whiting Lieut 2d Mass Regt
Corns v. Dyck, Lt Colo
Gouvion, Colel of the Corps of Engineers
Eben Huntington, L. Col. 1 Conn Regt
Saml B. Webb Colo 3d Conn Regt
Peter Woodward, Lt New York Artillery
Lewis Nicola, Col. Inn.
John Brooks LtCol Comdt 7th Mass Regt
High Maxwell Lieut. Colo 8th Mass Regt.
Walter Steward, Col Insp North. Army

---

[1] This is the document known in the Society of the Cincinnati as the "Parchment Roll." The signers were the general officers and others who were present when the Society was instituted. There are several other rolls of original members. Each State Society had such a roll, though all the original members did not sign, since they had dispersed before the roll was ready for signature. The Parchment Roll is the first document pertaining to the Society of the Cincinnati that General Washington signed.

General Washington's Correspondence

ALL LETTERS ARE FROM OR TO GENERAL WASHINGTON UNLESS OTHERWISE STATED.

From Colonel CHARLES ARMAND-TUFFIN, MARQUIS DE LA ROUËRIE.

Philadelphia, July 30, 1783

Sir

I am this instant favoured with a lettre of the baron de Steuben a copy of which I have the honor to inclose; as this is the first notice I have officially received relating to the society of *Cincinnati*, I have reason to be still at a loss to know whether the honor intended by the conference of that order on the americain's officers, extend to foreigners who have served in it with some reputation; and as in all cases where the advantage & interest of the legion & my own may be concerned in a military light, I wish they could be obtained with the approbation of your Excellency and through your patronage, I take the liberty to adress you on this occasion, and at the same time to declare our unlimited submission & confidence to whatsoever you may order, advise, or approve as soon as I am favoured with your answer I shall proceed agreable to it, and shall be allways anxious to be deserving of the esteem, & wear the testimony of it, of an army which I respect, in which I spented the most flourishing days of my life, & which was headed by the first military man of our age—I have the honor to be with the highest respect etc.[1]

[*Archives of the General Society*]

[1] This brilliant cavalry officer was, like most French officers, a profound admirer of General Washington. From La Rouërie, he wrote the General on 18 June 1789, congratulating him on his election as President of the United States: "We have had the confirmation that you are by your post at the head of affairs; in my former letter to your Excellency I complimented your country on that event, which surely will be like all those where circumstances have permitted you to be concerned in, the most advantageous & dear to America & the most renowned in her history—as to you, Sir, I do not think you have had any promotion—your influence over your country men & in public affaires and in many services & virtues which gave it to you, had placed and main-

[Enclosed in the above]:

Major-General THE BARON DE STEUBEN to Brigadier General ARMAND MARQUIS DE LA ROUËRIE.

West point July 19, 1783

Sir

I do myself the honor to forward you the Last Proceedings of the Convention, for Establishing the society of the Cincinnati; the former Proceedings you have Doubtless Received, from General Heath, long before this time.

the transactions relative to the society in future, you will have communicated to you, by General Knox; who is the acting secretary General

I am etc.

[*Archives of the General Society*]

From Major-General JOHN SULLIVAN.

Boston August 20th 1783

Dear General

The Inclosed Letter[1] is an answer to A Letter received from Baron Stubend inclosing the plans for forming the Society of Cincinnati. Since writing the inclosed I have had the pleasure of being informed that your Excellency has honored the Society by becoming The president. I therefore take the Liberty of forwarding to Your Excellency my answer for your perusal and Should be happy in receiving from you any directions which

tained you upon that mighty eminence from which the man who happen to be Born every three or four hundred years, look down with a holy pride and tranquility upon kings, & great dignitary while individuals & nations look up with respect and admiration to that man and regret, for the happiness & honor of humanity, he does not command over the whole world." (See *Letters of Col. Armand* (*Marquis de la Rouërie*) *1777-1791*, Collections of the New York Historical Society, 1879.

[1] Inclosed is a copy of the letter of 15 August 1783 from General Sullivan to the Baron de Steuben, see page 18.

2

you may think proper to give relative to the Establishment of that Society in New Hampshire—I have Notified the officers to Meet in october for the purpose of carrying the plans into Effect—

permit me Dear General to assure you that While I Lament the many trying Scenes which you pass even in the hour of Glory I feel the most unspeakable pleasure in finding you at Last Crownd. with those Laurels to which your own virtue & Military Talents so well intitle you.

I have the honor to be etc.

[*Washington Papers*]

This is a copy, in General Sullivan's writing, of his letter to the Baron de Steuben, who presided at the first meeting of the Cincinnati—when General Washington was chosen President General. This copy was sent General Washington in General Sullivan's letter to him, dated 20 August 1783, see page 17.

From Major-General JOHN SULLIVAN to the BARON DE STEUBEN.

Durham August 15th 1783—

Sir /

I was a few days since honored with your favor of the Last month inclosing a plan for the formation of the Society of the Cincinnati with a Copy of the Resolutions taken relative thereto.—

Nothing could afford me more Sensible pleasure than your Invitation to become a Member of a Society Established upon the most virtuous and Laudable principles Calculated to promote and cherish that harmony & Concord which cannot fail to Cement the union and add to the dignity of the united States.

I beg that you and the Gentlemen Officers will accept my most cordial Thanks for the polite Invitation and that you will believe that it is with the most Sincere Satisfaction I embrace this opportunity of giving you notice of my acceptance—

I shall not fail to pursue the measures pointed out for forming the Society in this State and Shall use every possible Effort for rendering it respectable

I have the honor to be etc.

[*Washington Papers*]

To Major-General HENRY KNOX.

Rocky Hill, 23 Sept. 1783

My dear Sir,

. . . I shall be obliged to you for pointing out in *precise terms* what is expected from the President of the Cincinnati previous to the General Meeting in May next. As I never was present at any of your Meetings, and have never seen the proceedings of the last, I may, for want of information of the part I am to act, neglect some essential duty which might not only be injurious to the Society, but Mortifying to myself, as it would discover a want of Knowledge or want of attention in the President [1]

[*Washington's Letter Books*]

---

[1] General Washington naturally turned to Knox for information about the Cincinnati, for Knox was the real founder, having first conceived the plan of the Society. Jefferson recorded in his diary, 16 March 1788, that Knox, in a conversation with Adams as early as 1776, expressed "a wish for some ribbon to wear in his hat or in his button-hole, to be transmitted to his descendants as a badge and proof that he had fought in defense of their liberties. He spoke in such precise terms as showed that he had revolved it in his mind before." Knox's "proposals" which were the basis of the Institution, were dated "Westpoint, 15 April 1783." (For Knox's "proposals," the Institution, and the Altered and Amended Institution of 1784 (see page 160), in parallel columns, see E. E. Hume, *Sesquicentennial History and Roster of the Society of the Cincinnati in the State of Virginia, 1783-1933*, Richmond, 1934, 26-41. Knox was Secretary General of the Cincinnati during the period that General Washington was President General.

Membership Certificate of Major L'ENFANT.[1]

I do hereby certify that Mr. L'Enfant of the Corps of Engineers in the service of the United States has acquired by his service during the War the Right of being acknowledged a Member of the Society of the Cincinnati, and having obtained permission to return to France on his own private Affairs he has at the same time undertaken to transact some necessary business relative to the Order of the said Society.

Given under my hand this 16th. day of Octobr. 1783

Go: Washington
Presidt Genl.

[*Archives of the General Society*]

[French translation of the last]

Major L'ENFANT's Credentials.

Je certifie par la présente que M. L'Enfant, du corps des ingénieurs au service des Etats-Unis, a acquis par ses services pendant la guerre le droit d'être reconnu comme membre de la Société des Cincinnati, et qu'ayant obtenu permission de rentrer en France pour ses affaires privées il a accepté en même temps de se charger de quelques affaires intéressantes relatives à l'ordre de ladite société.

Donné de ma main le 16 octobre 1783

Georges Washington
Président Général [2]

[*Archives of the French Cincinnati*]

---

[1] There is a copy, worded slightly differently, in Washington's Letter Books. See also certificate of 1 November 1783, page 30. L'Enfant was about to go to France on business for the Society of the Cincinnati, particularly to have the Eagles, or badges of membership, and the copperplate for the Diploma made. See the minutes of the first meeting of the Society for L'Enfant's letter anent the design for the Eagle, page 10.

[2] Translation attached to copy of the original.

I do hereby certify that Mr L'Enfant of the Corps of Engineers in the service of the United States has acquired by his service during the War the right of being acknowledged a Member of the Society of the Cincinnati. and having obtained permission to return to France on his own private Affairs he has at the same time undertaken to transact some necessary business relative to the Order of the said Society:

Given under my hand
this 16th day of Octobr 1783

Go Washington
Presidt Genl.

Major L'Enfant's credentials from General Washington attesting his membership in the Cincinnati and authorizing him to transact business in France for the Society.

[*Archives of the General Society*]

To Major-General Henry Knox.

Rocky Hill, 16 October, 1783

Dear Sir,

Major Shaw not returning so soon as I imagined, and the subject of your Letter of 28 September not admitting much delay, I take the opportunity of the Post to reply to it.

On referring to the Institution of the Society of the Cincinnaat I find that the Chevr. de la Luzerne, the Sieur Gérard, the Counts D'Estaing, Barras and De Grasse, the Chevalier Des Touches and the Count de Rochambeau with the Generals and Colonels of his Army are to be presented with the Order of the Society. [See page 7.]

As it is however proper that these Gentlemen should be made acquainted with the nature of the Society, I propose to write to each of those above named (except the Chevalier de la luzerne who was written to in first instance) and inclose them a Copy of the Institution, at the same time informing them that Major L'Enfant is charged with the execution of the Order, and has directions to furnish them from the first that are finished.

I propose also to inclose a Copy to the Marquis de la Fayette and request him to take the signatures of such of the French Officers in our Service who are entitled and wish to become Members—to receive their month's pay and deliver them the Orders on their paying for them.

These Letters Major L'Enfant will carry with him and deliver to each of those Gentlemen and must be directed to deliver them the Orders so soon as they are compleat, delivering to Count Rochambeau, for the Officers of his Command who will receive them of him—and to the Marquis de Lafayette sufficient for the French Officers in our Service who become Members.

I enclose to you the permission for Major L'Enfant to go to France, and a Certificate of his being a Member of the Society. However, before he sets off, I think it should be well explained and understood by him that the Voyage is not undertaken for the Society but that their business is committed to him only in consequence of his going there on his own affairs, and consequently he is not to be paid any Expenses of the Voyage or his stay—but only such Extra Expense as might be incurred by any person residing in France who transacted the same business for the Society—These are my sentiments—if they accord with yours and the rest of the Gentlemen, and he accepts these conditions I think the sooner he sets out the better.

I will be obliged to you to make out his instructions comprehending the objects I have mentioned above and such other as you may think necessary—and to make the necessary arrangements with him respecting the funds to be furnished. I am told subscriptions have been paid in by those who wish to have Orders—I propose taking seven, for which the Money is ready at any time—and it may not be amiss in this place to inform you that it has always been my intention to present the Society with 500 Dollars—if any part of this is necessary and can be applied with propriety in this business—I have no objection.

Maj. L'Enfant might also be directed to receive from the Marquis the Month's pay of the French Officers in our service who become Members.

I must request you to procure Six or seven Copies of the Institution to be made out neatly, to transmit to the Gentlemen above mentioned; Major L'Enfant can bring them on with him.

I intend immediately to write to the Commanding Officer of each of the State Lines, who have not yet made known their intentions respecting the formations of their State Societies pressing them to determination, for as I wish to adapt the place of the General Meeting to the convenience of all 'till I know which of the State form the Society I cannot fix it.

With great regard,

G^{o}. Washington

[*Archives of the General Society*]

To the MARQUIS DE LAFAYETTE.

Rocky Hill, October 20, 1783

Sir:

I do myself the honor to transmit to you herewith a Copy of the Institution of the Cincinnati, a Society formed by the American Officers before they separated and retired to private life.

The principles of the society the purposes for which it was

formed and the qualifications necessary to become Members will fully appear by the Institution. Should any of the Foreign Officers who are qualified by serving three Years in our Army, wish to become Members, I must take the liberty to request you to let them sign the Institution and pay the necessary sum into your hands.

Major L'Enfant who will have the honor to deliver you this, has undertaken to get the Order of the society executed in France, he has directions to deliver you one of the first that are compleated, and you will please also call on him for as many more as you may want. Maj. l'Enfant will inform you the price of them, the Deplomas shall be forwarded as soon as they can be made out.

I am etc.[1]

[*Archives of the General Society*]

The Society of the Cincinnati having been formally instituted at the cantonments on the Hudson, in May of 1783, the President General communicated with the senior officer in each of the thirteen states with the view of forming a branch in each. The following two letters are on this subject:

To the Senior Officer in Maryland, Virginia, North Carolina, South Carolina, and Georgia

Rocky Hill, October 24, 1783.

Sir,

At the Original Institution of the Society of the Cincinnati—Major General Heath who then presided was desired to transmit a copy of the Institution with the proceedings thereon to the Senior Officer in each of the Southern States, and to request them to communicate the same to the Officers under their commands and take such measures as might appear necessary for expediting the establishment of the society in their respective States—

[1] Draft in the handwriting of Benjamin Walker. See a similar letter dated 30 October 1783, page 29.

To the Letter sent on this occasion to the Senior Officer of your State—no answer has been received.—

At a subsequent meeting of the Society is was deemed expedient to appoint a president Genl. pro: tem. and the honor of the choice falling on me it becomes a part of my duty to name the place for the General Meeting in May next and in order to make it as Central as possible, for the general convenience it is necessary I should know in which of the States the Society is established—

I must therefore request that you would be pleased to inform me as soon as possible whether the Establishment has taken place in your State and what measures have been taken to effect it. I am etc.

[*Archives of the General Society*]

To Major-General LACHLAN MCINTOSH.

Rocky hill, October 24, 1783

Sir:

At the Original Institution of the Society of the Cincinnati, Major General Heath who then presided, was desired to transmit a copy of the Institution with the proceedings thereon to the Senior Officer in each of the Southern States to request them to communicate the same to the Officers under their command, and take such measures as might appear necessary for expediting the establishment of the Society in their respective States.

To the Letter sent on this occasion to the Senior Officer in your Statem no Answer has been received.

At a subsequent meeting of the Society it was deemed expedient to appoint a President General P. T., and the honor of the choice falling upon me, it becomes a part of my duty to name the place for the General meeting in May next and in order to make it as Central as possible, for the general convenience, it is necessary I should know in which of the States the Society is established.

I must therefore request, that you would be pleased to inform me, as soon as possible, whether the Establishment has taken place in your State, and what measures have been taken to effect it.

I am etc.[1]

[*Clements Library, University of Michigan*]

To the COUNT DE ROCHAMBEAU.

Rocky hill in New Jersey, 29 October 1783

Sir

The Officers of the American Army, in order to perpetuate that mutual friendships which they contracted in the hour of common danger and distress, and for other purposes which are mentioned in the instrument of their association have united together in a society of Friends under the name *Cincinnati*; and, having honored me with the office of president, it becomes a very agreeable part of my duty to inform you that the Society have done themselves the honor to consider you and the generals and officers of the army which you commanded in America as members of the Society.

Major L'Enfant, who will have the honor to deliver this letter to you, will execute the Order of the Society in France, amongst which he is directed to present you with one of the first Orders that are made, and likewise with Orders for the other gentlemen of your army, which I take the liberty to request you would present to them in the name of the Society. As soon as the diploma is made out, I will have the honor to transmit it to you.

[*Archives of the General Society*]

To the CHEVALIER DE GÉRARD.

Rocky hill in New Jersey, October 29, 1783.

Sir:

The Officers of the American Army, to perpetuate those friendships which have been formed during a time of common

[1] Draft in the writing of Benjamin Walker. See General McIntosh's letters, pages 34 and 141.

danger and distress, and for other purposes mentioned in the Institution, did before their separation associate themselves into a society of Friends under the name of the Cincinnati; and having done me the honor to elect me their President General, it becomes a pleasing part of my duty to acqaint you, that the society have done themselves the honor to enroll your name among their Members.

Major L'Enfant, who will have the honor to deliver you this Letter, is charged by the Society with the execution of their Order in France, and has directions to furnish you with one of the first that are compleated, and so soon as the Diplomas can be made out, I shall do myself the honor to transmit it to you.

With the greatest consideration, respect, &c.[1]

[*Huntington Library*]

From Major-General HENRY KNOX.

West point 29th October 1783

My dear General,

I have received your favor of the 16th Instant, enclosing a permission for Major L'Enfant to go to France, and a certificate of his being a member of the Cincinnati.[2] He had previously Set out for Princeton, where he will be able to obtain others. I have put the certificate, as a Copy upon the files of the Society.

Your Excellency appears to think, that the bald Eagle is to be presented to the Gentlemen in France, whose names are enumerated in the institution.[3]

—This construction appears natural from reading the insti-

[1] In the handwriting of Benjamin Walker.

Gérard's opinion of General Washington is expressed in his letter to the Count de Vergennes, French Minister of Foreign Affairs. Writing from Philadelphia, 8 March 1779, Gérard, the first French Minister to the United States said: "It is certain that if General Washington were ambitious and scheming, it would have been entirely in his power to make a revolution; but nothing on the part of the General or the Army has justified the shadow of a suspicion. The General sets forth constantly this principle that one must be a Citizen first and an officer afterwards" (*Dispatches and Instructions of Conrad-Alexandre Gérard, 1778-1780*, Baltimore, 1939).

[2] See pages 20, 21 and 30.

[3] See the Institution, pages 6 and 7.

tution itself. But there was an amendment, in consequence of Major L'Enfants intimations.

In addition to the *medal,* which was finally determined to be of *Silver,* instead of *gold,* it was resolved that there should be a *diploma,* which, with the *Silver medal* should be given to each member. The bald eagle of *gold. The Order* of the Society to be procured at the private expence of each member.

The diploma, and *Silver medal* to be given at the expence of the Society. To present the bald eagle at the rated price, would in the opinion of many exceed our abilities, and as the foreign Gentlemen Say, be contrary to the practice in Similar cases.—If however the general Society, when they meet, Should think proper, and Should find it convenient, *the Order* can be presented, without any time having been lost. Major L'Enfant has it in charge to get the *diploma* engraved, and the Dies for the *medals* executed in the most masterly manner.

He also will get *the order* for the Subscribers. And he Says, that he will have them in America by the first general meeting in May next. I hope I have been Sufficiently clear in explaining these Subjects.

Major L'Enfant will have laid before your Excellency his instructions, and orders from General McDougall, The Treasurer: if you should think anything in addition necessary, I hope you may find it convenient to give it to him.

I am fully of opinion with you, that the Marquis de la Fayette, would be the most proper person in France to interest in our affairs. I believe that Major L'Enfant has not any instructions which will interfere with Such an arrangement.

I will inform General McDougall of your Excellencys generous intentions to present the Society with 500 Dollars. This Sum, nor any other Similarly given, cannot in my opinion be appropriated but by the general meeting, in the manner pointed out in the institution.

I will endeavor, by the next post to have Six or Seven copies of the institution made out as well as possible, and transmit them to your Excellency.

I am my dear General etc.

[*Archives of the General Society*]

General Washington took General Knox's advice and left much of the Society's business in the hands of the Marquis de La Fayette. L'Enfant took with him the following letter of introduction to La Fayette:

To the MARQUIS DE LAFAYETTE.

Rocky Hill, October 30, 1783

Sir:

I do myself the honor to transmit You herewith a Copy of the Institution of the Cincinnati, a Society formed by the American Officers before they seperated and retired to private life.

The principles of the society the purposes for which it was form'd and the qualifications necessary to become Members will fully appear by the Institution. Should any of the Foreign Officers who are qualified by serving three years in our Army wish to become Members, I must take the liberty to request You to let them sign the Institution and pay the necessary sum into Your hands.

Major L'Enfant who will have the honor to deliver You this, has undertaken to get the Order of the society executed in France. He has directions to deliver you one of the first that are compleated, and you will please also call on Him for as many as You may want. Major L'Enfant will inform You the price of them; the Deplomas shall be forwarded as soon as they can be made out.

I am, etc.[1]

[*Washington Papers*]

The following letter of instructions to L'Enfant is interesting as shewing that General Washington desired a special Eagle made to his order. See Letter (page 100) anent the Eagle in diamonds presented to the President General by the officers of the French Navy.

[1] Contemporary copy in handwriting of George Augustine Washington. See similar letter, dated 20 October 1783, page 23. For LaFayette's reply, see page 37.

To Major PIERRE-CHARLES L'ENFANT.

October 30, 1783

Sir:

Herewith you will receive 250 Dollars in bank notes, with which you will please procure for me eight of the bald eagles. One of which if there shall appear (upon conversing[1] with gentlemen, better acquainted in these matters than I am) no impropriety in it, or any deviation from the intention of the Order. May not only be finished in a masterly manner but ornamented in an elegant, tho' not in a costly Stile. If, on the contrary, it should be thought best to have no difference between any of them, in the decorations (for I do not mean to depart in the smallest degree from the forms of the Order) then seven will be sufficient for me, as the ornamental one would only have been used on extra occasions.

I have in the Letter you are charged with to the Marquis de la Fayette, requested him to send me, by the earliest oppertunity, a sett of Silver plated ware, but as there is not only a possibility but a probability, that he may have left Paris for the country before you get there, or may be absent on some other occasion, I beg, in that case, that you would open my letter to him, and comply with the contents of it, if you can do it conveniently.

Wishing you a pleasant passage, and a prosperous voyage, I am, etc.

[From the copy in the Library of Congress made by Toner who copied it from the original then in the possession of Thomas A. Diggs of Maryland. Washington's Letterbooks also include a copy, but it differs in many details from the above.]

Membership Certificate of Major L'ENFANT.[2]

This is to certify that M. L'Enfant Major of the Corps of Engineers in the Armies of the United States of America, being

[1] "Canvassing," in the Letter Books.
[2] See also certificate of 16 October, 1733, page 20.

by virtue of his services in the said Armies entitled to be a Member of the Society of the Cincinnati is entitled to all the rights & privileges of the said Society—And having obtained permission to go to France on his own private Affairs—is charged with the execution of some important business of the said Society

Given under my hand this 1 day of Novr. 1783

Signd
G W———n
Presidt. General

[*Archives of the General Society*]

To Major-General HENRY KNOX.

Rocky Hill, November 3, 1783

Sir,

I do myself the honor to transmit you the proceedings of the society of the Cincinnati of the State of So. Carolina which I reced. yesterday. I am, etc.[1]

[*Archives of the General Society*]

From Major-General WILLIAM SMALLWOOD.

Annapolis, November 29, 1783

Dear Sir,

Your Letter dated the 24th of October[2] miscarried—I did not receive it untill the 27th. Inst.—as you will observe by the inclosed Letter from Genl. Gist—I have now the Honour of embracing the earliest Opportunity by Capt. Howe of transmitting the Proceedings of the Society of the Cincinnati of this State.—

I received Letters from General Heath and the Baron de Steuben on the Subject Matter of the Institution, which were communicated and the sense of all the Officers who were assem-

[1] These proceedings are attached to this letter in the Archives.

[2] This letter, to the President of the Maryland Cincinnati, is similar to that of 24 October 1783 to General McIntosh, page 25.

bled here in July last taken—but the Meeting not having been so general as might have been wished it was thought most eligible (from the remote and distressed situation of the Officers, and the Expences which might accrue upon drawing them to a Point on that single Object) to suspend all further Process therein untill the 20th. of November following, when we might also address the General Assembly upon the Subject of the Lands which have been pledged, the Redemption of our Depreciation Certificates, and Arrears of Pay &c—The Meeting on the 20th Inst. was not so full as was expected, but Numbers have fallen in since and subscribed the Institution—a list of whom is inclosed—

I have the Honor to be etc.

[*Archives of the General Society*]

Here is a letter written from a debtor's prison by a dismissed officer who hoped that membership in the Cincinnati might help him. His hope of being admitted to the Society was fruitless.

From Colonel HENRY BABCOCK.

Head Quaters
Little Rest Gaol Decr. 6, 1783—

May it Please your Excellency. . . .

The Glorious Institution of the Noble Order of Cincennati, does your Excellency great Honor;—when I presume to address so great a Character, my Pen faulters hesitates, & Blunders; I wish for some American Homer, only to do your exalted Character Justice; & no doubt Providence will raise up one, which will exceed the Monument, so well earned, that Congress have done themselves the Honor to be erected to your Memory; for when that has mouldered, & worn out, the bright Pages of the Historian will be remembered; not only for the Sublimity & Sentimental manner in which it will be wrote, but by the Magnitude of the Prize contended for, & so gloriously obtained, which will endure as long as Gratitude, the noblest Sensation of the human Mind will be held in Estimation.—

I have the Honor to be etc.

P. S.

The reason of the Letter being dated at a Gaol is, for not being able to pay my Debts, which Debts have been made, in consequence of taking a small Part, in the defence of my Country, having Leased out my Estate to a Tennant, who committed such waste with my Lands & Stock as hath disennabled me to make payment, together with some Excentrical Exhibitions;— But cou'd I be honor'd with a Medal of the Noble Order of Cincennati, it wou'd be more esteem'd than Money, Tho' I now stand in the greatest need of it; For honor ever was Esteem'd by me, more than Cash, & there I believe I shall have your Excellencys approbation

[*Washington Papers*]

From Brigadier-General GEORGE WEEDON.

Fredericksburg Decr. 12th
1783

Dear Sir

I had the honor of addressing a letter to Your Excellency from Baltimore on the subject of our State proceedings respecting the Order of Cincinnati. I have never been able to procure the printed copies till lately which are now inclosed with a Copy also of the proceedings of the Georgia line.—Wishing You the compliments of the Season

Am with every Sentiment of Esteem
Your Most Ob^t^. Servt.
G. Weedon [1]

His Excellency
Genl. Washington.
Fredericksburg Decr. 12th 1783
[Indorsed]
from Genl. Weedon
Proceedings of Cincinnati.
Read in Genl. Meeting May 6th '84
G. Turner, Sec^y^. pro. Tem:

[*Archives of the General Society*]

[1] General Weedon, first President of the Virginia Cincinnati, was at this time Postmaster at Fredericksburg, the post office being in the Rising Sun Tavern, built by General Washington's brother, Charles. In that building the Virginia Cincinnati first dined together, 6 October 1783.

This letter, from the President of the Georgia Cincinnati transmits the minutes of that branch of the Society, as requested by the President General:

From Major-General LACHLAN MCINTOSH.

Savannah [Georgia], December 20, 1783

Sir,

I was honored yesterday by your Excellency's favor of the 24th. October,[1]—and have directed the secretary of our state association of the Cincinnati to Copy such extracts from the minutes of our proceedings as will give you all the information you require, which he will inclose herewith,[2] as I am obliged to go out in the Country.—

The Reason I have not done myself the honor of writing to your Excelly. before on this subject is, that we were not informed of your acceptance of the appointment of President General of the Society, and some envious persons had asserted that you refused it, which made me at a loss who to direct to, as such, but for the deficiency, as well as to commence that communication and correspondence recommended in the original Institution with our Sister society, in the Neighbouring states, I have transmitted Copys of our proceedings to those of South & North Carolina and Virginia, and expected by that Means they would be conveyed through the other states.—

I have only to request your Excellency will inform me in time of the place of the General Meeting in May next, as we are at such a distance.—and have the Honor to be etc.

[*Archives of the General Society*]

Official French Announcement of the Institution of the Society of the Cincinnati.

[Translation by Edgar Erskine Hume]

Paris, 23 December 1783

The American vessel *Washington* arrived in Havre on the 8th of this month. On board this ship was Major L'Enfant,

[1] See also General McIntosh's letter of 20 April 1784, page 141.

[2] Extract from the proceedings of the Georgia Society, certified by Captain John Milton, Secretary of the Georgia Cincinnati, is with the letter.

charged with the duty of procuring the Orders of the Society of the Cincinnati.

This association, the rules of which will be published, was formed by the American officers as a monument to their fraternity in the cause which united them.

The distinctive Order of the Society is the Bald Eagle, the American eagle peculiar to that country. It bears emblems referring to the glory and the disinterestedness of Cincinnatus, whose position was analogous to that of the American officers. It will be suspended from a blue ribbon bordered with white, emblematic of the alliance of the United States with France, and of their gratitude.

General Washington, President of the Society, writes in this capacity to the Marquis de la Fayette for him to obtain the signatures of the officers of the American Army at present in Europe, who have complied with the prescribed conditions, and to deliver to them the insignia of the Order of Cincinnatus.

Major L'Enfant brought a letter to the Count de Rochambeau, in which the Society presents the insignia of the Order to the generals and colonels of the French Army who served with the Americans, as well as to the admirals who commanded the naval forces in those parts.

[*La Gazette de France,* 23 December 1783, No. 102]

This is the first of the many letters from French members of the Cincinnati telling of the success of the Order in France, and asking admission.

From the COUNT DE BOUGAINVILLE.

Paris, 24th December 1783

Sir,

Your Excellency will not be surprised that those who have had the happiness to co-operate by their services in the great act which gave Liberty to America, should express the greatest anxiety to enter into an association formed to commemorate forever the great event.

I declare to your Excellency that I do not see a Frenchman

who has been admitted into the illustrious Order of the Cincinnati without feeling the most earnest desire to participate in that honor.

As I am a general officer both in the Land and Naval Forces, M. le Comte d'Estaing, under whom I commanded a ship of 74 guns, was pleased, in my quality of brigadier-general of infantry, to intrust to my care in 1778 the defense of Natasket Roads, with a corps of 2000 men.

The works and batteries which I constructed for this purpose received the strongest approbation from the American generals who went to visit them.

I look on myself then to be in the same situation as the Colonels of the Army under M. le Comte de Rochambeau.

I had, afterwards, the honor to command the advance guard of the French Fleet in the naval action, which insured success to the important operations then being carried on in the Chesapeake Bay, and the praise of your Excellency bestowed on my conduct on that occasion has been my most glorious recompense.

Admission into the Society of the Cincinnati is also earnestly solicited by the general officers and captains of ships who have had the good fortune to serve in America, and our desire is better founded because, by serving in the Marine, we hope hereafter to return to those friendly coasts, and to enjoy the remembrance of those illustrious actions which have conferred liberty on a great people.

I beg of you, sir, that you will be pleased to lay before the honorable Society of which you have, with so much propriety, been made President, and explain and support my anxious wishes to be admitted to membership. It will be conferring a great honor on me if I owe this favor to the request which you will make in my behalf.

I am, with respect, your Excellency's very humble and very obedient servant,

de Bougainville[1]

[*Archives of the General Society*]

---

[1] The Count de Bougainville became an original member of the French Cincinnati.

Here is recorded the permission given by King Louis XVI for his officers to wear the Eagle of the Cincinnati. At that time the Order of the Golden Fleece was the only foreign decoration allowed to be worn in France.

From the MARQUIS DE LAFAYETTE.

Paris, December 25th, 1783

Sir:

On receipt of Your Excellency's letter[1] I took the measures to fulfill the instructions of the Society in which I have the honor to be a member.

As our institution was differently interpreted I wrote a letter to Count de Vergennes, of which the inclosed is a copy, and the account I gave was printed in a Court Gazette which I have the honor to send.[2]

At a King's Council, this day was a week, it has been decided that Count de Rochambeau, his generals and colonels, and who of the admirals should be permitted to wear the Order, and a very proper letter on the subject has been written by Maréchal de Ségur to M. de Rochambeau.

As to our American officers, I shall examine into the claims of every one. When the point is clear, deliver or refuse the Order, and in doubtful cases take the advice of a Board of American officers, members of the Society.

No foreign badge but the Golden Fleece is permitted to Frenchmen in this service.

From the distinction shown our Society, and the testimony it bears of having acted a part in this war, our badge is highly wished and warmly contended for by all those who hope they have some claim to it. The Nation has been very much pleased with the attention our Society has paid to the alliance and have found there is something very interesting in the brotherly affiliation.

Objections are made as in the case of every novelty. The hereditary part of the Institution has its comments, but the general voice is in favor of our Brotherly Society, and General Washington's name as President adds a weight to the Association.

[1] See page 29. [2] See page 34.

With the highest and most affectionate respect, I have the honor to be, my dear general,

Your obedient humble servant,

La Fayette

[*Archives of the General Society*]

L'Enfant reports to the President General his work in Paris for the Cincinnati.

From Major PIERRE-CHARLES L'ENFANT.

Paris, 25th December 1783

. . . . It is not less flattering to me to be able to inform Your Excellency of the success of my mission, and of the high appreciation which the French Nation entertain in general of the American Army for thus honoring an illustrious part of our army with such flattering distinction.

One single conversation with the French officers would at once convince you how thoroughly they appreciate in their hearts those brotherly sentiments which make them take so deep an interest in the happiness of America.

This institution, which they with reason consider as a monument erected to Republican virtues, as the fundimental basis of a cordial union between the different States, as a new tie which assures the duration of the reciprocal friendship which France has evinced to America cannot be looked upon in too advantageous a light.

The permission which this powerful Monarch, the Most Christian King, has already given to his subjects to wear in his dominions the Order of the Society of the Cincinnati, is not only a strong mark of his deference, but also an unmistakable proof of the sentiments of His Majesty toward America [1] . . . .

[*Archives of the General Society*]

---

[1] On the same day L'Enfant wrote to Steuben of the success of the Order in France. Text of his letter to Steuben is given in Gardiner's *The Order of the Cincinnati in France*, 13 n.

The Institution provided for the admission of officers of the French land forces, but officers of the French Navy were, seemingly, overlooked. Several letters on this subject were exchanged between General Washington and the French officers, and soon the officers of the sea forces were made eligible on the same basis as those of the armies.

From the COUNT D'ESTAING.

Paris, 25th December 1783

Sir:

I must beg leave to gratify a desire I cannot resist of paying Your Excellency, in a private letter, the most unfeigned homage of my unalterable attachment to you.

I shall take particular delight in carrying ye marks of an Association which you are President General of. It belonged to a chief of your merit, who gives to ye world in his person the example of everything that is great, to fasten more and more ye ties that link the citizen-soldier together, that unite ye civil and military virtues, and that put us constantly in mind of ye duties they impose on us.

Your portrait has hitherto served us as a Cincinnatus medal. I could wish it reproduced to ye life Your Excellency's features. It would alone be more expressive than the strongest and most elaborate inscriptions.

Our common friend, the Marquis de la Fayette, and I talk frequently of you. During our conversation we often cast our eyes on your picture, which makes a chief ornament of our respective houses.

We many times repeat to each other that among the celebrated men whom antiquity boasts of, none have performed actions of such difficulty and importance as those which you just so gloriously terminated. They reflect ye greater honor on humanity, as it was to defend its cause that you became a conquerer and that you had no other view whilst you were fighting to assert its rights. You are, Sir, the only such hero we know of.

Your excellency will not, I hope, be offended at my expressing so nakedly these truths, as every one of a Society has a privilege of opening freely his mind to his President.

I cannot but say something in favor of the gallant officers whom I conducted twice into North America. I'm perfectly satisfied that, upon recollecting ye proofs they gave of their courage and zeal, neither Your Excellency nor the Society should be surprised at my being mortified were they not as well treated as their fellow soldiers who went out under ye command of ye Count de Rochambeau.

It is impossible for me to tell you how much I should wish they could be made to believe, that, if they have not been specially named in the Institution of ye Cincinnati Society, it was a mistake, and they were supposed and looked on to be included therein.

This favor I most earnestly request you will be so kind as to grant me for four sea officers called ye Baillie de Suffren, d'Albert de Rioms, ye Chevalier de Borda, and ye elder of ye Chevalier du Rumain's nephews.

The motives that actuate me will, I hope, appear worthy of Your Excellency's attention. In every case ye captains of men of war are not to be comprised in the Association and that none are to be admitted but ye general officers who have served on your coasts, I shall beg you will make use of all your influence to obtain that particular honor for ye four gentlemen I have mentioned to your excellency.

I'm, by my rank, ye first officer of ye French marine. In this quality I have a right to represent the whole corps, and to point out those who have rendered ye greatest services and whom this mark of distinction would be of ye highest consequence to.

It was I who conducted to America the first fleet and ye first troops that were sent there. I took on myself, without any orders from my court, to bring back thither all ye forces I could muster up. They were not idle.

I say nothing of ye wounds I have received. I look on it as a most distinguished reward of my labors to have been ye only French general officer who has shed his blood for America.

Ye pain I shall feel, in consequence all my life, is a sensation I shall find happiness in, as it will constantly remind me that I have done for that country everything that lay in my power.

It was our arrival in Savannah that caused ye evacuation of Rhode Island. Had Count de Grasse executed as well as ye

Marquis de Vaudreuil ye orders I had given them both of going with their divisions to ye Bay of ye Chesapeake, Charlestown had not been attacked.

When I was called upon again to take the command, and that I was charged to form the plan of the following campaign, matters were so combined that peace immediately ensued. I was ye first that had ye pleasure of announcing it to the Americans.

The Marquis de La Fayette, who was the only one entrusted with ye secret, will make Your Excellency sensible of the infinite importance of ye articles concerning America. I'm ye more desirous of his explaining them fully to you, as they do great honor to the personal views of his Spanish majesty.

This prince was so gracious as to trust me with his land and sea forces when he permitted me to conduct them to America. I was really sending them to serve under ye command of your excellency.

I beg that you will be convinced that it is not self-love or vanity that has made me enter into this detail. I take ye liberty of looking on you in all this affair as my advocate. It was then but natural I should furnish you with arguments to plead and gain my cause.

I cannot sufficiently paint to you the worth manner that Major L'Enfant has acquitted himself of Your Excellency's commission. His conduct has given him a just claim to my esteem and friendship.

With the greatest consideration, respect and esteem, I have the honor to be, Sir,[1]

Your most obedient and most humble servant,

Estaing.

[*Archives of the General Society*]

---

[1] For General Washington's reply, 15 May 1784, see page 175.

To Major-General JEDEDIAH HUNTINGTON.

Circular [1]

Mount Vernon
Virginia Decr. 28th 1783

Sir

After taking the various circumstances into mature consideration, I have thought proper to appoint the City of Philadelphia to be the place for the general Meeting of the Society of Cincinnati on the first Monday in May next, agreeably to the original Institution. The object of this Letter is to communicate timely information thereof, that proper notice may be given to the Delegates of your State Society, whose punctual attendance will be expected at the time and place beforementioned.

Having made this Communication, I have only to suggest that it may perhaps be preferable to give the necessary notice to your Delegates by Letter, rather than by a public Notification. I would however wish, that whatever mode is adopted, measures may be taken to prevent a possibility of failure in the communication.

I have the honor to be Sir

Your very Hble Servant
Go. Washington

P. S. Please to acknowledge the receipt of this letter.
Majr. Gen. Huntington
Presdt of the State Society of
Cincinnati in Connecticut

[*Archives of the Connecticut Cincinnati*]

---

[1] Similar letters to each of the other State Societies were sent. Some are dated 28 December 1784 and some 1 January 1784 (see page 46). Washington had reached Mount Vernon on Christmas Eve, 1783. In Fitzpatrick's *The Writings of George Washington* (xxvii, 286), there is a copy of the letter to the Rhode Island Cincinnati, dated 28 December, 1783. For General Huntington's reply, 23 February 1784, see page 97.

To Major-General NATHANIEL GREENE.

Circular

Mount Vernon Virginia
Decr. 28th 1783

Sir

After taking all the various circumstances into mature consideration, I have thought proper to appoint the City of Philadelphia to be the place for the general Meeting of the Society of the Cincinnati on the first Monday in May next, agreeably to the original Institution—The object of this Letter is to communicate timely information thereof, that proper notice may be given to the Delegates of your State Society, whose punctual attendance will be expected at the time and place before mentioned.

Having made this communication, I have only to suggest, that it may perhaps be preferable to give the necessary notice to your Delegates by Letter, rather than by a public Notification; I would however wish that whatever mode is adopted, measures may be taken to prevent a possibility of failure in the communication—

I have the honor to be
Sir
Your Most Obedient Servt
G Washington

P. S. Please to acknowledge the Receipt of this Letter[1]

The President of the State Society
of Cincinnati in Rhode Island

[*Archives of the Rhode Island Cincinnati*]

---

[1] General Greene replied on 16 February 1784. See page 81.

From the COUNT DE GRASSE.

Paris, 29th December, 1783

Sir,

I have received from Major L'Enfant the letter[1] which Your Excellency has honored me with in your quality as President of the Society formed by the American officers and denominated the Cincinnati.

I am flattered by the honor done me in making me a member of said Society and I am charmed that His Majesty has been pleased to permit me to wear the decoration.

I hope you will believe me fully when I tell you that this visible symbol can add nothing to the sincere attachment which I feel for the brave defenders of American Independence, and that this further association with them and with yourself will ever be to me a source of boundless satisfaction.

I shall avail myself of every occasion to revive *all* the pleasant recollections of those days, but the one fact which I shall prize above all others is the fact of your personal friendship, which ever since the first moment I was permitted to enjoy it, has been freely extended to me. . . .

As to the fraternal Society, in the bonds of which you have kindly seen fit, in due form, to include me as a member, and as completing a correspondence that has been to me a delightful, friendly chat, I beg you will forward the decoration to M. le Chevalier de la Luzerne, who will see that it is delivered to me. . . .

Continue towards me, I beg of you, those sentiments of esteem which you have for me and which I shall ever endeavor to merit, and at the same time rest assured not only of the

[1] This was evidently one of several letters of introduction from General Washington to French officers and taken to France by Major L'Enfant.

friendship but of the most sincere and respectful attachment with which I have the honor to be, Sir, Your Excellency's

Most obedient and very humble servant,

Le Comte de Grasse

[*Archives of the General Society*]

Like the membership certificates issued to Major L'Enfant (see pages 20 and 30) these two provisional diplomas were given by General Washington European members about to depart for Europe. The regular diplomas were prepared from the copperplate brought from Paris to the General Meeting in Philadelphia in May 1784.

Provisional Diploma.

This Certifies that Caspar Schaffner Cornet in the First Partizan Legion, being in Virtu of his Services in the American Army, Entitled to become a Member of the Cincinnati, and having Signed and complied with the Regulations therein Specified, is accordingly admitted a Member, and is Entitled to all The rights and Privileges of the Said Society of the Cincinnati.

Wax Seal (Washington Arms)

Given under my hand
and Seal at Philadelphia
this —— Day of December 1783.

G°. Washington

[*Archives of the Virginia Cincinnati*]

Provisional Diploma.

(Seal in red wax: Washington Arms)

This certifies that Joseph Smith, cornet in the First Partizan Legion, being, in vertu of his services in the American Army, intitled to become a member of the Cincinnati, & having signed the institution & complied with the regulations therein specified, is accordingly admitted a member, & is intitled to all the Rights & Privileges of the said Society of the Cincinnati

Given under my hand & seal at Philadelphia this —— Day of December 1783

G^o. Washington

Attest
H. Knox Sec^ry [1]

[*Maryland Historical Society*]

The first General Meeting of the Society of the Cincinnati was clearly to be of the utmost importance. General Washington issued the following formal call to the several State Societies.

Circular Letter to the Presidents of the State Societies of the Cincinnati [2]

Mount Vernon, January 1, 1784.

Sir

After taking all the various circumstances into mature consideration, I have thought proper to appoint the City of Philadelphia to be the place for the general Meeting of the Society of Cincinnati on the first monday in may next, agreeably to the

[1] This document was bequeathed to the Maryland Historical Society by Colonel George A. Pearre of Cumberland, Maryland. Cornet Smith was an officer of Armand's Partisan Corps, and signed Armand's Roll (copy of the Institution). See *fac simile*, page 47.

[2] Some of these letters were dated 28 December 1783. See the letter to General Huntington, President of the Connecticut Cincinnati (page 42); the letter to General Greene, President of the Rhode Island Cincinnati (page 43); and that to General Sumner, President of the North Carolina Cincinnati (page 48).

This Certifies that Joseph Smith, Cornet in the first
Partizan Legion, being, in vertu of his services in the
American army, intitled to become a Member of the Cincinnati
& having signed the institution & Complied with the Regu-
-lations therein specified, is accordingly admitted a member
& is intitled to all the Rights & Privileges of the said Society
of the Cincinnati

Given under my hand & seal at
Philadelphia this Day of Dece-
-mber 1783.

G Washington

Attest

H Knox Secy

Provisional Certificate of Membership in the Society of the Cincinnati signed by General Washington as President and General Knox as Secretary. This was before the parchment diplomas were issued.

[*Maryland Historical Society*]

original Institution—The object of this Letter is to communicate timely information thereof, that proper notice may be given to the Delegates of your State Society, whose punctual attendance will be expected at the time & place beforementioned.

Having made this communication, I have only to suggest that it may perhaps be preferable to give the necessary notice to your Delegates by Letter, rather than by a public notification; I would however wish that whatever mode is adopted, measures may be taken to prevent a possibility of failure in the communication—I am etc.

[*Archives of the General Society*]

This is the letter regarding the first General Meeting that the President General addressed to the North Carolina Cincinnati. It is similar in text to those above quoted (pages 42, 43, and 46).

To Brigadier-General JETHRO SUMNER.

Mount Vernon, Jany 5th, 1784

Sir,

After taking all the various circumstances into mature consideration, I have thought proper to appoint the City of Philadelphia[1] to be the place for the general meeting of the Society of the Cincinnati on the first Monday in May next, agreeably to the original Institution. The object of this letter is to communicate timely information thereof, that proper notice may be given to the Delegates of your State Society, whose punctual attendance will be expected at the time and place before mentioned.

Having made this communication, I have only to suggest

[1] In a letter from Brigadier-General Sumner, President of the North Carolina Society of the Cincinnati, to the Baron de Steuben, dated Halifax, North Carolina, 28 October 1783, he says: "It appears to be the sense of the Societies to the Southward, that the first general meeting should be held at Fredericksburg, in Virginia. That place, it is tho't, is nearly central, and most convenient for the President-General. The compliance of the Northern Societies in this, will give us very great pleasure" (Bellas's *Sketch of the North Carolina Society of the Cincinnati,* 1896, 89-90).

that it may perhaps be preferable to give the necessary notice to your Delegates by letter rather than by public notification; I would, however, wish that whatever mode is adopted, measures may be taken to prevent a possibility of failure in the communication.

I have the honor to be, Sir, Your Ob[t] Hum Servt

G[o]. Washington.

P. S. Be pleased to acknowledge the receipt of this letter
Brigadier-General Sumner,
North Carolina

[*Archives of the North Carolina Society*]

From the Chevalier CHARLES DE LAMETH.

Paris, Janvier 6, 1784.

Monsieur,

Puis-je espérer que votre excellence voudra Bien de rapeller encore quelqu'un qui ne peut jamais oublier les Bontés flatteuses dont elle l'a honore, et qui ose aujourd'huy en Solliciter une nouvelle préuve.

L'amérique daigne admettre quelques officiers de l'armée De Rochambeau à L'association La plus honnorable et La plus chère aux cœurs des françois, Puisquelle fixe L'époque de la Gloire immortelle de votre excellence, et qu' elle est pour Eux Le Gage de son estime. L'amérique a cru devoir ne comprendre dans cette Grace que les officiers Généraux, et Colonels de L'armée française: malgré ce que j'ai souffert, et ce que je Souffrirai Probablement Le Resté de ma vie, pour La Liberté, et Le Bonheur de L'amérique, je n'ai Pas L'indiscrétion de demander à votre excellence qu'elle fasse en ma faveur une excéption qui pourait L'exposer à Des Réclamations, j'ose Seulement attendre de Sa Bonté une interprétation favorable au téxte même de la Loy portée par L'amérique: ma Position d'ailleurs est unique, elle ne peut être n'y Sous le rapport des Bléssures, n'y Sous celuy des Services celle d'aucun officier de l'armée francaise; que votre Excellence veuille Bien me perméttre de La luy éxposer. Je suis parti de france avec le grade de capitaine de Dragons; je n'avais pas L'age de Demander à être fait colonel: arrivé à l'amérique Mr. Le Cte De Rochambeau m'a nommé premier aide Maréchal Général des logis de Son armée: j'avais obtenu de marcher comme volontaire en virginie, contre arnold, et je me Suis trouvé au Combat de Mr. detouches du 16 mars, à new yorck j'ai marché à L'avant Garde de Lauzun qui était chargée de Replier La Légion de Dehancey qui voulait troubler La Reconnaissance de votre excellence. en quittant La Position de Philisbourg j'ai mené L'arrière Garde de L'armée. LePassage de La Rivière du nord, ainsy que tous Les détails fatigans de notre marche, embarquement à annapolis, débarquement dans La Rivière de james ont en partie Roulé Sur moy. à L'investissement D'yorck j'ai marché avec L'avant Garde de L'armée qui a Protégé—La première Reconnaissance que votre Excellence a fait de cette place: lors de L'ouverture de la Premiere parallelle, votre Excellence pourait Se rappeller que j'eu l'honneur de passez une partie de la nuit auprès de sa personne: Pendant le Siège j'ai montè La tranchée comme officier de La Ligne: enfin à l'attaque d'une des Redouttes de la Gauche des ennemis, marchant comme volontaire avec les travailleurs qui formaient La tête de l'attaque, je suis parvenu jusque sur le parapet, et ai été assez heureux de faire couper La fraize avant de recevoir deux coups de fusils dans les Deux Genoux, je me rapellerai toute ma vie avec une tendre et respectueuse reconnaissance L'extrême bonté qu'eut votre excellence de venir me visiter sur mon Lit de Douleurs.

Sur L'éxposé de mes Services, Le Roy de france a Bien voulu m'accorder La croix de St. Louis, et Le Grade de Colonel: mon Brevet est datté du mois de janvier, et ce n'est qu'au mois de fevrier que j'ai quitté L'amérique. *j'ai donc été Colonel à L'armée de Mr. Le Cte De Rochambeau, en même tems qu'aide Maréchal General des Logis de son armée, et me trouve dans Le Cas d'être compris dans La distinction que L'amérique veut bien accorder aux Colonels.* Cependant comme je n'en ai pas fait le Service (et comment aurai je pu le faire), puisque mes Blessures m'ont retenu au Lit plusieurs mois après mon retour en france), Mr. Le Cte De Rochambeau a poussé la rigoureuse exactitude jusqu'à attendre pour me comprendre La décision de votre éxcellence: il a L'honneur de vous écrire pour la Solliciter favorable: Mr. Le Mis de Lafayette aura pareillement l'honneur d'écrire à votre excellence, et de luy dire qu'il Pense que Mr. Le Cte de Rochambeau aurait pu Sans donner d'éxtension à La Loy me comprendre dans cette nomination cy. en éffet que votre excellence daigne Réfléchir un moment Sur ma position, elle Sentira combien il Serait Dur pour moy de voir des officiers qui n'ont Séjourné que Deux mois à l'amérique, Sans y entendre un coup de fusil, Recevoir une distinction militaire dont je Serais privé quoiqu'en étant Susceptible d'après La loy. quand les officiers francais ont autant à Se Louer des Bontés touchantes de L'amérique, votre excellence ne permettera pas que celuy de tous qui a le plus Souffert pour elle, que celuy à qui vous avez daigné montrer de L'intéret et de L'estime, trouve toujours dans les camarades des objets d'une Comparaison affligeante, et des motifs de Regrets qui ne finiraient plus, Si mon Oncle (Le Maréchal De Broglie) n'était absent, il aurait Surement eu L'honneur d'écrire dans cette circonstance à votre excellence pour me Recommander à Ses Bontés. Si, Comme je me plais à n'en pas douter, Le décision de L'assemblé Généralle m'est favorable, j'aurai à m'applaudir de La Rigueur de Mr Le Cte De Rochambeau, Puisqu'elle m'aura valu, avec cette Grace, à la qu'elle j'attache Le plus grand prix, un témoignage plus Particulier de L'estime de L'armée américaine, et de celle de votre Excéllence pour La qu'elle je donnerais ma vie.

Je Suis, avec une Réspectuéuse Reconnaissance, et une Profonde vénération, etc.

[*Archives of the General Society*]

[Translation by Edgar Erskine Hume]

Paris 6 January 1784

Sir:

May I hope that Your Excellency will still remember one who can never forget the flattering kindness with which he has been honored, and who hopes today to sollicit a new proof thereof.

America deigns to admit certain officers of the Army of Rochambeau into the Association most honorable and most dear to the hearts of Frenchmen, since it marks the epoch of Your Excellency's immortal glory, and because it is for them a mark of his esteem. America has thought proper to include in this body only the general officers and colonels of the French Army: In view of what I have suffered and shall probably suffer for the rest of my life, for the liberty and welfare of America, it may not be indiscrete for me to ask Your Excellency in view of this to make an exception in my favor that would not bring about criticisms. I hope only that there will be a favorable interpretation of the text of the law made by America: My position is moreover unique, for neither as to wounds received nor as to service is any other officer of the French Army in the same position, if Your Excellency permit, in the provision of the law. I left France with the grade of captain of dragoons. I was not old enough to ask to be made a colonel. On arrival in America, the Count de Rochambeau appointed me first Aide Marshal of Quarters for his army. I took part as a volunteer in the march to Virginia, against Arnold and I participated in battle with M. Destouches on 16 March in New York. I marched with the advanced guard of Lauzun who was charged with repelling the Legion of Dehancey, which sought to interrupt Your Excellency's reconnaissance. In leaving the position at Philisbourg [*sic*] I remained with the rear guard of the Army. The crossing of North River, as well as all of the fatiguing details of our march, embarkation at Annapolis, debarkation at James River were, in part, dependent on me. At the investment of York I marched with the advanced guard protecting Your Excellency's reconnaissance at that place. Aside from this, Your Excellency may recall that I had the honor of passing part of the night near his person. During the siege, I fought in the trenches as an officer of the line. Finally in the attack of one of the redoutes at the Enemy's left, marching as a volunteer with the sappers who formed the head of the attack, I advanced to the parapet, where I had the good fortune to be able to cut the entanglements before receiving two gunshot wounds in both knees. I shall retain all my life the tender and respectful memory of the extreme goodness with which Your Excellency came to visit me on my bed of pain.

On the basis of my services, the King of France was

graciously pleased to accord me the Cross of Saint-Louis and, the grade of Colonel. My commission is dated in the month of January, and it was not until February that I quitted America. *I was therefore a Colonel in the Army of the Count de Rochambeau, at the same time as being Aide Marshal General of Quarters for his Army, and so I believe myself to be eligible for the honor that has been accorded to Colonels.* However, since I have not served as Colonel (and how could I?, since my wounds kept me in bed for several months after my return to France) the Count of Rochambeau has, with strict exactitude, awaited the decision of Your Excellency. He has the honor to write you asking favorable consideration. The Marquis de Lafayette will also have the honor to write to Your Excellency, and say that it seems to him that the Count de Rochambeau might, without exceeding the provisions of the law, include my nomination. In fine, if Your Excellency will have the goodness to reflect a moment on my position, you will see how hard it is for me to see the officers who spent only two months in America, without having been struck by bullets, receive a military distinction of which I am deprived since I am not eligible under the law. Since French officers have received so much kindness from America, Your Excellency will not permit that one who suffered so much for her, one in whom you have deigned to display an interest and esteem, should go on finding in his comrades objects of painful comparison and motives of regret. Finally, if my uncle, the Marshal de Broglie, were not absent, he would certainly have the honor of writing the circumstances to Your Excellency and recommend me to your goodness. If, as I have no cause to doubt, the decision of the General Meeting will be favorable to me, I shall applaud the strictness of the Count de Rochambeau, for he will, in this way, have added value to the favor to which I attach the greatest worth, a most particular evidence of the esteem of the American Army, and that of Your Excellency for whom I would give my life.

I am, with the most respectful appreciation, and profound veneration, etc.[1]

[1] At the General Meeting, Monday, 17 May 1784, it was:

"*Resolved,* That Monsieur de Tarlé, Intendent and second officer of the French Auxiliary Army, and the Chevalier de Lameth, Colonel by brevet, also

From the COUNT DE ROCHAMBEAU.

[Translation by Edgar Erskine Hume]

Paris, 7 January 1784

Monsieur,

To-day I read to the generals and colonels who served under my orders in America the letter which you did me the honor to write me. As to the authorization of His Majesty for them to enter into the Society formed here under the name of the Cincinnati, His Majesty most graciously consents and interposes no conditions, as you will see from the text which I send you herewith.

Our purpose being to perpetuate that union which the alliance of His Majesty created beween our two nations and secure in case of need those officers of the American Army who have suffered in the war which we made in common, I hope that we will subscribe a sum worthy of this kingdom and of the object to which [the association] is directed.[1]

I am, dear Monsieur, Your Excellency's most obedient servant.

The Count de Rochambeau

[*Archives of the General Society*]

---

the Count de Sainneville, the Count de la Touche-Tréville, the Count de Kergariou Loc Maria, the Chevalier de l'Eguille, the Chevalier DeQuesne, the Count de la Prévalaye, the Chevalier de Colbert-Maulevrier, the Chevalier de Vallongue, the Count de Capellis, and the Chevalier de la Pérouse, Captains and Commanders of ships and frigates of the French Navy, who were employed on special service on the coast of America, and are particularly named and recommended to the Society by His Excellency the Minister of France, are entitled by the spirit and intention of the Institution to become members of the Cincinnati" (Minutes of the General Meeting of 1784).

[1] The French officers subscribed the sum of 60,000 *livres*, of which the Count de Rochambeau contributed 6000; the Chevalier de Chastellux 4000; each *maréchal de camp* 2000; each brigadier 1500 and each colonel 1000 *livres*—(Contenson, 32).

In the bicentennial year of Washington's birth, on 4 July 1932, two plaques

From the COUNT D'ESTAING.

[L'Orient, January 8, 1784]

Le Cte. d'Estaing a l'honneur de mettre sous les yeux de son Excellence, Le General Washington, les quatres Mémoires qui Lui ont été adressés, depuis la Lettre qu'il a eu L'honneur de lui écrire, en date du 25 décembre 1783.

Mr. de Choin, Colonel de dragons,[1]

Mr. Le Comte de Kergariou Locmaria, Cape. de vaisseau,

Mr. Le Comte Edouard Dillon, Colonel,

et Mr. Le Comte de Castellane Majastres, Cape. de vaisseau, ne sont pas les seuls qui ont demandé au Cte d'Estaing de faire parvenir Leur demande.

Le desir de partager l'association enflamme presque également tous Les officiers françois qui se flattent de pouvoir L'a meriter, et les motifs des autres officiers qui sollicitent sont compris dans la précédente Liste, ou dans Les Listes des Généraux sous lesquels ils ont servi.

[*Archives of the General Society*]

were unveiled at the former residence of the Count de Rochambeau, 40 rue de Cherche-Midi, in Paris. The tablet to the left of the door is inscribed:

Jean-Baptiste-Donatien de Vimur
Comte de Rochambeau
Maréchal de France, 1725-1807,
habitait cet hôtel quand il reçut le
commandement de l'armée envoyée par
le Roi Louis XVI en Amérique, 170
Pour aider les Etats-Unis
à conquérir leur indépendance

The tablet at the right of the door reads:

La section française de la
Société des Cincinnati a été
fondée dans cet hôtel, 7-16 janvier 1784,
en souvenir de la guerre de
l'Indépendance Américaine.

[1] The enclosure mentioned, from Mr. de Choin, is no longer with the collection.

[Contemporary English translation][1]

From The COUNT D'ESTAING.

[L'Orient, January 8, 1784]

The Count De Estaing has the Honor to submit to His Excellency Gl. Washington the four Memorials which have been sent to him since the last Letters He had the honor to address to him on the 25th of December 1783.

Mr. De Choin Colonel of Dragoons
Count De Kergariou Locmaria Captain of the Navy
Count Edwd. Dillon, Colonel
Count Castellane Majestres, Captn. of the Navy,

are the only Gentlemen who solicited Count De Estaing to present their demand.

To participate the honor of this association inflames equally all the French officers; and the motive for which I solicit in favor of the others are mentioned in the list of General Officers under whom they served.

[*Archives of the General Society*]

From the COUNT DE KERGARIOU DE LOCMARIA.

a l'hotel de Toulouse a paris ce 8 janvier 1784

[Enclosure in memorandum from the Count d'Estaing, 8 January, 1784]

Le Comte de Kergariou Locmaria Capitaine de vaisseaux, chargé pendant presque toute La guerre d'expeditions particuliaires, commandant toujours des fregates, a montré dans toutes Les Circonstances Son affection pour Les ameriquains, fournissant des Secours à Leurs fregates et autres batiments tout Sur Les Cotes de france qu'aux isles occidentales.

[1] Contemporary translation written in parallel with the original French. The four officers became original members of the French Cincinnati.

en 8bre 1781 La Sibille Lui fut confiée a brest chargée de plusieurs millions en or et argent ainsy que L'escorte d'une state chargée d'une valleur égale en équipements de troupes. il atteignit Le 4 janvier 1782 La Baye de chesapeack.—Se trouvant par Son ancienneté commandant des forces navales de france en amerique, il S'est, depuis L'instant de Son arrivée, Sans relache, occupé à proteger Le commerce de cette baye. il a décapé toutes Les flotes qui one désiré Sortir de La baye et La Sibille Se trouvant mieux disposée que Les Vaisseaux et fregates qui S'y trouvaient Sous Ses ordres, il Sest toujours tenu en Station à L'ouvert de cette baye, corvée dure et épineuse dont Les ordres de La Cour et Son ancienneté Le dispensaient puisqu'il etait destiné pour St dominque.

Sa conduite dans ce Lieu Lui a vallu Le Suffrage des gouverneurs et negotiants ameriquains et Le commerce de philadelphie Le Sollicita d'aller proteger L'entrée de La delavare.

au mois d'aoust Les Besoins de St dominque L'obligerent de Se charger d'y conduire une flote-americaine; et il revenoit en amerique escortant une nouvelle flote Lorsque Le 2 janvier 1783, attaqué par La magicienne Soutenue par Léndemion, il a par Sa maneuvre, ce jour, Sauvé Sa flote et Sa frigate apres avoir vazé et étaint Le feu de celle de L'enemis; un coup de vent Le Six janvier a dispersé Sa flote, a démati Sa frigate de tout mats, et L'a forcé Le 22 fevrier de rendre au centurion Secondé dune frigate et dune corvette, La Sibille Ses poudrés noyées et coulant bas. il n'est redevable des outrages et des mauvais procedes du Sr. Russell capitaine du hussard pour Son etat major et équipage qu a Son attachement pour Les ameriquains.

Cest en vertu de ce zelle, Des Blessures recues Le 2 janvier point encore guerries et dont il est couvert, de Son Rang de Colonel, ainsy que du poste de commandant des forces navalles qu'il a occupé pendant huit mois en amerique, qu'il reclame L'honneur d'etre, comme tous Les Colonels françois, agrégé à La Société de Cincinnatus.

[*Archives of the General Society*]

[Translation by Edgar Erskine Hume]

Hotel de Toulouse, Paris, 8 January 1784

The Count de Kergariou Locmaria, *Capitaine de Vaisseaux,* in charge of special expeditions during nearly the whole of the war, commandant of frigates during the whole time, has shown under all circumstances, his affection for the Americans, giving aid to their frigates and other ships as well on the coast of France as in the West Indies.

In October 1781 he was given command of *La Sibille* at Brest bearing several millions in gold and silver, as well as a vessel bearing equipment for the troops to an equal value. On 4 January 1782 he reached Chesapeake Bay. He assumed, by reason of his seniority, command of the naval forces of France in America, and from the moment of his arrival, without cease, gave his care to the protection of the commerce of this bay. He escorted all the fleets that wished to leave the bay, *La Sibille* being better suited for this than any of the other vessels and frigates placed under his orders, he always remained stationed at the mouth of the bay, a hard and trying task considering that the commands of his Sovereign and his seniority had destined him to Santo Domingo.

His conduct of this duty was appreciated by the American officials and merchants and the commerce of Philadelphia requested him to protect the entrance of the Delaware.

In the month of August the needs of Santo Domingo obliged him to bring an American fleet there. He was returning to America, escorting a new fleet when on 2 January 1783 he was attacked by the *Magician* supported by the *Endymion.* By his maneuvre on that day he saved the fleet, and his frigate, after he had grounded his ship and silenced the guns of the enemy. A storm of 6 January dispersed his fleet, and broken the masts of his frigate, forcing him on 22 February to surrender to the *Centurion* supported by a frigate and a corvette, *La Sibille* after he had flooded her powder. The outrages and mistreatment of Sir Russell, Captain of the *Hussar,* inflicted on his officers and crew were due only to his attachement to the Americans.

In virtue of this zeal, the wounds received on 2 January, not yet healed and with which he is covered, his rank of Colonel, as well as his post of commandant of naval forces which he held for eight months in America, that he asks the honor of being, like all French Colonels, admitted a member of the Society of Cincinnatus.

From the COUNT D'ESTAING.

[Enclosure in letter from d'Estaing, 8 January 1784]:

Mr. Le Comte Edouard Dillon était déstiné, en sa qualité de Colonel qu'il avait destais, à être employé dans L'Expedition de la Georgie. il avait sollicité avec la plus grande ardeur d'aller servir en Amérique. son zele et ses talens avaient décidé le Cte d'Estaing à seconder ses desirs: il aurait été à Savannah, blessé dans l'Expedition de la Grenade, son plus grand désespor, en ayant le bras cassé, fut causé par la décision des chirurgiens qui empêcherent de le transporter. Mr. Le Comte Edouard Dillon a chargé le Cte d'Estaing de demander son admission dans la société de Cincinnatus cet officier semble avoir, pour la meriter, le baptesme de desir et de sang.

[*Archives of the General Society*]

[Translation by Edgar Erskine Hume]

Count Edouard Dillon, in the rank of Colonel which he held, was employed in the Georgia expedition. He had requested with the greatest eagerness to serve in America. His zeal and his talents decided the Count d'Estaing to second his desires. He was present at Savannah, and wounded in the expedition to Grenada. His greatest regret was, on having his arm broken, caused by the surgeons who refused to transport him. Count Edouard Dillon has asked the Count d'Estaing to request his admission into the Society of Cincinnatus. This officer seems to merit it, having had his baptism of desire and of blood.

From the Count d'Estaing.

[Enclosure in letter from d'Estaing, 8 January 1784]:

Le Comte de Castellane Majastres, Cape. de Vau. du Roi, a l'honneur de représenter à son Excellence, Le Général Washington, que, commandant le vaisseau Le Marseillais, il a eu le bonheur d'êtré l'un des quatres vaisseaux de l'avant-garde, qui, au combat de la Chesapeak, se sont battus contre toute l'avant-garde angloise. le succès de cette journée ayant fortement contribué à la prise de L'armée de terre angloise, le Roi a honoré le Comte de Castellane d'une pension de cent pistoles, pour lui servir de témoignage de la satisfaction que Sa Majesté avait eue de sa conduite dans cette importante occasion; il prie son Excellence de lui faire obtenir de l'assemblée de la Société de Cincinnatus une Décoration qu'il a tâché de meriter; et il prie M Le Cte d'Estaing de faire parvenir sa demande.

Pour extrait, en date de L'Orient du 8 Janvier 1784.

Estaing

[*Archives of the General Society*]

[Translation by Edgar Erskine Hume]

The Count de Castellane Majastres, *Capitaine de Vaisseau* of His Majesty, has the honor to set forth to His Excellency, General Washington, that, in command of *Le Marseillais*, he had the good fortune to be in command of one of the four ships of the advance guard, which, at the battle of the Chesapeake, engaged the whole of the English advance guard. The success of this day having markedly contributed to the capture of the English land forces, the King honored the Count de Castellane with a pension of one hundred *pistoles*, to serve as a mark of the satisfaction which His Majesty had at his conduct on that important occasion. He begs His Excellency to obtain for him from the Assembly of the Society of Cincinnatus, a decoration which he has tried to merit; and he begs the Count d'Estaing to forward his request.

Extract. Dated l'Orient, 8 January 1784.

Estaing.

From the COUNT DE ROCHAMBEAU.

Paris ce 19 Janvier 1784.

Monsieur

Jai reçu la lettre dont Votre Excellence n'a honoré en datte du 29. 8bre. dernier par le major l'Enfant. Je ne peux mieux repondre à l'honorable invitation qu'elle veut bien me faire, ainsi qu'aux généraux et Colonels de l'armée française auxiliaire en amerique, qu'en lui envoyant 1o. la response de M. le mal. de segure, ministre de la guerre, portant la permission de mon souverain, de nous joindre à cette association respectable. 2o. La Liste des Généraux Brigadiers et Colonels que J'y ai admis, au suivant litteralement les pouvoirs qui m'ont été donnés par la société générale. 3o. un Liste de demandes qu'on m'a prié de Vous presenter, qui me paraissant dans des cas plus or moins favorables, suivant les notes que j'ai mises à leur article, en demandant une plus ample explication à leur sujet. 4o. une Liste des sommes qui ont été souscrites volontairement et unanimousment, pour concurir aux Vues bienfaisants de cet etablissement, ci remises à la disposition de la société générale.

Il me resté actuellement à assurer Voltre Excellence en mon nom et au nom de tous les Cincinnati de mon armée, que cet ordre peut perpetuer, mais n'ajoutera rien à la chaleur des sentimens tendres de fraternité et d'amitié que nous conservons pour nos freres de votre armée, et pour leur celebre chef que nous respecterons et que nous aimerons Jusqu'au dernier souper. C'est dans cette profession de sentiments que je Suis pour la vie

De Votre Excellence, etc.

[*Archives of the General Society*]

From the COUNT DE ROCHAMBEAU.

[Translation by Edgar Erskine Hume]

Paris, 19 January 1784

Dear Sir,

I had the honor of receiving your Excellency's letter, dated 29 October last, from the hands of Major L'Enfant.

I cannot better acknowledge the honor which you have done

me as well as the generals and colonels of the French Auxiliary Army which served in America than by sending you the following:

1. The reply of the Marshal de Ségur, Minister of War, giving us the authorization of our sovereign to enter this honorable association.

2. The list of generals, brigadiers and colonels which I have admitted to it, conforming literally to the powers which were given me by the General Meeting.

3. A list of the applications which I have been asked to place before you and which seem to me more or less admissible, to which I have added comments on each *dossier,* and to which I ask the action of the General Meeting.

4. A list of the amounts which have been voluntarily and unanimously subscribed as contributions to the charitable fund of the Institution and placed at the disposal of the General Society.

It is now my duty to assure Your Excellency, in my own name and those of all the Cincinnati of the army which I commanded that this order may perpetuate but it cannot increase the bonds of fraternal feeling and friendship which we hold for our brothers of your army and for their illustrious chief, whom we will cherish and respect to our last breath.

In professing these sentiments I have the honor to be, for all my life Your Excellency's most obedient and most humble servant.

The Count de Rochambeau [1]

[*Archives of the General Society*]

---

[1] Rochambeau's Memoirs are written with military brevity and do not often reveal his opinions of his friends and associates. He records, however, something of his feelings for Washington in the following note on the disbanding of the American Army and the institution of the Cincinnati: "The glorious peace, of such import to America, was proclaimed shortly afterwards. General Washington, at the head of an army to which nearly seven years' arrears of pay was due, found it no easy task to satisfy its demands with paper money, which its disbanding was talked of. An insurrection broke out amongst the troops, who persisted in maintaining themselves as a corps, and *in statu quo*, until the amount of pay should be acquitted in full by the different States in their respective shares.

This is the reply of the President of the Delaware Cincinnati to President General Washington's call for the first General Meeting of the Society.

From Surgeon General JAMES TILTON.

Annapolis [Maryland], January 20, 1784.

Sir,

It was with pleasure I received your communication of the 28 December 1783, appointing the city of Philadelphia to be the place for the general meeting of the society of Cincinnati, on the first monday in may next, agreeably to the original institution.

I am convinced, sir, you may rely on the punctual attendance of the delegates of the delaware state society. It was not without mature deliberation, in several meetings, the the officers of the delaware line entered into the association, and not before they had considered the objects of it as laudable, and the means of attainment as adequate to the ends proposed. I know therefore the delegates will consider themselves as inexcuseable for the least neglect. I have written a notification to Major James Moore (late Captn. Moore) who is one of the two appointed to represent our little society. He is a man of excellent character and can attend without inconveniency. And having myself the honor to be the other representative, I shall be ambitious to attend the first general meeting.

I have the honor to be, etc.

[*Archives of the General Society*]

General Washington, with that noble and patriotic character which ever formed the basis of his conduct, used his influential power over the minds of his soldiers to bring them round to those feelings of generosity with which they had been animated in the whole course of the Revolution. It was at his instigation that the *Cincinnatus association* was proposed, to commemorate the alliance of France, as an indissoluble bond of their mutual fraternity, and an honourable mark of their services. Having at last accomplished the disbanding of his army, he took leave of his military career by a letter which depicts with admirable precision the character of this great man, and which will certainly be handed down to posterity in the history of every country." (*Memoirs of the Marshal Count de Rochambeau relative to the War of Independence,* Paris, 1838, translation of the French edition of 1809.)

French officers, in many instances, considered *l'Ordre de Cincinatus* as a decoration to be conferred by General Washington just as the Royal and Military Order of Saint-Louis was conferred by the King. Many of their formal requests to be thus decorated are in the Archives. Some are addressed to General Washington. Others were addressed to General Knox, Secretary General. There is no record that the Baron de Fock was ever admitted to membership, though he is wrong is saying that he and the Count de Fersen were the only two Swedish officers who served in America.

From the BARON DE FOCK.

Paris, January 22, 1784.

My dear General,

The many favors, and particular marks, of His Excellence's kindness, and oblidging conduct, towards me, during the whole time, I spent in America; Gives me reason, to hope you will honor me with the order of Cincinnatus, of wich your Excellency is the President. As I was not a Colonel during the war, I can not get the order, wich is conferred only on Generals or Colonels in General Rochambeaus Army, without Your Excellences interposition—

Count de fersen, and I were the only two of our nation, which hat the Happiness, to be under His Excellences command, therefore I hopes my request will be most graciously granted, by His Excellency, and will be to me the Highest satisfaction, in my native Country, and an eternal remembrance, of His Excellency, for whom I have the greatest regard and attachment. All my wishes are, to be once my own master, to pay my respects to His Excellency in America, in the mean time, I pray Him, to give my most respectful Compliments, to Your Lady Mrs. Washington, and be sure that I am for Ever, with the Highest esteem etc.

[*Washington Papers*]

The Count de Barras, like other French naval commanders, felt keenly the apparent discrimination against them in not making them equally eligible to membership with the officers of the army. The Triennial of 1784 corrected this discrepancy.

From the COUNT DE BARRAS.

Paris, 23d January, 1784

Sir,

I received the letter which you did me the honor to write me, as well as the Institution of the Society of the Cincinnati formed by the American Army. I am most flattered to be comprised in a military society the members of which have, with so much glory, concurred under the orders of Your Excellency to establish American liberty, but it gives me grate pain to see that all the generals of the sea, as well as the captains of ships of war, who have cruised and fought on the coast of North America, and particularly those who were employed under my command, do not partake with me the honor to be admitted in the Society.

I will not here call to your mind the distinguished services rendered the America by the naval officers under the command of Count d'Estain, and of Monsieur de Grasse. I will confine myself to what regards the particular squadron which I commanded.

The frequent and honorable combats under the orders of Monsieur Destouches, the frequent cruisings and bloody battles of the frigates for the protection of American commerce, the very dangerous junction formed with the Count de Grasse in Chesapeake Bay which insured the success of the enterprise against Yorktown, are pretensions which may give to the captains of this squadron a right to the distinction conferred on the colonels of the land forces with whom they co-operated.

Persuaded, however that to repair this omission, the members of Society of Cincinnatus have only to know the names of the general officers and captains of ships who served on the American coast, I have the honor to send to Your Excellency a list of those who were employed under my orders, and I would not myself accept the decoration of the Society but that I look on it as certain that it will be very shortly in common with my ancient companions in arms.

Sir, your very humble and most obedient servant,

Barras.

P. S. M. le Vicomte de la Bretonnière has communicated to me a letter which he has the honor to write to Your Excellency,[1] in which he sets forth the services rendered by him to the United States in convoying American ships. He requests to be comprised in the Society. His request is well founded and I, with pleasure concur with this officer, and pray that he may be comprehended with the other officers for whom I have made application.

[*Archives of the General Society*]

From the Baron de Vioménil.

a paris Le 24 janvier 1784

Monsieur

Le Baron d'angilly qui ma Servi d'aide de camp pendant les campagnes que j'ay faites en amérique desirant tres vivement d'etre aggregé a la Société que préside Votre Exelence, c'est avec la plus grande confiance que je la Supplie de vouloir bien luy procurer cet agrément, il était colonel attaché au corps de La marine. L'orsque nous sommes arrivés a newport, M. le cte de barras La employé en cette qualité et cest avec Lagrement du ministre de ce departement que je prend La liberté de demander bonté, et protection a Votre Exelence pour le Succes de ma recommendation, na reconnoissance Sera vive et tout aussi durable que les Sentiments du tendre et respectueux attachement avec Lesquels j'ay lhonneur d'être etc.

[*Archives of the General Society*]

[Translation by Edgar Erskine Hume]

Paris, 24 January 1784

Sir,

The Baron d'Angilly,[2] who served me as Aide-de-Camp during the campaigns that I made in America, desires very deeply to be admitted to the Society over which Your Excellency pre-

[1] See the letter of the Vicomte de La Bretonnière, 1 February 1784, page 70. For General Washington's reply to the Count de Barras, 17 May 1784, see page 188.

[2] The Baron d'Angély, Colonel of Dragoons, became an original member of the French Cincinnati. See General Washington's reply to the Baron de Vioménil, 15 May 1784, page 180.

sides. It is with the greatest confidence that I ask that you will be good enough to procure for him this admission. He was a Colonel, attached to the Marine Corps. When we arrived in Newport the Count de Barras employed him in this capacity, and it is with the approval of the minister of this department that I take the liberty of requesting the goodness and the assistance of Your Excellency for the success of my recommendation. My gratitude will be as keen and as lasting as the sentiments of affection and tender attachment with which I have the honor to be etc.

General Washington's announcement of the time and place of the General Meeting is acknowledged by the President of the Pennsylvania Cincinnati.

From Major-General ARTHUR ST. CLAIR.

Philadelphia, January 29, 1784.

Sir

In Answer to your Circular Letter [1] of the 28th. ulto. I have the Honor to inform you—that Notice has been communicated to all the Delegates of the Society of this State (except Major [Evan] Edwards) of the Time and Place which your Excellency has fixed for the General Meeting of the Cincinnati agreeably to the original Institution.

It would be very proper that all the Delegates should attend, but I fear it will not be the Case—General [Walter] Stewart will probably be sailed for Ireland—Major Edwards is in Carolina, and may not be able to return in time, and it is doubtful as to myself. If a proper Number of the Society can be got together, a new Appointment in the Room of those who will necessarily be absent, may take Place; but the Members are now so dispersed, it is not easily done, besides that frequent Journeys to this City accord but ill with their Circumstances.—It was a great Mistake to appoint any Person whose Attendance could not be relied on.

I have the Honor to be etc.

[*Archives of the General Society*]

[1] See page 46. General Washington replied on 22 February 1784, see page 96.

The President of the New Jersey Cincinnati replies to the President General's circular letter.

From Brigadier-General ELIAS DAYTON.

Elizabeth Town [New Jersey], January 29, 1784

Sir,

I have been honored with your Excellency's letter of the 28th.[1] Ult. appointing Philadelphia to be the place of meeting for the general society of the Cincinnati.

I have since been particular in complying with your Excellency's request, by making that appointment known to the representatives of the society of this State and by urging in the most expressive terms, their punctual attendance.

With the most sincere wishes that your Excellency may enjoy uninterrupted health & happiness, I have the honor, etc.

[*Archives of the General Society*]

French officers who had served for three years in the American Army were, like their American comrades, eligible to original membership in the Society of the Cincinnati. Those who had served in the French land or sea forces were eligible if of the grade of Colonel in the Army, or corresponding rank in the Navy, or superior thereto. This rule was never changed, but there were several recommendations from French commanders that it be done. As with American officers, some of the French officers whose services had not qualified them for original membership, were made honorary members. In the following letter the Count de Rochambeau recommends extending the eligibility.

From the COUNT DE ROCHAMBEAU.

Paris, 29th January 1784

Sir,

Give me leave, my dear General, to entrust you with friendship in one observation which did not escape the regiments that composed our army. They find that the General Society has

[1] See page 46.

given too much or too little of its favor, in granting it to all the Colonels and staying to them.

I do not ask it for the Lieutenant Colonels and majors because it is to the choice or favour that they owe their advancement, as well as Colonels, but I think it would be convenient to grant forever and ever, the marck of "Cincinnati," not to the person, but to the office of the first captain actually in service under the colours of every regiment which has served in America under your orders and mine.

I deliver up this reflexion my dear Général, to your friendship, to use as it will be most agreeable to you.

I am with the most inviolable and respectful attachment My Dear Général,

Your most obedient and very humble servant,

Le Cte. de Rochambeau

[*Archives of the General Society*]

From Dr. DAVID STUART.

[1784? Jan.?]

Dear Sir,

. . . The purport of the Vicounts [Dillamant's?] [1] letter is, to inform you, that he was Coll: of the regiment of Agenois, wc. acted with you at he siege of Yorck and of the misfortune wc. detained him from being there; hoping you would be too just to add to this misfortune, by excluding him from the honor of an Order, that would be granted to so many of his regiment and that Count Rochambeau would not admit him, without a line

[1] "Dillamant" is evidently a corruption of "d'Allemans. Pierre-Marie, Viscount du Lac d'Allemans, was born at Champiers, diocese of Limoges. He was *Colonel-en-Second* of the Regiment of Agenois, 1781 and Colonel of the Regiment of Saintonge, 1 July 1783. Saint-Simon embarked in de Grasse's squadron, 3 August 1781, in command of a contingent drawn from several regiments in the French West Indies, among the number being 902 men from the Regiment of Agenois. Presumably d'Allemans was not among the officers embarking and felt aggrieved at not having earned the right to the Eagle of the Cincinnati.

from you. He further adds, the Chr: Lucern would interest himself with you, in his behalf his letter is dated at Paris, 15th January -84; and he signs himself Coll: of the Saintonge infantry.

I am etc.

[*Washington Papers*]

From the VISCOUNT DE LA BRETONNIÈRE.

Paris, Le 1er. fevrier 1784

Monsieur

Le Vte. De La Bretonnière Capitaine du vaisseaux du Roy a L'honneur de representer à Votre Excellence, qu'il commandait La frigatte La Tourterelle En 1779, & 1780, Avec La quelle Il a d'abord Escorté un convoy de Douze Batimens Americains, & plusieurs Batimens francois chargés de Munitions & d'officiers qui arriverent à Boston.

Ses ordres Luy prescrivaient de Se rendre directement à St. Dominque D'ou Il Escorta au mois de Juin 1780 un Second convoy de Batimens americains Jusqu'à La Bermude, ou Il S'Empara des Deux corsaires anglois *La Bellone* de 28 canons, & *L'ambuscade* De 18, & de deux prises qu'ils avaient faites dont Il remit En possession Les Proprietaires americains.

Il n'y avait point D'Escadre francaise à L'amerique à Cette Epocque dont La frigatte La Tourterelle fut Detachée, Ce qui met Le Sr. Vte. de La Bretonniere dans Le Cas de presenter Luy même cette adresse à Votre Excellence, Il Juge qu'elle Voudra Bien regarder Ses Services rendus au commerce des Etats Unis avec La même faveur que ceux des capitaines commandant Les Vaisseaux Des Escâdres En Station à L'amerique, qui comme Colonels reclament, & Sollicitent L'honneur d'etre associés à L'ordre de cincinnatus.

J'ay L'honneur d'Etre avec respect etc.[1]

[*Archives of the General Society*]

[1] See reference to this letter in that of the Count de Barras to General Washington, 23 January 1784, page 65. For General Washington's reply to the Count de Barras see page 188.

[Translation by Edgar Erskine Hume]

Paris 1 February 1784.

Sir,

The Viscount de la Bretonnière, *Capitaine de Vaisseaux* of the King has the honor to represent to Your Excellency that he commanded the frigate *La Tourterelle* in 1779 and 1780, in which he, in the first place, escorted a convoy of twelve American ships and a number of French ships bearing munitions and officers, which arrived at Boston.

His orders directed him to proceed directly to Santo Domingo whence he escorted, in the month of June 1780, a second convoy of American ships as far as Bermuda, where he captured two English corsairs, the *Bellona* of 28 guns and the *Ambuscade* of 18, and two prizes they had made; these he placed in possession of their American owners.

There was no French squadron in America at the period when the frigate *La Tourterelle* was detached; this makes it possible for the Viscount de la Bretonnière to place his case personally before Your Excellency. He believes that you will be good enough to regard his services rendered to the commerce of the United States with the same favor as those of the captains commanding the vessels of the squadrons stationed in America, who as Colonels claim and solicit the honor of being members of the Order of Cincinnatus.

I have the honor to be with respect, etc.

From Major THOMAS MULLENS.

Liege the 5th. of february 1784

Sir

I Received your favour of the 20th. of Last month with the Papers, I left with you inclosed. I am very much oblidged to you for the interest you have, and will be pleased to take for what regards me. I have no other proof of my Service in the american army. But my Commission and the resolve of Congress which you have Seen. all I Can Say is that I took on in the american Service in november 1776 with General Conway in paris. and that I Continued in the Service from that month till the end of november 1778, and Drew pay during the whole time. I parted with no other forlough or passport but my Commission and the resolve you have Seen, I do give you my word of honor I never resigned and that my intention was to go back the following Summer, if I had not been (as you know) imployed with you, in monsieur Devant army, and after that, if I had not been Sent as Captain of guides with General rochambeau to america I would have gone back to Serve there again, but you Know it was not in my power, as been employed for my own King and master, if any other person was charged with the Distribution of the order, and that they required proofs of my Service in that Country, I would not Know to who I should adres me Self to for a Certificat but to you as being very often eye wittness to my way of Serving, and Behaviour. Not Knowing personaly the gentlemen of the Committee I well ask it as a particular favour, of the marquis, to return them my hearty thanks for their good intintions in my behalf—I suppose they are Some of the gentlemen whom I had the honor of Serving with in that Country, if So, they have Seen how I have Served there, and may judge if I have merited the honor of wearing the Badge, with them or not.—

General La fayette had Shewed me a great deal of friendship where ever I met him, and ever honored me with a promise of his protection, now I reclaim it, and beg he will write for my favour to the Committee or to his excellency, Genl. Washington, who, I am Sure will not refuse me the honor of wearing the Badge I believe my Service in america with the french army, with the time I Served the american army, may count a Little in my favour—

In short I Leave all to your Judgement and goo[d]ness of heart, And remains with the humblest respect etc.[1]
[Major Mullens signs himself as " Capitaine D'infanterie Basse Sauvennière a Liège.]

[*Archives of the General Society*]

[1] Major Mullens was admitted to original membership in the French Cincinnati.

The President of the Maryland Cincinnati replies to the call of the President General for the first General Meeting of the Society.

From Major-General WILLIAM SMALLWOOD.

Mattawoman [Maryland], February 10, 1784

Sir,

I was honored with your Letter dated the 28th December [1] last, and agreeable to your request, communicated the Objects contained therein to the Delegates of our State Society of Cincinnati—and to obviate a possibility of failure in the communication, requested them to acknowledge the receipt of my Letters by the earliest Opportunity.

I have anxiously waited for an Opportunity of contriving an Answer to your Letter, but the extreme hard Weather still continuing to shut Communications, obliges me to lodge this at Piscattaway, with directions to contrive it by the way of Alexandria or George Town, as I imagine Passengers cross over upon the Ice at one or both those Places without any risque or difficulty.—

I have the Honor to be etc.

[*Archives of the General Society*]

From the COUNT DE ROCHAMBEAU.

Paris, February 13, 1784

here is, my dear Général, one demand for the order of Cincinnatus of the most remarkable Kind, and Which appears to me [to] deserve the attention of the Society. here is inclosed the letter that M. de Lilancourt, before a général commander in St. Domingo, has Wrote to me upon this Subject. all the facts are exact in it, and you know perfectly, even as me, how much obligations We owe to him for having Sent us the detachment under the Marquis de St. Simon's orders, that he

[1] See No. 46.

Was Strongly authorised, by the Silence of his instructions, to refuse us. I cannot then but particularly recommend his asking to your Excellency and to the général society.

I am with respect Sir etc.

[Enclosures:

a. Letter from the Count de Lilancour to the Count de Rochambeau, dated 8 February 1784

b. Letter from the Count de Rochambeau to the Count de Lilancourt, dated 13 February 1784.]

[*Archives of the General Society*]

From the COUNT DE LILANCOUR to the COUNT DE ROCHAMBEAU

Clairai, par Bordeaux, le 8 fevrier, 1784.

Monsieur,

Retenu dans le fond d'une province pour y rétablir ma Santé tres alterée du long Séjour que j'ai fait a St. dominique; Ce n'est que par les nouvelles publiques que j'aprens L'institution de l'ordre, ou La Confraternité de Cincinnatus et L'admission, jusqu'au grade de colonel, des officiers français qui ont Contribué aux Succés des armes Américaines.

S'il n'est pas indispensable pour participer a ces honneurs d'avoir eu Celui, Monsieur Le Comte, de Servir Sous vos ordres dans Ces Contrées, et Si d'autres Services, non moins Essentiels, peut-etre, peuvent le procurer, permettés-moi de vous Rapeller l'etat des affaires dans le Continent en 1781, votre lettre de providence a Mr. Le Cte. De grasse du 11. juin de la même année et le danger imminent dont les etats-unis etaient ménacés, Si l'on ne relevait par quelque Coup d'Etat qui les confirmat dans notre alliance, leur Courage Ebranlé par les revers.

j'avais l'honneur de Commander alors la Colonie De St. Dominique et quoique Mr. Le Cte. De grasse en me laissant tout le Convoi dans la rade du Cap m'exposat peut-etre a un peril plus grand, je n'hesitai pas, Sans être même nanti d'une autorisation qui justifiat ma Conduite, a lui fournir 3700 hommes dont je donnai le Commandement a Mr. Le Mqis. De St. Simon.

C'est à Cette resolution que j'osai prendre Sur moi et a Laquelle pouvait Seule me déterminer l'etat critique des affaires qu'est Specialement du Le Succés de l'Expedition d'yorck-town, qui ne pouvait etre Entreprise Sans ce renfort et la paix glorieuse qui En a été le fruit.

L'apréciation que vous fites vous même, Monsieur Le Comte, de ma Conduite en cette circonstance, la lettre dont vous m'honorates de philadelphie le 2 7bre. est la titre Sur lequel je prens la liberté de vous demander S'il ne Suffit pas pour etre agrégé a la dite confraternité. Si vous le jugez ainsi la recommandation auprès du Congrés dont vous honoreres mes Services me rendra Cette marque distinctive infiniment plus précieuse.[1]

I have etc.

[*Washington Papers*]

[Translation in writing of Lieutenant-Colonel David Humphreys.]

The Count de Lilancour to the Count de Rochambeau

Clairai near Bordeaux, February 8, 1784.

Sir

Confined at the extremity of a Province for the reestablishment of my health, which a long residence at St. Domingo had very much injured; it was only from the public Papers I learnt respecting the Institution of the Order or Fraternity of the Cincinnati, & the admission of those French Officers, (down to the rank of Colonel,) who contributed to the success of the American Arms.—

If to participate in this honour it be not indispensable to have had that of serving under your orders, M. le Count, in that Country; and if other services (perhaps not less essential) can procure it; permit me to recall to your remembrance the state of affairs on the Continent in 1781, your letter to the Cte de Grasse of the 11 of June in the same year, and the imminent danger with which the U. States were threatened, unless some stroke of policy should confirm their courage, shaken by adversity & fix them in our alliance.

[1] The Count Jean de Lilancourt-Taste, Brigadier of Infantry, was admitted to original membership in the French Cincinnati.

I had the honor of commanding then the Colony of St. Domingo, & altho the Cte de Grasse in leaving me all the convoy in the road of the Cape, exposed me perhaps to the greatest hazard, I did not hesitate at all (unsupported as I was with any authority that might justify my conduct) to furnish him 3700 men, of whom I gave the command to the Marquis de St. Simon.

It is to this resolution, which I dared to take upon myself & to which the critical state of affairs alone could decide me, that the success of the expedition of York Town is particularly due—This could not have been undertaken without the reinforcement; or could the glorious peace that was the fruit of it, have been obtained—

The merit which you yourself, M. le Compte, attached to my conduct in this circumstance, & the letter of the 2d of September with which you honored me from Philadelphia, are the titles upon which I take the liberty of asking whether I have not a sufficient claim to be admitted into the order. If you think I have, your recommendation of my services would honour them with Congress and procure me this mark of distinction so infinitely precious to me—

I have the honor etc.

[*Archives of the General Society*]

The COUNT DE ROCHAMBEAU to the COUNT DE LILANCOUR.

Paris, le 13 fevrier 1784.

Votre demande me parait Si juste, Monsieur, que je viens d'envoyer votre lettre[1] au général Washington en la lui Recommandant de la maniere la plus forte, ainsi qu'a la Société de Cincinnatus.

personne ne Sait mieux que lui et moi les obligations que nous vous avons de vous etre rendu de Si bonne grace a mes requisitions pour le détachement de troupes aux ordres de Mr. de S: Simon que vous nous avés Envoyé et qui nous a été trés grand Secours.

[1] See No. 75.

j'espere que Votre demande aura l'effet que je desire tout autant que vous.

j'ai etc.

[*Washington Papers*]

[Translation in writing of Lieutenant-Colonel David Humphreys.]

The Count de Rochambeau to the Count de Lilancour.

[Paris, February 13, 1784]

Your request appears to me so just, that I have sent your letter, Sir, to Genl. Washington, recommending it to him, as well as to the Society of the Cincinnati, in the strongest manner.

No one knows better than himself & me the obligations we are under to you, for having yielded to my requisitions with so good a grace, by detaching to our assistance the troops under the Mquis. de St Simon, & which proved a most powerful succour—

I hope your request will be complied with, indeed I desire it as much as you can—

I have the honor etc.

[*Archives of the General Society*]

The Chevalier de La Luzerne to the Count de Vergennes.

[Translation by Edgar Erskine Hume]

Philadelphia, 14 February, 1784

. . . Monseigneur, the object of the establishment of the Society of the Cincinnati was to perpetuate the memory of the courage and disinterestedness of the American and foreign officers who had taken part in the Revolution, and its honorable insignia were to be transmitted to their posterity. From this point of view, the Institution appears to be a means of recognizing a large number of citizens to whom the injustice of the people had refused remuneration for their services.

But, all of a sudden, certain disquieted writers displayed jealousy. These chevaliers are a body of nobles, the existence of which endangers the liberty of America; they wish to establish a feudal system; this is a patrician order of the kind which have birth of Catalines, Syllas, Cæsars, and finally Tiberiuses and Neros. These writers sounded the alarm and the Order began to become unpopular in several States; it is not likely that any Legislature will abolish it; but it is probable that in some States it is only necessary to belong to the Order to be refused election to public office or positions of honor or profit; the jealousy which these persons have for every unconstitutional establishment is an instrument which is almost never employed without success by those who wish to thwart everything not formally authorized by the Constitution. . . . [Affaires Étrangères, Paris, Vol. 26, Corr. Etats-Unis, fol. 133]

Two months later another report of de La Luzerne to Vergennes on the same subject contains the following passage:

[Translation by Edgar Erskine Hume]

The love of the Americans for liberty and equality has caused Massachusetts to proscribe the Society of Cincinnatus. A Commitee of both houses of the Legislature of this State has decreed that the Society will not be tolerated, and that if it is not destroyed, it will disturb the peace, the liberty and the safety of the United States in general and Massachusetts in particular. This act was read in the two houses assembled and approved by them after careful deliberation. The American papers are filled with reports of this sage resolution of Massachusetts and all tend to show that the Institution of Cincinnatus, the existence which neither Congress nor any of the States has recognized, is diametrically opposed to the fundamental principles of a republic and that the plan of this Order was put forward by ambitious men, embraced by the leaders, and adopted by the officers, and of which the state cannot foresee the political consequences.

Several writers have essayed to defend the Order of the Cincinnatus in the public press; they find nothing dangerous in the Order of Free-Masons or of any other Club or Tavern Society; but they have been answered that the Free-Masons never wear their emblems in society; and the majority of Free-Masons are not composed of military men; that Free-Masons do not meddle in affairs of state; that they were not created as protectors of the laws and that they have never sworn to defend the rights of humanity and public liberty, and that, in fine, the title of Free-Mason does not pass by primogeniture in families and their posterity, and does not give a sort of nobility which the United States, in Congress assembled, have not themselves the right to confer, according to Article VI of the Confederation.

[Affaires Étrangères, Paris, 27]

Shortly after this La Luzerne reverts to the same subject in another letter to Vergennes:

[Translation by Edgar Erskine Hume]

Mount Vernon, in Virginia, 12 April 1784

Monseigneur, From the estate of General Washington, not farther than fifteen leagues from Annapolis, where I repaired to pass some days, upon the invitation which he extended me, I have the honor to write you. After having seen him in the midst of his camp, and amid the tumults of arms, on my arrival on this continent, I have the pleasure of seeing him again as the simple citizen, enjoying, in the repose of his retirement, the glory which he has so justly earned. We felicitated each other that our cause had been finished so much sooner than we had dared to hope; the General took occasion to mention all the obligations and gratitude of the United States to His Majesty and expressed, with much touching feeling, appreciation for the services which the American cause received from us. He seems to consider the idea of a voyage to France, he told me that he would be pleased to go there if affairs which he desires to finish would permit. He is dressed in grey clothing like a Virginia farmer and nothing about him recalls the important rôle which he has played, except the great number of foreigners who come to see him.

His wife and her family form his usual society, and the happiness of those who surround him seems to be his principal thought. He is not unoccupied, however, and, independently of the affairs which remain to be completed, as a result of his command, I am led to think that he proposes to edit his mémoires or to put in order the material concerning the great events in which he has played such an important part. It must not be agreeable to him, after having so long been occupied in the world of his actions, to fall, all of a sudden, into a sort of state of being forgotten. He sincerely desired the end of this revolution, and no citizen worked harder for that result; but, after having been for eight years the first citizen of the Republic, it is difficult to return to the quality of planter.

The institution of the Society of Cincinnatus gives every day more umbrage to the inhabitants of the North. They do not wish to suffer any distinctions to exist. They find them incompatible with republican government, dangerous to liberty, and I think that their fears are not chimerical; they threaten to exclude the members of the Order from public office; it is in effect an institution diametrically opposed to the principles of equality and to the jealousy natural to these republicans; but the general in chief, without foreseeing this opposition, has done all in his power to give firmness to this institution. He will preside at the grand congress which the members of this Order will hold in Philadelphia next month, and, pressed from one quarter by the publicity which has attended his becoming its patron, and from another by the fear of becoming unpopular in supporting an institution abhorred in several States, I think that he is much perplexed as to the course that he should pursue. [Affaires Étrangères, Paris, Etats-Unis, fol. 282.]

The President General's letter anent the General Meeting of 1784 (see page 43) is thus answered by the President of the Rhode Island Cincinnati:

From Major-General NATHANIEL GREENE.

Newport [Rhode Island], February 16, 1784

Dear Sir,

I had the pleasure of receiving your letter of the 28th. of December last, and having had the Honor of being appointed President of the Cincinnati of Rhode Island, I embrace the earliest opportunity of giving you an Answer. General Varnum, Major Lyman and myself, are in the appointment to attend the annual General meeting of the order. It is not expected more than One will attend the meeting. I intend to be in South Carolina before that time.

General Varnum or Major Lyman will attend, and I have the pleasure to communicate to your Excellency that the measures necessary for the establishment of the Order is fully gone into, and all the Officers appointed agreeably to the Institution.

With esteem and affection, I am, sir.[1]

[*Archives of the General Society*]

Here is the first record of the famous Diamond Eagle of the Cincinnati, presented by French naval officers to President General Washington, and which has been worn by all of his successors in that office. General Washington's letter to Major L'Enfant, 30 October 1783 (page 30) directs him to obtain for him an Eagle "finished in a masterly manner and ornamented in an elegant tho' not costly stile." For the Count d'Estaing's letter presenting the Diamond Eagle to General Washington, dated 26 February 1784, see page 100.

The COUNT D'ESTAING to the CHEVALIER DE LA LUZERNE.

[Translation by Edgar Erskine Hume]

Paris, 18 February 1784

Monsieur le Chevalier,

I have the honor to send you copies of all the papers which I send to General Washington. The sojourn of M. L'Enfant

[1] For General Washington's reply, see page 121.

was several times prolonged but my own part was delayed. I hope that my requests and their motives might be entrusted to Major L'Enfant. His mission had its difficulties. This is explained by the way he worked and by the influence of the advice of the Marquis de La Fayette.

You will surely notice and I presume that General Washington will observe that I have conducted myself towards him and the assembly of the Cincinnati as I would with the King, placing before them justification for everything that I have requested. You will find, Monsieur le Chevalier, faults and gallicisms in the private letter in English which I wrote to General Washington; but I have had a copy made such as it is. The thought will always be understandable. I have thought it my duty to use my mother tongue in official letters and in Memoirs. My second letter was accompanied by a trinket. Learning by chance that an Eagle set with diamonds had been made for General Washington, I won over the jeweler. I obtained this Cincinnatus; I had a trophy and a banderole added, saying thereon that it was presented to *His Excellency General Washington by French sailors.* This trifle can neither displease nor embarass, nor can it be refused since it is offered in the name of all my comrades; one cannot deny that by their labors they added a few brilliants to the wings of the American Eagle and aided in assembling trophies. My little token nautically presented will acquire some value since it will be placed in the buttonhole of General Washington, and will never reduce the proportional and voluntary contribution due the fund of the Society of Cincinnatus; I shall attend to making my contribution so that all will be complete. If, as I hope, all captains of ships who served in America are admitted, I would strongly desire that the Assembly should determine absolutely that each member should send the sum which his ability and desire determine him to donate. Our captains of ships are for the most part younger sons, less rich than the colonels. It is particularly the general officers of the navy who, wishing to imitate those of the land forces, will be embarrassed and incommoded. I flatter myself, however, that our sailors will not consent to be humiliated by taxing themselves less. I feel that this pecuniary hint would be disagreeable and embarrassing to decline; moreover I confide the matter to your paternal prudence as concerning our other Frenchmen to the end that you will do as you think best.

I do not take the liberty of asking you again what was requested in the duplicate of the letter which I wrote you about grant of land which the State of Georgia made me. This mark of satisfaction is infinitely precious to me, and even though its value be zero, this does not diminish its worth in my eyes, I have only the ambition to possess the title to it executed in legal form. To accept it under the circumstances in which it was offered me would have been wrong.

It appears doubtful, according to all I hear, that M. L'Enfant will find you still in America, so that I must content myself by telling you that everything that interests you is going well. Madame the Baroness Montboissier, in drinking your health two days ago, expressed the hope that this time she would have a boy, seeing that you delivered a whole vigorous and healthy nation!

Accept the assurances of the attachment and respect with which I have the honor to be, Monsieur le Chevalier, your very humble and very obedient servant,

Estaing.

[*French National Archives, Affaires Étrangères: Etats-Unis*]

From Major WINTHROP SARGENT.

Boston, February 20, 1784.

Desirous of contributing to the Amusement of your Excellency I do myself the honor to transmit you a Poem of Eulogy on the Institution of the Society of the Cincinnati—[1] I hazard it to your Excellency's Judgment without more Preface than an Extract from its Accompanying Letter—

If your Excellency & Mrs. Washington (to whom I beg leave to present my Respects) deign to grant the approbating

[1] Inclosed with this letter were a letter (undated) and the Poem of Eulogy, see page 84.

Smile I shall have great Joy in that Felicity which I know it will bestow on the fair Poetess—

With sincere & warm Wishes etc.

[*Washington Papers*]

To Major WINTHROP SARGENT from his Sister:

Inclosure in his letter of 20 February 1784 (see page 83).

Give me leave once more to express my grateful Sense of your obliging Attention in forwarding me the several Pieces—The proposals for forming the Society are greatly worthy the amiable Character of Patrons of Liberty—May nought impede their Progress—I see resulting from their Amity as a Body the most benign as well as splendid Consequences—May their Order *indeed* endure as long as Nature herself shall endure—My Sentiments you will see more fully exprest in the Attempt at Poetry which I take the Liberty to transmit—An Itch for Rhyming hath a long Time been the Companion of your Sisters solitary Hours—Reading the Institution over last Evening I could not forbear seizing the Pen—I did not intend however to have run to such a Length—but an irresistable Impulse hurried me on—to your Candor Dear Sir I commit it, with the same Restrictions with which you inclosed me the— . . . .

[*Washington Papers*]

[Poem, enclosed in above letter]:

Hail glorious Period! Hail benignant Peace!
Now dinning Arms their hostile Clamour cease!
Now baleful Passions sheath the deathful Sword!
The Angel Amity is now restor'd.—

Long have I trembled for this younger World:
The british Thunder o'er our Head was hurl'd;
ALBION, who should have guarded! gave the Wound!
And Cut the Bands which sacred Nature bound!
Against her Sons, the Murd'rous Steel she rear'd!
And old in Conquest for their Death prepar'd!

They—now to Arms—to Battle all untrain'd,
Victory o'er Vetranes so unfrequent gain'd,
Who but must mourn for their Columbia's Fate,
And her impending Ruin deprecate—

I lov'd my Country—early own'd her Claims
But on my heart was 'grav'd dearer Name;—
A Brother fought in the ensanguin'd Field;
And O! thou God of Battle left thy Shield!
Spread round the Youth thy panoply divine!
For still to guard, O! Sire of Men is thine—

To the fond Matron while the flame ascends
Which her whole Interest in one Ruin blends,
Wildly exclaims—give me my infant Train!
Posses'd of them—those Strokes of Fate were vain:
Scap'd from the Wreck she sees her Girls & Boys
And one short Moment perfect Peace enjoys—
Thus (for I yield to none the Palm of Love)
My daily Orisons were mark'd above—
Th' Eternal heard—The Hero was his Care—
He smil'd propitious on my ardent Pray'r;
The Warrior fought & well earn'd Laurels gain'd,
His sacred honor unimpeach'd sustain'd.—

Thus, far the grateful retrospective Muse;
Now, op'ning Scenes with rapture she pursues.

If Liberty 's enthroned—if Reason sways!
Daughters of Light whom all that's food obeys,
Then Myriads, yet unborn shall hail the Day
To this auspicious Era Homage pay;—
Virtue shall grace our wide extensive shore,
And all its Sons the Rule of Right explore.—
Now, Arts & Sciences shall splendid rise,
Fair Fruits of Genius, Incense to the Skies:
Improvement hovers round the Steps of Youth,
To Crown its Labours, waits immortal Truth:—
This vernal World new Paths of Light shall send
And tow'r superior far to all Mankind.
Through a long Line of Ages yet to come

I see a Train of num'rous Worthies bloom,
Heroes, & Patriots, in one Int'rest join,
Poets, & Warriors, both alike combine:
While deep Philosophy adorns each Age
High are the Honors of the hoary Sage,
Writers of ev'ry Class shall weild the Pen,
And thou COLUMBIA boast the first of Men.

Imagination marks the historic Page
And scenes triumphant all her Pow'rs engage,—
In Arms victorious & in Peace renown'd—
With just Applause each useful Action's crown'd:
Far as old Ocean with impetuous Roll
Laves distant Lands—e'en to the frigid Pole,
So far they Deeds of Virtue shall extend
And Admiration with thy Name shall blend;—
Yea,—FAME shall ope for thee her hundred Gates
While at her Shrine th'aspiring HERO waits:
Her glittering Car thy Sons with Joy shall mount
And emulous their Val'rous Deeds recount;
With Steps assur'd ascend th'eventful Steep
And still the Eminence of Virtue keep.
A future Empire too I see Arise!
PRINCES & MONARCHS good & great & Wise,
Whose Care shall be to guard the public Weal:—
Who—for the people's Wrongs shall keenly feel,
PROTECTORS of the Rights of human kind.
Their Actions all be Rectitude confin'd;—
Sway'd by no Party—urg'd by no base End
But still determin'd Virtue to defend;—
Ennobled more by Dignity innate
Then all the Honors of their regal State;—
The Basis of whose Throne is Justice, found
By ever blooming Mercy, radiant, crown'd;
Amid the Glories of whose splendid Reign
Yet added Lustre ev'ry Art shall gain.
COMMERCE shall spread her broad—her swelling Sails
And Peace shall furnish the propitious Gale.
Fam'd AGRICULTURE as of old shall rise
And Shepherds chaunt beneath cerulean skies—

Amid their sylvan Shades shall gayly sing
The rural Blessings of a Patriot King.
A golden Ave once more shall bless the Race.
While every Chief—their Origin shall trace.
Back to that Order Cincinnati nam'd,
Whose Sons intrepid were for Valour fam'd.—

Thus the gay Vision skims athwart my Sight
And thus Emits prophetic Rays of Light.—
HAIL CINCINNATI! GUARD OF UNION HAIL!
O'er thy fair dawning may no Ill prevail;
First Fruit of Peace—by conq'ring Heroes form'd—
Heroes by Friendship, as by Valour Warm'd.—
Descend sweet Concord—from high heav'n descend—
And on this social Band with Care attend—
Guard ev'ry Avenue—each rising Scene.
And let no baleful Passion intervene—

My Bosom glows—I would exalt my Lays—
The first of Men deserve the first of Praise,
Tho' all unequal to the arduous Task,
I yet presume, celestial Aid to ask:—
As the untutor'd Bird advent'rous explores
Or feebly aiming, swells his little Throat,
To imitate some bold melodious Note.

So though untaught, & Rude, I still aspire,
Mistake my Zeal for true poetic Fire.

Impel'd by Veneration for thy Name
O Chief renoun'd—I hail thy spotless Fame!
How mark'd thy bright Career wth. worth unstain'd,
Unsully'd Rectitude, thy Triumphs gain'd—
Envy, cannot thy blooming Honors blast
Nor o'er thy virtues e'er a Shade can cast—
Happy retiring to thy peaceful Haunt
Malice her customary Dues shall want.—
Nor fear America—thy Warrier's Hand
From future Ills shall guard his native Land—
Upheld by Deity He'll rise to save
As TABIRIS cool, & yet as CESAR brave:—

Exper'ence circles now his honor'd Head,
And by fair Sapience he'll still be led.
Each vet'ran Chief (should dire Occasion rise)
Will coming Dangers—as the past—despise;
The CINCINNATI will its Aid combine,
To guard from Danger in strong Union join.—
Yes[1] social Friends,—undoubted is your Claim,
For Patriot Deeds deserve a Patriot's Name,
And CINCINNATUS from his azure Throne
Shall smile approving, & thy Order own.

(Thy Patronage illustrious Roman give!
And thy bright Altars shall our Vows receive
Diffuse thy Spirit 'midst the admiring Throng
And high to thee shall use the deathless Song.
Not thy ALLILLA could more fondly love
Or thy own Country e'er more grateful prove)

With conscious Joy I see Columbia's Pride—
Her unlike Sons in Amity ally'd;
Prime Source of Good the Nation's sure Defence,
Firmness & Union shall proceed from hence,
GUARDIANS of LIBERTY—august the Style—
Sweet Heav'n upon their ard'ous Efforts smile!
O! may those Rights they justly hold so dear
Still to their raptur'd View divine appear—
May they inviolate fair Honor guard,
May sacred Honor be their great Reward!—
Expressive Term—Word of no modern Date,
On which the Virtues all, obsequious wait;—

To guard the Innocent—to rev'rence Years—
From the swoln Eye to wipe the falling Tears—
To shelter Goodness, where so e'er tis found—
And in no feeling Breast to plant a Wound—
Against Oppression still to draw the Sword—
To see the Injured to their Rights restor'd—

[1] [Marginal note]: Alluding to that part of the Institution which is thus worded—"The Officers of the American Army think they may wth. Propriety denominate themselves the Society of Cincinnati."—

In one short Word—to Rectitude pursue
And its fair Dictates still as RULES to view—
These are the Out Lines—these delineate—
These are the graces which on Honor wait:—

Reverse the Scene—th'indignant Goddess wanes!
Fell Infamy the beaut'ous Image stains!—
Ignoble Views can ne'er deform that Breast
Which once admitted so divine a guest—
Her Charms celestial, must the Soul inspire,
And fill the Breast with emulative Fire—
GREAT SIRE OF ANGELS from thy heaven bend!—
The Cincinnati by thy power defend:—
To Honor may they still prefer their Claim
And may it strongly mark their rising Fame.

Thou too blest Charity—genial—benign,
Thy gentle Influence—thy soft Sway combine—
Aid the kind Efforts of each humane Chief—
'Tis time to bring the sighing heart Relief;
Born of Benevolence—celestial Fair,
The Boon of Heroes is thy choicest Care;—
Mark how the Cincinnati (gen'rous Race)
With thy benignant Worth their Order grace—
O! breath prolific on their lib'ral Store
And still with them the Sons of Want explore
Suppress their Wishes ere they yet arise
And wipe the Tear from the lone Widow's Eyes—
Guard the sweet Orphan with paternal Care,—
For Noble Efforts his Young Mind prepare,—
Say that his Father fought—& greatly fell,—
Oft in his Ear the Tale of Sorrow Tell!—
Twill stimulate to Deeds of high Renown,
Honor shall weave for him her laurel Crown—
Shall place him on the golden Car of Fame
And thus to CINCINNATI mark his Claim—

Nor leave the tender fair to ruthless Fate,
But on her steps with guardian vigils wait—
Give her to triumph o'er each baleful Wile—

(May nought her heav'nly Innocence Beguile
For while a spotless Character remains,
Twill rise sweet Incense to a Parents manes.)

Nor like the niggard—stinted Good bestow
But let Munificence unbounded flow—
At thy white Altar let no Suff'rer wait—
Compel no gentle Heart to supplicate,
Enough degraded is the noble Mind
E'en though unsought it should a Refuge find;—
Tis but a humble Life which Bounty yields—
The truly great from added Insults shield—
They seek unask'd each latent Cause of Woe
And still as broad will their Assistance flow—
They make Dependance wear a silken Band
And while they cherish with a lib'ral Hand
Disclaim all Title to that servile praise,
Which lone, the little Mind with Joy surveys.
Thus is you so—Applause shall wing its way
To the bright Regions of unclouded Day;—
So may the Aid the CINCINNATI grants
Be as extensive as the Suff'rer's Wants:—
Through the wide Circle of revolving Years,
Ages which rise till Nature disappears
May their just Pow'r no Diminution know
But still corral with their Virtues flow—
And those descendents of a polish'd Race,
Mark'd & adorn'd with ev'ry manly Grace,
Heroes of Gallic Fame of ancient Growth
Sons of Humanity & social Worth—
Your honor'd Names, to grace our Order give,
And from our Hand the votive Badge receive:—

In Bands of Amity with us you fought,
The sacred Flame by Freedom's Sons was caught—
FRIENDSHIP we hail'd—& Concord mark'd the Hour
That gave Emanicipation from that Pow'r
Which, how so e'er to Arms, or Conquest train'd,
Hath not o'er Liberty a Triumph gain'd:—
Then deign with us in Unity to join—

In sweet Affiance let us still combine,
So shall the CINCINNATI's annals swell
And to the latest Period proudly tell—
How thou Luzerne for blooming Sapience fam'd
And Sieur Gerard with equal Honor nam'd,
D'Estange—with Grasse—e'en by his foe belov'd
And tho' unfortunate, yet still approv'd.—
High are the honors of his laurel'd Head;
The brave entangled in the Toils of Fate
Seldom obtain the Plaudit of the great.
Yet on de Grasse his Prince acquitting smiles
And thus the Malice of his Fate beguiles—
These—with et ceteras, shall grace our Page
And loud proclaim to ev'ry distant Age
How broad the Brother-hood—how wide its claims,
How own'd & honor'd by the noblest Names.
Thus mark'd by Concord thus by Friendship join'd,
To one fair Order thus alike combin'd,
The Goddess Fame shall from celestial Pow'rs
Select a Garland of the fairest Flow'rs—
With nicest Art she shall the Texture raise—
Shall dip it in the sweet Perfume of Praise,
And to the fragrant ever beaut'ous Wreath,
Immortal Verdure—deathless Worth Bequeath—
Then while her Fav'rites for the Prize contend
While round her Altars distant Heroes bend,
Shall own the CINCINNATI's fairer Claim—
Its Right undoubted to the Gift of Fame,
And while her PLAUDITS thus bestow Renown
With her own hand affix the blooming Crown.

[*Washington Papers*]

From the COUNT DE LILANCOUR.

Clairai, February 20, 1784.[1]

Monsieur

L'admission dans La Confraternité de Cincinnatus, des officiers francais (jusqu'au Grade de Colonel) qui ont Eu Le Bonheur de Contribuer au Succés des armes Des Etats-unis de L'amérique est trop honnorable pour eux; pour qui ceux qui peuvent Etre autorisés a y aspirer par Leurs Services, ne le Recherchent pas avec L'Empressement le plus vif.

J'ai L'honneur, Monsieur, d'Etre Brigadier des armées du Roy, et j'avais celui de Commander en chef La Colonie de Saint domingue, Lorsque M Le Cte. de Grasse en 1781 Sur Les Instances de Votre Excellence et celles de M Le Cte. de Rochembeau; vint au cap me demander Les Secours que L'Etat des affaires vous Rendait Indispensables, et Les porter au Continent.

trois cent Batimens chargés dans La Rade de cette ville plus que Susceptibles d'attirer Les forces Ennemis qu'il Laissait derriere Lui; ne me Permettaient de me démunir Sans m'Exposer; et Rendaient ma Position d'autant plus délicatique dénué D'ordres de La Cour, il fallait prendre Les Evenemens Sur moi, consultant cependant moins une timide Prudence que L'utilité de La Cause commune; je n'hézittai pas a Lui fournir 3700 hommes dont je donnai Le Commandement a M Le Mis. de St. Simon, votre Excellence est mieux Instruite que personne, Monsieur, de Lheureux Effet de cette Resolution combien elle a contribué a La gloire des armes alliées et a La Paix honnorable qui en a été Le fruit.

tel est Monsieur, Le titre que j'ai prié M. Le Cte. de Rochambeau de vouloir bien Recommander a Votre Excellence, du moment qui j'ai Eté Instruit de LEtablissement de La confraternité. La Reponse que j'Avai Recu jointe a La Lettre que je Lui avais Ecrit, dont jai Lhonneur de mettre Les copies Sous Ses yeux me donnent tout Lieu DEsperer que Lappréciation qu'il fait de ma Conduite dans cette Circonstance critique et Le Soin quil veut bien prendre de vous en Rapeller Lutilité; dis-

[1] A duplicate of this letter (dated, however, February *22,* 1784), is in the General Society's Archives.

poseront favorablement Votre Excellence en faveur de ma demande; et quelle voudra bien me procurer Lhonneur que je Sollicite de Sa justice

Je Suis etc.

[P. S.] ozerais je Monsieur Supplier votre Excellence de vouloir bien faire parvenir a Mrs. de La Societé Generale Le pacquet que je prends La Liberté de mettre Sous Son couvert.

[*Washington Papers*]

[Translation in the writing of Lieutenant-Colonel David Humphreys]

From the COUNT DE LILANCOUR.

Clairai, near Bordeaux, February 22[20?], 1784.

Sir

The admission, into the Society of Cincinnati, of such French Officers, as have had the felicity of contributing to the success of the Arms of the U. States, is too honorable, for those who have pretensions, not to urge them to seek it with the most anxious solicitude.

I have the honor, Sir, of Being a Brigad. in the Armies of the King, and had that of commanding in Chief the Colony of St Domingo, when the Comte de Grasse in 1781, at the instance of your Excellency & the Comte De Rochambeau, came to the Cape to request those Succours which the state of your affairs rendered indispensable, & which he carried to the Continent.

The hostile force he left behind him; & 300 loaded vessels in the road—(more than capable of attracting the enemy) did not permit me to weaken my command without exposing myself infinitely—And my situation was rendered still more delicate, by having no orders from Court, & being of course obliged to take the consequences upon myself. Consulting less, however, a timid prudence, than the posterity [needs?] of the common cause; I did not hesitate to furnish 3700 Men. of whom I gave the command to the Marquis de St Simon. Your Excellency is better acquainted, than any other, with the happy issue of this resolution; & how much it contributed to the glory of the allied arms, and to the honorable peace which followed.

This, Sir, is the title, in virtue of which, As soon as I heard of the Institution of your Fraternity, I claimed the recommendation of the Count de Rochambeau to your Excellency. The answer which I have received, joined to the letter I wrote to him (both of which are laid before you) give me every reason to hope that the estimation in which the Count hath held my conduct on this critical occasion & the care he hath been pleased to take in recalling to your memory the utility of it, will happily dispose your Excy to favor my Petition, & that you will be pleased to procure me the honor I now solicit from your Justice.

I am with respect, etc.[1]

[*Archives of the General Society*]

To Major-General HENRY KNOX.

Mount Vernon, 20 Feb. 1784

My dear Sir,

. . . . .

It was amongst my first Acts after I got home to write to the Presidents of each State Society, appointing Philadelphia (and the first Monday in May) for the general meeting of the Cincinnati. Colo. [Benjamin] Walker took all the Letters to those Eastward of this before New Year's day; the others for the Southward I dispatched by the post, about the sametime; I have even sent duplicates for fear of miscarriage; yet, though it is the most eligable method, it is to be feared it will not prove so effectual a communication, as a general notification in the public Gazettes would have been. And, in case of failure, I shall be exceedingly sorry for not having adopted the most certain, as it would give me pleasure to have the first General Meeting a very full one. I have named Philadelphia (contrary to my own judgement, as it is not Central) to comply with the wishes of South Carolina, who being the most southern State have desired

[1] The Count de Lilancourt was, as already stated, admitted to original membership in the French Cincinnati.

it. North Carolina I have not heard a tittle from, nor anything official from New Hampshire. All the other States have acceeded very unanimously to the propositions which were sent from the Army. . . .

I shall be very happy, and I hope I shall not be disappointed, in seeing you at the proposed meeting in Philadelphia. The friendship I have conceived for you will not be impaired by absence but it may be no unpleasing circumstance to brighten the Chain, by a renewal of the Covenant. My best wishes attend Mrs. Knox and the little folks, in which Mrs. Washington most heartily joins me.

With every sentiment of purest esteem &c

P. S. I hope General Greene will be in the delegation from Rhode Island, and that we shall see him at the general meeting of the Cincinnati. Will you intimate this to him?

[*Massachusetts Historical Society*]

From Major-General HENRY KNOX.

Boston, 21 Feb. 1784

. . . The Cincinnati appears (however groundlessly) to be an object of jealousy. The idea is, that it has been created by a foreign influence in order to change our form of government; and this is strengthened by a letter from some of our ministers abroad. Burke's pamphlet[1] has had its full operation. The cool, dispassionate men seem to approve of the institution generally, but dislike descent. The two branches of the legisla-

[1] The attack on the Society of the Cincinnati was begun by the eccentric South Carolina judge, Ædanus Burke, who, under the pseudonym "Cassius" published: *Considerations on the Society or Order of Cincinnati; lately instituted by the Major-Generals, Brigadier-Generals, and other Officers of the American Army. Providing that it creates a Race of Hereditary Patricians, or Nobility. Interspersed with remarks on its Consequences to the Freedom and Happiness of the Republic* (Philadelphia, 1783, pp. 16). This book formed the basis of the longer work by the Count de Mirabeau. The attack was continued by a number of American politicians, notably Jefferson, the Adamses, Jay, and Gerry. For a full account of this opposition, see E. E. Hume, *Early Opposition to the Society of the Cincinnati,* Americana, October, 1936, XXX, 597-638.

ture of the State have chosen a committee "to inquire into any associations or combinations which have [been] or may be formed to introduce *undue* distinctions in the community, and which may have a tendency to create a nobility contrary to the confederation of the United States and the spirit of the Constitution of the Commonwealth." They have not reported, and perhaps will not. The same sentiments pervade New England. The Society have had a respectable meeting in Boston in the 16th inst., at which General Lincoln presided: General Heath was not present. A committee was chosen to attend the General Meeting at Philadelphia next May,—General R. Putmam, Colonel Cobb, Lieutenant-Colonel Hull, Major Sargent, and myself. Probably two only will attend. It was thought prudent not to make any honorary members at present.[1]

[*Archives of the Massachusetts Cincinnati*]

To Major-General ARTHUR ST. CLAIR.

Mount Vernon, February 22, 1784

Dear Sir,

Your favor of the 29th. of Jany.[2] in answer to my circular Letter of the 28th, of Decr. is at hand. I am sorry to find by it, that so many Delegates from your State Society are likely to be Non-attendants at the General Meeting in May. It would have an odd appearance (whatever may be the causes) for the Society of the State, in which the General Meeting is held, to be unrepresented upon such an occasion; and it would give me concern, I confess, to find any so; for it is my wish that the first meeting (at least) may be full. Not only for the purpose of bare representation then, but that the Abilities of the Society of the Cincinnati may be convened at that time, I hope your business elsewhere may, without much inconvenience, be made to yield to this call for your attendance.

With great truth and sincerity, I am, etc.

[*Washington Papers*]

---

[1] For General Washington's reply to this letter, see page 122.

[2] See page 67. For reply to the above letter, see page 39.

The Connecticut Cincinnati's President replies to the circular letter of the President General.

From Major-General JEDIDIAH HUNTINGTON.

Norwich [Connecticut], February 23, 1784

Dear Sir,

Your Favor of the 28th. of Decr.[1] did not reach me before last Week—I shall not fail to give Notice, either by Letter or in Person, to the Delegates from this States' Society, of the Time appointed for the General Meeting of the Cincinnati—

I have the Honor to be, etc.

[*Archives of the General Society*]

French and other European officers who had been admitted members of the Cincinnati, returning to Europe naturally desired documentary evidence of their membership, as seen by the following request. Diplomas were not available until Major L'Enfant brought from Paris the copperplate in May, 1784.

From Colonel FRANCIS JOHNSTON.

Philadelphia, February 23, 1784.

Sir

At the request of Captain [Frederick] Paschke of the Light Dragoons and Captains [Claude-Antoine Villet] De Marcellin and [Nicholas-George] Le Roy late of the 2d. P. Regt. I beg leave to inform Your Excellency that they are going to Europe and are desirous of receiving from your own hand a Certificate of their being Members of the Cincinnati Society—they have all signed the Institution in due form and lodged with me an Order on the Paymaster General for a months-pay respectively—this being the case I hope they will not fail in their present application. My most respectful Compts. attend Mrs. Washington & am with the highest sentiments etc.

[*Archives of the General Society*]

---

[1] See page 42.

From Major JEAN-DANIEL DE GAMBS.

Metz, February 24, 1784

Mon Général

Les bontés qui vous avés bien voulu me temoigner quand nous eûmes l'honneur de Servir sous vos ordres, mon général, me font prendre la liberté de reclamer vôtre Protection pour être admis à l'ordre de Cincinatus; qui me flatterait infiniment.

J'ai été le plus ancien major de L'armée de Mr. Le Cte. de Rochambeau, en Cette qualitié, j'ai fait les trois Campagnes de L'amerique septentrionale, Comme major de Brigade, et independement du siege d'york, le sort m'a si bien Servi, que je me suis trouvé avec Mr. Le Mis. de Laval, sur le vaisseau le Conquerant, au Combat de Chasapeak le 16 mars 1781, faisant partie du Detachement, qui deja pour lors, devoit aller en Virginie. Le Succés de Cette Expedition n'a pas repondu à nos desirs, mais vous n'ignorés pas, mon Général, que ce vaisseau a été beaucoup plus mal traité, et a beaucoup plus Souffert, que les autres de nôtre Escadre.

Je Saisi avec Empressement, L'occasion qui se presente, pour vous faire parvenir ma lettre, par le général Roberdeau,[1] avec lequel je suis en rélation depuis son arrivé à Londres, ayant eu L'honneur de faire sa Connaisance à nôtre Passage à Philadelphie, Je Connaits beaucoup son parent, le Colonel, qui demeure Chés moi, et qui a Servi le Roy trés long temps avec Distinction.

Sans Cette occasion, que je Crois la plus prompte pour vous faire parvenir ma lettre, j'aurais prié, Mr. Le Cte. de Rochambeau, d'Etre mon entrep[reneur] auprès de vous et du Congrès, Etant Convaincu des bonnes intentions de ce général à mon Egard. Comme le sejour que j'ai fait en Amerique, et le tems que j'ai eu L'honneur de Servir sous vos ordres, mon général, sera toujours une Epoque Chere en ma memoire, vous ai devés pas douter du plaisir que j'aurais, d'Etre decoré d'un ordre Comme Celui de Cincinatus.

J'ai l'honneur etc.

[*Washington Papers*]

[1] A copy of Major Gambs's letter to General Roberdeau, enclosed in the above letter to Washington, is in the Washington Papers.

[Translation in the writing of Dr. David Stuart.]

From Major Gambs

Metz February 24, 1784

General,

The kindness you were pleased to show me, when we had the honor of being commanded by you, encourages me to claim your protection for admittance into the Order of Cincinnatus. I should be much flattered with the honor—I have been the oldest Major in Count Rochambeau's army, and in America as Mjor of Brigade; and independant of the siege of Yorck, fortune was so kind to me, as to place me with the Marquis Laval, aboard the Conqueror, in the action in the Chesapeak the 16th. of march 81; making part of a detachment for Virginia—The success of this expedition was not answerable to our expectations, but you are not ignorant Sir, that this vessel was much worse treated than any in the Squadron—

I have seised with eagerness the opportunity that presents of sending you a letter by General Roberdeau with whom I have corresponded since his arrival in London; having first become acquainted with him on our journey through Philadelphia, and knowing well his relation, a Colonel who stays with me, and has served the King a long time with great honor, Without this opportunity, which I consider as the most ready, I should have begged Count Rochambeau to have interceded with you and Congress for me, as I am well convinced of this General's good inclinations towards me. As the stay I made in America, and the time I served under your orders General, will allways constitute an Epocha dear to me; you cannot doubt of the pleasure it will give me to be honored with such an Order, as that of Cincinnatus— [1]

I have the honor etc.

[*Washington Papers*]

This letter accompanied the Diamond Eagle presented to General Washington. This famous emblem, probably the most precious relic of

[1] Major Gambs, being below the grade of Colonel, was not eligible to membership, and was not admitted.

General Washington, except the estate of Mount Vernon, is inscribed: "D[ ]d in the Name of the french saillors to His Excellency the General Washington." A part of the first word has been chipped away, but may have been "Donated," probably a translator's term for "Donné." See, also, the Count d'Estaing's letter of 18 February 1784 to the Chevalier de La Luzerne, page 81.

From the COUNT D'ESTAING.

Sir: Paris, 26th February, 1784

It is in the name of all the French Navy that I take the liberty to request Your Excellency to accept an American Eagle, expressed rather then embellished by a French artist.

Liberty (of which it is the happy and august symbol) has risen of itself, supported by wisdom, talents and disinterestedness; by every virtue; by General Washington. Obstacles have only served to increase its strength.

The efforts of a patriotic army were irresistable when seconded by the King's troops, who have shown themselves by their discipline and conduct worthy of the choice of his Majesty. Those with his navy made everything possible.

It appears then to be proper in one of those who unites the titles of soldier and sailor, and whom you inspire with the sentiments of the most profound admiration and attachment, to entreat you to receive with indulgence an homage which must cease to be unimportant when it shall appeal to your sensibility.

One who has had the happiness to be the first of those whom the King sent to America, and who has been the last of those who were designed to lead thither the forces of two great monarchs, thereby acquiring the happy perogative of being entitled to express, though failtly, the sentiments of all his fellow sailors and soldiers,[1]

I have the honor to be, with respect, Sir,

Your Excellency's most obedient and
Most humble servant,

Estaing.

[*Archives of the General Society*]

[1] A detailed description of the Diamond Eagle, as it is always known in the Society of the Cincinnati, will be found in E. E. Hume, *General George Wash-*

From the COUNT DE ROCHAMBEAU.

Paris, March 1, 1784.

You will be, my Dear Général, Single confident of this letter. I did foresee the Ministry on the way Wherewith could be received here the different Demands that I have made to you, in order to increase or make Some additions in the Society of Cincinnatus, one did answer me that the King had a great repugnancy to permit to his Subjects any Stranger order, and it Was but by a particular consideration that he has permited to us to be aggregated in the form regulated by the général Society. but a considerable addition perhaps would not be So Well received, as it is not convenient to me to engage you in one proceeding Which may be Would have not here a Kind reception, I beg you to annul all the demands I have made to you be my foregoing letters, and I recommend only to you the two cases following as an explication to the deliberation already Settled by the général society and that do not Want any other consent in this country but that Which has been already given.

ington's Eagle of the Society of the Cincinnati, The Numismatist, Baltimore, December, 1933, xlvi, 749-759. In the inventory of the property at Mount Vernon at General Washington's death there are mentioned "three gold Cincinnati Eagles," valued at $30, and "one diamond Eagle" valued at $387. The Diamond Eagle was presented after General Washington's death, to his successor as President General, by Mrs. Washington. This was Major-General Alexander Hamilton. After his tragic death his heirs sent the Diamond Eagle to the third President General, Major-General Charles Cotesworth Pinckney. He, in turn, presented it to the Society to be worn as a badge of office of all future Presidents General. It is still used, having been worn by all thirteen of the Society's presiding officers. For General Washington's reply, 15 May 1784, see page 179. In Levasseur's journal of LaFayette's visit to America in 1824-5 he tells of the Marquis's reception of an Eagle of the Cincinnati that had once been Washington's. Cloquet lists LaFayette's American keepsakes including an Eagle in a Morocco leather case inscribed: "Washington's Cincinnati Badge." "This decoration," he says, "was once worn by Washington. Madame Lewis [Washington's sister, Betty, wife of General Fielding Lewis of Kenmore] had inherited this precious heirloom. She presented it in 1824 to Lafayette to be given to his second grandson, M Edmond Lafayette" (p. 201).

The Baron de l'Estrade Brigadier of the King's armies.	Has marched, being Lt. Colonel, to the attack of the Redoubts of York-town at the head of the first company of the french grenadiers, has been made Brigadier for this action on his return to St. Domingo.
The chevalier de Lameth aid quarter master-Général.	Has been Wounded by two shots in the attack of the redoubts of york-town, has been made Colonel for this action, While he Was yet in his bed at Williamsburg in consequence of his Wounds.

This two Caises appear to me alones Which may be comprised as an explication of the deliberation of the american army to Which the King has already given his consent, and Which consequently Will have no Want of New approbation of him.[1]

I am Sir With respect etc.

[*Washington Papers*]

The President of the Massachusetts Cincinnati replies to the letter of the President General anent the Triennial of 1784, and names the Massachusetts delegation.

From Major-General BENJAMIN LINCOLN.

Hingham [Massachusetts], March 2, 1784

Dear sir

Since I was honored with the receipt of your favor of this State society of the Cincinnati have had a meeting & have made choice of General Knox Gen Putnam Colo Cobb Colo. Hull & Majr. Serjeant to represent them in the General Meeting to be held at Philadelphia on May next. they are notified to attend I expect that two of them or more will have the pleasure

[1] Both officers became original members of the French Cincinnati.

of meeting your Excellency then—Our Citizens seem alarmed at the constitution of ye Cincinnati & our General Court have ye matter now under consideration I will do my self the pleasure of communicating to your Excellency their doing

With great esteem I have the honor etc.

[*Archives of the General Society*]

From Lieutenant-General LOUIS LEBÈGUE DUPORTAIL.

Paris, March 3, 1784

Dear general

i Cannot let so fine opportunity as major l'enfants going escape without Recalling me to your excellency's memory, probably this letter will find you on the bancs of potoomak; after having asurtained the liberty of your Country, and the fame of your name, you enjoyed the Tranquill pleasures of the rural Life like the patron of our society which you Represent more than any defensor of the Country—however there are certainly great differences between the dictator and your excellency, and one of them is that the Country which he defended was not then so large as the smallest of the 13 united states, but i am sorry i Cannot wish these last should act in future so great a part in the world proportionnately as Rome did, for it Cannot be but at our own expence—but i hope the americains will be wiser and more moderate in their ambition than the Romans, they shall be happier too—

i leave to Marquis de la fayette to tell your excellency the news of this country, the succes of the society of Cincinnatus—your excellency will judge of it by the demands presented by the Marquis as well as by Count de Rochambeau. i have been requested by many to support their demands with your excellency, but i refused to do it—as perfectly inutile. i know very [well] that if the demands are just or if the society is disposed to favours, your excellency will follow equal principles, and so those who have the same rights (or the same rights to favours) shall be treated in the same manner.[1] . . .

[*Washington Papers*]

The following letter is one of the earliest applications for hereditary membership. The writer was the son of General the Baron de Kalb, companion of La Fayette, who fell at the battle of Camden, 1780.

From the BARON FRÉDÉRIC DE KALB.[2]

Alsace, March 3, 1784

General,

I have just received the honor of the Order of Cincinnatus; wc. is conferred on those who have distinguished themselves in the service of America—You honor me with it, as Heir of an unfortunate & respectable parent—I return you my warmest acknowledgments for it, & wish the distance of your Country did not prevent me from paying my respects to you personally

I am etc.

[*Washington Papers*]

---

[1] Something of Duportail's personal attachment to General Washington may be gathered from a passage in his letter from Paris, 24 December, 1783: ". . . Everybody here, dear general, asks me if you intend to come over—i give them little hope after what you told me. your excellency may be certain that he would be received in france with great pleasure but no body could have a greater satisfaction to see you than myself—you may be an object of admiration from those who are at a distance and who know only your military and political life but for those who are so happy as to be particularly acquainted with your excellency's private character you are equally an object of veneration and attachment—however if i have little hope of seing you in france i hope to see you in america for i am far from renouncing from that country forever. may be i shall be able to tell you more about it a few weeks hence. i suppose this letter will find your excellency in Virginia. permit me to present my respects to Mrs. Washington and my compliments to the gentlemen our companions in the war who are so happy as to live near you." (Elizabeth Kite, *Brigadier-General Louis Lebègue Duportail, Commandant of Engineers in the Continental Army. 1777-1783,* Baltimore, 1933, 275-277.)

[2] English translation in the writing of David Stuart. The original is no longer in the Washington Papers.

Here two other original members of the Cincinnati request certificates of membership on their return to Europe and before the regular diplomas were ready.

From Captains ANTOINE-CLAUDE DE MARCELLIN and NICHOLAS-GEORGE LE ROY.

Philadelphia, March 4, 1784.

Sir

Having had the Glory of serving in the armies of the United States for near five years; and having seen the happy termination of the War, we are now preparing to return to Europe with the heart felt satisfaction of having Contributed a share of Service under your auspicious Command in the Establishment of a revolution so Brilliant and Extraordinary.

As the society of Cincinnati must be extremely respected in Europe, and as we Cannot Continue in America long enough to receive the Diplomas we take the Liberty to trouble your Excellency with our request that you will be pleased to sign the Certificates, which we have the honor to transmit as also that you will Condescend to accompany those Sign'd by General St. Clair, with certificates of your honorable approbation of our services

We now beg permission to take leave of your Excellency with our most ardent wishes for a prolongation of your health and Most Valuable life and are with every sentiment of Esteem and Veneration etc.[1]

[*Washington Papers*]

This is a letter on the success of the Cincinnati in France written by one of the great philosophers of his time:

[1] General Washington was not slow in complying with this request, at least as far as Captain de Marcellin was concerned. On 20 March 1784 he issued him a provisional certificate of membership. See page 120.

From the CHEVALIER DE CHASTELLUX.

Paris, March 6, 1784

Dear General,

P. S. . . . All the military gentlemen with the rank either of general or colonel, who have been in America, wear at present the order of Cincinnatus, and the nation sees the Decoration with pleasure, as it really to their mind [was] the most advantageous war, as well as the most valuable alliance they ever made. I am persuaded that this establishment being confined in proper bounds, will triumph over all the enemies it meets in America and I hope your country will understand how to unite the glory of the military to the liberty of the citizens.[1]

[*Washington Papers*]

---

[1] In his *Voyages dans l'Amérique Septentrionale dans les années 1780, 1781, 1782* (Paris, 1786), The poet, philosopher and soldier, Chastellux, gives us the following picture of Washington: "Here would be the proper place to give the portrait of General Washington: but what can my testimony add to the idea already formed of him? The continent of North America, from Boston to Charles Town, is a great volume, every page of which presents his eulogium. I know, that having had the opportunity of a near inspection, and of closely observing him, some more particular details may be expected from me; but the strongest characteristic of this respectable man is the perfect union which reigns between the physical and moral qualities which compose the individual, one alone will enable you to judge of all the rest. If you are presented with medals of Cæsar, of Trajan, or Alexander, on examining their features, you will still be led to ask what was their statue, and the form of their persons; but if you discover, in a heap of ruins, the head or limb of an antique *Apollo,* be not curious about the other parts, but rest assured that they all were comformable to those of a God. Let not this comparison be attributed to enthusiasm! It is not my intention to exaggerate, I wish only to express the impression General Washington has left on my mind; the idea of a perfect whole, that cannot be the produce of enthusiasm, which rather would reject it, since the effect of proportion is to diminish the idea of greatness. Brave without temerity, laborious without ambition, generous without prodigality, noble without pride, virtuous without severity; he seems always to have confined himself within those limits, where the virtues, by cloathing themselves in more lively, but more charitable and doubtful colors, may be mistaken for faults."

For General Washington's reply to this letter, 2 June 1784, see page 193.

La Fayette wrote General Washington three letters on 9 March 1784. One was to Washington as President General of the Cincinnati and intended to be read to the members at the General Meeting. The second was to Washington, his foster father and friend, the third was to General Washington as former Commander-in-Chief of the American Army. The letters are interesting in comparison.

From the MARQUIS DE LA FAYETTE.

Paris, March 9, 1784

Sir,

Your Excellency has been acquainted with my first measures respecting our Society. To my letter of Xber [December] the 25th I beg leave particularly to refer and entrust this with Major L'Enfant who is returning to America.

Having in a body waited upon Count de Rochambeau we delivered him and his officers the marks of the Association. A resolve of theirs for a voluntary subscription will arrive in time to be debated in the Grand Assembly.

Many claims have been raised by French officers, which is not my business to present. But I beg leave to observe that some of them, like in Chevalier de Lameth's case, are entitled to consideration. Count de Rochambeau, I am told, is writing on the subject.[1]

Former dispatches have apologized for the part we have taken respecting Count d'Estaing's officers; the neglect we know was not intended, and, as also in M. de Vaudreuil's case it would have produce a bad effect. The Captains in the navy, ranking as Colonels, have set up a claim to the Association. Some of them, Lapeyrouse, la Touche, Tilly, acted as Commodores. It might be observed that American trade will have to do with naval officers.

As a Board of officers met at my house, the claims of several gentlemen were introduced. Our opinions are submitted to the Assembly, and with them I inclose a list of members who have signed and paid, or to whom on account of their dispositions the instructions are as yet to be sent (etc). Count du Plessis convinced us that he had not resigned.

[1] See page 101.

Our brotherly association has met with general applause—not a dissenting voice to be heard, but in the point of heredity, that creates a debate wherein most of the Americans take the other part. Who can question but what we do not in any account wish to injure those sacred republican principles for which we have fought, bled, and conquered, and what sacrifice has not been made by us, in support of those principles? Which I am sure we are ready to repeat upon every occasion.

It had been my fond hope that I could have arrived in time for the beginning of May. But American claims, an account of which I gave to Congress, detain me for a few weeks. And now when I think this letter will be read among the representatives from all the lines of the Army, my heart is glowing with all the most unbounded sentiments of affection and gratitude. How pleasing it is for me to recollect our common toils, dangers, turns of fortune, our so glorious successes, and that lively attachment which united us with each other under our beloved General. Never can my heart forget the return of affection I have particularly obtained, the numberless obligations I am under my dear brother officers, and the happy hours, the happiest in my life, which I have pass [sic] in their company. Before the month of June is over, I shall, thank God, be again with them, and am impatient for the instant when I may be blessed with a sight of the American shore.

With the highest respect and unbounded affection, I have the honor to be, Sir, Your Excellency's

Most obedient humble servant,

LA FAYETTE [1]

[*Archives of the General Society*]

---

[1] For General Washington's reply to this and the other two letters from La Fayette, dated 9 March 1784, see his letter of 17 May 1784, page 183.

From the MARQUIS DE LA FAYETTE.

Paris, March 9th, 1784.

My dear General,

Had I not so perfect a confidence in your friendship, I should very much fear to tire you with my scribble of this day, but cannot leave my pen before I have again mentioned my tender respectful affection to my dear general. I want to tell you that Madam de LaFayette and my three children are well, and that all of us in the family heartily join to present their dutiful affectionate compliments to Mrs. Washington and yourself. Tell her, that I hope soon to thank her for a dish of tea at Mount Vernon. Yes, my dear General, before the month of June is over, you will see a vessel coming up the Potomac, and out of that vessel will your friend jump, with a panting heart, and all the feelings of perfect happiness. I intended to have gone sooner, but a few commercial matters still keep me here . . .

Most of the Americans here are violent against our Association. Wadsworth must be excepted, and Doctor Franklin said little. But Jay, Adams, and all the others, warmly blame the Army. You easily guess I am not remiss in opposing them; and, however, if it be found that the hereditary right endangers the true principles of democracy, I am as ready as any man to renounce it. You will be my compass, my dear general, because at this distance I cannot judge. In case you find, upon better consideration, that hereditary right will injure our democratic constitutions, I will join with you by proxy in voting against it. If you think hereditary right is a proper scheme, I shall be convinced that your patriotism has considered the matter in the best point of view. *To you alone* I would say so much, and I abide by your opinion in the matter. Let the foregoing be confidential, but I am sure your disinterested virtue will weigh all possible future consequences of hereditary distinctions. . . .[1]

[*Archives of the General Society*]

---

[1] For General Washington's reply to this and the other two letter from La Fayette, dated 9 March 1784, see his letter of 17 May 1784, page 183.

From the MARQUIS DE LA FAYETTE.

Paris, March 9th, 1784

My dear General,

Although I write another private letter, I must confidentially let you know my opinion upon matters relative to our society.

The captains of the navy have been much mortified to be left out of the institution. They rank as colonels, they have rendered great services, and, it is expected here, they will be admitted into the sociey. Some of them came with Count d'Estaing, among whom are Suffren, d'Albert, de Rioms, and some other great characters. The remainder went under Ternay, Destouches, and Grasse. A few have been sent to carry great news, such as the treaty, or have actually commanded in chief, such as Lapeyrouse, Latouche, &c. I know they are many, but how can a partial distinction be made? And as they will have much to do with American vessels, in preventing contraband trade, I suppose, or in receiving American ships into French harbours, I think it would be impolitic not to put them in a good humour. In the opinion I give, I oppose my own interests, for the fewer members there may be in the society, the more will it be valued. But I see a substantial public motive to be determined upon, and as the *captains de vaisseaux* are dispersed throughout the harbours, they will not so much crowd as land officers, because they very seldom come to the capital. M. d'Albert, de Rioms, Latouche, Lapeyrouse, Tilly, cannot but have it, and, I think, it could be general.

As to the land officers, many claims have been raised; some of them; I think, deserve consideration. M. de Lestrade. M de Menonville, such, in a word, as particular reasons may be assigned for, ought to be included; *above all the Chevalier de Lameth,* who has been so cruelly wounded in the redoubt; who was an aide-de-camp, and two months after was a colonel. I think we must avoid giving grounds of complaint. inclosed is a letter respecting Count Edward Dillon, who was going to Savannah when wounded in the engagement at sea, and was then a colonel. You will also find a note from M. de St. Simon respecting his brother. Menonville was his adjutant-general, and in that office they have the honours of brigadier paid to them when majors in the tranchées. M. de Corny has applied to me, and I could not give him the badge. I promised him I would mention his wishes, and send you his petition. His claims are set up in the capacity of an American officer.

In the resolutions of our committee, you will find a mention made of General Conway, which I am going to explain. I do not say that I have merit; but I say, I have its consequences—viz. enemies. My popularity is great throughout the kingdom, and in the city; but among the great folks I have a large party against me, because they are jealous for my reputation: in a word, the pit, to a man, is for me, and in the boxes there is a division. A plot was laid to draw me into a snare, and a Madame Conway was made a tool of to give me and yourself the air of an implacable revenge against that man who is considered here as having been abandoned and ruined by me in America. It might be well to grant him the decoration.

The French officers have offered money. I had rather is was not accepted; but at such a distance I cannot judge what is best to be done. The formation of a committee in Europe is very necessary, but it must, for obvious reasons, be quite separated from any society the French officers may form, as it is calculated only for American purposes, and ought to consist of but American officers for the time being in Europe.

After proper allowances have been made, both for the naval officers and particular cases, I will beg leave to represent that the members ought not to be too much multiplied. If a greater facility takes place, the institution will sink in proportion as it is bestowed upon too may people, and our officers must be upon their guard not to give the badge without proper motives.

I have been requested to present you with a new model and ribbon; and from the persons who gave it, could not refuse sending it to America. I need not say that this letter is confidential.

With the highest respect and tenderest affection, I have the honour to be, &c.,[1]

LA FAYETTE

[*Archives of the General Society*]

[1] For General Washington's reply to this and the other two letters from La Fayette, date 9 March 1784, see his letter of 17 May 1784, page 183.

The President or the New Hampshire Cincinnati replies to the President General's letter about the coming General Meeting.

From Major-General JOHN SULLIVAN.

Durham, March 12, 1784

Sir

Your Excellencys favor of the 28th of December respecting the attendance of our Delegates at the General Meeting of the Society of the Cincinnati on the first Monday of May; came to hand the first Instant—the Contents have been communicated & a meeting appointed on the second of April, at which time I doubt not, Delegates will be chosen & the proper steps taken, to insure a punctual attendance.

I have the honor to be, etc.

[*Archives of the General Society*]

From Colonel CHARLES ARMAND-TUFFIN, MARQUIS DE LA ROUËRIE.

Philadelphia, 14th March, 1784

Sir:

I have received a letter from Major General Duportail, dated from Paris the 24th December last, in which he gives me the following account of the success which the Order and Society of the Cincinnaty have in France.

The Order of the Cincinnaty has had great success here till this instant. The King has permitted the French officers who belong to it to wear the badge of it. Every man wishes to have it, and those who have not served the necessary time in the American Army endeavor to give a turn to their brevets and furloughs which may obtain them the honor of wearing it. I assure you that it has made and makes more noise here than it does in America. The officers of the French Army are much flattered by that honorable distinction and the Count de Rochambeau makes a superior affair of it. The Marquis de

le Quinze Mars 1785.

Louis Joseph de Bourbon Prince de Condé
Prince du Sang, Pair et grand Maître de France, Lieutenant général des armées du Roy, Chevalier de ses ordres, Gouverneur et Lieutenant général des provinces de Bourgogne et Bresse, Colonel Général de l'Infie. française et Étrangère.

Vu la présente lettre du Roy adressée à M. le Mis. de [illegible] portant que Sa Majesté a donné au [illegible] Barthélemy de Montlezun de la Barthette, Lieut. en [illegible], la charge de Lieutenant en premier de la Compie. de [illegible] dans le Régt. d'Infie. de Touraine vacante par l'abandonnement [illegible]

Nous [illegible] que nous [illegible] Colonel Général de l'Infie. française et Étrangère [illegible] Régt. de Touraine [illegible] de la Barthette en lad. charge de Lieutenant en premier de la Compagnie [illegible] dans led. Régt. [illegible] ainsi qu'il appartiendra. En foy de quoi nous avons fait expédier [illegible] signé et fait contresigner par le Secrétaire général de l'Infie. française et Étrangère.

Donné à Paris le 16. Juillet 1785.

Louis Joseph de Bourbon

Louis

Le Mis de Ségur

Par son Altesse Sérénissime
[illegible]

The Chevalier de Montlezun de la Barthette sent General Washington this commission from the King, in connection with his application for admission to the Society of the Cincinnati. The document bears the sign manual of His Most Christian Majesty, Louis XVI, and is countersigned by the Marquis de Ségur, Minister of War.

[*Archives of the General Society*]

Mons.r le V.te de Soudeux, ayant donné

à Barthelemy Escuier Du Moulin de Montlezun de La Barthette, Lieutenant

la Charge de Lieutenant en premier de la Compagnie de

Campan dans le régiment d'Infanterie de Touraine

que vous Commandez, vacante par l'abandonnement

d'Albenas

Je vous écris cette Lettre pour vous dire que vous ayiez a le

reçevoir et faire reconnoitre en lad. Charge de tous ceux et ainsi

qu'il appartiendra, et la présente n'étant pour autre fin, Je prie

Dieu qu'il vous ait, Mons. le V.te de Soudeux

en sa Sainte garde. Écrit à Versailles

Lafayette who is commissioned by the Order to receive in it the French officers who served in America, receives daily applications on the subject from persons who ought to be sensible that they have no right to be admitted.

As the character of the Cincinnatus, so well marked by nature, acquired habilitation and success in that of Your Excellency and is the most just and honorable foundation of the Order, I thought that the relation of my friend would be agreeable to you and indeed to say or do anything that may be agreeable to Your Excellency, is the superior wish governing my heart.

I have almost finished with success the affair of the Legion and Engineers, which gives me the expectation of being able to go soon and pay my respects to Your Excellency. In all probability it will be towards the latter end of this month.

I have the honor to be with highest respect, Sir, Your Excellency's most obedient humble servant.

ARMAND

His Excellency General Washington

[*Archives of the General Society*]

From the COUNT DE GRASSE.

My dear General:

I cannot at this time answer the friendship with which you honor me unless it is by a proof of my confidence in you, and I give it with pleasure.

I have the honor to send you the memorials which I have submitted to the consideration of the Court Martial for their better information of my conduct.[1]

The sincere desire I have to make you judge of this affair induces me to deviate from the order I have received not to communicate these memorials in print. I request you not to

[1] De Grasse was tried by court martial for his defeat at the battle of Les Saintes, 12 April 1782, by the British under Admiral Rodney, where he was taken prisoner. He was acquitted.

show them to anybody, or if you think proper to make use of them, I wish you would have them transcribed.

I hope, my dear General, that when you have read them attentively you will be sensible that I have not deserved that you should change your opinion of me; but that all my fault on the 12th day of April, 1782, was being unfortunate.

The Court Martial assembled at this place for the determination of this affair will, I hope, soon come to a finding. I request your leave, my dear General, to acquaint you with the issue whatsoever it may be.

I am waiting to hear from you with that impatience arising from the most sincere friendship. Do me the favor to let me hear from you the soonest possible. Depend always on the affectionate and respectful attachment with which I have the honor to be, my dear General,

Your Excellency's most obedient, humble servant,

The Count de Grasse
Associate in the Cincinnatus

L'Orient,
The 15th March, 1784.

[*Archives of the General Society*]

From Captain Le Gardeur de Tilly.

Rochefort ce 15 mars, 1784.

A Son Exelance

agrée je vous prie L'homage De mon Respect et me permite De vous Rappeler Les Sirconstances, qui M'ont procuré La Satisfaction De mettre En Evidance tout Le zele et Lamprescement a cegonder ceaux vu par mes Scitations Surveaux Cottes Comendant Le vaisseau de Sa Majesté LEveillé et Deux frigates avec Lesquels je me Suis Rendue Maitre Du vaisseau Le Romulusse, Le Duc De york, La Goilette La Revange Et plusieurs austre petite Batiments Dont je Remie Les prisoniers, au Commandant Demptone, qui me temoigna alors toutes Sa Satisfaction, par Les Déprédation quavoit Commes Ces Dernier,

Surtoutes vos Cotte javais désire mieux faire En Corre Sil mut Etre possible

jay Egalment eu La Satisfaction, Descorter La Corvette Le Wasington Du Cap françois a Larane, ou Elle prie un chargement En argent je continues alui Donner Lescorte jusque Sur Les Cotte de la Délaware, ou ayant Rencontré un vaisseau de Soixante et quatre Et Deux frigates Enemie je Crue Devoir Combatre Les Deux frigates pour faciliter La Retréte De Vôtre Corvétte, qui fut En, profiter avec Succes Cequi fait LEloge du Capitaine Dont les Differente Maneuvres pendant Le Cours De Nôtre Navigation merite Les plus Grand Eloge; je Navis jamais Rappelé a vôtre Exelance Daussy foible preuve Detous Mes Desir a Repondre a la confiance Dont on mavez honnoré Sy jusse pue partager La joix et La Satisfaction quont tous Seur que vous avez Bien voulue assossier a Lordre de Cincinatus je Repeux Donc vous Dicimiler tout Le Desir que jay Di Estre assossie Commun temoignage De Vôtre aprobation et Souvenir qui me cera toujour pressieux

je suis avec Respect etc.

[*Archives of the General Society*]

[Translation by Edgar Erskine Hume]

Rochefort, 15 March 1784

To His Excellency

Accept, I beg you, the hommage of my respect and permit me to recall to you the circumstances which brought me the satisfaction of demonstrating all the zeal and eagerness shown by my charges as commandant of His Majesty's ship *L'Eveillé* and two frigates with which I became master of the ship *Le Romulusse, Le Duc de York, Le Goilette, La Ravange,* and several other small boats in which I sent prisoners to Commandant Demptone, who showed me his every satisfaction

I have likewise had the satisfaction to escort the corvette *Le Wasington* [sic] from Cape François to Larane, where she took on a cargo of silver. I continued to escort her as far as the Delaware coast, and having encountered a vessel of sixty-four and two enemy frigates, I thought it my duty to engage the two frigates in order to facilitate the retreat of your corvette, and this done, to profit by the success which evoked the praise of the captain, to whom the different maneuvres during the course of our navigation merited the greatest praise. I have only recalled to Your Excellency these slight proofs of my every desire to respond to the confidence with which you have honored me, so that I might partake of the joy and the satisfaction which all those have who you have had the goodness to receive into the Order of Cincinnatus. I repeat, then, all the desire that I have of being admitted as an evidence of your approbation the memory of which will always be so precious to me.

I am with respect etc.

From the MARQUIS DE VIENNE.

[Contemporary Translation]

[March 1784]

To his Excellency General Washington

MAY IT PLEASE YOUR EXCELLENCY to admit the address of a French man, who had the honor of serving under you immediate command, and who—in hopes of obtaining by your Protection a favour which will make him happy, and save his honour and reputation begs leave to state his conduct whilst in your Excellency's Service.

The Marquis of Vienne left France in 1778 to join the General de la Fayette as Volunteer in America, to whome he was recommended. He embarked at Nants at his own expence on board a frigate belonging to the Congress, call'd the Queen of France, commanded by Captain Green. After a long and fatigueing voyage he arriv'd at Boston, where he remain'd only to make the necessary preparations. From thence he set off to join the Marquis de la Fayette, who was then at Valley Forge, where he arriv'd the day before the King's troops evacuated Philadelphia. He had the honour to be presented to your Excellency by the Marquis, who at the same time requested the permission of his serving under your immediate Command, to which you graciously condescended. He was of the detach'd party commanded by General de la Fayette to pursue the Enemy over Sandy-hook.—The day before the Action of Mon-mouth, he was dispatch'd by the General de la Fayette with four Dragoons to reconnoitre the Enemy's march in their retreat, and to examine the position of their Camp. He pursued them with such speed, that they were not sooner encamp'd, than thro' the favour of a storm, pass'd between two of their advanc'd Guards into their very Tents, and took two English Grenadiers prisoners, whome he sent to General de la Fayette. He return'd shortly after to make his report of his expedition. He was the next day with the Marquis de la Fayette in the action of Mon Mouth. The English having reimbark'd, the Marquis de la Fayette sent him from Brunswick to Philadelphia to be presented to the Congress, with letters of recommendation to the President Laurens. The Congres granted him the Degree and rank of a Colonel. Shortly afterwards he left Philadelphia and rejoin'd your Excellency at Old Plain, whence he set off the following day with the Marquis de la Fayette to march for Providence and Rhode Island, where he serv'd during the time the Troops of the United States remain'd there, under the command of General Sullivan, and return'd not to the Continent, 'till after their retreat from Providence; at which time he was sent by the Marquis de la Fayette to carry dispatches to the Count d'Estaing. War being declared at that period in his Native Country, he demanded your Excellency's permission to serve under its Banners, to which you agreed, and sent him a discharge dated Fredericks-Bourg Octobr. the 16th. 1778 together with a Certificate; both of which and one from the Marquis de la Fayette, he sends enclosed with this.—

The Marquis of Vienne set off at his own expence, and could not prevail on himself to receive any sort of recompence or appointment from the United States of America. His name & Family are well known in France, and his Father is honour'd by his Sovereign with the Rank of Lieutenant General—Under these Circumstances it is plain he could have no Motives to be mercenary; nor any Desire that his Services should be recompensed with Money.—He only sought the glory of spilling his blood, and exposing his life for the Cause and in the Service of the United States.

That Campaign cost him more than Twelve hundred Guineas, out of a Fortune not the most considerable, nor entirely free from Embarrassments.

He departed from Boston with M. le Comte d'Estaing, and wou'd certainly have return'd to America, had not both his health & fortune been impair'd, & render'd the Attempt impracticable.

The Marquis of Vienne having the honour of thus minutely stating his Case, leaves your Excellency to judge of his anxiety in not being admitted into the Order of Cincinnatus. He sees his Countrymen adorn'd with that honourable Badge, for having serv'd as Colonels in America. Have they done more for this mark of Distinction than the Marquis of Vienne? The Marquis de la Fayette charg'd by your Excellency with a power of confering this Dignity cannot (notwithstanding the great esteem with which he honours the Marquis of Vienne,) exceed his Commission, which impowers him to give it to those only, who serv'd three years, or as commanding Officers.

The Marquis de Vienne has expos'd his life freely as any other, nay he has serv'd at his own expence; wou'd receive nothing from the Congress—and yet cannot obtain the honour of being associated in an order, which wo'd be his greatest Glory & Satisfaction. He was among the first, who demonstrated that zeal, which afterwards drew so many of his Countrymen into the path of Glory, and which he, by his example, pointed out to them,—But, depriv'd of that mark of honour & distinction, he dare not boast of having serv'd under the great General Washington. It would perhaps, be inferred that he has not complied with his duty, that he has not shewn the Spirit of a Soldier and a Genleman—because, unlike others, he has not been honour'd with the Insignia of that respectable Order. The grief of the Marquis de Vienne, and that of his whole family is inexpressible.

At your Excellency's feet he lays his Grief, humbly prayg. you to regard his petition, and obtain for him as a Grace from the assembly of the Cincinnati that Badge which will rank him in that most respectable Society. He has already the honour of being in his own Country a Member of the honourable Order of St. Louis, his admission into that of Cincinnatus would compleat his desires.

The Marquis de la Fayette is pleas'd to charge himself with transmitting this to your Excellency, as the petition & testimonial of the sufferings of the Marquis de Vienne. Protected by a man so dear to the United States as the Marquis de la Fayette, who does not bestow his favours but on the Brave and the Worthy, he hopes that your Excellency will grant his request and crown his wishes by writing to the Marquis de la Fayette, that he may extraordinarily, and as an exception enroll the Marquis de Vienne in the Society of the Cincinnati. This would prove the most flattering moment of his life, while his acknowledgement and prayers for your Excellency's preservation could only end with the life of your Excellencys most humble etc.[1]

[*Archives of the General Society*]

Certificate of Service of Marquis de Vienne

[Attached to the Marquis de Vienne's letter, above]

Fredericksburg, September 29, 1778

I certify that the Marquis De Vienne served some time in the army under my immediate command in character of volunteer, during which his conduct was always such as became an officer and a gentleman, having embraced every occasion his situation offered to give proofs of his zeal and bravery—He received an appointment of brevet to the rank of Colonel in the army of the United States the fifteenth of July last.[2]

G: Washington

[*Archives of the General Society*]

---

[1] Only a rough English translation of this letter is in the Archives. It is undated but was probably written in March 1784. It is indorsed as having been read at the General Meeting in May, 1784. Attached to the translation is the certificate of service of the Marquis de Vienne, signed by General Washington.

[2] The Marquis de Vienne was not admitted to the Society of the Cincinnati, probably because his services as an American officer were not as long as the requisite three years.

As requested by Captain de Marcellin on 4 March 1784 (see page 105), General Washington issued him a provisional certificate of membership as he was about to depart for Europe. This document, unlike those previously recorded, is likewise signed by General Knox, Secretary General. Knox signed himself " Acting Secretary General," as he held the office only provisionally until permanently elected thereto at the General Meeting in May 1784.

Provisional Diploma of Captain DE MARCELLIN.

Wax seal: Washington Arms

This Certifies that Captain Claude Antoine Villet de Marcellin of the Pennsylvania Line being in virtue of his Services in the American Army entitled to become a Member of the Cincinnati and having signed the Institution and complied with the Regulations therein specified, is accordingly admitted a Member and is entitled to all the Rights and Privileges of the said Society of the Cincinnati.

Given under my hand, and
Seal at Mount Vernon, this
twentieth day of March 1784

G° Washington

H. Knox Actg. Secty General [1]

[*Archives of the General Society*]

From Lieutenant-Colonel DAVID HUMPHREYS.

New Haven, March 20, 1784

My dear General

I arrived at this place just a Month from the time of my leaving Mount Vernon, perfectly free from Misadventures, altho' attended with disagreeable roads & the coldest weather I ever experienced—in my route I had the pleasure of executing

[1] This document was purchased from a dealer by the late Mr. John Cropper, President of the Society of the Cincinnati in the State of Virginia and Assistant Secretary General. His widow presented it to the General Society in 1934.

all your commands, except that of delivering your verbal Message to Govr. Clinton, this, the impracticability of passing the Hudson below Kings-ferry prevented; I have however written a private Letter to His Excellency on the subject.

On the 17th. inst. the Connecticut State Society of Cincinnati convened at Hartford, they appointed Generals [Samuel Holden] Parsons, [Jedediah] Huntington, & [Heman] Swift, with Colo. [Jonathan] Trumbull & myself to attend the General Meeting in May next as their Delegation—in consequence of which I expect the honor of seeing you at that time.

It is with no small satisfaction I inform your Excellency that the disposition of the People of this State respecting political subjects seems to be changing for the better with great rapidity; there is scarcely a doubt but that the Legislature will adopt the Impost at their next Session [1] and I am told that the influence of General Greene is operating very favorably in the State of Rhode Island; so that I still hope (agreeably to your old prediction) that every thing will terminate happily. . . .

[*Pennsylvania Historical Society*]

To Major-General NATHANIEL GREENE.

Mount Vernon, March 20, 1784

My Dr. Sir,

From the purport of your Letter dated Feby. 16th.[2] at Newport (which only came to my hands yesterday)—I have little expectation that this reply to it will find you in the State of Rhode Island. If however the case be otherwise it is to express an earnest wish that you might make it convenient to take the Genl. Meeting of the Cincinnati in your way to So. Carolina.

I was concerned to hear you say, only one Delegate from your State would be there. It were to be wished on many accounts, that the ensuing Meeting might not only be full in

[1] Opposition in Connecticut to the Cincinnati was sufficiently weighty to prevent the Legislature granting the Society the charter for which they so often petitioned (*cf. Papers of the Connecticut Society of the Cincinnati,* 1916).

[2] See page 81. For reply to this letter see page 124.

representation, but that the best abilities of the Society might also be present.—There are, in my opinion very important reasons for this, & I cannot avoid an earnest wish, that yours may be among them.—I would add more were I not apprehensive that this will not meet you in time.—I have received Letters from France on this subject, which, with the sentiments which many seem disposed to entertain of the tendency of the Society, makes it, I repeat it again, indispensably necessary that the first meeting shou'd be full and respectable.

As there is time (supposing this letter gets to your hand in Rhode Island) to give me an acknowledgment of it, let me entreat an answer. My best wishes attend Mrs. Greene, yourself & Family, in which Mrs. Washington joins. And I am very sincerely, etc.

[*Washington's Letter Books*]

To Major-General HENRY KNOX.

Mount Vernon, 20 March, 1784

My dear Sir,

Your Letter of the 21st ulto.[1] did not reach my hands 'till yesterday. Having the governor here, and a house full of company, and the Post being on the point of setting out for the Eastward, I must confine the few lines I shall be able (at this time) to write, to the business of the Cincinnati.

From what you have said of the temper of your Assembly respecting this Society, from the current of Sentiment in the other New England States thereon, and from the official letter, which I have lately received from the Marqs. de la Fayette on this subject, I am more than ever of opinion, that the general meeting in Philada in May next ought, *by all means,* to be full and respectable: I was sorry to find these words, therefore, in your letter, after naming the delegates from your State, " Probably only two will attend."

[1] See page 95.

I think, not only the whole number chosen should attend, but the abilities of them should be coolly, deliberately, and wisely employed, when met, to obviate the prejudices and remove the jealousies, which are already imbibed, and more than probably, through ignorance, envy, and perhaps worse motives will increase in spread. I cannot, therefore, forbear urging in strong terms the necessity of the measure. The ensuing General Meeting is either *useful* or *useless*; if the former, the representatives of each State Society ought to be punctual in their attendance, especially under the present circumstances; if it is not, all ought to be exempted; and I am sure none can give the time, which this journey and business require, with less convenience to themselves than myself.

By a Letter, which I have just received from Genl. [Nathaniel] Greene, I am informed that himself, Genl. [James Mitchell] Varnum, and Majr. [Daniel] Lyman are chosen to represent the State Society of Rhode Island; that he intends to be in So. Carolina before the meeting; and it is not expected that more than one will attend it! I wish this could be otherwise, and that General Greene would attend. Private interest and convenience may be a plea for many, and the Meeting thereby be thin and unfit for the purpose of its institution.

I have heard nothing yet from New Hampshire, New York or New Jersey, to the eastward, nor anything from the southward; to the last, duplicates have long since have been sent.

As there can be no interruption of the post by bad weather now, and there is time for it, pray let me hear more fully from you on the subject of this letter by the return of it; particularly what the committees of your Assembly have reported. . . .

[*Washington's Letter Books*]

General Washington writes to his former Aide-de-Camp who is helping the President General in the seemingly difficult task of obtaining replies from several State Societies of the Cincinnati respecting the coming General Meeting of 1784.

To Lieutenant-Colonel BENJAMIN WALKER.

Mount Vernon, March 24, 1784

Dear Walker:

. . . I have obtained no answer yet to the Circular Letter you took with you for New Jersey, New York and New Hampshire, the two first certainly must have got to hand; but it may not be amiss nevertheless for you to enquire (by a line) of the Presidents of those two (State) Societies, whether they have or have not got them, accompanying the enquiry with information of the time and place of the Genl. Meeting.

I understand the Society of the Cincinnati is the cause of much jealousy and uneasiness in the New England States. Pray what is said of it in yours, and in the Jerseys. Will you (for a letter may arrive at this place before I set out) be kind enough to give me full information on this head, who your Delegates are, whether they will attend &ca. It were much to be wished that the Genl. Meeting might be full and respectable; that the several matters which may come before it, might be deliberately weighed, and wisely resolved on. A thin meeting will bring the Society into contempt. . . .[1]

[*Washington's Letter Books*]

To Major-General NATHANIEL GREENE.

Mount Vernon, March 27, 1784

My Dr. Sir:

A few days ago, by the post, on wch. of late there seems to be no dependence, I wrote you a few lines[2] expressive of an earnest wish that you could make it convenient to be at the Genl. Meeting of the Society of the Cincinnati, before you took your departure for South Carolina. I did not then, nor can I

[1] See Colonel Walker's reply, page 129.

[2] See General Washington's letter of 20 March 1784, page 121. For reply to the above, see page 141.

now, assign all my reasons for it; but it should seem in-despensable, that the Meeting in May next should not only be full, but composed of the best abilities of the representation. The temper, of the New England States in particular, respecting this Society, the encreasing jealousies of it, a letter from the Marquis, and other considerations point strongly to wise determination at this time. If then private interest or convenience will hold the first characters from the Meeting, what may be the consequence? 'tis easier, and perhaps better to be conceived than told. At any rate a bare representation will bring the Society into disrepute, and unfit it perhaps to decide upon the weighty matters which may come before it. besides, these excuses may be offered by one man as well as another, and sure I am none can urge them with more propriety than myself. I would add more, but that I fear this letter will not reach you in time and I am detaining a countryman of yours who has a fair wind, and I know is setting upon thorns from his eagerness to embrace it.

Most sincerely and Affectionately, I am, etc.

[*Washington's Letter Books*]

From Lieutenant-Colonel BENJAMIN WALKER.

New York, April 3, 1784.

My dear General

Your favour of the 12th of March[1] reached me the day before yesterday. . . .

I am surprized at your not having received any answers[2] to the Circular Letters. I kept those for the Eastward of this about a Week after I arrived here, when, finding no better conveyance, I forwarded them by the post;—least however any accident should have happend, I wrote yesterday, to the several persons to whom they were addressed, mentioning the purport

[1] This letter cannot now be found.
[2] See pages 42, 43, 46 and 48.

of them, and desiring to know if they were received and if their Delegates will attend—the enclosed will shew you how far the Society in this State have proceeded—. . .

[*Washington Papers*]

To Deputy Adjutant General JONATHAN TRUMBULL, JR.

Mount Vernon, April 4, 1784

My dear Sir:

The choice of your delegates to the General Meeting of the Cincinnati gave me pleasure, and I wish very sincerely you would all attend; Let me impress this upon you, with a request that you would impress it upon your Brothers of the delegation.

This meeting, taking into consideration the prejudices and jealousies which have arisen, should not only be respectable in number but respectable in abilities. Our measures should be deliberate and wise. If we cannot convince the people that their fears are ill-founded we should (at least in a degree) yield to them and not suffer that which was intended for the best purposes to produce a bad one which will be the consequence of divisions proceeding from an opposition to the currt. opinion, if the fact is so in the Eastern States as some have reported. Independent of this there are other matters which call for attention at the ensuing meeting.[1]

[*New York Public Library*]

---

[1] Fitzpatrick, in *The Writings of George Washington* (xxvii, 386), gives the following footnote: "Among these other matters was the admission of several French naval officers: La Peyrouse, La Touche, D'Albert de Rion, and Tilly, whose names had been sent in by Lafayette. Washington's short note, undated, to Knox concerning this is in the New York Public Library where it has been assigned the date of Apr. 4, 1784, and Trumbull is given as the addressee. Lafayette's letter to Washington mentioning these officers is dated Mar. 9, 1784, and is in the *Papers of the Society of the Cincinnati*."

From the COUNT DE ROCHAMBEAU.

Paris May the 4th. 1784

My Dear General

. . . The letter Which you have honoured me With, the 1er. of february ultime., has made the greatest pleasure to me, and your title of particulary citizen cannot but increases the Sentiments of veneration, and of the most tender affection that I have devoted to you all my life. It is the finest End of the highest employement that ever man has filled. . . .

you owe to have received, my dear Général, the little letter of confidence by which I did present you of all the repugnancy that the King has to admit Strange orders in his Kingdom, and that it Was only by a consideration for you and for the united States, he has permitted to us of being admitted in the Society of Cincinnatus. If you admit all the demands that the officers of the navy make to you, as well as that I Sent to you for my army, I fear that this great extension may displease to his majesty and I doubt he will accept it. I think then it would be convenient to Keep in two that I have designed to you, to wit, The chevalier de Lameth and the Baron de L'Estrade, The first having been Wounded in the attack of the redoubts of york, and the second having been ordered to march at the head of the first company of Grenadiers as a Lieutenant Colonel in the same attack. they have only been made, one Brigadier, and the other Colonel after the siege. They are both in So particulary cases that if you grant that favour to them, I Shall not Want a new permission of the King I shall consider it as an explication of the first deliberation that his majesty had already approved of.

my most tender respects, I beseech you, my Dear Général to Madame Washington, Let me know from you and from her as often as it will be possible to you, and be persuaded of the inviolable attachment and of the respect with which I am etc.[1]

[*Washington Papers*]

---

[1] For General Washington's reply, 20 August 1784, see page 203.

To Major-General HENRY KNOX.

[April 4, 1784?]

Dear Sir,

The names which follow are those mentioned in the Marqs. la Fayette's letter to me.

La' Peyrouse
La Touche
D'Albert de Rion, } I am not sure that these two Gentn. may
Tilly. . . . . } not be of the line, & thereby included in the Genl' descripn.

Enclosed it seems is the proper address to the characters therein mentioned,—I send it that you may be governed thereby—pray return it to me again.—The enclosed private letters be so good as to include under cover of the public ones.

Yrs affly

[*New York Public Library*]

From Brigadier-General RUFUS PUTNAM.

Rutland, April 5, 1784

Dear sir

Being unavoidably prevented from attending the General meeting of the Cincinnati, at Philadelphia as I had intended; and where I once more expected the oppertunity in person to pay my respects to your Excellency: I cannot deny my self the honnor, of addressing you by letter;—to acknowledge with gratitude the ten thousand obligations I feal my self under to your goodness, and most sincearly congratulate you on your return to Domestic happiness; to enquire after your health and wish the best of heavens blessings may attend you & your Dear Lady.— . . .

[*Washington Papers*]

From Major-General WILLIAM SMALLWOOD.

Mattawoman [Maryland] April 6, 1784

Dr. sir, . . .

I have received Answers to my Letters respecting the meeting of the Cincinnati in Philadelphia from Governor Paca and Colo. Ramsey (but none from Genl. Williams) whose punctual attendance you may depend on—. . .[1]

[*Washington Papers*]

From Lieutenant-Colonel BENJAMIN WALKER.

New York, April 6, 1784

Dear General

Your favor of the 24 March[2] was handed to me too late on Monday last to reply to it by that post—. . .

I had the pleasure to write to you a few days ago & inclosed the bye laws and proceedings of the Society of the Cincinnati for this State—I have not heard of any objections to it, either in this State or in Jersey—and I am told the Jealousies that existed in the New England States begin to die away—. . .

[*Washington Papers*]

From Lieutenant-Colonel JOHN ALLISON.

Charleston, South Carolina, April 6, 1784

Sir,

By comparing the date of the Letter[3] with which you honored me as Senior Officer in the State of South Carolina, with the period of Colonel Morris's arrival at Philadelphia it

[1] The delegates of the Maryland Cincinnati at the General Meeting of 1784 were: Major-General William Smallwood, Brigadier-General Otho Holland Williams (who was there elected Assistant Secretary General), Governor William Paca (honorary member) and Lieutenant-Colonel Nathaniel Ramsey.

[2] See page 124. For account of the early opposition to the Cincinnati, see Introduction, page xv.

[3] See page 46.

appears that the Dispatches from the Society of the Cincinnati of this State, with which he was charged came unfortunately too late to anticipate your Excellencys Enquiry concerning measures taken to Establish the society in South Carolina—

The Dispatches alluded to have I hope removed every Degree of uncertainty on this Head, and I take the Liberty of enclosing herewith the proceedings of this Society from its formation to the last meeting—[1]

I have also to acknowledge the receipt of Your Excellency's circular letter of the 1st of January last, and in conformity thereto, the Delegates to represent this Society in the General Society are required to appear in the City of Philadelphia on the first Monday in May next—for which purpose Lieu Colo [William Augustine] Washington has already sett out, and Colo [Anthony Walton] White will shortly follow—Lieu Colo [Lewis] Morris & Captn. [George] Turner, I am in hopes are Philadelphia, therefore persuade myself that the Society of this State will be fully represented on the Meeting of the General Society.

I have the Honor to be etc.

[*Archives of the General Society*]

General Washington, being troubled at the criticism of the Cincinnati, because of the supposed danger of its giving rise to an hereditary nobility, wrote to Jefferson, most powerful of the Society's enemies, asking for his views. In this letter the President General is particularly concerned with the attitude of Congress, for some of the State Legislatures were said to be considering steps against the Society—though no such measures were ever enacted.

To Mr. THOMAS JEFFERSON.

Mount Vernon, 8 April, 1784.

Dear Sir:

If with frankness, and the fullest latitude of a friend, you will give me your opinion of the institution of the Society of

[1] A manuscript copy of the proceedings, certified by Major John Sandford Dart, Secretary of the South Carolina Cincinnati, is with this letter.

Cincinnati, it would confer an acceptable favor upon me. If to this opinion, you would be so obliging as to add the sentiments, or what you *suppose* to be the sentiments of Congress respecting it, I would thank you.

That you may have the best materials on which to form a judgement, I send you a copy of the proceedings of the Society—consequent of their choice of me for President pro:tem:, and the direction therein; I sent the Institution to the French land and naval commanders, and to the Marquis de la Fayette (as the senior French officer in the American Army),—whose proceedings thereon, I also enclose.

These papers you will please to retain for fear of accidents, till I shall have the pleasure to see you at Annapolis, the week after next, on my way to Philadelphia, where this and other business will take me, but the sooner I could receive your sentiments on this subject, the more pleasing they would be.

The pamphlet ascribed to Mr. Burke,[1] as I am told, had its effect—people are alarmed, especially in the Eastern States—how justly, or how contrary to the avowed principles of the Society, and the purity of their motives, I will not declare; lest it should appear that I wanted to biass your judgement, rather than to obtain an opinion—which if you please, might be accompanied with sentiments, under the information here given respecting the most eligible measures to be pursued by the Society at their next meeting.

You may be assured, Sir, that to the good opinion alone, which I entertain of your abilities and candor, this liberty is to be attributed; and I can truly add, that, with very great esteem & regard, I am &c.[2]

[*Washington's Letter Books*]

General Knox, as Secretary General of the Society of the Cincinnati, was as awake as was General Washington to the importance of there being a full General Meeting at which to consider some of the problems facing the new brotherhood.

[1] See page xv.

[2] See page 135 for Jefferson's reply to this letter.

From Major-General HENRY KNOX.

Boston, April 12, 1784

My dear sir.

I received your favor of the 20th ultimo yesterday. I am fully persuaded of the importance of a general attendance at the meeting at Philadelphia, and I have now written to those concerned in this State, Rhode Island, Connecticut, and New-Hampshire, urging their attendance to the utmost of my power. If General Greene shall not be gone before I reach New York I will endevor to bring him along.

I wrote your Excellency on the 4th of this month, and enclosed the report of the committee of the Legislature of this State, which was accepted by the Senate and Assembly, but further measures were deferred untill the next session.[1] This was supposed to be in tenderness to the members, to give them time to abandon so dangerous an association. The prejudices against the society have received great additional strength, by the thundering speech of the Governor of South Carolina.

I shall set out for New York, from Providence by Water on the 21 instant—The roads are too bad to go by Land. It is not very probable this will reach you before I shall have the pleasure of seeing you in Philadelphia. . . .

[*Washington Papers*]

This letter from the French Minister to the United States to the Minister of Foreign Affairs in Paris is quoted here as throwing light on General Washington's problems as President General of the Cincinnati.

[1] The statement has frequently been made that Rhode Island disfranchised members of the Society of the Cincinnati (*cf.* McMasters—History of the People of the United States). This is untrue. Colonel Archibald Crary, an original member of the Society, was a member of the Rhode Island General Assembly, 1784-1786, and became its Speaker in 1797. Other Rhode Island members of the Cincinnati were members of the legislature and held other important State offices. But certainly disfranchisement was *threatened* (*cf.* Freeman's Journal of Philadelphia, 28 April 1784).

The Chevalier DE LA LUZERNE to the COUNT DE VERGENNES.

[Translation by Edgar Erskine Hume]

Mount Vernon in Virginia, 12 April 1784

Monseigneur,

To the estate of General Washington, not over fifteen leagues distant from Annapolis, I have come on the invitation which he extended me to pass some days, and it is from his home that I now have the honor to write you. After having seen him in the midst of his camp and amid the tumult of arms, at the time of my arrival in this continent, I now have the pleasure to see the simple citizen, enjoying, in the repose of his retirement, the glory which he has so justly acquired. We are mutually happy that our task was finished much sooner than we had dared hope; the General has taken occasion to speak of all the obligations and of the gratitude of the United States to His Majesty and spoke with most touching feeling the aid which the American cause received from us. He appears to be nearly ready to make a voyage to France and told me that he would be most happy to go there, if certain affairs of which he wishes to see the completion permit it. He is dressed in grey clothing like a Virginia farmer and nothing about him recalls the important rôle that he has played, except for the great number of foreigners who come to see him.

His wife and his relations are his habitual companions, and the happiness of persons surrounding him seems to be his principal care. He is not, however, unoccupied, and aside from the affairs which remain to be completed of his command, I have the impression that he intends to write his mémoirs or to put in order the material relative to the great events in which he has taken such an important part. It must not be agreeable to him, after having been so long occupied in the world of action, to fall all of a sudden into a sort of oblivion. He sincerely desired the end of the revolution and no citizen worked harder for that end than he; but, after having been for eight years the first citizen of the Republic, it is difficult to return to the condition of a planter.

The establishment of the Society of the Cincinnati gives

daily more umbrage to the inhabitants of the North. They will not suffer any distinctions. They find them incompatible with a republican government, dangerous to liberty, and I believe that their fears are not visionary; they threaten to exclude members of this Order from all public employment; it is, in effect, an institution diametrically opposed to the principles of equality and arouses the jealousies of these republicans; but the general-in-chief, without forseeing this opposition, has contributed all in his power to give stability to this establishment. He is expected to preside at the grand congress of the members of this Order to be held in Philadelphia next month, and, pressed on one side by the publicity given to his being the patron, and on the other by the fear of becoming unpopular and of supporting an institution abhorred in most of the States, I think he is most embarrassed as to which course to follow.[1]

[French National Archives, *Affaires Étrangères: États-Unis,* Vol. xxvii, folio 282]

The official French attitude towards the Cincinnati is shown in the following statement in *Le Journal Militaire*, published at Paris. This was at a time when, thanks to the writings of the Count de Mirabeau (See Introduction, page xv), the Society was under criticism in France no less than in America.

Tribute to the Cincinnati in *Le Journal Militaire* dedicated to Monsieur, brother of the King.

[Translation by Edgar Erskine Hume]

15 April 1784

All public papers have been given copies of the address by General Washington to the army which he commanded. It is the adieus of the father of his country to his cherished children to whom he gave their glory and their liberty. This moment was consecrated by a celebrated institution.

Nobody is so little informed as not to have admired in Roman history the character of Cincinnatus, that heroic citizen

[1] See page 79 for slightly different version of this letter.

of whom one of the most eloquent writers of ancient Rome said: *Gaudebat laureato vomere Tellus.*

At the moment when the Cincinnatus of America hung up his arms in the Temple of Peace and laid on the altar of Concord the sword with which his country had armed him to combat her oppressors, the army, which had shared the glory, the labors and the dangers of that great man, wished to preserve by an immutable institution the memory of their association, which gave to the whole world the most imposing spectacle of which history may record the memory.

Listen to what General Washington himself said of this institution. Here is the letter which he wrote on this subject to the Count de Rochambeau, lieutenant-general and commander-in-chief of the French troops in America

[Translation of Washington's letter of 29 October 1783 follows] [1]

[*Le Journal Militaire*, 15 April 1784]

Here is Jefferson's lengthy reply to General Washington's letter (see page 130) asking for his opinion of the Cincinnati. It sums up all Jefferson's objections and supposed fears.

From Mr. THOMAS JEFFERSON.

Annapolis, Apr. 16. 1784.

Dear Sir,—

I received your favor of Apr. 8. by Colo. Harrison. The subject of it is interesting, and, so far as you have stood connected with it, it has been matter of anxiety to me; because whatever may be the ultimate fate of the institution of the Cincinnati, as in it's course it draws to it some degree of disapprobation, I have wished to see you standing on ground separated from it, and that the character which will be handed to future ages at the head of our revolution may in no instance be compromitted in subordinate altercations. The subject has been at the point of my pen in every letter I have written to

[1] See page 130.

you, but has been still restrained by the reflection that you had among your friends more able counsellors, and, in yourself, one abler than them all. Your letter has now rendered a duty what was before a desire, and I can not better merit your confidence than by a full and free communication of facts & sentiments, as far as they have come within my observation. When the army was about to be disbanded, & the officers to take final leave, perhaps never again to meet, it was natural for men who had accompanied each other thro' so many scenes of hardship, of difficulty and danger, who in a variety of instances must have been rendered mutually dear by those aids & good offices to which their situations had given occasion; it was natural I say for these to seize with fondness any proposition which promised to bring them together again at certain & regular periods. And this I take for granted was the origin & object of this institution; & I have no suspicion that they foresaw, much less intended, those mischiefs, which exist perhaps in the forebodings of politicians only. I doubt however whether, in its execution, it would be found to answer the wishes of those who framed it, and to foster those friendships it was intended to preserve. The members would be brought together at their annual assemblies no longer to encounter a common enemy, but to encounter one another in debate & sentiment. For something I suppose is to be done at these meetings, & however unimportant, it will suffice to produce difference of opinion, contradiction & Irritation. The way to make friends quarrel is to put them in disputation under the public eye. An experience of nearly twenty years has taught me that few friendships stand this test, & that public assemblies, where every one is free to act & speak, are the most powerful looseners of the bands of private friendship. I think therefore that this institution would fail in it's principal object the perpetuation of the personal friendships contracted thro' the war.

The objections of those who are opposed to the institution shall be briefly sketched. You will readily fill them up. They urge that it is against the confederation—against the letter of some of our constitutions—against the spirit of all of them—that the foundation on which all these are built is the natural equality of man, the denial of every preeminence but that annexed to legal office, & particularly the denial of preeminence by birth; that however, in their present dispositions, citizens might decline accepting honorary instalments into the order, a time may come when a change of dispositions would render these flattering, when a well directed distribution of them might draw into the order, all the men of talents, of office & wealth, and in this case would probably procure an ingraftment into the government; that in this they will be supported by their foreign members, & the wishes & influence of foreign courts; that experience has shewn that hereditary branches of modern governments are the patrons of privilege & prerogative, & not of the natural rights of the people whose oppressors they generally are: that besides these evils, which are remote, others may take place more immediately; that a distinction is kept up between the civil & military, which it is for the happiness of both to obliterate; that when the members assemble they will be proposing to do something, & what that something may be will depend on actual circumstances; that being an organized body under habits of subordination, the first obstructions to enterprize will be already surmounted; that the moderation & virtue of a single character has probably prevented this revolution from being closed as most others have been, by a subversion of that liberty it was intended to establish; that he is not immortal, & his successor, or some of his successors, may be led by false calculation into a less certain road to glory.

What are the sentiments of Congress on this subject, & what line will they pursue, can only be stated conjecturally. Congress, as a body, if left to themselves, will in my opinion say nothing on the subject. They may however be forced into a declaration by instructions from some of the states, or by other incidents. Their sentiments, if forced from them, will be unfriendly to the institution. If permitted to pursue their own path, they will check it by side blows whenever it comes in their way, & in competitions for office, on equal or nearly equal ground, will give silent preferences for those who are not of the fraternity. My reasons for thinking this are: 1. The grounds on which they lately declined the foreign order proposed to be conferred on some of our citizens. 2. The fourth of the fundamental articles of constitution for the new states. I inclose you the report. It has been considered by Congress, recommitted & reformed by a committee according to sentiments expressed on other parts of it, but the principle referred to, having not been controverted at all, stands in this as in the original report. It is not yet confirmed by Congress. 3. Private conversations on this subject with the members. Since the receipt of your letter I have taken occasion to extent these; not indeed to the military members, because, being of the order, delicacy forbade it; but to the others pretty generally; and among these I have as yet found but one who is not opposed to the institution, & that with an anguish of mind, tho' covered under a guarded silence, which I have not seen produced by any circumstance before. I arrived at Philadelphia before the separation of the last Congress, & saw there & at Princetown some of its members not now in delegation. Burke's piece[1] happened to come out at that time, which occasioned this institution to be the subject of conversation. I found the same impressions made on them which their successors have received. I hear from other quarters that it is disagreeable generally to such citizens as have attended to it, & therefore will probably be so to all when any circumstance shall present it to the notice of all.

This, Sir, is as faithful an account of sentiments & facts as I am able to give you. You know the extent of the circle within which my observations are at present circumscribed, & can estimate how far, as forming a part of the general opinion, it may merit notice, or ought to influence your particular conduct.

It remains now to pay obedience to that part of your letter which requests sentiments on the most eligible measures to be pursued by the society at their next meeting. I must be far from pretending to be a judge of what would in fact be the most eligible measures for the society. I can only give you the opinions of those with whom I have conversed, & who, as I have before observed, are unfriendly to it. They lead to these conclusions: 1. If the Society proceeds according to it's institution, it will be better to make no applications to Congress

[1] See page xv.

on that subject or any other in their associated character. 2. If they should propose to modify it, so as to render it unobjectionable, I think this would not be effected without such a modification as would amount almost to annihilation; for such would it be to part it's inheritability, it's organization, & it's assemblies. 3. If they shall be disposed to discontinue the whole, it would remain with them to determine whether they would chuse it to be done by their own act only, or by a reference of the matter to Congress which would infallibly produce a recommendation of total discontinuance.

You will be sensible, Sir, that these communications are without all reserve. I suppose such to be your wish, & mean them but as materials with such others as you may collect, for your better judgment to work on. I consider the whole matter as between ourselves alone, having determined to take no active part in this by anything else, which may lead to altercation, or disturb that quiet & tranquillity of mind to which I consign the remaining portion of my life. I have been thrown back by events on a stage where I had never more thought to appear. It is but for a time however, & as a day labourer, free to withdraw, or to be withdrawn at will. While I remain I shall pursue in silence the path of right, but in every situation, public or private, I shall be gratified by all occasions of rendering you service, & of convincing you there is no one to whom your reputation & happiness are dearer.

[*Historical Society of Pennsylvania; draft in Jefferson Papers, Library of Congress*]

From Major-General ARTHUR ST. CLAIR.

Philadelphia, April 20, 1784

Dear Sir

I was favoured with your Letter of the 22d of February[1]—if any thing could have induced me to postpone my Journey it was your Wish that I should do so—indeed I should have

[1] See page 96.

been extremely glad to have met the Society of the Cincinnati, but I had made such Arrangements last fall, previous to my being appointed a Representative, that I cannot dispense with going to the back Country at this time, without suffering very considerable loss.

Strong Prejudices are conceived against the Institution but as they are ill founded I doubt not but they will be got over—I own however that the hereditary Descent of the Medal appears to me an objectionable part,—and could wish it might be altered in the Constitution, but I do not believe it is that has raised the cry so much as the Restriction with regard to honorary Members—had their number been left indefinite, or their proportion at least, it is probable they would never have exceeded that proposed in the Constitution.—It would also have been well, perhaps, if all political purposes had been avoided—and it is probable some Alterations may take Place on these Points. It is surely rediculous in the Legislature to interfere, as, was there any thing Dangerous in the Society, that kind of opposition is the most likely way to establish it—but as the purposes are surely benevolent and may have happy Effects too rigid an Adherence to the first outline should, in my Opinion, be avoided.

It would have aforded me a very singular Pleasure to have assured you personally with what sincere Respect and Esteem I am etc.

P. S.

I some time ago received a Letter from Capt. Paul Jones requesting that, at the general meeting he might be admitted a Member, and referring to Mr. John Ross, for the Money to be paid. I cannot at present lay my hand on the Letter, but think I gave it to Colo. [Francis] Johnson—shall I take the Liberty to request your interesting yourself in his Behalf.

[*Washington Papers*]

From Major-General LACHLAN MCINTOSH.

Savannah, Georgia, April 20, 1784.

Sir,

I had the honor of writing to your Excellency the 20th. December[1] in answer to your favor of the 24th. October[2] last which I hope you received—and since, your Circular Letter of the 1st. January with its duplicate came to hand at the same time, & only four days ago, which I laid before our state association of Cincinnati whose Quarterly Meeting was held here Yesterday and this Day—and in Consequence thereof, they have Chosen Majors [John Skey] Eustace, [John] Lucas, [Alexander Daniel] Cuthbert and Captain [James] Field to Represent them in the General society, who are to proceed immediately to Philadelphia if we can possibly make out as much Money as will bear their Expenses—and to whom I begg Leave to refer your Excellency for any information you may require as they will go fully Instructed, & are directed to carry Copy of all the proceedings of our state society from its commencement.—

I have the Honor to be etc.

[*Archives of the General Society*]

From Major-General NATHANIEL GREENE.

Newport, April 22, 1784

Dear Sir

Your two letters of the 20th and 27th of March[3] both came safe to hand. My indisposition is such I fear it will not be in my power to comply with your wishes if there was no other obstacle. I have a constant pain in my breast and am now so weak as to be incapable of bearing the fatigues of a Journey. Besides which the Doctor thinks it would be dangerous to go by water for fear I might burst a blood vessel as

[1] See page 34. [2] See page 25. [3] See pages 121 and 124.

I am very subject to sea sickness and the Vessels of the stomach are exceedingly uncoated. And he thinks it equally dangerous to ride for fear of the same end. My complaint arose from a strain I got in Providence last winter in making a violent exertion to save my self from a fall.— . . .

. . . . But was I well enough to travel I would certainly go by way of Philadelphia notwithstanding it would be attended with no small injury to my private affairs; and my necessities on this head are far different from yours. In addition to my own embarassments on this subject I am under such engagements to provide a Cargo for a vessel of my brothers expected in to Charleston that I should be at a loss how to accomodate that matter even if I had no calls of my own. And what makes me more anxious on this subject he has been unfortunate in trade at the close of the war which renders my obligation to fulfill my engagements the greater. You never felt embarrassments in matters of interest and god grant you never may. No body can feel but those that experience. It sinks the spirits and depresses the mind.

The uproar that is raised against the Cincinnati makes me more anxious to be at the Meeting than I ever expected to feel. It was uninteresting to me before. Assuming honors hurt my delicacy; but persecution bannishes the influence. The subject is important and it may be equally dangerous to recede or push forward; but I am decided in my opinion not to abolish the order from the prevailing clamours against it. If this is done away the whole tide of abuse will run against the commutation. The public seem to want something in New England to quarrel with the officers about, remove one thing and they will soon find another. It is in the temper of the people not in the matters complained of. I hope the meeting will not be hasty in their determination or in such a hurry to separate. It is yet uncertain what the politicks of America will lead to if they are not influenced by some collateral cause. It is necessary to create a jealosy in the people to bind them together. If they are not afraid of the Cincinnati local policy will influence every measure. If Congress is silent on the subject as I hope they will it will be a convincing proof they both see and feel its advantages. I am confident the tranquility of the public can only be preserved but by the continuance of the order. If I can come I will but whether I do or not I am for continuing the institution without alteration. To make any alteration in the present hour will be premature, injure its influence, and defeat all the good that may be expected from continuing it an object of public attention.

[*Washington Papers*]

In this letter one reads a forthright statement of the basis of eligibility of a representative of a class of officers not at first considered qualified for admission to the Cincinnati. Officers of Continental Marines were decided to be eligible as were also officers of the State Regiments (such as in Virginia), as distinguished from the Militia.

From Lieutenant-Colonel JOHN ALLISON.

Alexandria, April 26, 1784.

Sir

At a meeting of the Officers of the Continental line in October last to appoint officers of the State Society of Cincinnati; It was there resolv'd, that no officer not holding a Continental Commission should be entitled to become a member— As I view it in a different light from the Gentlemen that compos'd that Body; I beg leave to lay before your Excellency the State & progress of the Regiment to which I belong'd from its first rise to the close of War—

April 1st 1776 an order pass'd the Committee of Safety for raising nine Companies of Marines for the defence of the State, many of these Companys were compleated in less than a Month, & immediately enter'd upon Service—

In the October Session following an addition was made of six Regiments to the Continental Line, and those Regts. of Infantry was likewise order'd to be rais'd for the defence of the State; In which three Regts. was to be incorporated the Nine Marine Companies, they being found useless aboard small Vessels—

May 1777 the Assembly finding they were deficient in their Continental Quota—Ordered that a Regiment of the State troops should immediately march to join the Continental Army under the Command of Genl. Washington; which Regt. was chiefly compos'd of the Marine Companies (who readily turn'd out Volunteers) And were put under the Command of Colo. George Gibson—

The October Session of 1777 pass'd an act that the Regt. of State troops under Colo. George Gibson, then in Continental Service, should remain in place of the Ninth Virginia Regt. Captured at GermanTown, to be considered as part of their Continental quota; And to be entitled to every prevelige & emolument of Continental troops from this state, which Act was corroborated by several others of a similar nature—

In Jany. 1779 an application was made to Congress respecting our Regiment, and receiv'd the following proceedings for Answer viz—

[Proceedings for Sunday, 31st Jany. 1779]

A copy of the above proceedings was transmitted to Virginia, whereupon the House of Delegates came to the following Resolution—

[Extract from the minutes of the House of Delegates, May 24, 1780]

The Regiment in the Spring of 1780 consisting of 130 men for the War, Rendezvous at Petersburg; this number were properly officer'd & sent on to the Southard, where most of them ended their Military carreer in Continental Service; some of the Supernumerary Officers were incorporated with some troops then in the State & thrown into a Legion under Lt. Colo. Dabney, which Legion existed to the close of the War—

The proposals for establishing the Society of Cincinnati, Says: All Officers of the American Army &c. &c. have the right to become parties to this institution—had the Gentlemen that compos'd the meeting of the Virginia line attended to the above circumstance; perhaps there might [have] been no necessity of troubling your Excellency on the Subject—Though it was our misfortune throughout the course of the War, to labour under the disadvantage of State Commissions, (owing entirely to our own neglect at our first entering into Contl. Service,) I believe it is evident, we compos'd a part of the American Army, as well as those that held Continental Commissions—To your determination we submit the matter—

In behalf of myself & the Officers of the first and Second State Regiments, I am, etc.

John Allison Lt. Colo. 1st. S[tate] R[egiment].

[*Washington Papers*]

The writer of *The Rights of Man* and author of the line " these are times that try men's souls " approves of the Cincinnati and sends General Washington a song in its honor. Payne, twelve years later (1796) published his *Letter to George Washington* in which he accused him of bad faith!

From Mr. THOMAS PAINE.

New York, April 28, 1784

Dear Sir

. . . . As I hope to have, in a few days, the honor and happiness of seeing you well at Philadelphia, I shall not trouble you with a long letter. . . .

I present you with a new song [1] for the Cincinnati, and beg to offer you a remark on that subject. The intention of the name, appears to me either to be lost or not understood. For it is material to the future freedom of the Country, that the example of the late Army retiring to private Life on the principles of Cincinatus, should be commemorated, that in future ages it may be imitated, whether every part of the institution is perfectly consistent with a republic, is another question, but the precedent ought not to be lost.—

[*Washington Papers*]

---

[1] The song is not with this letter in the Washington Papers.

10

Major L'Enfant mission in France for the Cincinnati was executed successfully. He had the Eagles and the copperplate for the Diploma made, as well as delivering General Washington's letters to the senior French officers who were to have charge of the affairs of the Society in France. In this letter he gives a sort of preliminary report of his activities, and stresses the importance of the Cincinnati not overlooking certain of the French officers who had earned the right to membership. L'Enfant exceeded the money allowance mentioned in General Washington's instructions (see page 30), and the subject of his repayment was one that was before the General Meetings for some years.

From Major Pierre-Charles L'Enfant.

New York, April 29, 1784.

Sir

I take the liberty to inform your Excellency of my arrival at this place after a passage of 43 days from france which I left on the 16th of march last after having finish'd every thing respecting the society. the Diploma is engraved and many prints of it already drawn together with a number of stamps of the Bald eagle or sign of the association exceeding by more than *two hundred* the number for which I received the money issuing from the subscription which took place previous to my departure from america, those given to the french being included, the die for the medal is the only thing wanting, but will be sent after me.

a letter which I had the honnour to address to your Excellency in janary last[1] will have acquainted you with the particulars of my first steps to bring to a proper issue the matter trusted to me; with his most christian madjesty Kind reception, and graciouse assent to the wearing in his Kingdom the marks of an association already Beheld as one of the most recommendable among those formed on similar occassions and of wich the Basis established upon a characteristick Republican principle will leave to posterity a respected monument of fraternity, and a glorious testimony of a national and reciprocal union, never a token of honor even the most illustrated in the different kingdom of Europe could have fixed more the atten-

[1] No such letter is in the Washington Papers or the Archives of the Society of the Cincinnati.

tion, and been received with more gratitude than that which is Bestowed by the american army on that of france I will soon furnish your Excellency with proofs abundantly sufficient to vindicate my assertion, and could have done it at this moment had not the numbers of letters I am the bearer of, been to voluminous to be sent by this opportunity your Excellency will percive by thier differents contents what sensation the cincinnati has caused in france and petition coming from different sides will prove how much it has excited the pride of every persons who had the laist share in the last contest with great Bretagne; and I am apt to belive that tho' the limited numbers of foreigners the american army has resolved to admit into thier Brotherly association seems to leave no Room for aditional members, yet the rank and distinguished merite, as well as the eminente services Rendered to the United states, will be worthy of particular consideration and will move the society in favour of some gentlemen whose name can not but reflect honnour on the society, of this numbers are the captaine of the Roial navy who Rank as colonels in the armys, and some land officers whose particular Right are mentioned in the petitions formed in their behalf by the Counts d'Estaing and de Rochambeau. as for what concerns the officers who acted conjointly with us under the command of general Count d'Estaing and who were not personally named in the Resolve relative to foreigner, as it could not have been the intention of the society to cast any reflections upon gentlemen who nobly hazarded thier lives and shed thier blood on many occasions and of whom the galante Behaviour even in the much unfortunate attempt deserved the praise and gratitude of america, I thought it my duty to attend the purpose of the resolve as nearly as possible and construing its meaning to give to the world a publick testimony of the american army's fraternal friendship and gratitude towards the french, I looked upon these gentlemen as having been tacitly comprehended under the more usual denomination as expressed in the Resolve of the cincinnatus, who said all the general and colonels who served america in the armys under the commande of general counte De Rochambeau, your Excellency sensible how prejudicial such a forgetfulnes would have been to the chief aim of the resolve, will I hope approve my conduct towards those gentlemens to whom

I presented the marques of the associations as being directed by special command from the society it self.

previously to the day appointed to distribut the order of the Cincinnati general count de Rauchambeau communicated to the lands officers the King his permission to thier acceptance of it, and after the Reading of your Excellency official letter together with the included copie of the institution of the society those gentlemen being assembled made a motion to cause a sum of mony to be layd up by voluntary subscription the amount of to be thrown in to the funds of the general society.—Being acquainted with thier intention, I opposed it objecting that the title and marks of the cincinnati were to be considered as freely allowed to foreigner, and that the american army had not meant to comprehend the french in the assessement required only from her continental Brethren. but they insisted upon supporting thier motion by interpreting to its advantage the article of the institution which leaves a door open to donation even from personnes not reconised as members of the society, and arguing from this that it would be a Breach to the law of the association to oppose thier donnation they informed me of thier having unanimously agreed to compleat a sum to the amount of *60000* Livres and deliver it up to me, which notwithstanding thier instances I refused to accept previously to my reciving more particular direction from the general society to Whom I informed the Count de Rochambeau I should transmit thier intention at the first general meeting and it as been agreed that until thier desisive Resolution the sayd mony should be deposited in the hand of the treasurer of his army, after that matter had been setled in that way, al these gentlemen assembled again on the 16 of junary last the day appointed for thier being admited amongst the cincinnatus; on that morning I waited first on vice admiral count Desting and after having presented him with the marques of the association I procided from his hotel to that of the count De Rochambeau were al those gentlemen were waitting and they being there invested with the order, the ceremony inded with an Elegant Entertainment at which, toast suitable to the occasion were drink, until the compagnie divided,—that very day I dispatched the same included in letters, to the marin officers who were absent from paris and whose answer I shal have the honnour to communicat to your Excellency

As for what regards the french in the continental service the marquis de la fayette being at paris at the times of my arrival in that town I delivered up to him your Excellency dispatches, and he will have accointed you with his prociding towards them, I am only to mentione some particular, which are that although from the terms of the association we did not think our selves Hotorised [authorized] to forme a regular assembly, yet many petition having been made from gentlemen who had not serve the time required to be reconised as members of our association we formed a comity to examine thier particular pretention and some of them, being juged deserving to be distincguished from among the others, we agreed that they should be recommanded to the general society, and the marquis de la fayette as Chief of the commity is to communicat this resolution to your Excellency.

having al so considered the advantages which Would result from a regular corespondence with our Brother in america we al Expressed our wished to obtaine from the general society the permission to name a president and to forme a society similar to that of the respective lignes of the Continental army,—upon what it as been agreed to hotoraise [authorize] me to informe your Excellency with our prociding and to solicite the general society to comply with our demands Requiring al so that three of thier representative be admited to set in the general assembly—living to your Excellency to choose amongst those who are stil in america—whaitting for your Excellency ansuerd to this account of my proceding in france

I have the Honnour to be etc.

P. S.: the name of the officer of count desting army which were considered as comprehended into the resolve are

the marquis de Vaudreuil lieutenant general
de Bougainville brigadier, eschef descadre
Count Aartur Dilon Brigadier Commandant in second in his army at savana
de seting [Stedingk] suedois Colo. idem
Marquis de Rouvray Colo. idem

[*Archives of the General Society*]

From the BARON DE STEUBEN.

[April 1784]

Sir

On my arrival here I received a letter from Major L'Enfant an extract of which I have the honor to present your Excellency.

"It is with the greatest satisfaction that I announce the success of the Cincinnati in France, the difficulties which it was supposed would attend the introduction of this order (as no foreign orders are permitted to be worn with the Kings) are surmounted. His Majesty in his Council having decreed that this order shall be worn with the other orders of the Kingdom, willing by this to give to the Americans a proof of the friendship which he wishes to mentain [sic] with them.

"There are more wishes in France for the order of the Cincinnati than for that of St Louis."

Major L'Enfant proposed to leave France in Feby—so that we may expect him here the latter end of this month or begining of the next. I beg your Excellency will do me the justice to believe that I retain the most lucky sense of the many marks of friendship which I have had the honor to receive from you, & especially of those so recently confered.

I beg my respectfull Compliments may be offered to Mrs Washington, with the greatest respect etc.

[*Washington Papers*]

The question has sometimes arisen as to why the Society of the Cincinnati admitted all American Officers, including French officers serving under American commissions, to membership, if otherwise qualified by length of service, but only extended eligibility to French officers of the grade of Colonel or higher. This letter from the Count de Rochambeau throws light on this. The King, loath to permit his officers to wear foreign decorations, had made an exception for the Cincinnati. The French commander felt that His Majesty would hardly allow all his officers this privilege.

From the COUNT DE ROCHAMBEAU.

Paris may the 4th 1784.

My Dear Général

The letter which you have honoured me with, the 1st. of february ultimo.,[1] has made the greatest pleasure to me, and your title of particulary Citizen Cannot but increase the Sentiments of veneration, and of the most tender affection that I have devoted to you for all of my life. it is the finest End of the highest employment that ever man has filled.

I owe to let you Know, my Dear Général, that the King has given to me the Command in chief of the province of the Picardy, and the town of Calais will be my residence during the Summer. I Shall be very Neighbour with the people against which we have had so much fighting: but what politeness Soever the consequence of the peace will give me with them, my heart Shall be allways for the Général under the orders of which I did fight them, and it will be the height of the happiness for me, though I cannot flatter my-self of it, that to receive him in that residence.

You owe to have received, my dear Général, the little letter of confidence by which I did present you of all the repugnancy that the King has to admit Strange orders in his Kingdom, and that it was only by a consideration for you and for the united States, he has permitted to us of being admitted in the Society of Cincinnatus. if you admit all the demands that the officers of the navy make to you, as well as that I Sent to you for my army, I fear that this great extension may displease to his majesty and I doubt he will accept it. I think then it would be convenient to Keep in two that I has designed to you, to wit, The chevalier de Lameth and the Baron de l'Estrade, The first having been wounded in the attack of the redoubt of york, and the Second having been ordered to march at the head of the first Company of Genadiers as a Lieutenant Colonel in the same attack. they have only been made, one Brigadier, and the other Colonel after the Siege. They are both in So

[1] The letter does not mention the Cincinnati. It tells of General Washington's retirement at Mount Vernon. He invites the Count to visit him.

particulary Cases that if you grant that favour to them, I Shall not want a new permission of the King and I shall consider it as an explication of the first deliberation that his majesty has already approved of.

my most tender respects, I beseech you, my Dear Général to Madam Washington, Let me Know from you and from her as often as it will be possible to you, and be persuaded of the inviolable attachment and of the respect with which I am

My Dear Général

Your most obedient and
very humble Servant,

Le c[te] de Rochambeau

[*Washington Papers*]

The criticisms of the Cincinnati, particularly because of its establishing a fund and because of the hereditary succession, caused General Washington to resolve that these two provisions in the Institution (see page 1) should be changed. Accordingly he drew up the following suggestions for alterations. The Institution was duly altered (see page 160) to incorporate General Washington's changes. However in the end the State Societies did not ratify the alterations, so that the original Institution remains in force.

General Washington's Suggestions for Changes in the Institution.

[Philadelphia, May 4, 1784]

Strike out every word, sentence, and clause which has a political tendency

Discontinue the hereditary part in all its connections, *absolutely,* without any substitution which can be construed into concealment, or a change of ground *only*; for this would, in my opinion, encrease, rather than allay suspictions.

Admit no more honorary Members into the Society.

Reject subscriptions, or donations from every person who is not a Citizen of the United States.

Place the funds upon such a footing as to remove the jealousies which are entertained on that score.

Respecting the Funds.

It would be magnanimous, to place them in the first instance, in the hands of the Legislatures for the *express purposes* for which they were intended. This would shew a generous confidence in our Country, which might be productive of favorable sentiments and returns.

If it should be thought that this wd. be going too far, reserve them 'till our members are reduced to a certain ratio of what they now are, or, for a certain number of years; then to be disposed of as above.

The disposal of them by Will, or Deed, is too unimportant as object, in my opinion, for any member to be tenacious of. The Sums Subscribed were, in that moment, consigned to charitable purposes. No one ever expected to receive a farthing of it back, unless haplessly he should become an object of charity, and in this case whether he received the benefits mediately or immediately from the Society the effect to him, and obligation to them are precisely the same.

Authorize the foreign officers to hold meetings in France (if it shall be permitted by their Government). Empower them at these meetings to hear, and decide upon the pretensions of those, of their own body, who, under the letter, or spirit of the Institution, claim the privilege of becoming members of the Cincinnati. As also the pretensions of foreigners not of any particulr. State line whose claims are founded on being Officers in the American Army. Americans, in foreign countries who belonged to the line of any State, are to make application to the Society of that State, who shall hear, and decide thereupon.

Upon these principles

Let the Institution be formed in as clear, distinct and explicit terms as language can convey. Let the Secrety. transmit the same to the Senior Foreign Member in France, or the

Senior Land and Naval Officer in that Kingdom (if it shall be adjudged better) for their government. Send copies also to the President of each State Society. Accompany all of these with a well composed letter, expressive of the reasons which induced us to alter the constitution.

Then

Abolish that General Meetings altogether, as unnecessary; the Constitution being given, a continuance of them would be expensive, and very probably from a diversity of Sentiment, and tenacity of opinion might be productive of more dissention than harmony; for it has been well observed "that nothing loosens the bands of private friendship more, than for friends to pit themselves agst. each other in public debate, where every one if free to speak and act."[1] District meetings might also be discontinued as of very little use, but attractive of much speculation.

No alteration short of what is here ennumerated will, in my opinion, reconcile the Society to the Community, whether these will do it, is questionable.

Without being possessed of the reasons which induce many Gentlemen to retain the order or badge of the Society, it will be conceived by the public that this order (which except in its perpetuity still appears in the same terrific array as at first) is a feather we cannot consent to pluck from *ourselves,* tho' we have taken it from our descendants. If we assign the reasons, we might I presume as well discontinue the order.

[*Washington's Letter Books*]

When the General Meeting of 1784 opened, General Washington, with characteristic modesty, withdrew while the Cincinnati elected a President General. He had accepted that office only until the first General Meeting. He was, of course, immediately reelected, and thereupon again took the chair. The minutes recording this follow:

[1] These words are quoted almost literally from Jefferson's letter of 16 April 1784, see page 135.

General Meeting of 1784
General Washington, President General.

Wednesday, May 5th [1784]

. . . General Washington having moved that a resolution of the Society, dated at the cantonment of the American army, June 19th, 1783, requesting the commander-in-chief to officiate as president-general until the next general meeting of the Society, might be read; and the same being read accordingly, he laid the original resolution of the Society on the table, with the offical letters which he had written and received in consequence thereof, and retired. . . .

It was then unanimously,

Resolved, That General Washington be requested to preside at this general meeting until the whole business of the meeting be duly completed.

Mr. Williams [Brigadier-General Otho Holland Williams of Maryland], Mr. E. Dayton [Brigadier-General Elias Dayton of New Jersey], Mr. Ramsay [Lieutenant-Colonel Nathaniel Ramsay of Maryland], and Mr. Turner [Captain George Turner of South Carolina] were appointed to wait upon General Washington, and to inform him of the request of the meeting.

General Washington accepted, and took the chair. . . .

[*Minutes of the General Meeting of 1784*]

As General Washington had foreseen, the first General Meeting of the Cincinnati, held in Philadelphia in May 1784, was of great importance. The Minutes as preserved and published by the Society are rather barren and give little idea of the discussions that took place. Fortunately one of the delegates, Major Winthrop Sargent of Massachusetts, kept a confidential Journal of the meetings. This was published in 1858 by his grandson, Winthrop Sargent, with the title: " A Journal of the general meeting of the Cincinnati, in 1784." Published in the

Memoirs of the Historical Society of Pennsylvania, 1858, pp. 59. The following passages give something of General Washington's active part in the deliberations:

Action of the Triennial of 1784

Tuesday the 4th of May, 1784. After the credentials of the delegates were examined, and General Washington, as President General, had called the meeting to order,

> The President [General Washington] then arose;—express'd the opposition of the State of Virginia and other States;—observ'd that it had become violent and formitable, and called for serious consideration;—desired of the members of the several States to declare the ideas which prevailed in their countries with regard to our Institution, and the various manners which they had pursued to obtain this knowledge.
>
> Connecticut, by Colonel [David] Humphreys;—a very general disapprobation of the people.
>
> Massachusetts, by General [Henry] Knox;—expressed similar sentiments—with the difference, that some very sincerely wish its existence, but with alterations material.
>
> New York, by Colonel [William Stephens] Smith;—declared no opposition.
>
> Delaware, by Mr. [James] Tilton;—informed that the principal and indeed only enemies of the Cincinnati were among the class of people denominated Tories.
>
> Colonel [Anthony Walton] White, from South Carolina;—gave it as his opinion, that almost all the various classes in the State from whence he came, were opposed to the Institution in its present form.
>
> Georgia, by Major [Alexander Daniel] Cuthbert;—declared the very opposite.
>
> Captain [Jonathan] Dayton arose—and informed the Meeting that he did not know the sentiments of the People generally in the State of Jersey, but that it was the determination of the Society to preserve and support its dignity.

Pennsylvania, by Governor [John] Dickison;—as an objection of the People's, pointed out the hereditary part.

New Hampshire, by Colonel [Henry] Dearbourne;—declared that the opinions of the State were very generally in opposition to the Institution on its present Establishment.

[*Sargent's Journal*, 79]

It will be observed that no report was made by Maryland, Rhode Island or North Carolina. Bailey's *Freeman's Journal*, Philadelphia, April 28, 1784 says: "We hear that the State of Rhode Island is determined to disfranchise any and every person who is a member of the Order of Cincinnati, and render them incapable of holding any post of honour and trust in that government." On November 2, 1784, in the North Carolina Legislature, "Mr. Butler moved for leave and presented a Bill to render incapable all such persons that now are, or hereafter may be of or belong to, the Society of the Cincinnati of having a seat in either House of the General Assembly of this State. Ordered that said bill . . . lie on the table" (*N. C. State Records*, xix, 743).

Winthrop Sargent continues his account of this the first Triennial meeting of the Cincinnati. The importance attached to the deliberations is evident as parts of the journal were written in cypher, for the members thought that the public should not be informed of their secrets.

The President-General [General Washington] arose, and acknowledg'd the information from all the States—endeavoured to prove the disagreeable consequences which would result to the Members of the Cincinnati from preserving the Institution in its present form—illustrated the force and strength of opposition to it in a variety of examples, supported by his knowledge, and the informations from confidential friends—proposed as the most exceptionable parts and that require alteration in their very essence, the following viz:—the hereditary part—interference with politicks—honorary members—increase of funds from donations—and the dangers which would be the result to community from the influence they would give us—declared that it was not for the connection we stood in with the very distinguished Foreigners in this Institution, he would propose to the Society to make one great sacrifice more to the world, and abolish the Order altogether—the charitable part excepted—that considering the connection which we stood in with France, the particular situation in which our Society had placed some of their Officers, he was willing, provided we could fall on a middle way, that would neither lead us to the displeasing of them on encouraging the jealousies and suspicions of our countrymen, to adopt it. But he doubted if this was possible, and if it should so appear on a full investigation, he was determined at all events to withdraw his name from amongst us.

The General here in confidence introduced a report of a Committee of Congress, that no persons holding an hereditary title or order of nobility should be eligible to citizenship in the new State they are about to establish, and declared that he knew this to be levelled at our Institution—that our friends had prevented its passing into resolution, till the result of this meeting should be known; but if we do not make conformable to their sense of republican principles, we might expect every discouragement and even *persecution* from them and the States severally. That ninety-nine in a hundred would become our violent enemies.

Here the General introduced a private letter from the Marquis de Lafayette, objecting to the hereditary part of the Institution, as repugnant to a republican system and very exceptionable.[1] Jersey and New York take up the matter on this letter, and in the strongest terms oppose the entire abolition of the hereditary rights and honours of the Society.

. . . Thursday, May the 6th, 1784—A private letter was introduced by General Knox from the Chevalier, General Chateauxleau [Chastellux] the sentiments of which seemed opposed to the hereditary part of the Institution of Cincinnati. General Washington arose, and again opposed this part as particularly obnoxious to the peoule. In a very long speech, and with much warmth and agitation, he expressed

[1] This was La Fayette's letter of 9 March 1784, see page 109.

himself on all the Parts of the Institution deemed exceptionable, and reiterated his determination to vacate his place in the Society, if it could not be accomodated to the feeling and pleasure of the several States.

[*Sargent's Journal,* 80]

The Committee appointed by the meeting reported in favor of changes in the Institution in view of public opposition. The proposed alterations were discussed paragraph by paragraph and finally arranged in a form that the meeting accepted. The changes included the abolition of the hereditary succession, the placing of the funds under control of the State Legislatures, etc.

Taking into consideration the reports by the delegates from many of the thirteen States as to opposition to the Cincinnati, and in view of General Washington's recommendations (see page 152), the General Meeting of 1784 adopted *The Altered and Amended Institution.* It omits the hereditary feature and is otherwise considerably simplified. The placing of the Cincinnati's fund in the hands of the State Legislatures was a step thought necessary, though it will be observed that this establishment of a fund to care for needy members and their dependents was the only thing of its kind in the country. This was long before the first pensions were established by the United States Government.

The *Altered and Amended Institution,* though adopted by the General Meeting, could not be effective until ratified by the State Societies of the Cincinnati. The action of these several branches of the Cincinnati is worth reviewing. The New Hampshire Society from the first declined to ratify any changes in the Institution, and though other State Societies also opposed changes, none were so articulate as that of New Hampshire, which is therefore properly credited by the Society with having had much to do with its remaining an hereditary body. The Massachusetts Society accepted the change, but in 1786 reversed that action. The Rhode Island Society did the same. The Connecticut Society, after many delays, ratified the new Institution in 1795. The New York Society's committee, of which Colonel Alexander Hamilton was chairman, reported " that they highly approved of the motives which dictated these alterations, they are of opinion that it would be inexpedient to adopt them." The New Jersey Society adopted the Altered and Amended Institution by a close vote. The Pennsylvania Society ratified the changes but in 1789 voted to consider the original Institution " the criterion by which to act" until the several State Societies should adopt the changes. The Delaware Society voted against any change. The Maryland Society unanimously approved of the new Institution, but its committee had recommended the return to the original Institution when the General Society itself dropped the new document. The Virginia Society not only ratified the Altered and Amended Institution but never returned to the principles of hereditary succession. No hereditary members were admitted in Virginia during the lives of the original members. Such was Mr. Jefferson's power in his native State. The North Carolina Society ratified the changed Institution, as did also the South Carolina Society, but the latter went on record as having done so out of respect to popular opposition and not because of any sense of self-accusation. The Georgia Society ratified the alterations, but later voted to return to the old Institution. The Society in France accepted the Altered and Amended Institution, but at the same time the meeting "declared itself in favor of the hereditary transmission of the title of member . . . and expressed the opinion that this right should be reëstablished."

So the changes failed of ratification and were without effect. However the Altered and Amended Institution is an interesting document and of importance in the Society's history. Since it bore General Washington's approval and signature it is here quoted in full. Compare it with the original Institution, page 1. For more complete consideration of the action of the Altered and Amended Institution, see E. E. Hume, Early Opposition to the Cincinnati, *Americana*, October, 1936, xxx, 597-638. In E. E. Hume, *Sesquicentennial History of the Society of the Cincinnati in the State of Virginia, 1783-1833*, there are given in parallel columns General Knox's "Proposals" on which the Society was based, the Institution, and the Altered and Amended Institution (pp. 26-41).

The Institution of the Society of the Cincinnati as Altered and Amended at their first General Meeting

It having pleased the Supreme Governor of the Universe to give success to the arms of our country, and to establish the United States free and independent: Therefore, gratefully to commemorate this event; to inculcate to the latest ages the duty of laying down in peace, arms assumed for public defence, by forming an Institution which recognizes that most important principle; to continue the mutual friendships which commenced under the pressure of common danger; and to effectuate the acts of beneficence, dictated by the spirit of brotherly kindness towards those officers and their families, who unfortunately may be under the necessity of receiving them; the officers of the American Army do hereby constitute themselves into a Society of Friends: and possessing the highest veneration for the character of that illustrious Roman, LUCIUS QUINTUS CINCINNATUS, denominate themselves the SOCIETY OF THE CINCINNATI.

SECTION 1. The persons who constitute this Society are all the commissioned and brevet officers of the Army and Navy of the United States, who have served three years, and who left the service with reputation; all officers who were in actual service at the conclusion of the war; all the principal Staff Officers of the Continental Army; and the officers who have been deranged by the several resolutions of Congress, upon the different reforms of the army.

SECTION 2. There are also admitted into the Society, the late and present Ministers of his Most Christian Majesty to the United States; all the Generals and Colonels of regiments and legions of the land forces; all the Admirals and Captains of the Navy, ranking as Colonels, who have co-operated with the armies of the United States, in their exertions for liberty; and such other persons as have been admitted by the respective State meetings.

SECTION 3. The Society shall have a President, Vice President, Secretary and Assistant Secretary.

SECTION 4. There shall be a meeting of the Society, at least once in three years, on the first Monday in May, at such place as the President shall appoint.

The said meeting shall consist of the aforesaid officers (whose expenses shall be equally borne by the State funds) and a representation from each State.

The business of this general meeting shall be to regulate the distribution of surplus funds, to appoint officers for the ensuing term, and to conform the by-laws of the State meetings to the general objects of the Institution.

SECTION 5. The Society shall be divided into State meetings; each meeting shall have a President, Vice President, Secretary and Treasurer, respectively, to be chosen by a majority of votes annually.

SECTION 6. The State meetings shall be on the Anniversary of Independence. They shall concert such measures as may conduce to the benevolent purposes of the Society, and the several State meetings shall, at suitable periods, make applications to their respective legislature for grants of charters.

SECTION 7. Any member removing from one State to another, is to be considered in all respects as belonging to the meeting of the State in which he shall actually reside.

SECTION 8. The State meeting shall judge of the qualification of its members, admonish, and (if necessary) expel any one who many conduct himself unworthily.

SECTION 9. The Secretary of each State meeting shall register the names of the members resident in each State, and transmit a copy thereof to the Secretary of the Society.

SECTION 10. In order to form funds for the relief of unfortunate members, their widows and orphans, each officer shall deliver to the Treasurer of the State meeting one month's pay.

SECTION 11. No donations shall be received, but from citizens of the United States.[1]

SECTION 12. The funds of each State meeting shall be loaned to the State by permission of the legislature, and the interest only annually to be applied for the purposes of the Society, and if, in process of time, difficulties should occur in executing the intentions of the Society, the legislatures of the several States shall be requested to make such equitable dispositions as may be most correspondent with the original design of the Institution.

[1] The 60,000 *livres* contributed by the French members had been tactfully declined, see La Fayette's letter, page 111, and General Washington's letter of 15 May 1784 to the Count de Rochambeau, page 176.

SECTION 13. The subjects of his Most Christian Majesty, members of this Society may hold meetings at their pleasure, and form regulations for their policy conformably to the objects of the Institution and to the spirit of their government.

SECTION 14. The Society shall have an order, which shall be a bald eagle of gold, bearing on its breast the emblems hereafter described, suspended by a deep blue ribbon edged with white, descriptive of the union of America and France.

"The principal figure Cincinnatus, three Senators presenting him with a sword and other military ensigns. On a field in the back ground, his wife standing at the door of their cottage: near it a plough and other implements of husbandry. Round the whole, omnia reliquit servare rempublicam. On the reverse, sun rising, a city with open gates and vessels entering the port; Fame crowning Cincinnatus with a wreath inscribed virtutis præmium. Below, hands joined, supporting a heart with the motto esto perpetua. Round the whole, Societas Cincinnatorum Instituta, A. D., 1783."

SECTION 15. A silver medal representing the emblems to be given to each member of the Society, together with a diploma on parchment, whereon shall be impressed the figures of the order and medal as above mentioned.

RESOLVED, That the Institution, as amended and altered, be forwarded to each State meeting and to the meeting in France, and that it be accompanied with a circular letter to each, explanatory of the reasons which produced the amendments and alterations, and recommending the same to their observance.

RESOLVED, That a committee of three be appointed to prepare the circular letter, to whom also be referred the Institution as amended for critical and grammatical correction and engrossment.

The members chosen were Messrs. Dickinson, Lee and Humphreys.[1]

---

[1] These members were Governor John Dickinson, honorary member of the Pennsylvania Cincinnati, Colonel Henry Lee ("Lighthorse Harry") of the Virginia Cincinnati, and Lieutenant-Colonel David Humphreys of the Connecticut Cincinnati The circular letter that they prepared for General Washington's signature is given on page 170.

The wording of the parchment diplomas of the Society of the Cincinnati is in accordance with the vote of the General Meeting. For description of the design, see page xiv.

DIPLOMA.

Be it known that.................... is a member of the Society of the Cincinnati, instituted by the Officers of the American Army at the Period of its Disolution as well to commemorate the Event which gave Independence to NORTH AMERICA, as for the laudable Purpose of inculcating the Duty of laying down in Peace Arms assumed for public Defense and of uniting in Acts of Brotherly Affection and Bonds of perpetual Friendships the Members constituting the same.

IN TESTIMONY whereof I the President of the said Society have hereunto set my Hand at Mount-Vernon in the State of Virginia this Day of in the Year of the Independence of the United Stattes.

By order

H. Knox, Secretary

G°. Washington, President

The President of the Rhode Island Cincinnati could not attend the General Meeting as he here explains to the President General. The meeting was long since over by the time the letter reached General Washingon.

From Major-General NATHANIEL GREENE.

Newport May 6th 1784

Dear Sir

Since I wrote you by Col Henley I took a ride to Boston to try my strength and see how travelling would affect me. It increased my complaint [1] but not so much as to discourage my

[1] General Greene again alludes to his poor health in his letter of 29 August 1784 to General Washington, see page 204.

attempting to be at the Cincinnati had not my complaint increased since my return. The Doctor thinks my life would be endangered by attempting to cross the Water and my pain in my stomach increased by riding by land. In this Situation prudence forbids my coming; but that the Society may not be unrepresented Col Ward has agreed to go altho not in the original appointment. He is sensible and prudent and deserves every degree of confidence you may think proper to repose in him. He is a young Gentleman of a liberal education and great observation.

The clamour against the order rather increases in Massachusetts and Connecticut States. In this little is said about it but in one County. Many sensible people are anxious for the continuance of the order—Many more wish the Hereditary part loped off as the most exceptionable part of the whole institution. Others again are offended at the Hereditary part on account of the French Officers. It is thought it may lead to an improper influence in our National affairs. But what ever objections are raised against the order it is evidently paving the way for the commutation. People begin to say they should have no objection to paying the commutation but for the dangerous combination of the Cincinnati Drop the Cincinnati and the old question will revive; but continue the order and I am confident the commutation will go down. It is the wish of many that the order should be altered and admit no honorary Members and terminate with the present Generation. But I fear any alteration in the present state of things would go far to defeat the influence upon the federal connection and the business of the commutation. It is worthy some consideration to attempt giving reasonable satisfaction to the apprehensions of the people; but I am at a loss to determine what will affect it. I hope the Meeting will not rise hastily and the Moment my health will permit I shall leave this for Philadelphia. My breast will not permit me to write more and I have written in much pain already.

I am dear Sir with esteem & affection etc.

[*Washington Papers*]

While the General Meeting of 1784 was in session, the French Minister to the United States presented a letter asking that French naval officers be made eligible to membership in the Cincinnati. This was done. The number of such requests that were made to General Washington shows the importance attached to the proposal by the French King's Government and officers.

From the CHEVALIER DE LA LUZERNE.

Philadelphia, 6th May 1784

Sir:

The Counts de Grasse and d'Estaing have desired me to say that they have had the honor of obtaining the official permission for the properly qualified officers of the navy of the King to be admitted into the Society of the Cincinnati.

These gentlemen have added some memoranda setting forth the distinguished services of those officers for whom they desire to obtain that honor.

I know too well the justice of Your Excellency, and that of the Honorable Delegates who compose the Assembly to consider that it is necessary for me to join my solicitations to theirs.

The extreme eagerness of the French naval officers to be admitted into the Society of the Cincinnati is most natural if one will but consider the principles of honor on which it is founded and the military and patriotic virtues which so distinguish the members who compose it.

The Admirals, who have commanded fleets on this Continent, request that the capitains of ships (capitaines de vaisseau) who have served immediately under their orders be permitted to wear the decoration the same as army officers of like grade.

There are also several capitains of frigates who, although not having been employed in the great squadrons, have nevertheless been extremely useful in furthering the common cause either through the missions which they have filled or in actual combats in which they have been engaged on the American coast.

These officers having, under the instructions of the Minister, concerted their operations with me, it remains for me to recite their services.

I take the liberty of addressing Your Excellency a memorandum in this matter and request that you will be good enough to bring it to the attention of the committee charged with the examination of the different memorials.

I have the honor to recommend to you the Chevalier de Lameth. His services are well known to you; he was badly wounded at the siege of Yorktown. His Majesty was pleased to reward him by giving him the grade of Colonel, but as this promotion was not made until two months after the siege he finds himself excluded from the Society if he be not admitted by special dispensation.

On account not only of his wounds but because of his zeal, his case deserves special consideration, and with no apprehension of disappointment, I leave it to the considerate attention of Your Excellency and of the Delegates.

I also take the liberty of sending you a memorandum on behalf of the Sieur de Tarlé, Intendant of the Army, the circumstances of whose case are peculiar, and I verilie believe, merit some consideration.

I entreat Your Excellency to receive this assurance of the sentiments of attachment and respect, with which I am, Sir,

Your very humble and very obedient servant,

Le Chevalier de La Luzerne

[*Archives of the General Society*]

Colonel Armand presents anew the claims of French naval officers as to eligibility to the Cincinnati.

From Colonel CHARLES ARMAND-TUFFIN, MARQUIS DE LA ROUËRIE.

philadelphia may. 10th. 1784.—

Sir

when mr. l'enfant returned lately from france, he communicated to me a lettre which he was to lay before the Grl.

assembly of the Cincinnati & of which I have the honor to inclose an Extract—as he does Express the desire of the Cincinnati in france to form a society there similar to those of the respective states of américa, & that their représentatives, at this time, be taken from amongst the french at présent here which belongs to the Cincinnati—my-self & the other gentlemen in the same circumstances who consist of 12th or 13th, thought it was proper we should wait in américa for the answer which the grl. assembly would give to mr. l'enfant's lettre, that in case the Cincinnati in france were formed in to one state society and of course had représentatives either by an appointment from your Excellency or an appointment by their own votes, we might be here to represent them—

we do not présume to express here our desire to be admitted or not admitted as représentatives of the Cincinnati in france. the grl. assembly has *alone* to *determine* on the altérnative & we are sensible they will détérmine for the best, but it concern us much to know what is their determination, that in case the Cincinnati in france were not formed in to a state's society, or it should not be thought proper to admit at *this time* its représentatives, we might be at liberty to go from here.

having received no official lettre from france relative to the interest of the Cincinnati there, I do not mean to intimate here any desire or ideas of their own further than what may be understood from the above mentioned lettre of mr. l'enfant; the step I take here concern more immédiately the french officers who are present in philadelphia—they have desired me to state their ideas to your Excellency & request an answer—

I have the honor to be etc.

[Enclosure in the above:]

Extract of a lettre from mr. l'enfant to his Excellency grl. washington concerning the Cincinnati in france—

having also Considered the advantages which would result from a regular Correspondence with our brethren in américa, we all expressed our wishes to obtain from the grl. society the permission to name a president & to form a society similar to those of the respective states or lines of the Continental army—upon which it has been agréed to authorise me to inform your Excellency with our procéedings & to sollicite the grl. society to Comply with our demands, requesting that representatives be admitted in the grl. assembly leaving to your Excellency to chose amongs those who are still in america—

[*Archives of the General Society*]

One of the reports made to the General Meeting by Major L'Enfant had to do with the admission of French naval officers. This letter was presented to the meeting by Colonel Armand.

From Major PIERRE-CHARLES L'ENFANT.

Philadelphia, 10th May, 1784

. . . As the reading of the several letters of thanks and petitions which are now before you, may easily convey to you an idea of the high consideration which the Cincinnati enjoy in Europe, give me leave, in the name of all my Countrymen, to assure you of their sincere and heartfelt gratitude.

No pledge of friendship can be dearer to them than that which they have received at the hands of the Society of the Cincinnati.

I am particularly charged by them with supporting the several demands which have been addressed to you. . . .

The captains of His Majesty's ships, who all have the rank of Colonel, have no doubt acquired your favor, by their repeated services in the different squadrons of Messieurs d'Estaing, de Grasse, de Barras, de Vaudreuil, and Destouche, and they hope that you will pay some attention to their demands.

Several captains of frigates, who are designated by the Minister of France as having had particular commissions on the American Coast, have acquired a title to be destinguished from those of the same rank who have not rendered the same services.

It is in order to enable you to obtain the object which you have proposed to yourselves that the French General Officers have recommended the above mentioned gentlemen to your illustrous Assembly. It is with the same view that the Counts d'Estaing and de Rochambeau have recommended to your favor the particular services of some land officers, who, on account of those services and of their wounds, have been promoted since the War to the rank required by our Institution.

[*Archives of the General Society*]

In compliance with the action of the General Meeting of 1784 (see page 163) a committee prepared the following circular letter of information to the State Societies. It was signed, in fourteen copies, by President General Washington.

WASHINGTON'S CIRCULAR LETTER AFTER THE MAY 1784 MEETING.

To the State Society of the Cincinnati in [Each State]

Gentlemen.—We the delegates of the Cincinnati after the most mature and deliberate discussions of the principles and objects of our Society, have thought proper to recommend that the inclosed Institution of the Cincinnati as altered and amended at their first meeting, should be adopted by your State Society.

In order that our conduct on this occasion may stand approved in the eyes of the world; That we may not incur the imputations of obstinacy on the one hand, or Levity on the other, and that you may be induced more cheerfully to comply with our recommendation, we beg leave to communicate the reasons on which we have acted.

Previous to our Laying them before you, we hold it a duty to ourselves and our fellow Citizens to declare, and we call heaven to witness the veracity of our declaration. That, in our whole agency on this subject, we have been actuated by the purest principles.

Notwithstanding we are thus conscious for ourselves of the rectitude of our intentions in instituting or becoming members of this fraternity; and notwithstanding we are confident the highest evidence can be produced from your past, and will be given by your future behaviour, that you could not have been influenced by any other motives than those of friendship, patriotism and benevolence; yet, as our designs, in some respects, have been misapprehended; as the instrument of our association was of necessity drawn up in a hasty manner at an epoch as extraordinary as it will be memorable in the annals of mankind—when the mind, agitated by a variety of emotions, was not at liberty to attend minutely to every circumstance which respected our social connection, or to digest our ideas into so correct a form as could have been wished; as the original Institution appeared, in the opinion of many respectable characters, to have comprehended objects which are deemed incompatible with the genius and spirit of the confederation; and as, in this case, it would, eventually frustrate our purposes, and be productive of consequences which we had not foreseen,—Therefore, to remove every cause of inquietude; to annihilate every source of jealousy; to designate explicitly the ground on which we wish to stand; and to give one more proof, that the late Officers of the American Army have a claim to be reckoned among the most faithful Citizens, we have agreed that the following material alterations and amendments should take place.

That the hereditary succession be abolished; That all interference with political subjects should be done away, and That the funds should be placed under the immediate cognizance of the several Legislatures, who should also be requested to grant Charters for more effectually carrying our humane designs into execution.

In giving our reasons for the alteration in the first article, we must ask your indulgence while we recall your attention to the original occasion which induced us to form ourselves into a Society of Friends.

Having lived in the strictest habits of amity, through the various stages of a War, unparallel'd in many of its circumstances; Having seen the objects for which we contended happily attained; in the moment of triumph and separation, when we were about to act the last pleasing, melancholy scene in our military drama; pleasing because we were to leave our country possessed of Independence and peace; melancholy, because we were about to part perhaps never to meet again; while every breast was penetrated with feelings which can be more easily conceived than described; while every little act of tenderness recurred fresh to the recollection.—it was impossibe not to wish our Friendships should be continued; It was extremely natural to desire they might be perpetuated by our posterity to the remotest ages. With these impressions, and with such sentiments, we candidly confess we signed the Institution. We know our motives were irreproachable; but, finding it apprehended by many of our countrymen that this would be drawing an unjustifiable line of descrimination between our descendants and the rest of the community and averse to the creation of unnecessary and unpleasant distinctions, We could not hesitate to relinquish everything but our personal Friendships, of which we can not be divested, and those acts of beneficence which, it is our intention, should flow from them.

With views equally pure and disinterested, we propose to use our collected influence in support of that Government, and confirmation of that union, the establishment of which had engaged so considerable a part of our lives; But, learning from a variety of information that this is deemed an officious and improper interference, and that, if we are not charged with having sinister designs, yet we are accused of arrogating too much and assuming the Guardianship of the Liberties of our Country. Thus circumstanced, we could not think of opposing ourselves to the concurring opinions of our fellow Citizens, however founded, or of giving anxiety to those whose happiness it is our Interest and duty to promote.

We come next to speak of the charitable part of our Institution, which we esteem the basis of it. By placing your fund in the hands of the Legislature of your State, and letting them see the application is to the best purposes, you will demonstrate the integrity of your actions, as well as the rectitude of your principles. And having convinced them your intentions are only of a friendly and benevolent nature we are induced to believe they will patronize a design which they cannot but approve; That they will foster the good dispositions, and encourage the benevolent acts of those who are disposed to make use of the most effectual and most unexceptionable mode of relieving the distressed. For this purpose it is to be hoped that Charters may be obtained, in consequence of the applications which are directed to be made.

It is also judged most proper that the admission of Members should be submitted to the regulations of such charters; because, by this acting in conformity to the sentiments of Government, we not only give another instance of our reliance upon it, but of our disposition to remove every source of uneasiness respecting our Society.

We trust it has not escaped your attention, Gentlemen, that the only objects of which we are desirous to preserve the remembrance are of such a nature as cannot be displeasing to our Countrymen, or unprofitable to posterity; We have retained accordingly those devices which recognize the manner of our returning to our Citizenship; not as ostentatious marks of discrimination, but as pledges of our friendship, and emblems, whose appearance will never permit us to deviate from the paths of virtue.

And, we presume, in this place it may not be inexpedient to inform you that these are considered as the most endearing tokens of Friendship, and held in the highest estimation by such of our allies as have become entitled to them, by having contributed their personal services to the establishment of our Independence; that these gentlemen, who are among the first in rank and reputation, have been permitted by their Sovereign to hold this grateful memorial of our reciprocal affections; and that this fraternal intercourse is viewed by that illustrious Monarch and other distinguished characters, as no small additional cement to that harmony and reciprocation of good offices, which so happily prevail between the two Nations.

Having now relinquished whatever has been found objectionable in our original Institution: having by the deference thus paid to the prevailing sentiments of the community, neither, as we conceive, lessen the dignity nor diminish the consistency of character, which it is our ambition to support in the eyes of the present as well as of future generations; having thus removed every possible objection to our remaining connected as a Society and cherishing our mutual friendships to the close of Life; and having, as we flatter ourselves, retained in its utmost latitude, and placed upon a more certain and permanent foundation that primary article of our association which respects the unfortunate. On these two great original pillars, Friendship and Charity, we rest our Institution; and we appeal to your liberality, patriotism and magnanimity,—to your conduct on every other occassion as well as to the purity of your intentions on the present, for the ratification of our proceedings. At the same time we are happy in expressing a full confidence in the candor, justice, and integrity of the public, that the Institution, as now altered and amended, will be perfectly satisfactory, and that acts of Legislative authority will soon be passed to give efficiency to your benevolence.

Before we conclude this address permit us to add, that the cultivation of that amity we profess, and the extension of this charity, we flatter ourselves will be objects of sufficient importance to prevent a relaxation in the prosecution of them: to diffuse comfort and support to any of our unfortunate companions, who have seen better days, and merited a milder fate—to wipe the tear from the eye of the widow, who must have been consigned with the helpless Infants to indigence and wretchedness, but for this charitable Institution—to succor the Fatherless—to rescue the female orphan from destruction—to enable the son to emulate the virtues of the father, will be no unpleasing task. It will communicate happiness to others, while it increases our own; it will cheer our solitary reflections, and soothe our latest moments. Let us then prosecute with ardor what we have instituted in sincerity. Let heaven and our own consciences approve our conduct; let our actions be the best comment on our words; and let us leave a lesson to posterity that the glory of soldiers cannot be completed without acting well the part of citizens.[1]

Signed by order.

G. Washington, President.

Philadelphia, May 15th, 1784.

[*Copy in the Archives of the Virginia Cincinnati*]

---

[1] This circular letter was prepared for Washington's signature by a committee consisting of Governor John Dickinson of Pennsylvania, an honorary member, Colonel Henry Lee of Virginia ("Light Horse Harry") and Colonel

General Washington informs the Count d'Estaing, President of the French Cincinnati, of the General Meeting's vote to admit certain French officers whom the Count had recommended.

To the COUNT D'ESTAING.

Philadelphia, May 15, 1784

Sir:

I cannot, my dear General, express to you all the gratitude which I feel for your very great politness manifested for me in your letter of the 25th. of Decr.; [1] which I now have the honor and pleasure to acknowledge. The very tender and friendly regards which you are pleased to mention as possessing your mind, for my person and character, have affected me with the deepest sensibility; and will be forever remembered as a most agreeable token from the Count D'Estaing, for whose character as a Gentleman and a soldier, and for whose attention to the American interests and cause, I have ever been impressed with the highest veneration.

I feel myself happy that your Excellency countenances with so much cordiality, the association formed by the officers of the American army, a bond of cement Sir, which if anything could be wanting for that purpose, will I trust serve, to render durable and permenent those mutual friendships and connections, which have happily taken root between the officers of your Army and ours. And I am peculiarly happy to be able to inform you that the wishes expressed in your letter are more than fulfilled; since by the institution of our Society, as amended and altered at their General Meeting in this City held during the present month, and which will be officially forwarded to the Society in France; your Excelly. will find that the honors of it are ex-

David Humphreys of Connecticut. It was unanimously approved. (Sargent's Journal of the Cincinnati, 1784, p. 105.) The circular was printed under the following title: "A Circular Letter, addressed to the State Societies of the Cincinnati, by the General Meeting, convened at Philadelphia, May 3, 1784. Together with the Institution, as altered and amended. Philadelphia, Printed by E. Oswald and D. Humphreys, at the Coffee-House, M, DCC, LXXXIV." 8vo. pp. 8. (See Minutes of the General Meeting of 1784.) See General Washington's letter, 22 October 1786, to Colonel Humphreys, page 256.

[1] See page 39.

tended, not only to the few Gentlemen honor'd by your particular mention, but to all the Captns. ranking as Colonels in your Navy; which, altho' not clearly expressed in the original Constitution, is now in the fullest terms provided for and not left to doubtful implication.

I am much pleased with the prospect of soon having the pleasure of seeing in this country our mutual worthy friend de la Fayette. Be assur'd Sir, I shall be among the warmest of his friends who will welcome him to the American shore; and rejoice in an opportunity to embrace him in my arms. I am pleased that our confidence in Majr. L'Enfant has been so honorably placed, and that the business entrusted to that Gentlns' conduct has been executed to so great satisfaction.

With high regard, &c.

[*Washington Papers*]

To the COUNT DE ROCHAMBEAU.

Philadelphia, 15th May, 1784

Sir,

The letters with which you have honored the Society of the Cincinnati have been read with attention, and several subjects regarded with the most respectful consideration.

It is a circumstance pleasing to this Society that the Count de Rochambeau has so willingly become a member and interested himself in its reputation.

The very liberal subscriptions made by the gentlemen of the French army [1] merit our grateful acknowledgement, but, as it

[1] The subscription here mentioned was made by certain officers of the Auxiliary Army, and amounted to 52,000 *livres*. The list of subscribers was sent President General Washington in a communication from the Count de Rochambeau, dated Paris, 19 January, 1784. This subscription list is indorsed by Major George Turner, secretary *pro tem.*, as having been read in the General Meeting, 6 May 1784, and "to be politely refused, and the money placed in the funds of the French Society." The epilogue of this incident is given in a letter from the Count de Rochambeau to the Marquis de Ségur, Minister of War, dated 20 July 1784, in which the following paragraph occurs: "You will observe, Monseigneur, that the General Society refuses most politely the subscriptions which we have throught to offer them, from which you will conclude that we have done well to offer them, and they have done still better to refuse" (Contenson, *La Société des Cincinnati de France,* 91).

is inconsistent with the spirit of the Confederation of the United States and contrary to the original Institution to this Society, to receive sums of money from foreign nations, though in alliance, we trust the gentlemen will not conceive it any want of affection of them if we are obliged to decline the acceptance.

Your request in favor of Count de Lillancour[1] will be fully answered by a just construction of the Institution which includes all officers of his rank who co-operated with the armies of the United States.

The Count manifestly co-operated by sending a considerable detachment of his command from St. Domingo at his own risque, and, therfore the opinion of the Society is that the Count de Lilliancour is a member of right. It is not in the ability of this meeting of the Society to comprehend the justice of all the claims which have been made, and therefore they are submitted to the meeting of the Society in France to be taken into consideration. The several memorials, petitions and letters relative to those claims will be transmitted to the Society in France, together with a copy of the Institution as it is amended and a Circular letter communicating the reasons for those amendments.

By order of the General Meeting of the Society of the Cincinnati.

George Washington
President General

[*French National Archives*: *Affaires Etrangères*: *Etats-Unis, vol. xxvii. Copy in Archives of the General Society*]

To Governor JONATHAN TRUMBULL.

Philadelphia, May 15, 1784

Dear Sir:

It was with great pleasure and thankfulness, I received a recognizance of your friendship in your letter of the 20th. of last month.[2]

[1] See page 92.

[2] A copy of this letter is in Washington's Letter Books. He sends General Washington his good wishes on his retirement, and expresses the hope that their correspondence, begun during the war, may continue.

No corrispondence can be more pleasing than one which originates from similar sentiments, and similar Conduct through (tho' not a long War, the importance of it, and attainments considered) a painful contest. I pray you therefore to continue me among the number of your friends, and to favor me with such observations as shall occur.

As may good friend Colo. Trumbull [1] is perfectly acquainted with the proceedings of the meeting which brought us together, our embarrassments, and final decisions, I will refer the detail of them to him.

With the most perfect esteem, etc.

[*Connecticut Historical Society*]

To Major-General PHILIP JOHN SCHUYLER.

Phila., May 15, 1784

My dear Sir:

It has long been my wish, and until lately my intention to have proceeded from this meeting of the Cincinnati to the Falls of Niagara, and probably into Canada. Two causes however prevent it. My business is of such a nature that I cannot, without great inconvenience, be long absent from home, at this juncture; it is indeed, exceedingly inconvenient to be away from it at all; the other is, that I am not disposed to be indebted for a Passport into that Country to the British whose *convenient speed* has not permitted them to surrender the Western Posts to us yet. . . .

We have been most amazingly embarrassed in the business that brought us here.[2] It is now drawing to a conclusion, and will soon be given to the Public, otherwise I would relate it in detail. Mrs. Washington is not with me at this place, otherwise I am sure she wd. join me in best respects to Mrs. Schuyler and yourself.

With the greatest esteem, etc.

[*Harvard College Library*]

[1] This was, of course, Governor Trumbull's son, Jonathan Trumbull, Jr., an original member of the Connecticut Cincinnati.

[2] The embarrassing business to which General Washington refers was the revision of the Institution under pressure of public criticism.

General Washington was deeply touched by the gift of the Diamond Eagle by the Count d'Estaing on the part of the officers of the French Navy (see d'Estaing's letter of presentation, 26 February, 1784, page 100). He thenceforth wore his Eagle instead of one of those he had purchased.

To the COUNT D'ESTAING.

Philadelphia, May 15, 1784

Sir:

Any token of regard of whatever intrinsic worth in itself, coming from the Count D'Estaing, must [be] stamped with dignity and respect; but when attended with the esteem and regards of all the Sailors of your Nation, the companions of your honorable Toils in America, is not only agreeably acceptable, it becomes absolutely inestimable. As such I receive the American Eagle, which your Excellency has been pleased to present me in the name of all the Sailors of the French Nation. And at the same time that I acknowledge myself hereby inexpressibly honored by that most respectable Body of men. I beg you to assure them in my name of the very high estimation in which I shall ever hold this particular mark of their regard and attention.

To the Navy of France sir, this Country will hold itself deeply indebted: its assistance has rendered practicable those enterprizes, which without it could not with any probability of success, have been attempted. I feel myself happy in this opportunity thro' your Excellency's favour, of paying to the Officers and sailors of His Most Christian Majesty, this tribute of grateful acknowledgement, which I beg you sir to be so obliging as to convey to them, and at the same time to assure yourself of possessing in my breast, every sentim. of inviolable attachment and respect, with which your character has impressed my mind.

I have the honor, etc.

[*French National Archives, No. c*[8] *1; copy in Washington's Letter Books*]

To the COUNT DE BOUGAINVILLE.

Philadelphia, May 15, 1784

Sir,

The letter which you wrote to the President of the Society of the Cincinnati relative to your claim to become a member has been read in this General Meeting, and it is their opinion that Brigadier General de Bougainville is comprehended in the Rules of Admission expressed in the Institution and sent to the Society of France.

Signed in General Meeting.

By Order

George Washington
President General

B. General Bougainville [1]

[*Archives of the General Society*]

The General Meeting of 1784 being adjourned, General Washington, as President General, wrote answers to a number of letters, several from French officers, which he had been holding until the action of the Society had been taken. The following is a typical reply to a French officer who had applied for admission to the Cincinnati.

To the BARON DE VIOMÉNIL.

Philadelphia, 15th May, 1784

Sir,

The Baron d'Angely, for whom you ask admission [2] into the Society of the Cincinnati, having been, as you inform the Society, a colonel in the Auxiliary Army, is in consequence entitled to become a member according to the Rules of the Institution.

[1] Bougainville became an original member of the French Cincinnati. His formal application for admission is in the Archives of the General Society.

[2] See the Baron de Vioménil's letter of 24 January 1784, page 66.

The members of the Society in France will, in future, hold meetings there, as we do in these States. Baron d'Angely will please to make his application to the former.

Signed in General Meeting,

By Order; George Washington
President General

[*Archives of the General Society*]

To Colonel CHARLES ARMAND-TUFFIN, MARQUIS DE LA ROUËRIE.

Philadelphia 15th May 1784

Sir

The letter which was address'd by you to the President of the Society of the Cincinnati was read with attention on the 10th Instant—

As the revision of the Institution [1] was then under consideration of a Committee no answer could be given to your letter until their report was made.

The Society have not heretofore formed a meeting in france, and as there was no delegation from that Country, there could not, consistently, be any *particular* representation admitted into the general meeting—which, being a full representation of the Society at large, hath given due attention to the particular circumstances of the Members in france, who are provided for in the Institution as amended by this meeting.

[*Archives of the General Society*]

Here, again, L'Enfant transmits an application for membership in the Cincinnati on the part of a French officer.

[1] See pages 152 and 160.

From Major PIERRE-CHARLES L'ENFANT.

Philadelphia, May 17, 1784

Sir

I take the liberty to adresse your Excellency with the inclosed letter from Mr. du Bouchet, who is one of the officers whose particular cases have moved the french comitee in favour of thier claims, his suspecting that there has been in the assembly some opposition to his claims, is the occasion for is troubling your Excellency with a second adresse—and I could not but be confident that your Excellency and the whole communite are dispose to render justice to his merite, and will considere How heart full a disappointement to his Expectation should be to his military character, it is upon the same Considerations that I intreat your Excellency to be favorable to the wishes that the french continantal officer have shew to protect the gentlemans whiche they have taken upon themselves to recommande to the general society—and I will go as far as to assure your Excellency that those personnes are the only ones in whose behalf they intend to petition, and that from the communication of thier opinion they may be considered as being already name in france from which idea the assembly not positively explaning their intention would be looked as if thier opinion was contrary to thier wishes

as I expect your Excellency opinion will move the assembly in favour of those gentlemen, I beg that in a view to prevent any further application the assembly will be pleased to personnally designate name by name those who shal have a sufficient suport, for to merite so particular a proof of your attention and unapreciable favour—whose personnes names I beg to be mentione only in the ansuers to the frenche continental officer commite held at the marquis de la fayette Hotel at paris—

with great respect etc.

[*Archives of the General Society*]

From the MARQUIS DU BOUCHET.

Philadelphia. mai. 17th. 1784.

Sir,

Being of all the petitioners for Becoming Members of the association of the cincinnati, the only officer Whose case stands so pecular as to advocatise for an exception to the General Rules of the Society, I ardently Beg your Excellency to Be pleased to Recollect, that I have on no other purpose that [*sic*] to Get admittance to the order Cross'd the atlantick, and that returning home disapointed in my expectation, Would ruin Both my Carracter and all prospect, I may have of prefferement in the army.

am I, Sir, so infortunate, as to have Been too sanguine and confident in your Excellency's esteem and Goodness? am I so infortunate as to have Been in the Wrong, When I indulged myself in the thought, that having since 1776. almost at any time, Being employ'd for the cause and more, Being the only french man Who Was at Both the surrenders of the two British armyes taken on this continent, you Would Graciously Look on and Grant my petition?—Disapointement Would Be a Stain upon my honour, Wich could never Be Blotted out.

I am, Sir. With the highest Respect etc.[1]

[*Archives of the General Society*]

To the MARQUIS DE LAFAYETTE.

Philadelphia, 17th May, 1784

Sir,

The Society of the Cincinnati in a General Meeting of delegates from the respective States, now held in this City, have had before them the letters which were addressed by you to the President General.[2]

[1] At the General Meeting on Monday, 17th May 1784, it was

Resolved, That it is the opinion of this general meeting that Lieutenant Colonel de Bouchet is entitled, from his services, to be admitted a member of the Cincinnati, and he is hereby admitted accordingly" [Minutes of the General Meeting of 1784].

[2] For Lafayette's three letters, all dated 9 March 1784, see pages 107, 109, and 110.

The measures you have taken to fulfill the intentions of the Society are proofs of your attachment and obligations on the Society.

The permission of His Most Christian Majesty for his Generals and Colonels and also for the Admirals to wear the Order of the Cincinnati, is a real distinction to the Society, and is considered as an obliging instance of His Majesty's condescension.

You will see, Sir, by the papers which will be sent to the Society in France, that the Institution of the Society of the Cincinnati has necessarily undergone some alterations and amendments, and you will see also, in the Circular letter, the reasons for such alterations being made.

By the Institution as it is now recommended for concurrence and confirmation to all the State Meetings and to the Meeting in France, it is provided that all the Generals and Colonels of Regiments and Legions in the Land Forces, and all the Admirals and Captains of the Navy, ranking as Colonels, who cooperated with the Armies of the United States, etc., are admitted to the Society, and it was so expressed as well to comprehend all the gentlemen mentioned in the Memorial of the Count d'Estaing as several others, Commanders and Captains of Squadrons and Frigates, who had done essential service under the orders of His Excellency, the Chevalier de la Luzerne; and also Mr. De Tarlé and Colonel Lameth, who were heretofore supposed not eligible to become members.

An explanatory resolve of the meeting hath been entered into purposely to express the sense of the Society respecting the claims of those gentlemen, a copy of which will also be sent to you with several memorials, upon which this meeting cannot decide.

The Meeting of the Society in France, being now distinctly considered in all respects of the same authority as the State Meetings, no claims will in future be determined in the General Meeting, and all claimants must apply to the meeting of the State or Country where they reside.

Those meetings alone are to judge of the qualifications of members of this Society.

It is a subject of concern to this meeting that so good an

officer as Admiral de Vaudreuil should have been omitted by mistake, but as he is now included in the Society, an error which we lament should not induce him to decline the Association.

You have the thanks of this meeting for your attention to the Honor of the Society.

Signed in General Meeting:

By Order

George Washington
President General

[*Archives of the General Society*]

General Washington writes the Count de Rochambeau that thenceforth French officers are to be admitted members of the Cincinnati upon application to the French branch of the order, rather than upon application to the President General or the General Meeting.

To the COUNT DE ROCHAMBEAU.

Philadelphia, May 17, 1784

My dear Count:

From the official letters and other proceedings of the general meeting of the Society of the Cincinnati, held at this place, and of which you have copies; you will observe a thorough knowledge of what the Society has been doing, and the ground upon which it was done; to enter therefore into a further detail of the matter, in this letter, would be mere repetition, alike troublesome and unnecessary.

The Society could not go into too minute a discrimination of characters, and thinking it best to comprehend its members by general description, those who will constitute the Society in France must, hereafter, decide upon the pretensions of their Countrymen upon the principles of the institution as they are now altered and adopted.

I will detain you no longer than while I can repeat the assurances of sincere respect and esteem &c.

[*Washington's Letter Books*]

The French Minister to the United States is informed by the President General of the action of the General Meeting of the Cincinnati.

To the CHEVALIER DE LA LUZERNE.

Philadelphia, 17th May, 1784.

Sir,

The letter addressed by Your Excellency to the President General of the Society of the Cincinnati, and the Memorials referred to that Body, have been laid before the General Meeting.

The Institution, as it is amended, admits into this Society "the late and present Ministers of His Most Christian Majesty to the United States; all the Generals and Colonels of Regiments and Legions of the Land Forces; all the Admirals and Captains of ye Navy ranking as Colonels, who have co-operated with the Armies of the United States, in their exertions for Liberty; &c."

And to testify to Your Excellency, that it was the intention of this Meeting to comprehend, in the words "Captains of the Navy," those officers who had the command of Squadrons and Frigates, and who did essential service on the *Coast of America,* they have entered on their proceedings and explanatory resolve, which includes also Monsieur de Tarlé, second in the French Army, and Colonel Lameth, who, notwithstanding the peculiarity of their cases, the Society consider as evidently included in the Association.

Signed in General Meeting.

By Order: George Washington
President General

[*Archives of the General Society*]

To the COUNT D'ESTAING.

Philadelphia, 17th May, 1784

Sir,

All the letters and memorials which have been sent by you addressed to the President General of the Society of the Cincinnati have been laid before a General Meeting now held in this City and were conducive to the extensive latitude in that article of the Institution (as amended) which denominates the characters to be admitted into the Society. "All the Admirals and Captains of the Navy, ranking as Colonels, who have co-operated with the Armies of the United States," are literally included, and it is the expectation also of the Society that it will effectually comprehend all the officers of the French Navy who have been particularly recommended by Your Excellency.

The Generals and Colonels of the Land Forces are provided for in the previous part of the same article, and the Society careful that those gentlemen who had already received the Order should not be omitted through mistake, have added "and such other persons as have been admitted, &c."

The meeting of the Society in France is conceived to be in a situation similar and parallel in all respects to those in the States of America, and as they are respectively empowered to judge of the qualification of their members, this General Meeting are of opinion that they cannot do better than to refer all cases which require examination to the respective meetings to be held as well in France as in America.

Signed in General Meeting.

By Order: George Washington
President General

[*Archives of the General Society*]

To the COUNT DE BARRAS.

Philadelphia, 17th May, 1784

Sir,

It was intended to comprehend in the Original Institution of the Cincinnati, many officers who, through want of better information and a peculiarity of circumstances, were omitted. The Institution as now amended and published will fully include in the Society all Generals and Captains of ships of war, for whom you have applied to the President General.

The Count de la Bretonnière, having had the command of a Royal ship and rendered services in America, is included without doubt.[1]

Signed in General Meeting.

By Order: George Washington
President General

[*Archives of the General Society*]

General Washington, in his letter of instructions to Major L'Enfant, 30 October 1783, commissioned him to purchase eight Eagles of the Cincinnati in Paris. This L'Enfant did, and the President General presented his principal Aides-de-Camp with one each. This letter accompanied the Eagle given to Lieutenant-Colonel Tilghman. The "Tilghman Eagle," as it is known in the Society, is one of the best preserved copies known. It was the Eagle from which the official replicas were made upon the Society's order in 1935.

[1] See the letters to General Washington from the Count de Barras 23 January 1784 (page 65), and from the Viscount de La Bretonnière, 1 February 1784 (page 70).

To Lieutenant-Colonel TENCH TILGHMAN.

Philadelphia, May 18, 1784

My dear Sir

I pray you to accept the enclosed[1] (if a member of the Society of Cincinnati)—I sent for one for each of my aids de Camp

In haste I am, etc.[2]

General Washington's expense account for his attendance at the General Meeting of 1784, entirely in his handwriting, is one of the most interesting mementoes of his service as President General. It will be recalled that although General Washington accepted no pay as Commander-in-Chief of the Army, he was repaid his expenses.

[General Washington's] Expense Account of Attending the Cincinnati Meeting in Philadelphia.

[Mount Vernon], May 24, 1784

The Society of the Cincinnati Dr to General Washington

		Pensa.	Cury.	
Apl. 26th	To ferriage, crossing Potomk. River		9.	6
	Dining &ca. at Upper Marlborh.		19.	9
	Lodging &ca. at Rawlins's	2.	0.	7
27	To Ferriage at South River		9.	4
28	To Expenses at Annapolis	4.	11.	3
	Ferriages to Rock hall pr. Middleton[3]	5.	10.	

[1] This Eagle, or order of the Society of the Cincinnati, is at present in the possession of Colonel Harrison Tilghman of the Maryland Cincinnati, representative of his great-great-grandfather, Colonel Tench Tilghman. (Entire extract above copied from S. A. Harrison's *Memoir of Lieut. Col. Tench Tilghman*, . . . , Albany, 1876, p. 111.) The original letter cannot now be found.

[2] Colonel Tilghman replied on 7 June 1784, see page 195.

[3] Fitzpatrick in notes to *The Writings of George Washington,* xxvii, 405-6, gives the following information about the persons and places noted, *viz.* Middleton was Gilbert Middleton. Spencer's Tavern was Richard Spencer's. At New Town Washington stopped at the tavern of Edward Morrell. Mr. Hiltzhimer was Jacob Hiltzhimer. Mr. Mann was George Mann. The ferryman who ferried Washington across from Rock Hall to South River was named Hodges.

Date	Item	£	s.	d.
	Oats &ca. for the passage		8.	
	Servants at Annapolis		3.	9
29	To Expenses at Spencers Tavern [1]	2.	3.	4
	Ditto at New Town Chester [1]	1.	7.	6
30	To Ditto at the cross roads	1.	19.	6
	Ditto at Middle Town		12.	9
	Ditto at New castle	1.	11.	9
May 1	To Ditto at Wilmington	2.	1.	7
	Ditto at Chester	1.	4.	6
	Servants at Difft. Stages		7.	6
	Ferriage at Schoolkill		1.	8
17	To Barber sundry times	1.	5.	10
	Washing—during my stay in Phila.	2.	15.	8
	Livery Stable—Mr. Hiltzimer [1]	16.	6.	7
	Servants Board	9.	3.	2
	Mr. Morris's Servants and other Exps. there	5.	15.	
	Exps. at the City Tavern	3.	10.	
18	To Ferriage over the Schoolkill		1.	8
	Exps. at Chester	1.	1.	3
	Ferriage over Christiana		2.	2
19	To Exps. at Newcastle	1.	10.	10
	Ditto at Middle Town		12.	9
20	To Ditto at New Town Chester	2.	18.	4
	Ditto at Rock hall	3.	8.	4
	Ferriages to Annapolis	5.	13.	8
22	To Exps. in Annapolis—pr. Mr. Mann [1]	3.	17.	4
	Carried Over	£84.	4.	10
May 22	To Ferriage over South River [1]		8.	4
	Expenses at Rawlins's Tavern		17.	
	Ferriage over Patuxent		5.	
23	To Ditto—over Potomack		9.	6
		£86.	4.	8

Errors Excepted

pr. Go: Washington

[*Washington Papers*]

[1] See footnote 3, page 189.

The Society of the Cincinnati Dr. to Genl. Washington for his Expences attending the General Meeting in Philadelphia
May — 1784.

Date	Item	Penns. Curr.
Apl. 26th.	To Ferriage crossing Potomk. River	9.6
	Dining &ca. at Upper Marlboro	19.9
	Lodging &ca. at Rawlins's	2.0.7
27.	To Ferriage at South River	9.4
28.	To Expences in Annapolis	4.11.3
	Ferriages to Rock-hall & Middleton	5.10.–
	Oats &ca. for the passage	8.
	Servants at Annapolis	3.9
29.	To Expences at Spencers Tavern	2.3.4
	Ditto at New Town Chester	1.7.6
30.	To Ditto at the Cross Roads	1.19.6
	Ditto at Middletown	12.9
	Ditto at Newcastle	1.11.9
May 1.	To Ditto at Wilmington	2.1.7
	Ditto at Chester	1.4.6
	Servants at diff. Stages	7.6
	Ferriage at Schoolkill	1.[illegible]
17	To Barber sundry times	1.5.10
	Washing during my stay in Phila.	2.15.8
	Livery Stable — Mr. Hiltzimer	16.6.7
	Servants Board	9.3.[illegible]
	Mr. Morris's Servants & other Exps. there	5.15.–
	Exps. at the City Tavern	3.10.–
18.	To Ferriage over the Schoolkill	1.[illegible]
	Exps. at Chester	1.1.3
	Ferriage over Christiana	2.[illegible]
19.	To Exps. at Newcastle	1.10.10
	Ditto at Middletown	12.9
20	To Ditto at New Town Chester	2.18.4
	Ditto at Rock hall	3.8.4
	Ferriages to Annapolis	5.13.8
22.	To Exps. in Annapolis — pr. Mr. Mann	3.17.4
	Carrd. over	£84.4.10

General Washington's Expense Account for attending the first General Meeting of the Society of the Cincinnati, Philadelphia, May, 1784.
The entire document is in his handwriting.

[*Washington Papers*]

Dr

1784.	Amount brot. over . . .	£84 . 4 . 1
May 22.	To . Ferriage over South River	8 . 4
	Expences at Rawlins's Tavern . . .	17
	Ferriage over Patuxent	5 .
23.	To . Ditto . over Potomack	9 .
		£86 . 4 .

Errors Excepted

May 24th. 1784 Pr. G. Washington

[*Washington Papers*]

To the CHEVALIER DE CHASTELLUX.

Mount Vernon, June 2, 1784

My Dr. Sir:

I had the honor to receive a short letter[1] from you by Majr. L'Enfant. My official letters to the Counts D'Estaing and Rochambeau[2] (which I expect will be submitted to the members of the Society of the Cincinnati in France) will inform you of the proceedings of the Genl. Meeting held at Philada. on the 3d. inst.; and of the reasons which induced a departure from some of the original principles and rules of the Society. As these have been detailed, I will not repeat them, and as we have no occurrences out of the common course, except the establishment of ten New States in the Western Territory, and the appointment of Mr. Jefferson (whose talents and worth are well known to you) as one of the Commissioners for forming Commercial Treaties in Europe; I will only repeat to you the assurances of my friendship, and of the pleasure I shou'd feel in seeing you in the shade of those trees which my hands have planted, and which by their rapid growth, at once indicate a knowledge of my declination, and their disposition to spread their mantles over me, before I go hence to return no more, for this, their gratitude, I will nurture them while I stay.

Before I conclude, permit me to recommend Colo. [David] Humphreys, who is appointed Secretary to the Commission, to your countenance and civilities while he remains in France; he possesses an excellent heart, and a good understanding.

With every sentiment of esteem, etc.

[*Washington's Letter Books*]

---

[1] See Chastellux's letter of 6 March 1784, page 106.

[2] Both letters are dated 15 May 1784, see pages 175 and 176.

From Colonel JAMES WOOD.

Richmond 5th. June 1784.

Sir

At the Arrangement of the Virginia Line made at Cumberland Old Court House in the year 1782, a Number of Officers of Different ranks were Declared Superseded, which Bars Such Officers from Obtaining Certain Portions of Lands under the Act of Assembly of this State, Provided the Proceedings of the Board of Arrangement were Approved by the Commander in Chief. Applications are Daily Making by those Officers for Bounties in Lands, their Right to which, Cannot be Determined by the Assembly till they are informed whether the Proceedings Were Approved by you. May I beg the favor of you, Sir, to give Me the Necessary information by Post. I Intended Myself the Honor of Meeting you in Philadelphia, but was Prevented by the Advice of a Number of Officers, who were Anxious that I shou'd Attend the Assembly,[1] and who Assured Me there Wou'd be a full Representation from this State. I am happy to inform your Excellency that the Alterations Made in the Articles of the Institution of the Society,[2] meet with a very General Approbation here. My Best Respects wait On your Amiable Lady. I have the Honor to be etc.

[*Washington Papers*]

---

[1] The " Assembly " was the General Meeting of the Society of the Cincinnati, held in Philadelphia in May, 1784.

[2] Colonel Wood was a member of the Standing Committee of the Virginia Cincinnati at this time, and voted for the Virginia Society's ratifying the Altered and Amended Institution (see page 160). General Washington answered this letter on 12 June 1784, see page 197.

From Lieutenant-Colonel TENCH TILGHMAN.

Baltimore June 7, 1784

Dear Sir

Upon the receipt of your Excellency's favr. of the 28th. ulto. giving me a greater latitude than you had before done, in regard to the qualifications of the Bricklayer and Joiner wantd by you. . . .

I beg leave to take this opportunity of acknowledging the rect. of your Excellency's letter of the 18th. of May from Philada.[1] accompanied by a Badge of the Order of the Cincinnati, of which Society I have the honor of being a Member. I pray your Excellency to accept my warmest and most grateful thanks for this distinguishing mark of your attention and regard. I had before received many proofs of your Esteem, but I must confess you have by this last instance of your goodness, made the most flattering addition—I shall now wear my Badge with a full conviction of having deserved it, or it would never have been presented by the illustrious hands of him, whose modest Nature—unsullied honor—and true Glory it was the object of the Institution to commemorate—

I have the vanity to think that whatever contributes to the increase of my happiness will not be uninteresting to your Excellency—I therefore take pleasure in informing you that Mrs. Tilghman presented me with a Daughter a fortnight ago, and that she and her little Charge are both perfectly well—I entreat your Excellency to make her and my most respectful Compliments to Mrs. Washington—

I have the honor to be etc.

[*Washington Papers*]

Colonel Hawkins, who had been one of General Washington's Aides-de-Camp, writes him that there appears to be no opposition in North Carolina to the Cincinnati.

[1] See page 189.

From Colonel BENJAMIN HAWKINS.

North Carolina June 10, 1784

Sir,

. . . . I have not in this State heard a single objection to the commutation or rendering simple justice to the army.—early in the spring there was circulated the pamphlet said to be written by Burke[1] of South Carolina against the Institution of the Cincinnati which gave some uneasiness to some people who were apprehensive the institution would be productive of an aristocracy dangerous to the principles of our Governments.—but a little reflection with the remembrance of the patience perseverance and sufferings of the army in defence of their just rights and liberties has worn down the suspicions in some measure; and will I hope teach them to put their trust in them, who in the worst of times stood the constant centinels over the liberties of their Country, and to suspect those only, who have themselves in the of danger and now step forth to revile the virtuous welldoer and his endeavours to adopt wise and equitable measures.— . . .

[*Washington Papers*]

One of Maryland's Signers of the Declaration of Independence writes General Washington of his approval of the Institution of the Society of the Cincinnati, after its amendment and alteration.

From Mr. THOMAS STONE.

Haberdeventure[2] [Maryland], June 12, 1784

Sir

I have considered the Institution of the Cincinnati as amended and am happy to find every objection to the order removed by the late alterations—. It has given me much pleas-

[1] See page xv, for account of Burke's pamphlet.

[2] This estate is one of the most beautiful examples of Colonial architecture in Maryland.

ure to find all sensible men with whom I have conversed on the subject concur in this opinion.—. with sentiments of perfect Esteem & respect I am sir, etc.

[*Washington Papers*]

General Washington answered Colonel Wood's letter (see page 194) one week after it was written. He always approved of the action of the Virginia Cincinnati with respect to hereditary membership, though on one occasion he is said to have expressed the hope that his eldest collateral descendant would succeed him in membership.

To Colonel JAMES WOOD.

Mount Vernon, June 12, 1784.

Dr. Sir:

In answer to your favor of the 5th., I have to inform you that I can find nothing in my letter or orderly books confirmatory or disapproving the arrangements which have been made of the Virginia line of the army in the year 1782. the presumption therefore is, if they ever came to hand, that they either obtained a silent acquiescence, or that I did not care to intermeddle in them at all, as part of the line was in So. Carolina, and the whole (by a resolve of Congress) were considered as belonging to the Southern army. If I should hereafter come across anything which can illucidate the point more fully, it shall be transmitted to you[1]

It gives me pleasure to hear that the alterations in the institution of the Society of the Cincinnati meet general approbation, if a sincere disposition in those who composed the general Meeting to remove all the objectionable part of it, and give satisfaction to their Country, could have a claim to its approbation; their conduct cou'd not fail of this reward.

With very great esteem, etc.

[*Washington's Letter Books*]

[1] Fitzpatrick, in a footnote says that this refers to the right of superceded Virginia officers to be awarded Virginia land grants. (*Writings of George Washington*, xxvii, 420.) See Colonel Wood's letter of 5 June 1784, page 194.

From the Count de Rochambeau.

paris ce 16 juin 1784

je ne veux pas, mon cher général, laisser partir le mis. de la fayette, sans le charger de mes plus tendres complimens pour vous, et de vous renouveller les assurances de l'attachement le plus eternel que je vous ay voüé. je voudrois bien qu'il eut le talent de vous persuader de venir nous voir, et que tout cela put s'arranger sans se brouiller avec madame Washington.
nous avons icy le roy de Suède prince fort aimable, mais je ne luy pardonne pourtant pas de ne pas souffrir que ses Suedois qui etoient colonel a notre armée, portent l'ordre de cincinnatus, sous le pretexte qu'ils etoient cy devant si républicains qu'il ne veut point d'ordre qui le leur rapelle.[1]
nous construisons un port a cherbourg dont la pre. pile a eté fondée par un apareil de nouvelle invention qui a eu le succés le plus complet, Les anglois le voyent avec beaucoup d'inquietude, ils travaillent avec beaucoup de rigueur a leur marine. le gouvernement est le maitre, mais l'opposition est toujours forte plus en qualité, qu'en quantité des individus.
revenés avec le marquis et le chr. de la luzerne, et soyés bien persuadé que quoique vous ne soyés pas roy, vous serés aussi bien reçu qu'eux. mes respects, je vous prie a madame Washington. je suis avec le plus respectueux et le plus inviolable attachement

mon cher général

votre tres humble
et tres obeissant Serviteur
le cte de Rochambeau

[*Washington Papers*]

[1] See footnote on page 203.

[Translation by Edgar Erskine Hume]

From the COUNT DE ROCHAMBEAU.

Paris 16 June 1784

I do not wish, my dear General, that the Marquis de LaFayette depart without charging him with my most tender compliments to you, and to renew the assurances of the most eternal attachment which I have vowed to you. I could wish that he had the talent to persuade you to come to us here, and that all this might be arranged without upsetting Mrs. Washington.

We have here the King of Sweden, a most amiable prince, but I cannot pardon him for not allowing that his Swedes who were colonels in our army should wear the Order of Cincinnatus, under the pretext that they were erstwhile republicans, and that he does not wish an order which recalls this.

we are constructing a port at cherbourg of which the first pile has been placed by a new invention which has had the most complete success. The English view it with much inquietude, and they work with much precision in their navy. The government is master, but the opposition is always stronger in the quality than in the quantity of its members.

Return with the Marquis and with the Chevalier de La Luzerne, and be well persuaded that though you may not be a king, you will indeed be received as one. My respects, I beg you, to Mrs. Washington. I am with the greatest respect and the most inviolable attachment.

my dear General

Your very humble and
most obedient servant

The Count de Rochambeau

The President of the Pennsylvania Cincinnati feels that the changes being made in the Institution (see page 160) are too far reaching.

From Major-General ARTHUR ST. CLAIR.

Philadelphia, July 9, 1784

Sir,

The circular letter from the General Society of the Cincinnati addressed to the several State Societies on the 15th. of May 1784[1] has been received, and laid before the Society of this State, and they have at their annual meeting held on the 5th. of July, and continued by adjournment, agreed to accept the Institution, as altered and amended, that accompanied the said letter: But, Sir, it is their opinion that the ground of the Society has been too much narrowed, and that without some farther alterations, the Society itself must necessarily, in the course of a few years, reach its final period; they have therefore directed me to lay before the General Society, the following additions and amendments, which they wish may take place, and which, they, with great deference, are of opinion would not only tend to render the Instititution more permanent, but more extensively useful.

I have the Honor to be with the greatest Respect Sir, etc.

That this be added to the 2nd. Section.

And where any vacancy or vacancies are occasioned by the death or expulsion of any member or members belonging to any of the State Societies, such State Society shall have power to fill said vacancy or vacancies at the annual meeting, next, after such vacancies may happen, or some subsequent meeting.

The second clause of the 4th. Section, after each State.

add "The expences of which to be borne from the State funds respectively, and that on all questions, each State shall have but one vote.

Section 10th. after the words "widows and Orphans" add and their distressed descendants.

[*Washington Papers*]

[1] See page 170.

The President of the Massachusetts Cincinnati reports that the Society in that State have approved the Altered and Amended Institution (see page 160).

From Major-General BENJAMIN LINCOLN

Hingham [Massachusetts], July 15, 1784

My dear General

I may not omit so good an opportunity as now offers p[er] Major Baylies [1] to inform your Excellency that at the meeting of the Cincinnati of this State they with great pleasure adopted the system as altered and amended by the general meeting and it appears to give great satisfaction to the citizens at large.—. . .

[*Washington Papers*]

From Major-General HENRY KNOX.

Dorchester [Massachusetts], July 26, 1784

My dear Sir,

A fear of intruding upon your more important concerns has prevented my writing to you since my return. I found here your kind favor of the 2d of June,[2] with its enclosure for General [Rufus] Putnam which I delivered. . . .

I presume that General [Benjamin] Lincoln informed you the alterations of the Cincinnati are generally satisfactory in this state. The opposition to it is dead. One or two persons it is said however still grumble. Our State Society on the 4th of July was respectably full, and adopted it unanimously, one vote excepted. . . .

[*Washington Papers*]

---

[1] Major Hodijah Baylies, original member of the Massachusetts Cincinnati; formerly one of General Washington's Aides-de-Camp.

[2] The letter tells of General Washington's return home. It deplores the lack of sovereign power to act under the present form of government. The Cincinnati is not mentioned.

Major L'Enfant feared the attempts of many ineligible foreigners, claiming service as officers in the late war, to gain admission to the Cincinnati. General Washington invariably referred such claims to the Society in France for decision.

From Major PIERRE-CHARLES L'ENFANT.

Philadelphia, August 4, 1784

Your Excellency

having since my arrival at this place been informed that a number of foreigner claims the Reight to be reconised cincinnati, and being all so confident that many of those who applayed to the marquis de la fayette and whose demands were rejected by a colected body of members of the society as expressed in my last account of our prociding. and considering a great number of person which held commission in the continental army must al since the begining of the war, and who without leave absented themselves, retourning to thier country, or remaining in america on & trading way. assuming now and then the character of officer watching for the oppertunity of gething mony, or anny Rewards what so ever, such as are due only to lasting services.

I in the name of the comity held at the marquis de lafayette hotel on the ten day of march last, beg from the general assembly that no persons not comprehended in thier resolution of the same date, or not specially recommended by a majeur parts of the french members stil remaining in america, could be admited into the association if not suported by such an hotority, and if provided with sufficient recommendation thier petition to be presented by me to the assembly. Being directed to this by the mentioned comity, un til a fixed number of thier representative be admited to set in the general assembly—

With great respect etc.

[*Archives of the General Society*]

To the Count de Rochambeau.

Mount Vernon, Augt. 20, 1784

My dear Count:

I thank you for your favor of the 16th. of June[1] by the Marquis de la Fayette, who arrived here three days ago; and for your other letter of the 4th. of May[2] which, also came safe. permit me to offer you my sincere congratulations on your appointment to the Government of Picardy. It is an honorable testimony of the approving smiles of your Prince, and a just reward for your Services and merit. Should fortune ever put it in my power to come to France, your being at Calais would be an irresistible inducement for me to make it a visit.

My letters from Philadelphia (public and private) would give you a full acot. of every matter and thing respecting the Society of the Cincinnati, and upon what footing all claims to the order were, therefore, to be decided; to these referring I shall save you the trouble of reading a repetition. Considering how recently the K—g of S—ed-n[3] has changed the form of the Constitution of that Country, it is not much to be wondered at that his *fears* should get the better of his *liberallity* at any thing which might have the semblance of republicanism; but considering further how few of this Nation had, or could have, a right to the Order, I think he might have suffered his complaisance to have superceded his apprehensions. . . .

[*Rochambeau Papers in the Library of Congress*]

---

[1] See page 198.

[2] See page 127.

[3] Gustavus III, King of Sweden, had declined to permit Swedish officers to *wear* the Order of the Cincinnati, a number of whom served in French regiments in America. He, however, appears to have offered no objection to their being *members*, and several were. Some are now represented in the Society by their eldest descendants. The present Crown Prince, Gustavus Adolphus, is an honorary member of the Cincinnati.

From Major-General NATHANIEL GREENE.

Charleston Augt 29 1784

Dear Sir

My ill health and the distressing situation of my private affairs for some time past has claimed too much of my Attention to afford me either time or inclination to attend to any thing else. At the time of the meeting of the Cincinnati in Philadelphia I had a dangerous and disagree pain in my heart. It had hung about me then upwards of two months; but by the use of balsam of firr soon after I wrote you from Newport [1] I got better of it. And the very day that Col- [Samuel] Ward returned from the Meeting I set sail for Philadelphia upon some matters very interesting to my Southern affairs; and was in hopes to have arriv'd in time to have had the pleasure of seeing you. On my return from Philadelphia and my stay was short. I got information that my fortune was much exposed from the situation of sundry debts which I had guaranted for the Contractors of the Southern Army while I had the command in this Country. The amount of the debts and the Situation of the Contractors affairs made it seriously alarming and brought me to this Country without a moments hesitation notwithstanding the season and climate. I have been under great apprehensions of heavy losses; but I have now got matters in so happy a train that I have little to fear but from partial inconveniencies. It has given me much pain and preyed heavily upon my spirits. My stay I expected would have been short in this Country; but from the peculiar situation of concerns it will be protracted to a much greater length than I wish or expected.—After the war I was in hopes of repose; but fortune will not allow me what I most wish for. Some good natured Acts done for individuals and the low state of public credit in this Country has drawn me into many inconveniencies and some heavy losses. By Baron Glaubeck whom Congress noticed for his conduct in Morgans affair I expect to loose a thousand dollars having endorsed his bills and had them to settle. And if I suffer no loss by the

[1] The letter is dated Newport 6 May 1784. See page 164.

Contractors, the uncertainty will hang over me like a Cloud until the whole affair is closed.—

While I feel much for my self I feel for you. You have had your troubles since you left public life. The clamour raised against the Cincinnati was far more extensive than I expected. I had no conception that it was so univerasl. I thought it had been confined to New England alone; but I found afterwards our Ministers abroad and all the Inhabitants in general through-ut the United States were opposed to the order. I am happy you did not listen to my advice. The measures you took seemed to silence all the jealosies on the subject; but I wish the seeds of discontent may not break out under some other form. However it is hardly to be expected that perfect tranquility can return at once after so great a revolution: Where the Minds of the people have been so long accustomed to conflicts and subjects of agitation. In this Country many discontents prevail, Committees are formed and correspondences going on, if not of a treasonable nature highly derogatory to the diginity of Government as well as subversive of the tranquility of the people. And I wish they may not break out into acts of violence and open rebellion against the Authority of the State—Nor am I without some apprehensions that the situation of our public credit at home and abroad and the general discontent of the public creditors may plunge us into new troubles. The obstinacy of Rhode Island and the tardiness of some other States seems to presage more Mischief. However I can but hope the good sense of the populace will correct our policy in time to avoid new convulsions—but many people secretly wish that every State should be completely independant; and that as soon as our public debts are liquidated that Congress should be no more. A plan that would be as fatal to our interest at home as ruinous to it abroad. I see by the Northern Papers that the Marquis de la Fayette had arrived at New York and set out for Mount Vernon. Doubtless you will have a happy Meeting. "It will be the feast of reason and the flow of soul." Present him my respectful compliments of congratulation upon his safe arrival in America and my affectionate regards to Mrs Washington.

I am dear Sir with esteem & affection etc.

[*Washington Papers*]

The Count de Rochambeau reports to General Washington the promotion of a group of officers to the grade of Colonel, which under the French interpretation of the Institution, rendered them eligible for admission to the Cincinnati.

From the Count de Rochambeau.

Paris the 9th September 1784.

My dear Général

I have the honour of Sending to you the New-promotion Which has been done lately for the order of Cincinnatus according to the resolutions of the last meeting of the général Society. I also inclose in it the copy of a letter from M. le Mal. de Ségur [1] bearing the permission of his majesty for these new aggregated, you will See by it, at the same time, that his majesty Stops all kind of farther demand, Which Will disingage you,—my Dear Général, of great many demands Which certainly have been very troublesome to you.

I profit with the loveliest pleasure of all—these opportunities for giving to you the new assurances of the respect and inviolable attachment With Which I am my Dear Général, etc.

the Prince Henry, the brother of the King of Prussia Which has dined at my house has Seen your Picture With great pleasure.[2]

[*Washington Papers*]

[1] There is also a duplicate original of the letter in the Washington Papers. Enclosed with the letter are:

1. Copy of letter from Ségur to Rochambeau, dated 28 August 1784, see page 207.
2. List of officers promoted to the rank of Colonel and admitted into the Society, dated 9 September 1784.

[2] General Washington replied on 25 November 1784, see page 120. He also refers to this letter in his letter of 7 September 1785 to Rochambeau, see page 234.

[Enclosure in the letter of 9 September 1784 from Rochambeau]

Copy of the letter from M. le Mal. de Ségur to the Count de Rochambeau.

Versailles the 28th. August 1784.

I have received, Sir, the letter that you made me the honour of Writing to me the 23th. of this month With a List inclosed in it. We agreed on with M. le Mal. de Castries to Establish an Equal march in the two Districts. By the intentions that the King has made known upon the associaion of Cincinnatus, his majesty consents that the officers, mentioned in the List Which you have directed to me, bear the distinctive marks of that Society, and he approves that you authorise them to it, but his majesty thinking not convenient that this association be perpetuated in the Kingdom he gives me order to prevent You he Will permit no more for the future that any of his subjects be yet admitted in it. As it appears that you, Sir, and M. le Count d'Estaing have been look'd upon, by the Général Washington as the chiefs of this Society in Europe, I refer it to you to make him an answer conform to the dispositions of his majesty.

I have the honour to be &c.

Sign'd Le Mal. de Ségur.

pour copie le cte de Rochambeau

[*Washington Papers*]

[Enclosure in the letter of 9 September 1784 from Rochambeau]

List of the officers Which have been promoted to the rank of Colonel Since their Return from america, for the Services that they have rendered thither, and Which have been admitted in the Society of Cincinnatus according to the last deliberation of the General Society of the 15th. may ulto.[1]

—The Baron de l'Estrade
—The chr. de Lameth

[1] All of the officers in this list became original members of the French Cincinnati.

—M. de Menonville
—The Baron de St. Simon
—The chr. de Mirabeau
—The Baron de Montesquieu
—The Viscount D'osmond
—M. de Macmahon
—The chr. de Tarlé
—The Count de Loménie
—The Count de chabannes
—The Baron D'Esebeck
—M. D'anselme
—M. de Ricey [Riccé]
—M. Lynch
—The Viscount de Vaudreuil
—The Viscount de fleury
—M. Goulet de la Tour
—The Marquis de Montmort.
—The Count Henry de St. Simon.
—M. de Tarlé, Intendant
—M. de Lilancourt formerly Commander in Chief in St. Dom.
—M. D'angely.

le cte de Rochambeau

[*Washington Papers*]

From Captain ALEXANDER-CÉSAR DE GENEVY DE PUSIGNAN.

A Roanne en forest le 16 8bre. [Octobre] 1784.

Monsieur

Jaloux de partager les honneurs militaires avec Les officiers de votre nation ou j'ai Servi Sous les ordres de mr de rochambeau pendant Le Sejours qui a fait L'armée Françoise; je m'estois addressé au docteur Franklin, persuadé que vous luy aviez laissé les pouvoirs de Faire délivrer de L'ordre Cincinnatus les officiers qui en Sont Susceptibles. Il m'a renvoyé a vous, monsieur, Comme estant le président de Cette Sçociéte. j'ose donc vous

Supplier de me procurer L'honneur de Cette décoration que je n'ai osé réclamer que Lorsque j'ai vu plusieurs particuliers François dans les postes. a la vérité monsieur, je n'éstois pas Capitaine lorsque je Fus Bléssé au Siège d'york; mais Cette Considération n'a point apporté d'obstacles aux graces du Roy de France, Come vous les verrez par la lettre du ministre qui me Fut écrite a ce sujet et que supplie votre éxcelence de me renvoier; mais immédiattement apprez le Siége le Capitaine passat en France et je Commendai pour luy la Campaigne, et la division des huit pièces de Campagne. de la brigadde de Soissonnois, jusqua má rentré en France ou j'ai été Fait Capitaine en arrivant. j'éspere assais aux bontés de vostre excelence pour ésperer que Ce ne Sera pas une exclusion, et qu'elle m'accordera la grace que j'ai l honneur de luy demander

je Suis avec un tres profond respect Monsieur etc [1]

[*Washington Papers*]

[Translation by Edgar Erskine Hume]

Roanne en forest, 16 October 1784

Sir,

Jealous of sharing military honors with officers of your nation where I served under the orders of M. de Rochambeau during the time spent there by the French Army; I have addressed myself to Doctor Franklin, persuaded that you had given him the power to confer the Order of the Cincinnatus on eligible officers. He has referred me to you, Sir, as being the President of this Society. I take the liberty of asking you to procure for me the honor of this decoration which I hope to obtain for I have seen many Frenchmen possessing it. In truth, Sir, I was not a Captain when I was wounded at the siege of York; but this circumstance has never been any obstacle to the graces of the King of France, as you may see from the letter of the Minister which he sent me; but immediately after the siege the Captain departed for France and I commanded the company in his stead, and the battery of eight field pieces, until my return to France where I was made Captain on arrival. I count greatly

[1] General Washington replied on 25 September 1785, see page 235.

on the kindness of Your Excellency in order to hope that I will not be excluded, and that there will be accorded me the honor that I ask.

I am with most profound respect, Sir, etc.[1]

As usual, General Washington referred the request for admission by a French officer, to the French branch of the Cincinnati.

To Monsieur DE VENIE.

Mount Vernon, Nov. 25, 1784.

Sir,

I had the honor to receive your favor of the of last.—At the general meeting of the Society of the Cincinnati held in May at Philada., general principles respecting the right to that order, were established; the members of it in the armies & navy of his most Christian Majesty were requested to hold meetings in France to examine rights &ca., & decide upon the equity of Claims.—To the decision of this meeting Sir, permit me to refer you; in full confidence that due attention will be given to your merit & services.—

I have the honor to be Sir etc.

[*Washington's Letter Books*]

To the COUNT DE ROCHAMBEAU.

Mount Vernon, November 25, 1784

My dear Count:

Your favor of the 9th. of Septr, enclosing the copy of a letter from the Marqs. de Segar[2] is this moment received. The repeated instance of the honor, conferred on the Society of the

[1] Pusignan was, of course, ineligible for admission to the Cincinnati. Even as a Captain his rank would not have entitled him to membership, under the terms of the Institution.

[2] See pages 206 and 207 for Rochambeau's letter and a copy of the letter of the Marquis de Ségur of 28 August 1784.

Cincinnati by His Most Christn. Majesty's indulgent recognition of it, is highly flattering to the Order; and merits the most grateful acknowledgements of all its Members.

The pleasure with which you say Prince Henry of Prussia viewed my Picture at your house, is very flattering. I can never too often assure you of my Affectionate regard, and of the respectful attachment with which I have the honor etc.

[*Rochambeau Papers, Library of Congress*]

To Major-General HENRY KNOX.

Mount Vernon, December 5, 1784,

My Dr. Sir,

Apologies are idle things: I will not trouble you with them; that I am your debtor in the epistolary way I acknowledge, and that appearances indicate a disposition to remain so, I cannot deny; but I have neither the inclination nor the effrontery to follow the example of great men of St—s to withhold payment altogether. To whatever other causes therefore my silence may be attributed, ascribe it not, I beseech you, to want of friendship, for in this, neither time nor absence can occasion a diminution; and I regret that fortune has placed us in different States and distant climes, where an interchange of sentiments can only be by letter. . . .

P. S. Had you an agreeable tour to the Eastward? Are the State-societies [of the Cincinnati] in the New England Governments making any moves towards obtaining Charters? If they are, with what success? [1]

[*Washington's Letter Books*]

---

[1] The "charters" were not so easily obtained from some of the New England "governments." The New Hampshire Cincinnati was incorporated in 1897; Massachusetts in 1806; Rhode Island in 1814; Connecticut in 1895. See General Knox's reply, 31 January 1785 (page 212) to the effect that "charters" had not as yet been sought.

This letter from the Assistant Secretary General refers to the text of the diploma (see page 164), which was added in Philadelphia. The pictorial designs were engraved on the copperplate in Paris under Major L'Enfant's supervision.

From Brigadier-General Otho Holland Williams.

Baltimore, 24th. Jany 1785.

Sir,

Major [George] Turner of Philadelphia to whom, and Captn. [Abraham George] Claypole, was committed the business of having the Diploma of the Society of the Cincinnati engraved on Copperplate, has sent me a bundle containing eighty three Diplomas on parchment, with a list of fourteen members who have advancd to him one dollar each for the expence—

Major Turner has importuned me exceedingly to pay him the money he has advanced on account of the Society; But I cannot do so without the means of reimbursing myself.

If you Sir, will please to sign the Diplomas most of the members will be glad to have them, and a regular and true account shall be rendered of all monies received and paid by me.—

I have the honor to be Sir, etc.[1]

[*Washington Papers*]

From Major-General Henry Knox.

Boston 31st January 1785

I have the satisfaction, my dear Sir, to acknowledge the receipt of your kind of favors of the 5th of Decr[2] and of the 5th instant[3] for which I beg you to receive my warmest thanks.

[1] General Washington's reply to this letter, 2 February 1785, see page 214.

[2] See page 211.

[3] This letter is in the Washington Papers. It is not about the Cincinnati, but concerns private aid to Potomac navigation.

I regard these letters as fresh proofs of your unchanging friendship and kindness, which I shall ever esteem among the chief blessings of my Life. . . .

You are so good as to ask whether General [Benjamin] Lincoln and myself had an agreable tour to the eastward? and whether the State societies and [*sic*] making moves towards obtaining charters? We Went to the eastern Lines of this State, and found that the British had made excessive encroachments on our territories. . . .

As to the Cincinnati, the objections against it, are apparently removed—But I believe none have yet applied for charters. In this State it is pretty evident from communicating with the members of the Legislature that we should not succeeed—However we shall attempt it previous to our next meeting in July—. . .

[*Washington Papers*]

General Washington recorded his signing the diplomas of General Williams, Assistant Secretary General, in his diary.

Extract from General Washington's Diary

2 Feb 1785

Wednesday, 2d February, 1785 The Snow this morning is about 9 Inches deep and pretty well compressed. Mr. Scott went away after Breakfast. Employed myself (as there could be no stirring without) in writing Letters by the Post and in signing 83 Diplomas for members of the Society of the Cincinnati, and sent them to the care of Colo. [Peregrine] Fitzgerald in Alexandria, to be forwarded to General [Otho Holland] Williams of Baltimore, the Assistant Secretary General.

To Brigadier-General OTHO HOLLAND WILLIAMS

Mount Vernon, 2^{d} Feby 1785.

Dr Sir:

Your letter of the 24th ult^{o} with eighty three Diplomas came to my hands on Monday last. I have signed and returned them to Colo. [Peregrine] Fitzgerald to be forwarded to you.

It would be hard indeed upon Maj^{r} Turner & Captn Claypoole[1] not only to give them the trouble of producing the Diplomas, but to saddle them with the expence of it also. Was there no provision made therefor at the General Meeting? Do not the minutes of that meeting devise some mode of payment? I well remember that the matter was agitated, but I recollect also that I desired Genl Knox when difficulties arose with respect to the busi^{n}ess which had been entrusted to Maj^{r} L'Enfant to suggest, that the sum which I had proposed to subscribe for the purposes of the Society might be applied to any uses the meeting should direct; but what the result of it was, I know not. It was observed at that time, but there was money in the hands of the Treasurer General—but not having the proceedings to refer to, and a bad memory to depend on—these things appear like dreams to me. With great esteem and regard I am, etc.

[*Washington's Letter Books*]

Extract from General Washington's Diary

Friday, 11th February, 1785—Employed all day in marking the ground for the reception of my Shrubs.

In the Evening a Mr. Andrews, Jeweller in Philadelphia, called to shew me an Eagle Medal, which he had made, and was about to offer as a specimen of his Workmanship to the Members of the Society of Cincinnati in hopes of being employed by them in that way. He was accompanied by a Mr.—, name not known.[2]

[1] See General Williams's letter of 24 January 1785, pages 212.

[2] As late as 1788 there were still a number of the Eagles that Major L'Enfant had had made in Paris not yet taken by members. No record is found of Mr. Andrews being successful in his project.

A Prussian officer in the French service seeks membership in the Cincinnati.

From the BARON DE HOLTZENDORFF.

Nymegen June the 4th. 1785

Sir!

This Letter will come to your hands by favour of Colonel Senf, who is returning to america very soon. I thought it incumbent to me to take that opportunity in order to renew to you, Sir, my most grateful thanks for all the marks of Benevolence you shewed to me during my Stay under your Commands in the american army. The Satisfaction about my military Character, as well as the Reports about my Leaving the said Service you was pleased to manifest even by your latest Letter, I was honoured with in answer of that by wich I informed you of my returning to France, make me hope you will be glad to learn, that I stay as yet in the Service of the united States of Holland, having been granted by the General Count de Maillebois with a Place of Lieutenant Colonel in the Legion which he is raising for this Service.

I'll allways regret sincerely, that circumstances did not allow my terminating with you, Sir, a war by yourself so gloriously ended; for, the French Regiment, I was from, though destined in the year 1780 to go to america with the corps of army of the Gal. Rochembeau, which becaim one of them of his 2nd. Division, that could not be carried over for want of vessels, I was obliged to see myself disappointed of that hope. I'm the more sorry as I believe I would have been granted with the admission to your association of Cincinnatus, which favour would have flattered me particularly, as I would have considered it not only as a recompense of my zeal I shewed, you know Sir, whilst I served your own country, but of the rest hopes, Even the unjustice, I proved by the particular Illwill of Mr. Lovel, whose influence prevented their good intentions to me, as well as the fulfilling of one of their Resolveds, which I Keep in original, and according to which I should be indemnified.

Will you, Sir, give me leave to beg your influence about both them Subjects?—If you think it possible I should be very happy to be honoured with the admission to your association of Cincinnatus.—for the rest, it would be indeed an act of justice and Even of honour to congress to fulfill a resolved they gave in favour of myn [*sic*] in the beginning of 1778.

this new mark of your Benevolence, Sir, shall increase the gratitude consecrated to you forever, which I have the honour to remain very respectfully

Sir

your most obedient humble servant Lewis Casimir Baron de holtzendorff Lt. Coll. of the Legion of Maillebois, in garrison at Nymegen[1]

[*Washington Papers*]

A slightly different copy of the Baron de Holtzendorff's letter is in the Archives of the Cincinnati.

From the BARON DE HOLTZENDORFF.

Nymegen June the 4th. 1785.

Sir:

This Letter will come to your hands by favour of Colonel Senf, who is returning to america very Soon. . . .

I'll allways regret Sincerely, that circumstances did not allow my terminating with you, Sir, a war by yourself so gloriously ended; for, the French Regiment, I was from, though destinated in the year 1780 to go to america with the corps of army of the Gal. Rochambeau, which became one of them of his 2nd. Division, that could not be carried over for want of vessels, I was obliged to see myself disappointed of that hope.—I'm the more Sorry as I believe I would have been granted with the admission to your association of Cincinnatus, which favour would have flatterd me particularly; as I would have considered it not only as a recompense of my zeal I showed, you Know Sir,

[1] For General Washington's reply, 31 July 1786, see page 248.

whilst I served your own Country, but of the real hopes, Even the injustice, I proved by the particular Illwill of Mr. Lovel, whose influence prevented their good intentions to me, as well as the Fulfilling of one of their Resolveds, which I keep in original, and according to which I should be indemnified.

Will you, Sir, give me leave to beg your influence about both these Subjects?—If you think it possible, I should be very happy to be honoured with the admission to your association of Cincinnatus.—for the rest, it would be indeed an act of justice and even of honour to congress to fulfill a resolved they gave in favour of me in the beginning of 1778.—

this new mark of your Benevolence, Sir, shall increase the gratitude consecrated to you for ever, with which I have the honour to remain very respectfully etc.[1]

[*Archives of the General Society*]

From the MARQUIS DE BARBÉ-MARBOIS.

New York, June 12th 1785.

Sir,

I beg leave to trouble your Excellency about the request of Mr de Corny a gentlemen who in the character of a commissary general preceeded the French army in the year 1780. The 5th of June of the same year congress resolved *That a brevet commission of lieutenant of Cavalry be granted to Mr. Louis Ethis de Corny.* Mr. de Corny has been since employed in the services of both armies either here or in france to procure & forward their supplies: he now is commissary general of the Swiss infantry in france. He informs me that he is desirous to be a member of the cincinnati Society in the State where your Excellency resides[2] & at he has sent to me his quota of the subscription according to his rank: I take the liberty to send you his bill—one M. Wadsworth for the [ ]? you'll excuse me Sir, for troubling you about this affair: I would not have

[1] For General Washington's reply, 31 July 1786, see page 248.

[2] Lieutenant-Colonel Ethis de Corny was admitted to the Virginia Cincinnati. He later transferred to the French Cincinnati.

done it if I had had the honour to be acquainted with the officers of the Society in Virginia.

According to very late intelligence from Europe the Emperor impressed with the danger of staying alone of his party seems desirous to compromise the matter. There is little doubt but we should support the Dutch in case they were attacked.

Mr Gardochi is not yet arrived. Congress are uncertain what exception to make to him as his character of a *chargé des affaires plenipotentiaire* is a novelty in the diplomatic style. There is no doubt however that he will be made an envoy as soon as the States shall have resolved to send one to Spain.

The governor of georgia informed the delegates of the States that there has been an encounter between the Spaniards at & the inhabitants there, & that persons have been killed on both sides.

No determination about the [ ] Treaty with the Indians. Congress cannot come to a resolution as to the funds: there are eight States & two half States who are for providing all [ ] expenses but it is said some individuals are opposed to this measure from private motives.[1]

With great respect, I have the honour to be, Sir,

Your Excellency's

Very humble obedient servant

De Marbois[2]

[1] General Washington replied on 21 June 1785 (see page 221). On 23 July 1785, General Washington wrote to General Weedon, President of the Virginia Cincinnati, about the subscription of Colonel Ethis de Corny, see page 228.

[2] François Marbois, later Count and Marquis de Barbé-Marbois, left the following estimate of General Washington: "Washington remains greater in the eyes of his fellow citizens than Alexander or Cæsar ever were for the Greeks and the Romans. His natural moderation was such, that after defeating the enemies of his country, unlike so many men who have acquired military glory, he had not to overcome his own ambition. He was satisfied to put away his sword in order to devote himself to the government of a republic at last at peace. Desolation and ruin are the monuments which commemorate the careers of conquerors and mark their passage on this earth. Men's happiness, such is the unperishable monument that will remind future generations of the name of Washington. His glory is purer than the conqueror's; in fact it is greater than the fame of the so-called sons of the gods. When the war was over, the

I have been told that Mr de Corny on advice of some of the members of the Society in france has taken the insignia of the order, as they saw no doubt of his being a member in consequence of his commission.

[*Washington Papers*]

The Eagle of the Cincinnati was usually known in France as the *Order of Cincinnatus,* variously spelled. One officer called it the *Cross of Saint Signatus!*

From Lieutenant ALEXANDRE DE GUBIAN.

A Monsieur De Wasington
Général Des Etats Unis de la Merique

Mon Général—

Je prend la Liberté de Mêtre sous vos yœux mes Services, pour vous Suplier de m'accorder vos Bonté Comme mes Comarades ont obtenu.

Etant Embarqué sur le Vaisseau du Roi le Scipion dans l'armée De Monsieur Le Comte de Grasse, Lorsque nous fumes à Chezapeak, le Général ma Chargés de La Coréspondance du Camp, par Bac-River, que Jai continue tout Le long du Siège. Apré la Capitulation de York Jeu L'honneur de Vous porter avec Le Canot de Bac River à Bord de la Ville de paris; avec M. De Rochambeau, le Marquis de Lafayette, M. de Laurens, Le Comte Chalus, & le Comte de LaValle.

Un pareil Bonheur n'est pas sans Désir, Grand Général. Jai Eté assé heureux D'avoir Sauvé des Mains de nos Ennemies un Brigatier de votre Nation allant au port-au-prince Dans le tems que Je Commandé La Corvette du Roi, le Saint-Louis en Station à Saint Domingue [sic] Déstiné à Convoyer les Batiments de votre Nation, Espagnolle, & Francaise, du Cap, au molle Saint nicolas, & au port-au-prince. Si Je pouvoit Etre assé heureux Grand Général le faible Service peut me faire obtenir de Vous Lhonorable Croix de Saint Singnatus, ce Seroient ajouter aux

American people took to heart to pay a special tribute to his civic virtues." (*The Letters of François, Marquis de Barbé-Marbois, during his residence in the United States as secretary of the French Legation,* 1779-1785 (New York, 1929).

Marque Dhonneur Distinctive d'un Bon Officier dont Vous En-Ete Le vraij modelle, Je suis avec Le plus profond Respect, Mon Général

Votre très humble & très obeissant Serviteur Alexandre De Gubian ancien Lieutenant De fregate de Marseille [1]

Marseille le 13 Juin 1785

[*Washington Papers*]

[Contemporary Translation]

A Monsr. De Washington
Genl. of the United States of America

My General

I take the liberty of giving you an account of my Services, for to beg of Your Excellence to Grant me, what my Companions have obtain'd; Having been embarked aboard the King's Ship, the Scipion, In the Army of M^{r}. the Compte de Grasse, Whilst we were in the Chessapeak, that General gave me charge of the Correspondence, with the Camp, by the Back River, & I continued in that Situation, all the time of the Siege. After the Capitulation of York; I had the Honour of carrying you, with a Boat of the Back River, aboard the Ville de Paris, with Monsr. de Rochambeau, the Marquiss de lafayette, M^{r}. Laurence, the Comte de Chatus,[2] and the Comte De la Valle. I have been sufficiently happy, to have Saved from the Hands, of our Enemy's, a Brigantine of your Nation, Bound to Port au Prince, during the time I Commanded an advice Boat of the Kings, The S^{t}. Louis Station'd at S^{t}. Dominiqu[e] Destined

[1] For General Washington's reply, 20 November 1785, see page 236.

[2] A misreading of the original, where the name is erroneously spelt "Chalus." The Comte de Charlus was evidently intended. At the time he was known by this title, but later became Marquis, and still later Duc, de Castries. He was an original member of the French Society. (See Contenson, La Société des Cincinnati de France.) The translation of St. Domingue into St. Dominique is another error.

Endorsed by General Washington:

From / Monsr. Alex^{r}. de Gubian / 13th. June 1785

In another had has been repeated "Gubian" on a line with "From."

to Conduct the Ships of your Nation, Spanish & French, from the Cape, or Mole of St. Nicolas, to Port au Prince.—If I Could be Sufficiently happy, Great Genl. that these little Services, could make me obtain of you, the Honourable Cross of St. Singnatus, It would be adding those Marks, of Distinguish'd Honour, of a Good Officer, of which you have been the True Pattern. I am with
the most Profound Respect

My General

Your Very Humble & Very Obedt.
Servant
Alexander De Gubian formerly
Lieutenant of Marseille
Frigate

Marseilles 13th. June 1785

[*Washington Papers*]

To Marquis de Barbé Marbois.

[June 21, 1785]

Sir:

The last Post brought me the honor of your favor of the 12th inst:—I am made happy by occasions which induce you to write to me, & shall take pleasure in rendering Mr De Corney any service in my power.—I will immediately inform myself of the name & residence of the Treasurer of the Cincinnati in this State, & transmit Mr De Corney's [1] Bill on Colo. Wadsworth [2] to him. . . .

[*Washington's Letter Books*]

---

[1] Lieutenant-Colonel Louis-Dominique Ethis de Corny, original member of the Virginia Cincinnati and later of the French Cincinnati.

[2] Colonel Jeremiah Wadsworth, Vice-President of the Connecticut Cincinnati at this time.

From Commodore JOHN PAUL JONES.

Paris July 18, 1785

Sir,

I avail myself of the departure of Mr. Houdon to transmit to your Hands two sets of Certificats in favor of Captain Stack and Captain McCarty, who in consequence of their Service under my Orders pray to be admitted as Members of the Society of the Cincinnatus. Although Count de Rochambeau has made difficulties about giving those Officers his Certificate to support their pretentions,—I am persuaded that you will, from the very honorable testimony I now transmit you, think they have deserved the gratification they ask; which I shall consider as a favor confered on me by the Society. If their prayer is granted, the Diplomas may be sent to Mr. Jefferson or Colonel Humphreys, who know their address.

I beg Pardon, if this mode of Application is irregular, and I beseech you support the Object of the Certificates, if you think, they deserve your protection.

I am, wishing you perfect Happiness, Sir, etc.[1]

[*Historical Society of Pennsylvania*]

[Enclosure No. 1 in Commodore John Paul Jones's letter of 18 July 1785]

Edward Stack sub Lieutenant in the Regiment of Walsh in the ervice [sic] of his most Christian Majesty had leave from the court of Versailles in the begining of the year 1779 to serve on board the squadron which his Majesty then put under my command; as I had made it a condition with the Minister of Marine that the Squadron should carry the flag of America because I could not as an American Officer accept the commission of Captain in the royal Navy of France all the Officers of the squadron received from me (with the consent & approbation of Mr. Franklin) Brevets that had been signed & sent *blank* to Europe by Mr. Hancock as president of Congress. The

[1] For General Washington's reply, 25 November 1785, see page 238.

Commission of Mr. Stack was that of Lieutenant of Marines in the Navy of the United States,—he served in that quality on board the Bon-Homme Richard & was in the engagement between that Ship & the Seraphis on the coast of England the 23d day of September 1779. At the Texel in the month of November following he received orders from France to join his Regiment then ordered to embark for the West Indies, & on producing at Versailles the certificate I gave him at the Texel, his Majesty promoted him immediately to the rank of Captain with a pecuniary gratification for the loss he sustained when the Bonhomme-Richard Sank after the battle. But there can be no clearer proof of the high sense his Majesty entertains of the merit of that Battle than his having confered on Captain Stack on that account the pension of four hundred livres a year the 27th of February last.

Captain Stack has applied to me & wishes to become a member of the Society of Cincinnatus. There is no doubt in my mind but that he has merited that distinction. I am of opinion that the order he received at the Texel ought to be considered as operating his derangement & placing him in a similar predicament with the officers of the American Army who were reformed by particular Acts of Congress & who are notwithstanding entitled to become members of the Cincinnati. If Mr. Stack therefore can obtain a similar opinion from their Excellencies Count D'Estaing & Count De Rochambeau & from the Marquis de la Fayette, the Marquis de Saint-Simon & Colonel Humphreys in writing at the foot hereof I have no doubt but that he will be considered in America as a Member of the Society when he has paid a months pay into the hands of Colonel Humphreys for the charitable fund of the Society.

[Signed] Paul Jones

Paris, April 13th. 1785

Upon the circumstances represented by Commodore Jones I am of opinion that Captain Stack ought to be considered as entitled to become a member of the society of the Cincinnati.

[signed] D Humphrys
late Colonel in the Service of
the United States & aid de
camp to the Commander

Je pense de meme que Mr. Le Colonel humphrys Aide de camp du General Washington et je crois meme qu'en ma qualité de Marin, il m'est permis de joindre mes prieres à mon opinion, et de solliciter l'admission du Capitaine Edouard Stack. Avoir autant contribué que cet officier l'a fait au succès du plus beau Combat maritime dont non seulement la derniere guerre, mais dont l'histoire de toutes les Nations ait jamais parlé, semble donner à tout homme de Mer le droit de demander en son nom.[1]

[signé] Estaing

Je joins a la meme opinion que celles de Monsieur le Colonel Humphreys, et de Monsieur le Comte D'Estaing, le plus vif desir de voir le Capitaine Edouard Stack admis a l'association americaine de Cincinnatus—j'en fais des prieres et les solliciations les plus vives, ayant été temoin de la valeur et du zele avec laquel cet officier a servi en Amerique,—À Paris ce vingt Avril, mil sept cent quatre vingt cinq.[2]

[signé] St. Simon

Les bons services de Monsieur Stack, l'opinion des Generaux, celle du Commodore Paul Jones, et du Colo. Humphreys aid de Camp du Gal. Washington, qui a pu mieux que personne connoitre les vrais principes de l'institution tout s'accord a placer Monsieur Stack au rang des officiers *reformis par certaines Resolutions* et de ceux qu'on doit voir avec plaisir admis dans la Société[3]

[signé] La Fayette

The foregoing is a true Copy from the Original in my Hands given at Paris July 18th. 1785.

Paul Jones.

[*Washington Papers*]

[1] For translation see page 226.
[2] For translation see page 227.
[3] For translation see page 227.

[Enclosure No. 2 in Commodore John Paul Jones letter of 18 July 1785]

Eugene Maccarthy sub-Lieutenant in the Regiment of Walsh in the service of his most Christian Majesty had leave from the Court of Versailles in the beginning of the year 1779 to serve on board the Squadron which his Majesty then put under my command. As I made it a condition with the minister of Marine that the Squadron should carry the flag of America because I could not as an American Officer accept the commission of Captain in the royal Navy of France, all the Officers of the Squadron received from me (with the aprobation & consent of Mr. Franklin) Brevets that had been sent *blank* to Europe by Mr. Hancock as President of Congress. The Commission of Mr. Maccarthy was that of Lieutenant of Marines in the Navy of the United States. He served in that quality on board the *Bon-homme-Richard*, & was in the engagement between that Ship & the *Seraphis* on the coast of England the 23d. day of September 1779. At the Texel in the month of November following he received orders frfom France to join his regiment them ordered to embark for the west Indies & on producing at Versailles the Certificate I gave him at the Texel his Majesty promoted him immediately to the rank of Captain with a pecuniary gratification for the loss he sustained when the *Bon-homme-Richard* sank after the battle. But there can be no clearer proof of the high sense his Majesty entertains of the merit of that battle than his having confered on Captain Stack on that account the pension of four hundred livres a Year, the 27th. day of February last, & as Mr. Stack was also a Lieutenant of Marines on board the *bon-homme Richard*, there is no doubt but that Mr. Maccarthy (who is just arived at Paris from his Regiment) will immediately receive a similar pension.

Captain Maccarthy has applied to me & wishes to become a member of the society of Cincinnatus. There is no doubt in my mind but that he has merited that distinction. I am of opinion that the order he received at the Texel ought to be considered as operating his derangement & placing him in a similar predicament with the Officers of the American Army who were reformed by particular acts of Congress & who are notwithstanding entitled to become members of the Cincinnati.

If Mr. Maccarthy therefore can obtain a similar opinion from their Excellencies Count D'Estaing & Count de Rochambeau, & from the Marquis de la Fayette, the Marquiss de Saint-Simon & Colonel Humphreys in writings at the foot hereof I have no doubt but that he will be considered in America as a member of the society when he has paid one months pay into the hands of Colonel Humphreys for the charitable fund of the society.

[signed] Paul Jones

Paris April 13th. 1785

[Following this there are the same statements from each of the four officers named above, *viz,* Lieutenant-Colonel David Humphreys, the Count d'Estaing, the Marquis de Saint-Simon, and the Marquis de LaFayette, as to Maccarthy's service. The wording is identical with the certificates concerning Stack, see pages 224 and 227 in the same order, as those following the Jones statement about Captain Stack. They are identical, except that " Maccarthy " is of course in the place of " Stack," so they are not repeated here.]

The foregoing is a true Copy of the original in my Hands, given at Paris July 18th. 1785.

Paul Jones.

[*Washington Papers*]

[Translation of the Count d'Estaing's Indorsement]

I agree with Colonel Humphreys, Aide-de-Camp of General Washington, and I feel the same as a sailor. I take the liberty of joining my request to my opinion and of asking the admission of Captain Edward Stack. To have contributed as this officer has to the most splendid maratime combat, not only the last war but of the whole history of nations, it would seem to give every seafaring man the right to ask this in his name.

[signed] Estaing.

[Translation of the Marquis de Saint-Simon's Indorsement]

I hold the same opinion as Colonel Humphreys and the Count d'Estaing, the most keen desire that Captain Edward Stack be admitted to the American Association of Cincinnatus. I make the request the more strongly having been witness to the valor and zeal with which this officer served in America. Paris 20 April 1785.

[signed] St. Simon.

[Translation of the Marquis de LaFayette's Indorsement]

The good service of Mr. Stack, the opinion of the Generals, that of Commodore Paul Jones and of Colonel Humphreys, Aide-de-Camp of General Washington, who knows better than anyone else the true principles of the Institution, all agree in placing Mr. Stack in the category of officers deranged by certain resolutions, and of those who have the right to be admitted into the Society.

[signed] LaFayette

From Major-General ARTHUR ST. CLAIR.

Philada. July 21st 1785

Dear Sir

This is accompanied by a Letter from the State Society of the Cincinnati which was written to you more than a Year ago and by some inadvertance of the under Secretary was never forwarded. I am very sorry that it has so happened, because it would have been some satisfaction to you to have known, at an early period, that this State Society had come into the proposed Alterations[1]—It was not however without great Reluctance

[1] See the text of the Altered and Amended Institution, page 160.

The Pennsylvania Cincinnati accepted the new Institution at its adjourned meeting in Philadelphia, 9 July 1784. At the same time, they adopted the report of the committee composed of Major-General Arthur St. Clair, Major-General Anthony Wayne, and Colonel Thomas Hartley, that by the proposed

the first Institution was parted with: yet it was happy that it was parted with, for the Prejudices against the Society have since entirely subsided, and, if the paper Medium that has been introduced in this State can be supported, We are in the receipt of the Interest of our Funds. I have very often the Pleasure to hear of your Excellency and never fail to enquire after You with all the earnestness of Friendship and Affection. I request You to present my best Respects to Mrs. Washington and to believe me ever with the greatest Respect and Esteem etc.

[*Washington Papers*]

To Brigadier-General GEORGE WEEDON.

Mount Vernon, 23^d July 1785.

Dr Sir:

It is some time since I received the enclosed Bill, under cover from the Drawer: among a multiplicity of other letters it got buried and forgot; until a line from Mr de Marbois the other day, forwarding the third bill of same tenor and date, reminded me of it.

As I do not know who the Treasurer of the Society of the Cincinnati of this State is, I take the liberty of committing the Bill to your care, with a request that you would be so obliging as to ask him personally if he is near you, or by letter if he is at a distance for a receipt for it, that I may transmit the same to Col^o De Corney,[1] with an apology for my long silence. If I

alterations "the ground of the Society has been too much narrowed . . . ," and in order to perpetuate it, the committee proposed certain additions and amendments." On 6 July 1789, the Pennsylvania Cincinnati resolved that it should "consider its original Constitution as the criterion by which to act until all alterations of said Constitution shall be unanimously agreed to by the several State Societies" (*Institution of the Society of the Cincinnati of State of Pennsylvania*, 1863, p. 36).

[1] Lieutenant-Colonel Louis-Dominique Ethis de Corny, at this time a member of the Virginia Society. He transferred later to the French Cincinnati. See the letter about him from the Marquis de Barbé-Marbois, 12 June 1785 (page 217), and General Washington's reply, 21 June 1785 (page 221). The Treasurer of the Virginia Cincinnati at this time was Colonel William Heth.

knew who the State Treasurer is, I would not give you any trouble in this business; but as I really do not, I hope it will be received as an excuse for having done it.

I am, etc.

[*Washington's Letter Books*]

The Assistant Secretary General reports the theft of signed blank diplomas, and his finding three of them in the possession of inmates of a Baltimore jail.

From Brigadier-General OTHO HOLLAND WILLIAMS.

Bath August 15, 1785

Dear Sir,

Your Letter dated Mount Vernon, July 26th.—is the only one that I have had the pleasure to receive from you since the return of peace.

I could not imagine why the Diplomas were not returned, and, having written to you once or twice on the subject, concluded that it would be more respectful to wait until you should please to send them to me than to give any unnecessary trouble by sending for them.

When I discovered that they had got into the hands of improper persons I made very diligent search after them—found only three, and wrote you a circumstantial account of all I could discover respecting them, which was, indeed, very little. A Fellow detected and committed to Baltimore Gaol for a theft had two taken from him by a justice of peace, who finding your name to them enquired of me what they were—I examined the gaol and found one more—The fellow (who had many marks of the knave about him) told me that he had found them in a part of the town to which I immediately went. I think I never saw a more abandoned set of Mortals of both Sexes collected together; after an hours fruitless search I went from thence to the Stage office, for I conjectured that they had been sent by that conveyance, But could not find any Letter receipt for the delivery which is common, nor entry in the Office books, All these matters were reported in a letter which I had the honor of addressing to you last April—which went by a Gentleman to Georgetown—

If Colonel [Peregrine] Fitzgerald or any other person can prove the delivery I can recover the cost of the Diplomas which is still due to the Gentlemen who advanced money to Major Turner on that account. But I do not think it possible ever to recover the parchments not do I think it probable that any attempts have been, or will be, made to apply them to any purposes of imposition—Those I found were much abused—dirty—rumpled, and bore no marks of forgery, and from the situation in which a wretched old Woman shewed me the others had been, it is impossible that they could be fit for the uses intended.

With the most sincere and respectful Esteem and regard, I am, Dear Sir, etc.[1]

[*Washington Papers*]

The Minister of the Netherlands to the United States writes to General Washington forwarding a petition of Joseph Mandrillon of Amsterdam for admission to membership in the Cincinnati. Mandrillon was one of the most persistent candidates for this honor. He was not considered eligible and never became a member of the Society. See also Mandrillon's letter to General Washington of 24 January 1787, page 288.

To His Excell[enc]y P[IETER] J[OHAN] VAN BERCKEL.

Sir,

The letter which your Excellency did me the honor to write to me on the 5th. of last month,[2] came to this place whilst I was from home—or I should have paid my respects to you at an earlier period.—

I thank your Excelly. for your care of Mr. Mandrillon's

[1] For General Washington's reply, 25 September 1785, see page 234.
[2] This letter is not in the Washington Papers.

letter, & take the liberty of troubleing you with the enclosed answer to it; and of congratulating you on the safe arrival of Miss Van Berkel who I hope enjoys good health.—I have the honor, etc.

Mount Vernon
22d. Augt. 1785. [*Washington's Letter Books*]

To M. Joseph Mandrillon.

Mount Vernon, 22^{d}. Augt. 1785.

Sir:

Thro' the hands of M^{r}. Van Berkel, I had the honor to receive your letter of the first of March.

It rests with a General Meeting of the Society of the Cincinnati to admit foreigners as honorary members; tho' it has been done by many of the State Societies, where the subject proposed was a Resident. The general Meeting is triennial, and will not assemble again before May 1787 . . . but if my memory serves me, there were some particular reasons given at the last, which induced a resolution to suspend the further appointment of honorary members, as well citizens as foreigners: but if I should be mistaken in this, I shall have great pleasure in proposing you as a member of that body, which have associated for the purpose, amongst others, of commemorating the great events to which, under providence, they owe the deliverance of their country from systematic tyranny.

With a grateful sense of the flattering expression of your letter, and with much esteem and regard, I have the honor, etc.[1]

[*Washington's Letter Books*]

[1] Mandrillon wrote the following tribute to General Washington: "Oh, that I had received at birth the genius and the eloquence of the famous orators of Greece and Rome! Why can I not steal their brush for a moment in order to draw with quick strokes the portrait of the greatest man that has ever appeared in America, and one of the greatest that has ever lived! With what energy, with what enthusiasm would I not celebrate his splendid virtues! Who could be jealous of the tribute I am paying him? Who could ever tax me with being a flatterer?

"We no longer live in those barbarous ages when tyrants received incense,

To Major-General ARTHUR ST. CLAIR.

Mount Vernon, 31 August, 1785.

I am perfectly convinced, that if the first institution of this Society had not been parted with, ere this we should have had the country in an uproar, and a line of separation drawn between this Society and their fellow-citizens. The alterations, which took place at the last general meeting, have quieted the clamors, which in many of the States were rising to a great height; but I have not heard yet of the incorporation of any Society by the State to which it belongs, which is an evidence, in my mind, that the jealousies of the people are rather asleep than removed on this occasion. . . .

[*Washington's Letter Books*]

---

when people would call heroes men indulging in every vice and so much feared that nobody dared to give them offense. We no longer live in those ages when cruel monarchs paid hired writers to disguise their crimes and lend them virtues. Our age, more enlightened, portrays in its history monarchs and individuals such as they were; truth characterizes it. The reverence in which General Washington is held by the public results from the most severe scrutiny of his conduct. Careful of his reputation and eager to receive the approbation of his fellow countrymen, he enjoys it without taking pride in it and without ostentation. He is fair enough to himself to believe that he deserves his fame, and he also knows that posterity which erects and overthrows statues will never overthrow the trophies raised in his honor. Only an illiterate barbarian or a savage ignorant of our history could mistake his statue for that of a tyrant and strike it with his axe. But even if from the fragments of the inscription one could save only the name of Washington, the chieftain of this savage or of this barbarian, informed by tradition of the American revolution, would punish this outrage and restore the monument; and on the pedistal one would read: *Ignorance has overthrown it, justice has raised it again: Mortals revere his memory.*" (Mandrillon, *Fragments de politique et de literature . . . offerts comme étrennes a mes amis, le 1er janvier 1788* (Paris et Bruxelles, 1788).

For Mandrillon's reply to General Washington's letter, 24 October 1786, see page 257.

To the MARQUIS DE LAFAYETTE.

Mount Vernon, September 1, 1785

My dr. Marqs.,

Since my last to you, I have been favored with your letters of the 11th. and 13th. of May by young Mr. Adams, who brought them to New York, from whence they came safely to this place by the Post: the first is a *Cypher*; and for the communications therein contained I thank you: My best wishes will always accompany your undertakings; but remember my dear friend it is a part of the military art to reconnoitre and *feel* your way, before you engage too deeply. More is oftentimes effected by regular approaches, than by open assault; from the first too, you may make a good retreat; from the latter (in case of repulse) it rarely happens. . . .

If I recollect right, the letter [1] which was written by the Marquis de St. Simon was on the business of the Cincinnati, and was laid before the general meeting at Philad[a]. in May 1784; consequently, the answer must have proceeded from the Society either specially to him, or generally, thro' the Counts de Estaing & Rochambeau, who were written to as the heads of the naval & military members of that Society in France; but as all the papers relative to the business of the Society were deposited in the care of the Secretary, General Knox, or the assistant Secretary, Williams, I have them not to refer to; but will make enquiry and inform you or the Marq[s] de St. Simon more particularly of the result. . . .

[*Washington's Letter Books*]

---

[1] This letter is not in the Washington Papers, nor in the Archives of the Cincinnati, though it was read to the General Meeting of 1784.

To the COUNT DE ROCHAMBEAU.

Mount Vernon, Sepr. 7th. 1785.

My dear Count,

Since I had the honor to address you last, I have been favored with your letters of the 9th. of Septr.[1] and 24th. of Feby.[2] The first enclosing a list of the New promotions, and the additional members of the Society of the Cincinnati as consented by the King; for which I thank you, as it will enable me to give answers to those Gentlemen who, unacquainted I presume, with his Majesty's pleasure, are still offering to me their pretensions to be admitted into this Order. . . .

[*Rochambeau Papers, Library of Congress*]

The President General again writes the Assistant Secretary General about the diplomas of members.

To Brigadier-General OTHO HOLLAND WILLIAMS.

Mount Vernon, 25th. Sepr. 1785.

Dear Sir,

Your letter of the 15th. of Augt. from Bath,[3] only got to my hands on Sunday last. The one alluded to, of April, as giving an acct. of the miscarriage of the Diplomas, & the best information you could obtain respecting them, nor any other since that which accompanied the Parchments, and wch. received an immediate acknowledgement, have reached me at all.

In a word, I never had the least intimation, or knowledge of the accident until Major [William] Jacksons Letter (copy of which I sent you) was delivered to me.

I have since enquired of Colo. [Peregrine] Fitzgerald if he could recollect in whose care they were placed—his memory

[1] See page 206.

[2] This letter, in the Washington Papers, does not concern the Cincinnati. It mentions the chances of France being involved in war.

[3] See page 229. The letter of April, 1785, is not in the Washington Papers.

he says does not serve him on this occasion, but he is sure they were entrusted to safe hands, or such as appeared to him at the time to be so. It is a little extraordinary therefore that this person, whoever he may be, should not have given notice of the loss either to him, from whom the parcel was received, or to you, to whom it was intended.

It is to be feared, under these circumstances, that neither the Diplomas, or the money advanced for them, will ever be recovered.—however, if you conceive that an advertisement will effect any valuable purpose—or be satisfactory to the Gentlemen for whose benefit they were designed, you can, as Secretary, recite the event and request information from any who may have it in their power to give it. With great esteem etc.

[*Pennsylvania Historical Society*]

General Washington received numerous letters from French officers seeking the Eagle of the Order of the Cincinnati, which appeared to many a decoration. The General always referred such requests to the French Cincinnati.

To Captain DE GENEVY DE PUISGNAN.

Mount Vernon, 25th. Septr. 1785

Sir,

It is not fourteen days since I was honored with your letter of the 16th. of the last Octr.[1] to what cause the delay is to be ascribed I am unable to inform you; but lest this answer with the inclosure should meet with any accident, I dispatch it under cover to the Count de Rochambeau at Paris.

I am sorry Sir, it is not in my power to comply with your wishes in regard to the Order of the Cincinnati. The institution itself points out the different grades of Officers who are to be admitted into this Society; and at its last General Meeting, the members thereof in France, of which the Counts de Rochambeau & de Estaing were placed at the head; one in the

[1] See page 208.

military, the other in the naval Line, were empowered to hold meetings & to decide upon the Claims of Officers belonging to either department in that Country.

It is there Sir, your pretensions must be offered; & if they are not precluded by the determination of your Sovereign, will I doubt not, meet with the liberal & favourable interpretation to which your merit entitles you.

I have the honor to be, etc.

[*Washington's Letter Books*]

Extract from GENERAL WASHINGTON'S DIARY.

Monday, 31st October, 1785—A Captn. Fullerton[1] came here to Dinner on business of the Society of the Cincinnati of Pennsylvania; for whom I signed 250 Diplomas as President. Went away after.

This is another letter from a French officer seeking admission to the Cincinnati.

To Lieutenant ALEXANDER DE GUBIAN.

Sir,

I have had the honor to receive your favor of the 13th. of June[2] from Marseilles.—If the right of admitting Members into the order, or Society of the Cincinnati rested with me, I should be happy in adding to its number a gentleman of your merit.—But as this is not the case, & as a Society is established in France, at the head of which the Counts de Estaing & Rochambeau are placed—to examine the pretentions of gentlemen of

[1] Captn. Fullerton was Brevet Captain Richard Fullerton, First Pennsylvania Regiment and Assistant Adjutant-General of the Southern Army. He was Assistant Secretary of the Pennsylvania Cincinnati, and as such had the duty of obtaining the President General's signature on the diplomas. As usual, General Washington signed them in blank, and the State Society inserted the date and the member's name.

[2] See page 219.

your nation—I beg leave to refer you to it, where I am persuaded your services & merits will have the weight they deserve.

I am, etc.

Mt. Vernon—
20th. Novr. 1785.

[*Washington's Letter Books*]

From Major-General HENRY KNOX.

New York 22 Novr 1785

My dear Sir

I have often been on the point of acknowledging your kind favor of the 18th of June,[1] and have as often deferred it, from the hope of having the pleasure of visiting you at Mount Vernon, on my way to James River, at which place there is a quantity of public stores . . .

Major Fairlie[2] will give you a detail of the proceedings of the new York Society of the Cincinnati with respect to the reception of the new institution proposed by the General Meeting on the 12th of May 1784. I flatter myself that the Society of this State will receive the alterations notwithstanding any appearances to the contrary I am uninformed how many of the states have adopted it, but New Hampshire has rejected it as it respects the funds, and it is said Connecticut have also declined adopting it— I am apprehensive that it may be as difficult to get in universally adopted as it is to obtain an universal assent of the respective legislature assemblies to any recommendation of Congress. . . .

[*Washington Papers*]

---

[1] This letter, in the Washington Papers, congratulates General Knox on being appointed Secretary of War, and asks what Congress is doing about the Western Territory. It does not mention the Cincinnati.

[2] Major James Fairlie was Secretary of the New York State Society of the Cincinnati at this time.

The father of the United States Navy writes the President General about the admission of two of his former officers. This is General Washington's reply.

To Commodore JOHN PAUL JONES.

Mount Vernon, November 25, 1785.

Sir,

I have been honoured with your letter of the 18th. of July from Paris,[1] enclosing certificates in favor of Captns. Stack and Macarthy.[2] I pray you to be assured that I should have pleasure in doing justice to the merits of these Officers, and in obliging you if the power of deciding lay with me. But, though I am in sentiment with the Gentlemen who have declared in favor of the pretensions of Captns. Stack and Maccarthy's right to become members of the Cincinnati, yet, in matters of opinion I have no authority to pronounce them such. As French Officers, having borne Continental Commissions, my opinion is that their best mode *would* have been, to have got themselves admitted as members of some State Society before the Kings edict, or order in Council took effect, for if I mistake not all Officers in the Service of France whose names are not particularly enumerated in that order are excluded thereby.

This however is a matter of which they, or you, can be better ascertained of than I. At any rate nothing can be done in this Country until the next *General* Meeting; and that cannot happen in less than Eighteen months, and may be much longer delayed.[3] I have the honor etc.

[*J. P. Morgan Library, New York*]

---

[1] See page 222.

[2] Captains Edward Stack and Eugene MacCarthy had served as volunteers on the *Bon Homme Richard.* (Fitzpatrick, Vol. xxviii, 325 n.) The former became a member of the Cincinnati of France.

[3] The second General Meeting of the Society of the Cincinnati was held in Philadelphia, in May 1787.

To Mr. SAMUEL VAUGHAN.

Mount Vernon, 30 November, 1785.

. . . I have received the pamphlet, which you were so obliging as to send me, entitled "*Considerations on the Order of Cincinnatus,* by the Count de Mirabeau."[1] I thank you, my good Sir, for this instance of your attention, but wish you had taken time to have perused it first, as I have not yet had leisure to give it a reading. I thought, as most others seemed to think, that all the exceptionable parts of that institution had been done away with at the last general meeting; but, with those who are disposed to cavil, or who have the itch of writing strongly upon them, nothing can be made to suit their palates. The best way, therefore, to disconcert and defeat them, is to take no notice of their publications. All else is but food for declamation.

There is not, I conceive, an unbiassed mind, that would refuse the officers of the late army the right of associating for the purpose of establishing a fund for the support of the poor and distressed of their fraternity, when many of them, it is well known, are reduced to their last shifts by the ungenerous conduct of their country in not adopting more vigorous measures to render their certificates productive. That charity is all that remains of the original institution, none, who will be at the trouble of reading it, can deny. . . .

[*Washington's Letter Books*]

[1] Mirabeau's pamphlet attacking the Society of the Cincinnati was based on that of Judge Ædanus Burke of South Carolina ("Cassius"). Indeed Burke, in an article in the Charleston Gazette complained bitterly that Mirabeau had stolen his thunder and had given him no credit for his priority. Mirabeau's book appeared first in London with the title *Considérations sur l'Ordre de Cincinnatus, ou Imitation d'un Pamphlet Anglo-Americain,* par le Comte de Mirabeau (1784). In the following year the work was published in London in English, *Considerations on the Order of Cincinnatus as well as Several Original Papers relative to that Institution.* There were several other editions of this book, including one published in Philadelphia, 1786, and a German edition published in Berlin and Libau, 1787. Burke was right in claiming that Mirabeau had merely warmed over the arguments he had himself advanced. The younger brother the Count de Mirabeau, the Viscount de Mirabeau, was an original member of the French Cincinnati.

To Lieutenant-Colonel LOUIS-DOMINIQUE ETHIS DE CORNY.

Mount Vernon, 5th. Decr. 1785

Sir,

I am really ashamed to have been so long in acknowledging the receipt of your letter of the 3d. of August of last year;[1] but circumstances which would be more tedious in the recital, than important when told, have been the cause of it.

I have now the honor of enclosing you the receipt of the Treasurer of the Society of the Cincinnati of this State, for your Bill on Colo. Wadsworth,[2] & wish it was in my power to have accompanied it with a Diploma: but it has so happened, that except a few which were struck at Philadelphia for the Members of that State at their own expence, none have yet been presented to me by the Secretary, for signing.

[*Washington's Letter Books*]

General Washington continued to favor the changes in the Institution voted by the General Meeting of 1784, until it became evident that opposition on the part of the public had subsided. For the text of the Altered and Amended Institution, and the action thereon by the several State Societies, see page 159. Here he writes to Hamilton, who was destined in 1800 to succeed him as President General.

[1] This letter is not in the Washington Papers nor the Cincinnati Archives.

[2] The minutes of the Society of the Cincinnati in the State of Virginia for 17 November 1786 contain this entry:

"On motion, Resolved, that the Treasurer be directed to purchase Military Certificates of this State, at the best rate they can be got, with 22: 10 specie, now in his hands, rec'ed from Colo. De Corny for his months pay" (E. E. Hume, *Papers of the Society of the Cincinnati in the State of Virginia, 1783-1824*, Richmond, 1938, 28). De Corny became an original member of the Virginia Cincinnati and, of course, was required to contribute one month's pay to the Permanent Fund.

To Major-General ALEXANDER HAMILTON.

Mount Vernon, 11 December, 1785.

Dear Sir,

I have been favored with your letter of the 25th of November by Major [James] Fairlie.

Sincerely do I wish that the several State Societies had, or would, adopt the alterations that were recommended by the General meeting in May, 1784—I then thought, and have had no cause since to change my opinion, that if the Society of the Cincinnati mean to live in peace with the rest of their fellow citizens, they must subscribe to the alterations which were at time adopted.

That the jealousies of, and prejudices against this Society were carried to an unwarrantable length, I will readily grant. And that *less* than was done, ought to have removed the fears which had been imbibed, I am as clear in, as I am that it would not have done it. But it is a matter of little moment whether the alarm which siezed the public mind was the result of foresight—envy and jealousy—or a disordered imagination; the effect on perseverance would have been the same; wherein there would have been found an equivalent for the separation of the Interests, which (from my best information, not from one state only but from many) would inevitably have taken place?

The fears of the people are not yet removed, they only sleep, and a very little matter will set them afloat again. Had it not been for the predicament we stood in with respect to the foreign officers, and the charatable part of the Institution, I should on that occasion, as far as my voice would have gone, have endeavored to convince the narrow-minded part of our Countrymen that the Amor Patriæ was much stronger in our breasts than theirs—and that our conduct through the whole of the business was actuated by nobler and more generous sentiments than were apprehended, by abolishing the Society at once, with a declaration of the causes, and the purity of its intention. But the latter may be interesting to many, and the former, is an inseparable bar to such a step.

[*Washington's Letter Books*]

To Major-General HENRY KNOX.

Mount Vernon, December 11, 1785

. . . I am sorry the State Societies should hesitate to comply with the recommendation of the General Meeting of the Cincinnati, holden at Phil[a] in 1784. I then thought & have no cause since to change my opinion, that nothing short of what was then done would appease the clamours which were raised against this institution. Some late attacks have been made upon it; amongst which a Pamphlet written by the Count de Mirabeau, a French Gentleman, has just made its appearance.[1] It is come to my hands translated into English, but I have not had time yet to read it. . . .

[*Washington Papers*]

Extract from General WASHINGTON'S Diary.

Monday, 12th December, 1785—Majr. Farlie[1] went away before breakfast, with 251 Diplomas which I had signed for Members of the Cincinnati of the State of New York, at the request of General McDougall[2] President of that Society.

The matter of Colonel Ethis de Corny's subscription to the Permanent Fund of the Cincinnati necessitated a number of letters to and from General Washington. See page 240.

[1] See page 95, note, concerning Mirabeau's pamphlet.

[2] Captain James Fairlie had been an Aide-de-Camp to Major-General the Baron de Steuben. Major-General Alexander McDougall was the first President of the New York State Society of the Cincinnati and the first Treasurer General.

From Colonel WILLIAM HETH.

Wales near Petersburg 24th. Decr. 85

Sir

I have some time since recd. Colo. De Corny's first bill on Jeremiah Wadsworth esqr. for 75 Dlrs. together with your letter to General Weedon on the subject, & advising that you were in possession of the third bill, of the same tenor & date.—expecting of which, hath hitherto prevented my forwarding the first for paiment, and which, I hope, will plead my apology for troubling you with this.

I have the honor to be
Yr Most Ob. Servt.

From Will. Heth

Colonel Heth 24th. Decr. 1785
His Excellency
General Washington
By Stage
Mount Vernon

[*Washington Papers*]

The matter of the payment for the original Eagles, or badges of membership, occurs frequently in General Washington's correspondence. Apparently both Major L'Enfant and the actual jeweler had to wait for payment.

From Mr. THOMAS JEFFERSON.

Paris Jan. 7. 1785 [misdated for 1786]

Dear Sir

A conversation with the Count de Rochambeau yesterday obliges me to write a supplementary letter to that of the 4th.[1] instant. he informs me that he has had applications for paiment

[1] This letter from Jefferson is in the Washington Papers. It contains no reference to the Cincinnati, but concerns plans for canals to open the Potomac and James Rivers. It also mentions Bavarian and Russo-Turkish affairs.

from the person who furnished the badges for the Cincinnati, as well the Americans as French. that this person informed him they were not paid for, that he had furnished them indeed on the application of Major L'Enfant, but that he did not do it in reliance on his credit, for that he should not have trusted so much to Major l'Enfant of whose means of paiment he knew nothing, but that he considered himself as working for a society who had delivered their orders thro' Major l'Enfant, and always expected the Society would see him paid. Count Rochambeau has written to Major l'Enfant, and the answer is that he has never received the whole, nor expects to be able to collect it, & that being without resources he is obliged, as fast as he collects it, to apply it to his own sustenance. Count Rochambeau told the workman he would pay for the badges delivered him for the French officers (I think he said about 40. in number) but that for the others he must apply to the Marquis de la fayette and Count d'Estaing, as L'Enfant's letter gives room to suppose a misapplication of these monies, and in the mean time the honour of the American officers stands committed, and in danger of being spoken of publicly, I thought it my duty to apprise you of this, that you might take such measures herein as you think best. I have the honour to be with sentiments of the most perfect esteem Dear Sir etc.

[*Washington Papers*]

To the MARQUIS DE SAINT-SIMON.

Mount Vernon, May 10, 1786.

Sir,

I received with great pleasure (a few days ago in a letter from the Marquis de la Fayette) the news of your being in good health. The recollection of your gallant services, and the happy moments I have had the honor to spend with you in this country, will always be dear to me.

It appears by the Marquis's letter that the answer to a letter which you did me the honor to write to me (now more than two years) respecting the order of the Cincinnati, had never come to your hands. I cannot tell how to accot. for it, as all the papers are in the hands of the Secretary General. I well remember however, that at the general meeting which was held at Philadelphia in May 1784, that I laid all the letters with which I had been favored on that subject, before the members which constituted it; and that the Secretary was ordered to communicate the determinations which that meeting had come to, to the gentlemen who had written to the President, one of which was, that the members of the Society in France were to constitute a meeting of themselves in order, among other things, to investigate the claims of those who conceived they were entitled to the order, and to decide on them accordingly; in as much as the Meeting in this Country was not intended to be held oftener than triennially; and could not well at those times enter into the detail of a business which with more propriety would be taken up by the several State Meetings, and the one it had just authorized to be held in France. . . .

[*Washington's Letter Books*]

Again the Eagles are considered. Several American goldsmiths made copies, varying in accuracy, of the Eagles L'Enfant procured in Paris for the Society.

To Major-General HENRY KNOX.

Mount Vernon, June 1st, 1786.

My dear Sir,

The Post of last week brought me (by way of New York) a letter of which the enclosed is a Copy.[1] I transmit it, not only for your perusal, but for information, and advice. All the papers respecting the Society of the Cincinnati being in possession of the Secretary Genl. or the Assistant Secretary, and my memory very defective, I cannot speak with precision to Mr. Jefferson, or decide on any thing which is pleasing to myself. From what I can recollect of the matter, all the

[1] The inclosed copy was of Jefferson's letter of 7 January 1785 (for 1786), see page 243.

officers who chose to make use of Major L'Enfant's agency to obtain the badge of the Society, not only commissioned him to bring them from France, but furnished him with the means. I did this myself for 6 or 8. He brought many more. I have some reason to believe on a speculating scheme; and demanded so much for them, as, if my memory serves me, to disgust many members of the Society, and induce them to apply to an Artist in Philadelphia, who, it was said, would not only execute them as well, (and without the defect which was discovered in the French ones) but furnished them cheaper. This and L'Enfant's misapplication of the money (if the fact is so) for those he did receive, may have been the Sources of the present difficulty. On the one hand, it will be very disagreeable to the American Officers to be freely spoken of on this occasion. On the other, it may not only be hard but distressing to comply with the demands of the Parisian Artisan, as we are not only unacquainted with the extent but in some measure with the nature of them. What is become of L'Enfant? I have not seen him since the general meeting of the Society which was held in Philadelphia in May 1784, nor that I recollect, have heard of him 'till Mr. Jefferson's Letter[2] came to hand.

Mrs. Washington joins me in every affectionate wish for M[rs] Knox, yourself & family. And with sentiments of the warmest friendship

I am ever
Your's

G[o] Washington.

Major General Knox

By forwarding the enclosed you will oblige

G W

[*Washington's Letter Books*]

---

[2] See Jefferson's letter from Paris, 7 January 1786, page 243.

Once more General Washington refers the claims of a French officer for membership in the Cincinnati to the French Society.

To the COUNT DE GROUCHET.

Mount Vernon, June 19, 1786

Sir,

I have had the honor to receive your letter of the 20th. of Octr. 1785. to-gether with the certificate of the Duke de Richelieu, Marechall of France.—

The high estimation in which I hold the French nation in general, & the particular respect which I have for those Gentlemen who served in America in the late war, would lead me to grant to a person of your merit every request which I could consistently comply with; but at the last general meeting of the Cincinnati (which is holden but once in three years) those Gentlemen in France who are of that order, were empowered to examine the claims of those of their countrymen who should apply for admission into it, & judge of their qualifications.—

I have not the last doubt Sir, but that upon an application to those gentlemen, (at the head whom are the Counts d'Estaing & Rochambeau) you will meet with every attention you could wish.—

I am Sir etc.

[*Washington's Letter Books*]

Baron de Holtzendorff, having served only two years under an American commission was not eligible to membership in the Society of the Cincinnati. But he was a frequent applicant. General Washington in this letter shows the difference in qualifications required of European officers who served under American commissions and those of the French forces.

To the BARON DE HOLTZENDORFF.

Mount Vernon, July 31, 1786

Sir,

The letter of the 6th. of June 1785 [1] which you was pleased to address to me by Colo. Senff, has very lately put into my hand; in answer to which I have the honor to observe, that having divested myself of an official character and retired to private life, I can have no agency whatever in matters of a public nature. This, I thought, had been made known extensively enough by the manner of my resignation and retirement. The want of being acquainted with these facts seems however, to have involved some gentlemen at a distance in unnecessary and unavailing applications. All therefore, that I have it in my power to advise you on the two objects of your letter, is, that application for admittance into the Society of the Cincinnati, must be either to the Society of the State in whose line the officer served; or, if the officer was a foreigner, to the Society in France; and with respect to pecuniary claims, recourse must be had either to the Paymaster General, or Secretary for the Department of War. With due consideration and regard I have the honor, etc.

[*Washington's Letter Books*]

A French officer, original member of the Pennsylvania Cincinnati, is informed by the President General where he may obtain his insignia and diploma.

To Lieutenant-Colonel ANTIONE-FELIX WUIBERT DE MÉZIÈRES.

Mount Vernon, July 31, 1786

Sir,

I have been favored with the receipt of triplicate copies of your polite letter dated at Cape-francois the 15th. of Novr. last.[2] . . .

As to medals and Diplomas for the Cincinnati, the former

[1] The letter was dated 4 June 1785, see page 215.

[2] This letter cannot be found.

I believe are to be purchased in Philada., and the latter to be obtained thro' the State Society of wch. an officer is member. I have none of either at my disposal. With sincere wishes for your health and happiness, I remain, etc.

[*Washington's Letter Books*]

General Washington writes to Mr. Jefferson in Paris anent the statue of himself by Houdon, now in the Capitol at Richmond. He also refers to the matter of the payment for the Eagles.

To Mr. THOMAS JEFFERSON.

Mount Vernon, August 1, 1786.

Dear Sir,

The letters you did me the favor to write to me on the 4th.[1] and 7th of Jany.[2] have been duly received. In answer to your obliging enquiries respecting the dress, attitude &ca. which I would wish to have given to the Statue in question, I have only to observe that not having sufficient knowledge in the art of Connoisseiurs, I do not desire to dictate in the matter; on the contrary I shall be perfectly satisfied with whatever may be judged decent and proper. I should even scarcely have ventured to suggest that perhaps a servile adherence to the garb of antiquity might not be altogether so exepedient as some little deviation in favor of the modern costume, if I had not learnt from Colo. [David] Humphreys that this was a circumstance hinted in conversation by Mr. West to Houdon. This taste, which has been introduced in painting by West, I understand is received with applause and prevails extensively.

I have taken some pains to enquire into the facts respecting the medals of the Cincinnati, which Majr. L'Enfant purchased in France. It seems that when he went to Europe in 1783 he had money put into his hands to purchase a certain number, and that conceiving it to be consonant with the intentions of

[1] See footnote on page 243.

[2] See page 243.

the Society, he purchased to a still greater amount; insomuch that a Committee of the Genl. Meeting, upon examining his Acct. reported a balle. due to him of Six hundred and thirty dollars, wch. report was accepted. This money is still due, and is all that is due from the Society of the Cincinnati as a Society. General Knox has offered to pay the amount to Majr. L'Enfant, but as it has become a matter of some public discussion, the latter wished it might remain until the next Genl Meeting, which will be in May next. In the mean time Genl. Knox (who is Secretary Genl) has, or will write fully on the Subject to the Marquis de la Fayette, from whom he has had a letter respecting the business. . . .

[*Jefferson Papers, Library of Congress*]

The china, bearing the emblems of the Cincinnati, is considered in this letter from "Lighthorse Harry" Lee to General Washington. See page 266 for note on this china.

From Major-General HENRY LEE.

Dear Gen[l].

I have not written to you for a long time having nothing important or agreable to communicate.

Nor have I now any thing agreable, but alas the reverse.

The [ ] which have for some time past distracted the two eastern states, have risen in Massachusetts to an alarming height. In New Hampshire the journeys of their president the late General Sullivan has dissipated the troubles in that state. I enclose a full narration of his decided conduct, and the effects which it produced. But affairs are in a very different situation in Massachusetts. After various insults to government, by stopping the courts of justice &c, the insurgents have in a very formidable shape taken possession of the town of Springfield, at which place the supreme court was sitting. The friends to government arrayed under the Militia General of the district Shephard in support the court, but their exertions were not affectual. The court removed and broke up, the insurgents continued of the town & General Shephard has retired to the United States Arsenal one mile from Springfield. This Arsenal contained a very important share of our munitions of war. Congress have sent their Secretary of this department, General Knox, to take the best measures of his power in concent with government for the safety of the Arsenal. What renders the conduct of the insurgents more alarming is that they behave with decency & manage with system, they are encamped and regularly supplied with provisions by their friends & have lately given orders to the delegates in assembly from their paticular towns, not to attend the Meeting of the Legislature.

It might give you pleasure to hear in this very distressing scene, the late officers & soldiers are on the side of government unanimously. The insurgents it is said are conducted by a captain of the late army, who continued but a small period in service & possessed a very reputable character.

This event produces much suggestion as to its causes. Some attribute it to the weight of taxes and the decay of commerce, which has produced universal idleness.

[ ] councils the vicinity of Vermont & the fondness for novelty which always has & ever will possess more or less influence on man. The rent accounts will I hope produce favorable intelligence, but present appearances do not justify this hope—

Has your china arrived, & does it please M^{rs}. Washington. Be pleased to present my best respects to her and accept the repitition of my unceasing regard with which . . .

I have the honor to
be most sincerely
your ob ser

Henry Lee

General Washington
The Honble. Henry Lee about 1st. Oct. 1786.

[*Washington Papers*]

[Enclosure]

Col°. Henry Lee

1786 Bo^t^ of Constable, Rinker & C°

Augt. 7th.

1 Sett of Cincinnati China Cont^y^
1 Breakfast
1 Table Service of 302 p^s^. £60
1 Tea . .

Rec^d^. New York 7th. Augt. 1786 the Amount

Constable, Rinker & C°

[*Washington Papers*]

Here is further reference to the Cincinnati china, procured by Captain Samuel Shaw in China for General Washington and other members of the Cincinnati.

From Major-General HENRY LEE.

My dear Genl.

By Col. [David] Humphrey I had the pleasure to receive your letter acknowledgin the receipt of the china account paid here by me, and at the same time got one hundred and fifty dollars payment in full for the money advanced. Before this M^r^. Gardoquis box must have reashed you; it was sent to the care of M^r^. C. Lee in Alexandria and I hope your china has also got to hand—It had left this for Norfolk addressed to Col°. Parker before your letter respecting the mode of conveyance got to me, or I should have obeyed your wishes.

The period seems to be fast approaching when the people of these U. States must determine to establish a permanent capable government or submit to the horrors of anarchy and licentiousness.

How wise would it be, how happy for us all, if this change could be made a friendship [ ]ducted by reason. But such is the tardiness of the and worthy part of society in matters of this importance, and such the concert & zeal of the vicious, that is to be apprehended that wickedness and audacity will triumph over honor & honesty—the enclosed proclamation just come to hand will show you the temper of the eastern people—it is not confined to one state of to one part of a state, but pervades the whole. The decay of their commerce leaves the lower order unemployed, idleness in this body, and the intriguing [ ] of another days whose desperate fortunes are remedeable only by the [ ] of society produce schemes portending the dissolution of order & good governments. Weak and feeble governments are not adequate to resist such high handed offences. It is not then strange that the sober part of mankind will continue to prefer this incertitude & precariousness, because their jealousys are alarmed and their envy encited when they see the officers of the Nation possessing that power which is indispensably necessary to chastise vice and reward virtue. But thus it is and thus it has been, and from hence it follows that almost every nation we read of have drank deep of the misery which flow from despotism or licentiousness—The happy medium is difficult to practice.

I am very unhappy to hear by Mr Shaw that your health declines; I must hope he is mistaken and cannot help thinking so, as Col. Humphrey tells me that you look very hearty, and use vigorous exercise. If the potomac navigation succeeds in the manner these gentlemen mention, it is another strong evidence that difficulties vanish as they are approached, and will be a strong argument among the politicians, in favor of the Spanish treaty and the occlusion of the Mississippi.— M^rs^. Lee joins me in most respectful compliments to Mount Vernon—with unceasing and affectionate attach-

ments I am dear gen^l^ your
most ob h ser

Henry Lee Jun.
New York Sepr. 8th 1786

Genl. Washington
From
The Honble. Henry Lee
8th. Sepr. 1786

[*Washington Papers*]

From Lieutenant-Colonel DAVID HUMPHREYS.

Hartford Septr. 24th. 1786

My dear General,

I had the pleasure, before I left New York, to receive your favor containing the enclosures respecting Asgil's affairs, and am taking measures for their publication. . . .

Not having found in my journey Genl Knox (who was at the eastward) or any of our particular friends, with whom I might converse unreservedly on the subject of the Cincinnati; I have delayed writing to you until I could have an opportunity of advising with Colo. Trumbull, Colo. Wadsworth & Mr Trumbull of this town—and now I have to inform, that it is their unanimous sentiment, that it would not be of any good consequence, or even advisable for you to attend he next General Meeting. Agreeably to your desire in this case, I forward you the draft of a circular letter, of which you will, of course, My dear General, make such use as you shall judge most expedient, either by altering, suppressing, or communicating it. I am sensible the subject is a very delicate one, that it will be discussed by posterity as well as by the present age, and that you have much to lose & nothing to gain by it in their estimation—Under this persuasion, caution was the primary point, & it has consequently been the object to avoid as much as possible every thing that will be obnoxious to censure on the part of the public as well as of the Society. Whatever communication is made, it ought to have the property of a two-edged weapon & to cut both ways. We have had a State Meeting at New Haven since my return, in which, I found there was no disposition to adopt the Institution as altered and amended—I moved therefore to postpone the discussion until after the next General Meeting; this was unanimously carried, and they appointed Genl [Samuel Holden] Parsons, Col [Jeremiah] Wadsworth, Mr [Ralph] Pomeroy, Dr [Ezra] Styles (Presidt of the [Yale] College) & my self their Delegates. Having learnt it was wished & expected the General Meeting would be holden at New York, I have ventured to propose that place accordingly. . . .

This State, which seems rather more tranquil & better disposed than those before mentioned, has had an election of representatives for the Assembly since my arrival. More gentlemen, lately belonging to the Army, have been elected than on any former occasion. Amongst these are Genl [Jedediah] Huntington, Cols. [Jeremiah] Wadsworth, [Samuel] Wyllys, [Philip Burr] Bradly, myself, & many others who may be personally unknown to you. But what appears most singular & proves some revolution of sentiment, is, that Major [William] Judd, who 3 years ago was driven by an armed Mob out of the town to which he belonged on account of commutation, should now have a seat in the Assembly from the same town.—. . .[1]

[*Washington Papers*]

To Major WILLIAM JACKSON.

Mount Vernon, September 28, 1786

Dr. Sir,

I have received your letter of the 20th, ulto. together with the pamphlets enclosed. I consider your sending the latter to me as a mark of attention wch. deserves my warmest acknowledgments.

I cannot join with you in thinking that the partiality of your friends in assigning to you so honorable a task,[2] prejudiced their discernment. The subject is noble, the field extensive,—& I think it must be highly satisfactory, & indeed flattering, to a man that his performance, upon such an occasion, is approved of by men of taste and judgment.

I am Dr. Sir etc.

[*Washington's Letter Books*]

[1] General Washington replied on 22 October 1786, see page 256.

[2] The "task" mentioned in the second paragraph was the delivery of the oration before the Pennsylvania Society of the Cincinnati, 4 July 1786. It was published under the following title: "An Oration to Commemorate The Independence of The U. States of N. A. delivered at the Reformed Calvinish Church in Phila. July 4, 1786 and published at the request of the Penna. Soc'y of the Cincinnati. Philadelphia, Oswald, 1786" Pages 29.

To Lieutenant-Colonel DAVID HUMPHREYS.

Mount Vernon, October 22, 1786

My D^{r}. Humphreys,

Your favor of the 24th. ulto.[1] came to my hands about the middle of this month. For the enclosures it contained I pray you to receive my warmest acknowledgments & thanks.—. . .

With respect to the circular letter,[2] I see no cause for suppressing or altering any part of it, except as to the place of meeting. Philadelphia, on three accots. is my opinion must be more convenient to the majority of the delegation, than New York—1st. as most central—2dly because there are regularly established packet-boats, well accomodated for Passengers, to it from the Southern States; & 3rdly. because it appears to me that the seat of Congress would not be so well for this meeting.—When you have digested your thoughts for publication, in the case of Captn. Asgill, I would thank you for a copy of them; having arrested the account I had furnished Mr. [Tench] Tilghman, with an assurance of a more authentic one for his friend in England.—

I am pleased with the choice of Delegates which was made at your State meeting;—& wish the representatives of all the State societies may appear at the Genl. Meeting; with as good dispositions as I believe they will.—It gives me pleasure also to hear that so many officers are sent to your Assembly: I am persuaded they will carry with them more liberality of sentiment, than is to be found among any other class of Citizens. . . .[3]

[*Washington's Letter Books*]

---

[1] See page 254.

[2] This was the President General's circular letter, 15 May 1784, explaining to the State Societies the reasons for altering the Institution, see page 170.

[3] Colonel Humphreys replied on 9 November 1786, see page 269.

From M. Joseph Mandrillon.

Amsterdam ce 24. 8re. 1786.

Monsieur le Général

Votre Excellence m'a Fait espérer dans sa dernière lettre[1] si les Statuts de la *Société de Cincinnatus* pouraient tolérer mon aggrégation; vous vous feriez un plaisir, Monsieur, de me proposer dans le prochaine assemblé de 1787.

Permettez moi de rappeller à Votre Excellence, combien je Serais flaté d'appartenir par *ce nouveau lieu* à un pays et à des citoyens qui ont tant de droits à mon dévouement et à mon admiration. En conséquence je prends la liberté, Monsieur le président, de vous envoyer ma Soumission pour cette illustre assemblée. Il m'est bien doux d'y paraitre sous des auspices aussi respectables que ceux de Votre Excellence. Si je suis assez heureux pour obtenir cette faveur, il me sera également bien agréable de l'annoncer à Mr. le Marquis de la Fayette qui Sera charmé de mon adoption.

Souffrez, Monsieur, que j'ajoute qu'un membre de plus en Europe ne Saurait devenir d'aucune conséquence pour l'Amérique, et qu'il est Souvent des cas où l'on fait taire pour un moment le Sévérité des loix & des Statuts, Surtout quand il Sagit de ne faire que le bien.

J'ai oüi dire que chaque membre de la Société avait contribué pour former un Fond tendant à Soulager les pauvres familles qui avaient perdues leurs époux, ou leurs peres en deffendant la patrie: Jugez, Monsieur, combien je Serai heureux d'avoir part à de bienfait si patriotique et si humain.

J'ai eu dernierement la visite de Mr. le Colonel Vernon qui voyage avec Milady Hamilton et retourne en Angleterre; Nous avons beaucoup parlé de l'Amérique et surtout de Votre Excellence, dont il prise, *autant que moi,* les rares vertus et la noble modestie. Quel plaisir n'ai-je pas eu de converser avec une personne qui connait si bien l'Amérique et son libérateur!

Agréez, *avec les vers ci joints,* les assurances du profond

[1] General Washington's letter was date 22 August 1785, see page 231.

respect avec le quel je ne cesserai davoir l'honneur d'être de Votre Excellence

Le très humble & très obéissant Serviteur

P. S.: Je recommande à vos bontés la liste des membres dont je fait mention dans mon mémoire. Agréez en, je vous prie, d'avance ma gratitude je n'attends que cela pour publier la nouvelle édition de mon ouvrage.

[*Archives of the General Society*]

[Contemporary Translation.]

Amsterdam, 24 October 1786

My dear General

Your Excellency made me hope in your last letter that if the Rules of *the Society of the Cincinnati* could tolerate my admission, you would with pleasure Sir, propose me at the next General Meeting of 1787—Permit me to remind your Excellency, how much I should be flattered, in beg. united *by this New Tie* to a Country and Citizens who have so great a right to my admiration and devotion—Of course I take the liberty of sending you Mr. President my submission to this illustrious assembly [1]—It will be very pleasing for me to appear under such respectable auspices as those of your Excellency—If I am so happy as to obtain this favor, it will be equally agreeable to announce it to the Marquis de la Fayette who will be charmed at my adoption—

Suffer me Sir, to add that one Member more in Europe can be of no consequence to America, and that in some cases the Severity of laws may be suspended to procure a more beneficial Result.

I have heard that each Member of the Society has contributed towards forming a fund for the succour of poor families who

[1] Mandrillon's formal petition to the General Meeting for admission to the Society as an honorary member is attached to this letter (see page 259).

have lost husbands or Fathers in defence of their Country: Judge Sir how happy I shall be to bear a part in so patriotic and humain a devotion—

I have at least had a visit from Col. Vernon who travelled with Lady Hamilton and returned to England; We have had a good deal of conversation about America, and, above all, Your Excellency, whose rare virtues and noble modesty formed the pleasing subject of our conference—What pleasure I experienced in thus conversing with a man so well acquainted with America and her Deliverer! Agreeable to these assurances of profound respect I have the honor to be Your Excellency's Very humble and obedient Servt.

[P. S.]: I would remind you of the list of the Members of whom I made mention in my memoir. If agreed on advance my gratitude for I wait for that only to publish the new edition of my work—[1]

[*Archives of the General Society*]

Memorial from J[OSEP]H MANDRILLON to "l'Honnorable Assemblée de la Société de Cincinnatus." Enclosed in his letter, October 24, 1786, to General Washington.

Amsterdam, 24 Octobre 1786

Messieurs!

Si j'avais eu, comme vous, la gloire de verser mon Sang pour la noble cause de la liberté américaine: j'aurais espéré, Messieurs, de mériter mon admission dans votre illustre Société. Mais, n'ayant pour obtenir cette faveur, que l'énoncé de mes veilles et de mon zele à Soutenir et deffendre cette cause, dans un tems et dans un pays òu l'independance divisait encore les esprits: ce mérite, je l'avoue, Messieurs, n'approche pas d'une telle recompense. Cependant le vif desir que j'ai d'appartenir par un nouveau lien à un pays qui m'interesse à tant d'égards, m'enhardit à Solliciter aujourd'hui mon aggrégation, *comme associé honnoraire de la Société de Cincinnatus.* Agréez à cet

[1] See page 261 for a contemporary translation in the Washington Papers. It differs somewhat from this one.

effet, Messieurs, ma Soumission entiere à vos Statuts.[1] Mais soit, que j'obtienne ou non cette faveur, me permettez-vous, de m'honorer du titre de votre *historiographe* et d'imprimer en français (à la Suite de la nouvelle édition du *Spectateur Américain* que je dois publier dans le courrant de 1787,) tout ce qui appartient aux Status et réglemens de votre illustre Société. Pour cet effet, Messieurs, Je desire une liste exacte des membres qui la composent tant en Amérique qu'en Europe. On ne Saurait donner trop de publicité à cette liste pour empêcher surtout, certains étrangers de se décorer impunément d'un titre aussi respectable.

En attendant avec respect & Soumission le résolution & les ordres de votre illustre Société: J'ai l'honneur d'être, Messieurs, etc.

[*Archives of the General Society*]

[Contemporary Translation.]

Amsterdam, October 24, 1786.

Gentlemen:

If, like you, I had had the glory of spilling my blood in the noble cause of American freedom, I would hope, Gentlemen, to merit admission in your illustrious Society—But having nothing towds. obtaing. the favor, but by my zeal in supporting and defending this cause, at a time and in a Country where the Minds of people were yet too divided, it is a merit, I fear, Gentlemen, far short of such a recompense—Nevertheless the lively desire I entertain for a new Tie to unite me to a Country which interests me so feelingly, emboldens me to sollicit you for admission as *an Honorary Member of the Society of the Cincinnati.* But I Leave this Matter entirely Gentlemen to your Rules—Whether I obtain this favor or not, permit me to be honored with the title of your *Historiographer,* and to print in french (at the end of a new edition of the *American Spectator* which I shall publish this current year of 1787) every thing which concerns the Rules and regulations of your illustrious Society—

[1] This petition is attached to Mandrillon's letter of 24 October 1786, see page 257.

To accomplish this Gentlemen I desire an exact list of the Members who compose it, as well in America as in Europe— They cannot give it too public an authenticity, as it will particularly prevent certain Strangers from decorating themselves with so respectable a title with impunity—

Waiting with respect and submission the Resolutions and orders of your illustrious Society, I have the honor to be etc.[1]

[*Archives of the General Society*]

The contemporary translation of Mandrillon's letter, in the Washington Papers differs somewhat from that in the Archives of the Cincinnati, as does also the translation of his petition to the General Meeting. Both of the translations are here given.

From M. JOSEPH MANDRILLON.

General

Your Excellency gave me reason to hope, by your last letter, that if the Statutes of the Society of the Cincinnati permitted it, you would do me the pleasure Sir to propose me in the next assembly of 1787.

Permit me to repeat to your Excellency how much I shall feel myself flattered by being connected, by a new bond, to a Country & to Citizens who have had so much of my devotion & admiration. In consequence, I take the liberty, M^{r}. President, to send you my address to that illustrious Assembly.[2] It will be peculiarly agreeable to me to appear there under auspices so respectable as those of your Excellency. If I am so happy as to obtain this favour, it will be equally agreeable to me to announce it to the Marquis de la Fayette, who will be charmed at my adoption.

I understand that each Member contributes something towards establishing a fund for the relief [*sic*] of the Widows & families of those who perished in the defence of their Coun-

[1] See footnote on page 260.
[2] Enclosure: see pages 259, 260 and 262.

try.—Think, Sir, how happy I shall be in taking a part in that humane & patriotic Contribution! . . .

Amsterdam 24th. Octr. 1786 Mandrillon

I recommend to your care the list of the members which I have made mention of in my memorial. Accept, I beseech you, beforhand, of my gratitude for it. I wait only for that to publish a new Edition of my work.

[*Washington Papers*]

[Enclosure]

To the Honble Assembly of the Society of the Cincinnati.

Gentlemen:

If I had had the honor, as you have, of sheding my blood in the noble cause of American liberty: I should have hoped, Gentn to have merited an admission into your illustrious Society. But, having no other means of obtaining that favor, but the declaration of my labours & my Zeal in supporting & defending that Cause, at a time & in a Country where the Independence of America was viewed in no very favourable light, I confess Gentlemen that it hardly deserves so great a recompence. Nevertheless, the strong desire which I have of connecting myself by a new bond to a Country in which I have so much interested myself, emboldens me, this day, to solicit my admission, as an honorary member, into the Society of the Cincinnati. Accept, therefore, Gentlemen, my entire submission to your Statutes.—But, whether I obtain this favor or not, will you permit me to honor myself with the title of your Historiographer, & to publish in French (at the end of a new Edition of the American Spectator which I am about to publish in the year 1787) all that appertains to the Statutes & rules of your illustrious Society.—To effect which, Gentlemen, I request an exact list of all the Members both in America & Europe. The publication of this list will prevent certain Strangers from arrogating to themselves so respectable a title with impunity.

Waiting with respect & submission this resolution & orders of your illustrious Society,

I have the Honor to be

Gentlemen

Your very H^ble^ & most Obed^t^ Servt

J^h^ Mandrillon, neg^t^

Amsterdam 26th Octr. 1786

Member of the Philosophical Society at Philadelphia, of the Academy of Sciences at Holland, & of that of Bresse &^ca^

[*Washington Papers*]

To Governor [Major-General] WILLIAM MOULTRIE.

Mount Vernon, October 31, 1786

Dr. Sir,

As soon as your Excellency's favor of the 7th. of Augt.,[1] came to my hands, I forwarded the enclosure therein, to Mr. Brindley, under cover to Saml. Hughes Esqr.— . . . .

Presuming that your Excely. is President of the Society of the Cincinnati in the State of South Carolina, I have the honor of addressing the enclosed circular letter to you.—If I am mistaken, I pray you to forward it to the right person.— . . .[2]

P. S.—Permit me to request the favor of you to direct the blank cover herewith sent, to the President of the Georgia Society of the Cincinnati,[3] & cause it to be forwarded by the first safe conveyance that may offer.

[*Washington's Letter Books*]

[1] This letter is in the Washington Papers. It concerns the South Carolina Canal, and makes no reference to the Cincinnati.

[2] Major-General William Moultrie was President of the South Carolina Cincinnati until his death. The circular pertained to the Altered and Amended Institution, see page 170.

[3] Major-General Lachlan McIntosh, first President of the Georgia Cincinnati was still in office at this time.

This is apparently the first of several letters General Washington wrote expressing his desire not to be reelected President General. Since General Gates was the Vice-President General, it was probably General Washington's thought that Gates would succeed him. As it turned out, General Washington reconsidered and continued to hold the President Generalcy to the end of his life.

To Major-General HORATIO GATES.

Mount Vernon in Virginia October 31st 1786
(Circular)

Sir

I take this early oppertunity, in my character of President of the Cincinnati, of announcing to you that the triennial General Meeting of the Society is to be convened at Philadelphia on the first Monday of May in the year 1787—

As it will not be in my power (for reasons which I shall have the honor of immediately communicating) to attend the next General Meeting; and as it may become more & more inconvenient for me to be absent from my Farms, or to receive appointments which will divert me from my private affairs, I think it proper also to acquaint you, for the information of your Delegates to the General Meeting, that it is my desire not to be elected to the Presidency, since I should find my self under the necessity of declining the acceptance of it.

The numerous applications for information, advice, or assistance which are made to me in consequence of my Military command; the multiplicity of my correspondencies in this Country as well as in many parts of Europe; the variety and perplexity of my own private concerns, which having been much deranged by my absence through the War, demand my entire & unremitting attention; the arduousness of the Task, in which I have been as it were unavoidably engaged of Superintending the opening the navigation of the great rivers in this State; The natural desire of tranquility and relaxation from business, which almost every one experiences at my Time of Life, particularly after having acted (during a considerable period) as no idle spectator in uncommonly busy & important Scenes; and the present imbecility of my health, occasioned by a violent attack of the fever & ague, succeeded by rheumatick pains (to which till of late I have been an entire stranger); will, I doubt not, be considered as reasons of sufficient validity to justify my conduct in the present instance.—

Although the whole of these reasons could not have before operated; yet, in conformity to my determination of passing the remainder of my days in a state of retirement, I should certainly have refused to accept the Office of President with which I was honored in 1784, but from an apprehension that my refusal, at that time, might have been misrepresented as a kind of dereliction of the Society on my part, or imputed to a disapprobation of the principles on which it was then established. To convince the opposers of the Institution, should any such remain, that this was not the fact; and to give no colourable pretext for unreasonable attacks I prevailed upon myself to accept the appointment with a view of holding it only until the next election: before which time I expected the Jealousy that had been excited, would subside—and this, I am happy to be informed, has universally taken place.—

Highly approving as I do, the principles on which the Society is now constituted; and pleased to find, so far as I have been able to learn from reiterated inquiries, that it is acceptable to the good people of the United States in general; it only remains for me to express the sense I entertain of the honor confered by the last General Meeting in electing me their President, and to implore in the future the benediction of Heaven on the virtuous Associates in this illustrious Institution.—

During the residue of my continuance in Office, I shall be constantly ready to sign such *Diplomas* as may be requisite for the Members of your State Society, being sincerely desirous of giving every possible proof of attachment, esteem, & affection for them; as well as of demonstrating the sentiments of perfect consideration and respect with which

I have the honor to be
Sir

Y^{r} most Obed. and
most H^{ble} serv.

G. Washington

P. S.

I have thought it expedient to forward a transcript of this circular address to Maj^{r}. Genl. Gates, Vice President of the Society: In order that the General Meeting may suffer no embarrassment for want of an Official character to Preside at the opening of it.

G. W.

Horatio Gates Esq.

Vice President of the General Meeting of the Society of the Cincinnati—and President of the said Society in the State of Virginia—

[*Archives of the Virginia Cincinnati, Contemporary Copy in Archives of the General Society*]

The Cincinnati china ordered by General Washington (see pages 250 and 252) was finally received safely. It was carefully preserved and in Mrs. Washington's will (see page 401) bequeathed to her grandson George Washington Parke Custis, father of Mrs. Robert E. Lee. The china was at Arlington during the War Between the States, when much of it was destroyed by hostile troops.

To Major-General HENRY LEE.

The China [1] came to hand without much damage; and I thank you for your attention in procuring & forwarding of it to me.—M^{rs}. Washington joins me in best wishes for M^{rs}. Lee and yourself and I am very affectionately

Dear Sir

Y^{r}. Most Obed^{t}. & Obliged

G^{o}. Washington

The Honble. Henry Lee
31st. Oct. 1786

[*Washington's Letter Books*]

---

[1] There have been a number of accounts of the Cincinnati china, see, for example, Alice Morse Earle's *China Collecting in America* (1924), 224-248.

To Governor [Brigadier-General] GEORGE CLINTON.

Mount Vernon, November 5, 1786

Dear Sir,

Not having heard, or not recollecting who the President of the Society of the Cincinnati in the State of New York[1] is, I take the liberty of giving you the trouble of the enclosed. . . .[2]

[*Collection of Edward Ambler Armstrong, Princeton, New Jersey*]

To Brigadier-General ELIAS DAYTON.

Mount Vernon, November 6, 1786.

Dear Sir,

Presuming you are Presidt. of the Society of the Cincinnati in the State of New Jersey,[3] I give you the trouble of the enclosed address.[4]—If I am mistaken, you will be so good as to hand it to the right person.—

Months ago, I received a number of blank Diplomas for my Signature, which was affixed & held in readiness for Mr. [John] Peck or his order.—No call has yet been [made] for them.—If a good conveyance should offer, I will forward them; but I am not much in the way of meeting this.—With great esteem and regard I am etc.

[*Huntington Library; copy in Washington's Letter Books*]

---

[1] At the time of this letter the Baron de Steuben was President of the New York Cincinnati and Brigadier-General (Governor) George Clinton its Vice-President. General Clinton succeeded the Baron de Steuben as President in 1794.

[2] The enclosure was General Washington's circular letter of 31 October 1786 (see page 264) anent not accepting further election as President General.

[3] General Dayton was President of the New Jersey Cincinnati at this time, being succeeded in 1808 by Major Joseph Bloomfield.

[4] This was General Washington's circular letter of 31 October 1786 (see page 264) about not being reelected President General.

Mount Vernon Novr. 5th. 1786

Dear Sir,

Not having heard, or not recollecting who the President of the Society of the Cincinnati in the State of New York is, I take the liberty of giving you the trouble of the inclosed.

I am endeavouring by the sale of Land, to raise money to pay for my Moiety of the purchase on the Mohawk River — So soon as this is effected I will write your Excellency more fully. In the mean time, with every good wish for Mrs. Clinton and the rest of your family, in which Mrs. Washington cordially unites.

I am Dear Sir
Yr. Most Obedt. and
Affecte. H'ble Servt.

G: Washington

His Excelly.
Govr. Clinton

General Washington's letter to the President of the New York Cincinnati.

[*Ambler Collection*]

To Major-General BENJAMIN LINCOLN.

Mount Vernon, November 7, 1786

My Dr. Sir,

I have seen, I think, your name as President of the Society of the Cincinnati in the State of Massachusetts.[1]—I therefore give you the trouble of the enclosed address. . . . [2]

[*Washington's Letter Books*]

To Major-General HORATIO GATES.

Mount Vernon, November 8, 1786.

Sir,

Expecting this letter will be handed to you in Richmond at the Meeting summoned to be holden there; you will please to receive the enclosure [3] in your double capacity of Vice President of the Genl. Meeting of the Society of the Cincinnati, & President of the said Society for this State.

I am Sir, etc.

[*Washington Papers*]

From Lieutenant-Colonel DAVID HUMPHREYS.

New Haven, Novr 9th. 1786

My dear General

I have this moment been honored with your letter of the 22nd of Octr.[4] I am thereby relieved from some anxiety for fear mine of the 24 of Septr.[5] had miscarried.—For the reasons

[1] General Lincoln was President of the Massachusetts Cincinnati from the time of its institution until succeeded in 1810 by Lieutenant John Brooks.

[2] The enclosure was the President General's circular letter about not being re-elected to that office.

[3] The enclosure was probably Washington's circular letter to the Presidents of the State Societies, dated 31 October 1786. Neither this letter nor the enclosure is in Fitzpatrick's *Writings of George Washington.* General Gates replied on 19 January 1787, see page 286.

[4] See page 256. [5] See page 254.

you mention, I think it will be best that the General Meeting of the Cincinnati should be holden at Philadelphia. I am happy that the enclosures have met with your approbation. . . .

[*Washington Papers*]

From Mr. THOMAS JEFFERSON.

Paris Nov. 14, 1786

Sir,—

. . . The author of the Political part of the Encyclopedie Methodique desired me to examine his article "Etats Unis." [1] I did so. I found it a tissue of errors, for in truth they know nothing about us here. Particularly however the article "Cincinnati" was a mere Phillipic against that institution; in which it appears that there was an utter ignorance of facts & motives. I gave him notes on it. He reformed it as he supposed & sent it again to me to revise. In this reformed state Colo. Humphreys saw it. I found it necessary to write that article for him. Before I gave it to him I showed it to the Marq. de la Fayette who made a correction or two. I then sent it to the author. He used the materials, mixing a great deal of his own with them. In a work which is sure of going down to the latest posterity, I thought it material to set facts to rights as much as possible. The author was well disposed: but could not entirely get the better of his original bias. I send you the article as ultimately published. If you find any material errors in it & will be so good as to inform me of them, I shall probably have opportunities of setting this author to rights. What has heretofore passed between us on this institution, makes it my duty to mention to you that I never heard a person in

[1] When writing his *Encyclopédie Méthodique*, M. Meusnier applied to Jefferson for information about the United States. On the proofs of that article Jefferson prepared lengthy notes. The article itself was separately printed. Jefferson's notes, incorporating his arguments that the Cincinnati was dangerous, are published in *Writings of Thomas Jefferson*, edited by Worthington Chauncey Ford, iv, 169-177. It was a copy of his notes, together with Meusnier's sketch, that Jefferson sent to General Washington in the above letter.

Europe, learned or unlearned, express his thoughts on this institution, who did not consider it dishonorable & destructive to our governments, and that every writing which has come out since my arrival here, in which it is mentioned, considers it, even as now reformed, as the germ whose developments is one day to destroy the fabric we have reared. I did not apprehend this while I had American ideas only. But I confess that what I have seen in Europe has brought me over to that opinion; & that tho' the day may be at some distance, beyond the reach of our lives perhaps, yet it will certainly come, when a single fibre of this institution will produce an hereditary aristocracy which will change the form of our governments from the best to the worst in the world. To know the mass of evil which flows from this fatal source, a person must be in France, he must see the finest soil, the finest climate, the most compact state, the most benevolent character of people, & every earthly advantage combined, insufficient to prevent this scourge from rendering existence a curse to 24 out of 25 parts of the inhabitants of this country. With us the branches of this institution cover all the states. The Southern ones at this time are aristocratical in their disposition: and that that spirit should grow & extend itself, is within the natural order of things. I do not flatter myself with the immortality of our governments; but I shall think little also of their longevity unless this germ of destruction be taken out. When the society themselves shall weigh the possibility of evil against the impossibility of any good to proceed from this institution, I cannot help hoping they will eradicate it. I know they wish the permanence of our governments as much as any individuals comprising them. An interruption here & the departure of the gentleman by whom I send this obliges me to conclude it, with assurances of the sincere respect & esteem with which I have the honor to be, Dear Sir, your most obedt. & most humble servt.

[*Jefferson Papers, Library of Congress*]

From Lieutenant-Colonel ANTOINE-FÉLIX WUIBERT DE MEZIÈRES.

Hispaniola Cap-français. 15. of November 1785

. . . .

P. S. Being one among he members of the Society of the Cincinnati, I do Stand in Need of the Engraved Patent or Diploma & the Silver medal of our Order, for Such piece Cannot be Dispensed With: the french do much Cavilling upon that Head. I do Belong to the Committee of the State of Pennsylvania. Pardon, General, Pardon, if I take upon mySelf to be So free & Give you So many Troubles [1]

Wbt.

[*Washington Papers*]

General WASHINGTON to the Virginia Cincinnati.

[Minutes of the Virginia Society, Richmond, 15 November, 1786]

A Letter addressed to the President, was laid before the Meeting from George Washington, Esq. President General of the Society, signifying his desire not to be again elected President General, on account of the variety of affairs to which he is under the necessity of attending, as well as of his present ill state of health; and expressive of his full and entire approbation of the principles of the Society, and of his readiness to sign the diplomas which should be offered by the members for that purpose; Whereupon

[1] Duplicates, dated 15 and 25 December 1785 are also to be found in the Washington Papers. The body of the letter is signed: "Colonel Wuibert, Cinctus of the Late Continental Corps of Engineers." The writer's s's are uniformly capitals, even in "myself" above.

Ordered, That Mr. Vice President,[1] Mr. McClurg, Mr. Eggleston, and Mr. Matthews, prepare and report to the Meeting tomorrow, an answer thereto.

[*Archives of the Virginia Cincinnati*]

The Committee of the Virginia Cincinnati prepared the following letter to General Washington, in response to his letter declining re-election as President General.

From Brigadier-General GEORGE WEEDON.

Richmond November 17th. 1786

Sir

Your circular Letter of the 31t. of October[2] having been communicated to the annual Meeting of the Virginia Cincinnati, they have directed me to assure you, that while they regret the loss the Society sustains by your relinquishing the Presidency, they are fully sensible of the justness of those motives which have determined your Retreat. They lament however, that to the causes which might have operated to produce this resolution before, is added a more afflicting one, the ill state of your health. They can never sufficiently express their gratitude for the patronage you afforded the Society in its insecure and infant state; and they trust that they shall never deviate from those principles of their constitution, which, as they procured your approbation, must dispel every idea of jelousy from the minds of the good people of these United States. They receive with pleasure the information of your being ready to sign Diplomas during your continuance in Office; As they apprehend those papers might lose much of their value, in the opinion of the members, if marked with any other signature—This circumstance induced them to wish that you could be

[1] The committee chosen to prepare the reply to President General Washington were: Brigadier-General John Peter Muhlenberg (Vice-President of the Virginia Cincinnati), Surgeon James McClurg, Major Joseph Eggleston, and Colonel George Mathews.

[2] See page 264.

prevailed upon, to sacrifice so much of your valuable time to the interests of the Institution, as might be necessary for this purpose, without subjecting yourself to any other duty of the Presidency; supposing that the other labours of the Office, might without inconvenience be transferrd to the Vice President of the Society.

I have the honor to be with much esteem
Your Ob[t]. Serv[t].
G. Weedon Pres[t].

George Washington Esq[r].
President General of The Society
of the Cincinnati
Mount Vernon
From
Gen[l]. Weedon
17th. Nov[r]. 1786 [*Washington Papers*]

General Washington having decided to decline reelection as President General of the Society of the Cincinnati, this nearly prevented his attending the Constitutional Convention, held in Philadelphia at the same time, for he did not want to offend his comrades of the Cincinnati by attending the Convention after declining to attend the General Meeting of the Cincinnati. This letter to the "Father of the Constitution" was the first of several that General Washington wrote on the subject. To the great good of his country he was at length persuaded to attend the Constitutional Convention, and his influence had much to do with the adoption of the Federal Constitution. He also attended the General Meeting of the Cincinnati and accepted reelection as President General, to the lasting good of the Order. (See E. E. Hume, The Rôle of the Society of the Cincinnati in the Birth of the Constitution, *Pennsylvania History*, April, 1938, v, 101-107.)

To Mr. JAMES MADISON.

Mount Vernon, 18 November, 1786

My dear Sir,

.... Although I had bid adieu to the public walks of life in a public manner, and had resolved never more to tread on public ground, yet if, upon an occasion so interesting to the well-being of the confederacy, it should have appeared to have been the wish of the Assembly to have employed me with other associates in the business of revising the federal system, I should, from a sense of the obligation I am under for the repeated proofs of confidence in me, more than from any opinion I should have entertained of my usefulness, have obeyed its call; but it is now out of my power to do this with any degree of consistence. The cause I will mention.

I presume you heard, Sir, that I was first appointed, and have since been rechosen, President of the Society of the Cincinnati; and you may have understood also, that the triennial general meeting of this body is to be held in Philadelphia the first Monday in May next. Some particular reasons combining with the peculiar situation of my private concerns, the necessity of paying attention to them, a wish for retirement and relaxation from public cares, and rheumatic pains which I begin to feel very sensibly, induced me on the 31st ultimo to address a circular letter to each State society, informing them of my intention not to be at the next meeting, and of my desire not to be rechosen President. The Vice-President is also informed of this, that the business of the Society may not be impeded in my absence. Under these circumstances it will readily be perceived, that I could not appear at the same time and place on any other occasion, without giving offense to a very worthy and respectable part of the community, the late officers of the American army. I feel as you do for our acquaintaance Colo. Lee; better never have delegates than left him out, unless some daring impropriety of conduct had been ascribed to him. I hear with pleasure that you are in the New choice.[1] With sentiments of the highest esteem and affection, I am, &c.[2]

G. W.

[*Washington's Letter Books*]

[1] "It is not very clear why Henry Lee was dropped from the Virginia delegation; but his supposed heterodoxy on the Mississippi question was mentioned as one reason. Jones, the delegate chosen, declined to serve, and Lee was unanimously named in his place" (Ford's *Writings of George Washington,* xi, 88 n.).

[2] Mr. Madison replied on 7 December 1786, see page 279.

To Dr. David Stuart.

Mount Vernon, November 19, 1786

Dear Sir,

I have been favoured with your letters of the 8th. & 13th. Instt.,[1] but not having sent to the Post office with my usual regularity, I did not receive them so soon as I might have done from the date of the former.

I thank you for the interesting communications in both.—It gives me sincere pleasure to find that the proceedings of the present Assembly are marked with wisdom, liberality & Justice.—These are the surest walks to public, & private happiness. The display of which by so respectable a part of the Union, at so important a crisis, will, I hope, be influential, and attended with happy consequences.

However delicate the revision of the federal system may appear, it is a work of indispensable necessity.—The present constitution is inadequate.—The superstructure totters to its foundation, and without helps, will bury us in its ruins.—Although I never more intended to appear on a public theatre, and had in a public manner bid adieu to public life; yet, if the voice of my Country had called me to this important duty, I might, in obedience to the repeated instances of its affection & confidence, have dispensed with these objections, but another now exists which would render my acceptance impracticable, with any degree of consistency—It is this

The triennial General Meeting of the Society of the Cincinnati is to be holden in Philadelphia the first Monday in May next.—Many reasons combining—some of a public, some of a private nature, to render it inpleasing, & inconvenient for me to attend it; I did on the 31st. ulto. address a circular letter to the State Societies, informing them of my intention not to be there, and desiring that I might no longer be chosen President.—The Vice Presidt. (Gates) has also been informed thereof, that the business of the meeting might not be impeded on acct. of my absence.—Under these circumstances, I could

[1] Neither of these letters concerns the Cincinnati. The former contains news of the session of the Virginia Legislature; the latter of the treaty with Spain.

not be in Philadelphia precisely at the same moment on another occasion, without giving offence to a worthy, & respectable part of the American community,—the late Officers of the American Army.

I will do as you advise with respect to the Certificates, & trouble you with them again.—Colo. Mason[1] it is said, expresses an inclination to give his attendance, but I question much his leavg. Gunston this Weat[her?]. . . .

[*Historical Society of Pennsylvania*]

To Don Diego de Gardoqui.

Mount Vernon, December 1, 1786

Sir,

I have had the honor to receive the letter which your Excellency did me the favor of writing to me on the 18th. ulto. together with the enclosure from the Prime minister of Spain, for which, and the translation, I pray you to accept my grateful thanks.— . . . .

Rheumatic pains, with which of late I have been a good deal afflicted, and some other causes, will render it inconvenient for me to be in Philada. in May next as seems to be expected, & where one of my first pleasures would have been to have paid my respects to your Excellency. . . .

[*Washington's Letter Books*]

Major L'Enfant's long overdue account against the Cincinnati again comes up.

From Major Pierre-Charles L'Enfant.

New York December 6th 1786.

Sir

the inclosed memorial which my actual circumstances has made necessary, rendering it useless I should enter here into

[1] Colonel George Mason of Gunston Hall.

any of the particular of its content I confine myself with requesting your Excellency will excuse the length of it. unable to be concise in an explanation where in it is essential to me to give account of the differents sensations which actuated me I have need of much Indulgence—and the good testimony of your Excellency being alone to persuad of my real principles in such an Extraordinary a conjuncture I claim its support with the more Confidence that I promise myself from your goodness as well as from the details which I take the liberty to submit to you that if in juging me after the event I am found culpable it will at any rate be only of too much Confidence and liberality and Convinced I did not bring myself into so unfortunate a situation but through a wish to give a truly brotherly proof of my affection to the interest of the Cincinnati—your Excellency being placed to apprise the valu of the sacrifices which I have made will do me the justice to believe that if I have not done honor to the Engagements which I have been induced to contract in france for the Cincinnati it has not been from a want of my own good will neither through fear that the incapacity of the fund, of the Society to reimburse would Expose me to remain the dupe of my advances.—had my fortune allowed me to make an immediate sacrifice or could the present State of my personal resources enable me to borrow a sum such as would be necessary to do honor to the principal to gether with the interest of the sum of the advances that have been made to me in france for the Society and also to reimburs the loans to which I have been forced to have recourse here I would not hesitate one moment to pay both the one and the other. a regard to myself as well as for the Society which it is my wish not to bring in to the question acting conjunctly would surely led me to that measure, but it is with regret I see that with personal means in view—the actual derangement of my affair however Cross my inclination so far has to oblige me to intrud upon your Excellency by a relation of facts which nothing but the necessity of exculpating myself from charges which seem authorised by my failure to discharge those engagements which by accident are become personal could only make me resolve to bring to light

doubtles I ought to have begun this address by an apology

for my apparant negligence in not having taken some opportunity during my residence here to have paid my respect to your Excellency agreable to the persuasion which you so complaisantly gave me—but full of the subject on which I have the honor to address you, it appeared most proper to explain my motives—and then Confiding in your Excellency sensibility of the cause which have taken from me the power of undertaking a journey to virginie I flatter myself your Excellency will remain persuaded that this dissappointment has not little added to the bittereness of many other unhappiness

With the most profound respect I have the honor to be etc.

P. S. a picture directed to your Excellency and which has been left to me, in the cours of last Sumner, by mr Senf Col in the service of the So carolina—has not been forwarded to your Excellency for want of direct opportunity by watter which had appeared to us to be the much proper way of conveyance I had proposed to myself being the bearer of it but circumstances not permitting I should if your Excellency will give me directions which way I may send it I will comply.[1]

[*Archives of the General Society*]

From Mr. James Madison.

Richmond Decr. 7. 1786

Dear Sir

Notwithstanding the communications in your favor of the 18th ulto.[2] which has remained till now unacknowledged, it was the opinion of every judicious friend whom I consulted, that your name could not be spared from the Deputation to the Meeting in May at Philadelphia. It was supposed in the first place, that the pecularity of the Mission, and its acknowledged

[1] Enclosed in this letter was a 40-page memorial from L'Enfant, addressed to Washington and dated 1 December 1786, stating his claims upon the Cincinnati. The memorial was read at the General Meeting of the Society, 12 May 1787. See Minutes of that meeting. General Washington replied on 1 January 1787, see page 285.

[2] See page 274.

pre-eminence over every other public object, may possible reconcile your undertaking it, with the respect which is justly due, & which you wish to pay to the late officers of the Army; and in the second place, that although you should find that or any other consideration an obstacle to your attendance on the service, the advantage of having your name in the front of the appointment as a mark of the earnestness of Virga. and an invitation to the most select characters from every part of the Confederacy, ought at all events to be made use of. In these sentiments I own I fully concurred, and flatter myself that they will at least apologize for my departure from those held out in your letter. I even flatter myself that they will merit a serious consideration with yourself, whether the difficulties which you enumerate ought not to give way to them. . . .

[*Autograph draft, James Madison Papers, Library of Congress*]

To Mr. JAMES MADISON.

Mount Vernon, 16 December, 1786

Dear Sir,

. . . Besides the reasons, which were assigned in my circular letter[1] to the several State societies of the Cincinnati, for my non-attendance at the next general meeting to be holden at Philadelphia on the first Monday in May next, there existed one, of a political nature, which operated stronger on my mind, than all others, and which in confidence I will now communicate to you.

When this Society was first formed, I am persuaded not a member of it conceived, that it would give birth to those jealousies, or be charged with those dangers, real or imaginary, with which the minds of many, and of some respectable characters in these States, seem to be agitated. The motives, which induced the officers to enter into it, were, I am positive, truly and frankly recited in the institution; one of which, and the

[1] Dated 31 October 1786, see page 264.

principal, was to establish a charatable fund for the relief of such of their compatriots, the widows and descendants of them, as were fit objects for such support, and for whom no public provision had been made by the public. But, the trumpet being sounded,[1] the alarm was spreading far and wide. I readily perceived, therefore, that, unless a modification of the plan could be affected (to annihilate the Society altogether was impracticable to account of the foreign officers who had been admitted), irritations would arise, which would soon draw a line between the Society and their fellow citizens.

To avoid this, to conciliate the affections, and to convince the world of the purity of the plan, I exerted myself, and with much difficulty effected the changes, which appeared in the recommendation that proceeded from the general meeting of those of individual States. But the accomplishment of it was not easy; and I have since heard, that, while some States have acceded to the recommendation, others are not disposed to do so, alleging that unreasonable prejudices, and ill-founded jealousies, ought not to influence a measure laudable in its institution, and salutary in its objects and operation.

Under these circumstances it may readily be concerved, that the part I should have had to have acted would have been delicate. On the one hand, I might be charged with dereliction of the officers, who had nobly supported me, and had even treated me with uncommon attention and attachment; on the other, with supporting a measure incompatible with republican principles. I thought it best, therefore, without assigning this (the principal) reason, to decline the presidency and to excuse my attendance on the ground, which is firm and just, of necessity of attending to my private concerns, and in conformity to my determination of spending the remainder of my days in a state of retirement; and to indisposition occasioned by rheumatic complaints with which at times I am a good deal afflicted; professing at the same time my entire approbation of the institution as altered, and the pleasure I feel at the subsidence

[1] The phrase "the trumpet being sounded" refers to Judge Ædanus Burke's pamphlet attacking the Cincinnati. On the title-page was the passage from the Bible, "Blow ye the Trumpet in Zion." See page xv.

of those jealousies, which have yielded to the change, *presuming* on the general adoption of it.

I have been thus particular, to show, that, under circumstances like these, I should feel myself in an awkward situation to be in Philadelphia on another public occasion, during the sitting of this Society. That the present moment is pregnant of great and strange events, none who will cast their eyes around them can deny. What may be brought forth between this and the first of May, to remove the difficulties, which at present labor in my mind against the acceptance of the honor, which has lately been conferred on my by the Assembly, is not for me to predict; but I should think it incompatible with that candor, which ought to characterize an honest mind, not to declare, that, under my present view of the matter, I should be too much embarrassed by the meeting of these two bodies in the same place at the same moment, after what I have written to be easy in my situation, and therefore that it would be improper to let my appointment stand in the way of another. . . .

[*Washington's Letter Books*]

To Lieutenant-Colonel David Humphreys.

Mount Vernon, 26 December, 1786.

My Dr. Humphreys:

. . . I had scarce despatched my circular letters[1] to the several State Societies of the Cincinnati, when I received letters from some of the principal members of our [Virginia] Assembly, expressing a wish, that they might be permitted to name me as one of the deputies of this State to the convention proposed to be held at Philadelphia the first of May next. I immediately wrote to my particular friend Mr. Madison, and gave similar reasons to the others. My answer is contained in the extract No. 1; in reply I got the extract No. 2. This obliges me to be more explicit and confidential with him on points which a recurrence to the conversations we have had on this

[1] Dated 31 October 1786, see page 264.

subject will bring to your mind and save me the hazard of a recital in this letter. Since this interchange of letters I have received from the Governor the letter No. 4 and have written No 5 in answer to it. Should this matter be further pressed, (which I hope it will not, as I have no inclination to go), what had I best do? You, as an indifferent person, and one who is much better acquainted with the sentiments &d views of the Cincinnati than I am (for in this State, where the recommendations of the general meeting have been agreed to, hardly anything is said about it), as also with the temper of the people and the state of politics at large, can determine upon better ground and fuller evidence than myself; especially as you have opportunities of knowing in what light the States to the eastward consider the convention; & the measures they are pursuing to contravene or give efficiency to it. On the last occasion, only five States were represented, none East of New York. . . .

[*Washington's Letter Books*]

FROM THE VIRGINIA CINCINNATI.

Sir

Your Excell^{cys} Letter of 31st of Oct. [1786] [1] having been laid before the State Meeting of Cincinni. they have directed me to assure you that while the regret exceed^{y} your determin^{s}. to—

They are throughly satisfied of the justice of your reasons for this Determint.

They are afflicted to know that the reasons which might have operated before is added the ill state of yr. health.

They are suffic^{y} sensible of the sacrifice you made of your tranquill^{y} & favority pursuits to their Society estabd. in great measure by your patronage. Trust they shall never deviate from thos principles, which attracted your Approbation.

Are gratified to hear that the Diplomata will continue to be signed by your Excelly for a certain period as their value

[1] See page 264.

might diminish in the eyes of the Members if they had any other Signature.[1]

[Endorsed on back of sheet]

(Trial letter to G. Washington regretting his resignation from the Presidency)

[*Archives of the Virginia Cincinnati*]

To Brigadier-General GEORGE WEEDON.

Dear Sir,

I have been favored with your official letter of the   ulto.[2] in answer to my circular one of the 31st. October; but will you permit me, in a private & friendly manner, to ask if my letter[3] or a copy of it has been sent to the vice President, General Gates? You would have perceived that that letter was intended to have met him in the double capacity of President of the State Society, & Vice President of the Genl. Meeting. In the former case, as he did not attend the State Meeting in Richmond, it was unnecessary that he should be furnished with a copy of it;—but as Vice President he ought to be made acquainted with my intention of not attending the latter—the reasons therefore of this inquiry is, that if it has not been by the State Society, I may do it from hence—

I should be glad to know the names of the Delegates from this State to the general Meeting to be held in May next at Philada.

I shall be ready at all times between this and the appointment of my Successor, to sign any Diplomas which may be presented to me; but it will be readily occur to you that after this event takes place my powers wou'd cease, & the signature would be invalid.—

With great esteem &c
I am
G. Washington

Mount Vernon
29th. Decr. 1786

[*Washington's Letter Books*]

[1] The Minutes of the Virginia Society for November 17, 1786, give another and more complete version of this letter.

[2] See draft, page 283.

[3] See page 269.

General Washington writes L'Enfant regretting that he should have got into financial difficulties through expenditures for the Cincinnati, but hints that L'Enfant exceeded the authority given him (see General Washington's letter of instructions, 30 October 1783, page 285).

To Major PIERRE-CHARLES L'ENFANT.

Mount Vernon, Jan. 1, 1787

Sir,

The Letter which you did me the honor of writing to me the 6th. ulto.[1] together with the Memorial which accompanied it came safe, after some delay.—

Without entering into the merits of the latter, which I could only do as an individual, I shall regret that your zeal for the honor, & your wishes to advance what you conceived to be the interests of the Society of the Cincinnati, should have led you into difficulties which are attended with such embarrassing circumstances, & from which none but the general meeting (to be held at Philada. in May next) can afford you relief.— It shall be my care to hand the Memorial to that body for consideration.—. . .

[*Washington's Letter Books*]

From the MARQUIS DE LA FAYETTE.

Paris, January 13, 1787

. . . You have heard mention of a certain Beniowski[2] who wished to command a legion in our army, and who, since then, engaged in an expedition to Madagascar in which, despite my

[1] See page 277.

[2] Maurice August Beniowski was born of Polish descent in Hungary in 1741. He took part in the first Polish war for freedom, and being captured by the Russians in 1769, was exiled to Kamchatka with other Polish prisoners. He escaped and reached France in 1772. He later induced the French government to send him with an expedition to Madagascar where he won the confidence of the natives who made him "king," but disagreeing with the French he returned to France. He took part in the War of the Bavarian Succession as a Colonel of Austrian Hussars. At the beginning of the American Revolution he embarked for America but was captured by the British and was imprisoned

advice to the contrary, certain merchants of Baltimore have invested funds. Beniowski pillaged the French establishment at Madagascar. Some men were sent from l'Ile-de-France to attack him, and he was killed. I shall go to Versailles and ask the minister to send back to the United States the Americans who may be there; for I hear among the prisoners there is one wearing the decoration of the Cincinnati. The entire force of Beniowski did not exceed forty white men. . . .

[La Fayette, *Mémoires*, II, *192*]

General Gates, Vice-President General, like all other members, regrets General Washington's desire not to be reelected President General.

From Major-General HORATIO GATES.

Travellors Rest

19th. January, 1787

Sir

By the last Alexandria Post I had the Honour to receive your Excellencys Letter of the 8th. of November,[1] inclosing your Circular Letter of the 31st. of October.[2] I am truly sorry Your

at Portsmouth. After escaping thrice, and being each time recaptured, he finally managed to gain his freedom through the intervention of the Count d'Almadovar, and, arriving in America, joined the Count Pułaski to whom he was related. Unfortunately for him Pułaski was killed a few days later. Beniowski's plan to organize a legion of Germans for a consideration of 518,000 *livres* (about $100,000) was not accepted by the Continental Congress, possibly because there was no liking for German mercenaries. He was never commissioned in the service of the United States. He returned to France and tried without success to induce the Count de Vergennes to accept a scheme for the colonization of Madagascar, and thereupon went again to America in 1784. In October of that year he sailed with an American ship, the *Intrepid*, for the island, under circumstances stated in La Fayette's letter. There he tried to overthrow the French authorities and was killed in an encounter with French troops on 23 May 1786. He became a popular hero in Polish literature, particularly in the poems of Julius Slowacki. The name of his companion who La Fayette heard was a member of the Cincinnati is not known. (E. E. Hume, *La Fayette and the Society of the Cincinnati*, 1934, 43 n.)

[1] See page 269.

[2] See footnote, page 264.

Excellency Declines the Presidency of The Cincinnati, as I conceive your continuing at the Head of the Society, indispensibly necessary to the Support of The Order. The very high consideration, and Respect, in which the whole Continent agree to place Your Excellency, is absolutely requisite, to defeat the ungenerous Designs of the Enemies of the Order from prevailing against it.—I am happy to find that in this Critical Hour, The Legislature have thought proper to call upon Your Excellency, to step forth to Rescue us from Anarchy, by placing you at the Head of that Committee, which is to meet the 2^{d}. of May, in Philadelphia; this is so important a Station & the Crisis which calls for it so alarming; that I will not believe Your Excellencys Patriotism, & High Regard for Civil Liberty, will permit you to Decline it; you will there Sir, be upon the Spot, where the Representatives of the Cincinnati so Ardently desire to see their President. I think with Your Excellency, that the Malevolence, & Illiberal Jealousy, which attacked The Order is in great measure done away, and good Men are ashamed it ever was countenanced.—Unconnected, & unsupported, I cannot think of being even for a day, placed at the Head of The Institution; For unless You Excellency continues there The Dignity of The Order will be Diminished. Heaven Grant that may not be a prelude to the Greatest Misfortune that can befall a Free People.—With the Sincerest Sentiments of the Highest Consideration, & Respect,

I have The Honor to be
Sir
Your most Obedient
Humble Servant

Horatio Gates

His Excellency
George Washington Esqr.
President of The Cincinnati.

[*Washington Papers*]

The persistent Joseph Mandrillon tries again to obtain the Eagle of honorary membership in the Cincinnati.

From M. Joseph Mandrillon.

Amsterdam 24 Janvr. 1787

Monsieur

Le 24 Octobre dernier,[1] j'ai eu l'honneur d'envoyer à Votre Excellence Un mémoire contenant ma Soumission rélative à la résolution de la prochaine assemblée générale de Cincinnatus. Je suis rempli d'espérance, puisque c'est sous les auspices respectables de Votre Excellence que la proposition Se fera, Savoir Si l'on peut m'admettre. Mr. Le marquis de la Fayette m'écrit que je ne Saurois avoir dans l'assemblée un plus grand protecteur que vous, Monsieur, puisque vous en êtes le président. Quoiqu'il en Soit, Si absolument les Statuts de la Société S'oppose à mon élection comme membre honnoraire, Je prie, Votre Excellence, d'être persuadée, que je n'en aurai pas moins le même zele, et le même desir de travailler à m'instruire Sur les interêts des 13 Républiques et pas moins d'empressement à publier le triomphe, la gloire,—& les exemples de Sagesse que l'Amérique offre à l'Europe.

Votre Excellence Sait qu'un écrivain est toujours insatiable quand il a besoin de renseignemens Sur une matiere qu'il veut traiter: Elle me pardonnera Sans doute la demande que je fais *d'une liste exacte des membres de la Société,* et tout ce qui a rapport *à Sa constitution et à Ses Statuts.* J'ai deja plusieurs objets intéressans mais ils ne me Suffisent pas, et je n'attends que ces Supplemens—pour terminer le nouvel ouvrage que je me propose de publier.

L'Europe est actuellement occupée du nouveau monument de gloire que la justice vous reservoit, Monsieur, en ornant votre heureuse patrie de la Statue de Votre Excellence: permettez moi de lui donner ici copie d'une lettre intéressante inserrée dernierement dans *le journal de Paris,* Je me suis empressé d'y répondre, et de payer publiquement à Votre Excellence un nouveau tribut de mon respect & de mon admiration Si le Sentiment Suffisoit pour Savoir bien dire, assurément personne n'auroit mieux réussi que moi à faire une belle inscription: mais avec le Sentiment il faut des talens bien Supérieurs, et je

[1] See footnote to translation.

n'ai malheureusement que beaucoup de zele: reçevez-donc, Monsieur, et cette pièce de vers, et cette inscription avec indulgence et bonté.

En rappellant à Votre Excellence qu'elle est mon héros,—que je porte Sans cesse Son image Sur moi, & que je m'estime heureux d'avoir pu l'intéresser un instant.

J'ai l'honneur d'être avec l'admiration la plus parfaite etc.[1]

[*Archives of the General Society*]

[Contemporary Translation]

Amsterdam 24th. Jany. 1787-

Sir

The 24th. October last,[2] I had the honor to send your Excellency a memorial containing my entire submission to any resolution of the next General Meeting of the Cincinnati—Since it is under the respectable auspices of your Excellency that the proposition is made, I am filled with the hope of hearing that I am admitted—

The Marquis de la Fayette has written to me, that I could not have in the General Meeting a greater Protector than yourself, Sir, as you are the President—Be it as it may, if the statutes of the Society are absolutely against my election as an Honorary Member[3] I beg your Excellency to be persuaded, that I shall not have the less Zeal for and desire to be instructed in the Interests of the thirteen Republics nor be less impressed with the design of publishg. the Triumphs, the Glory and the Examples of Wisdom which America offers the admiration of Europe—Your Excellency knows how anxious a Writer is, who has need of information on a Subject he wishes to treat of. I hope for pardon then for the Request I must make, of *an Exact list of the Members of the Society,* and every thing respectg. *its Constitution and Statutes.* I have already many interesting objects, but

[1] See also Mandrillon's letter of 22 August 1785, page 231.

[2] This letter is neither in the Washington Papers nor the Archives of the General Society of the Cincinnati.

[3] Mandrillon was not made an honorary member as he several times requested.

as they are not sufficient, I only wait for those documents to finish the new work which I propose to publish—Europe is now attentive to the new Monument of glory which justice has reserved for you Sir, in adorning your happy Country with the Statue of Your Excellency—permit me to give herewith a Copy of an interesting letter inserted lately in the *Paris Journal,* I feel myself impressed with a desire to answer it, and to offer publicly to Your Excellency a new tribute of my respect and admiration—Were my Abilities equal to the Task I should most certainly would have written a *handsome* Inscription:—but, unfortunately, superior talents are wanting, I have Only the Wish & a Great Share of Zeal: Receive then Sir: these Verses and the Inscription with kindness and indulgence—Reminding your Excellency that he is my Hero, His image is ever before me, and I shall esteem myself happy if I interest him for a moment. I have the honor to be with the most perfect admiration etc.[1]

[*Archives of the General Society*]

General Washington writes the Secretary General of the Cincinnati that against his will he had been elected one of the Virginia delegates to the Constitutional Convention in May 1787 and persists in his intention not to attend the General Meeting of the Cincinnati at the same date. He, in the end, attended both.

To Major-General HENRY KNOX.

Mount Vernon, February 3, 1787

My dear Sir,

I feel my self exceedingly obliged to you for the full, & friendly communications in your letters of the 14th. 21st. & 25th. ult;[2] and shall (critically as matters are described in the latter) be extremely anxious to know the issue of the Movements of the forces that were assembling, the one to support, the other to oppose the constitutional rights of Massachusetts.—. . .

[1] No attempt has been made to reproduce the numerous words crossed out in this contemporary translation. The poem is not in the Archives.

[2] These three letters do not concern the Cincinnati, but tell of the insurrection in Massachusetts.

In your letter of the 14th. you express a wish to know my intention respecting the Convention, proposed to be held at Philada. in May next.—In *confidence* I inform you, that it is not, at this time, my purpose to attend it.—When this matter was first moved in the Assembly of this State, some of the principal characters of it wrote to me, requesting to be permitted to put my name in the delegation.—To this I objected—They again pressed, and I again refused; assigning among other reasons my having declined meeting the Society of the Cincinnati at that place, about the same time,—& that I thought it would be disrespectful to that body (to whom I ow'd much) to be there on any other occasion.—Notwithstanding these intimations, my name was inserted in the Act; and an official communication thereof made by the Executive to me, to whom, at the same time that I expressed my sense of the confidence reposed in me, I declared, that as I saw no prospect of my attending, it was my wish that my name might not remain in the delegation, to the exclusion of another.—To this, I have been requested, in emphatical terms, not to decide absolutely, as no inconvenience would result from the non-appointment of another, at least for some time.—Thus the matter stands, which is the reason of my saying to you in *confidence* that at present I retain my first intention—not to go. In the meanwhile as I have the fullest conviction of your friendship for, and attachment to me;—know your abilities to judge;—and your means of information,—I shall receive any communications from you, respecting this business, with thankfulness.—My first wish it to do for the best, and to act with propriety; and you know me too well, to believe that reserve or concealment of any circumstance or opinion, would be at all pleasing to me.—. . .[1]

[*Massachusetts Historical Society*]

---

[1] The Minutes of the General Meeting of 1787, Monday, May 14, contain this paragraph: "A letter from General Washington, stating the causes which may probably prevent his attending the present general meeting, accompanied with a bundle of papers which were committed to the secretary, *pro tem,* to be indorsed and arranged previous to their being read."

Brigadier Duplessis is usually confused with Colonel Mauduit Duplessis, who returned to France in 1778 and never revisited America. The Brigadier was admitted to membership in the Georgia Cincinnati as he here writes to General Washington.

From Brigadier JEAN-BAPTISTE VIGNOURNIN DUPLESSIS.

Savannah, 12, fevre. 1787.

Monsieur

pendant que J'étois agonisant, le 19. 8bre. dernier Le general MacIntosh, d'aprés la lettre que vous lui aves écrit, et la demande que lui en a fait Mr. Le Comte d'Estaing, a cause qu'une assemblée extraordinaire, à la quelle J'ay eté admis a la Société de Cincinnatus, et le general Mc. Intosh y a mis toute la grace imaginable. vous sentes, combien Je suis reconnoissant, a votre Excellence, del'honneur que J'ay reçu de mon admission, et que je lui raporte en entier. . . .

[*Washington Papers*]

[Contemporary Translation]

Savannah 12th. Feby 1787

Sir,

While I lay sick I sent for Genl. McIntosh & gave him the letter which you wrote to him, as well as that of the Count de Estaing—in consequence, an extraordinary meeting was called in which I was admitted into the Society of the Cincinnati; [1] General McIntosh showed me every attention imaginable. Think what obligations I am under to your Excellency for the honor which I have received by my admission!—. . .

[*Washington Papers*]

---

[1] Colonel de Mauduit Duplessis, with whom this officer is often confused, was an original member of the Society to the Cincinnati of France.

This letter, from the son of Baron de Kalb who fell at the battle of Camden, is one of the earliest from an hereditary member of the Society of the Cincinnati in France.

From Lieutenant the BARON DE KALB.

Alsace, 3rd March 1787

General:

I have just received the honor of the Order of Cincinnatus, which is conferred on those who have distinguished themselves in the service of America.

You honor me with it as heir of an unfortunate and respected parent.

I return you my warmest acknowledgements for it and wish the distance of your country did not prevent me from paying my respects to you personally.

I am,

Your humble and obedient servant,

Frédéric de Kalb

[*Washington's Letter Books*]

The committee of the Pennsylvania Cincinnati reply to the President General's circular letter anent his reelection.

From Colonel THOMAS MCKEAN, Major WILLIAM JACKSON and Lieutenant-Colonel FRANCIS MENTGES.

Philadelphia March 6. 1787.

Dear General,

In obedience to a resolve of the Standing Committee of the Pennsylvania Society of the Cincinnati, we do ourselves the honor to inform your Excellency that your circular letter of the 31st. of October last,[1] addressed to the President of our State-Society, was laid before the Committee at their last meeting.

They desire to communicate their respectful thanks for the

[1] See page 264.

early information which you have been pleased to give of the triennial general-meeting—and to express, with heartfelt concern, their regret at the necessity, which induces your desire not to be re-elected to the Presidency.

While they admit the cogency of those reasons which are assigned for your determination—they lament, with the sorrow of sincere affection, that impaired health should be numbered among them—and they prefer the prayer of grateful regard for its speedy restoration.

Your Excellency's wishes will be intimated to our Delegates to the general-meeting—and your letter will be laid before a Meeting of the State-Society which is called on the 26th. instant.

With profound respect and attachment We have the honor to be etc.

[*Washington Papers*]

Again the President General writes of his hesitation about attending the Constitutional Convention, having previously declined attending the General Meeting of the Society of the Cincinnati.

To Major-General HENRY KNOX.

Mount Vernon, 8th March 1787

. . . I am directly and delicately pressed to attend this Convention [to frame the Constitution of the United States]. Several reasons are opposed to it in my mind; and not the least, having declined attending the General Meeting of the Cincinnati, which is to be held in Philadelphia at the same time, on account of the disrespect it might seem to offer to that Society were to attnd on another occasion.[1]

[*Washington's Letter Books*]

General Washington explains to Judge Mercer that his desire to attend neither the Constitutional Convention nor the General Meeting of the Society of the Cincinnati arose from his wish to retire from public life.

[1] General Knox replied on 19 March 1787, see page 296.

To Judge JAMES MERCER.

Mount Vernon, March 15, 1787

Dear Sir,

Your favor of the 10th.[1] came duly to hand, and with very sincere concern I read the acct. of your ill health; but if your other complaints have left you, the Asthma, though troublesome & distressing, is not a dangerous one; I will hope therefore that the agreeable season which is fast approaching, will perfect restore you good health. . . .

However desirous I am, & always shall be, to comply with any commands of my Country, I do not conceive that I can, with consistent conduct, attend the proposed Convention to be holden in Philadelphia in May next.—For besides the declaration which I made in a very solemn manner when I was about to retire, of bidding adieu to all public employment; I had just before the appointment of delegates to this Convention, written and dispached circular letters to the several State Societies of the Cincinnati informing them of my intention not to attend the General Meeting which was to take place about the same time and in the same City.—and assigned reasons which apply as forcibly in the one case as the other.—Under these circumstances, to attend the Convention might be considered disrespectful to a worthy set of men for whose attachment and support on many trying occasions, I shall ever feel the highest gratitude & affection.—. . . .

[*Collection of Major-General Preston Brown, U. S. A., Vice-President of the New Hampshire Cincinnati*]

General Knox, as Secretary General, seeks to disssuade General Washington from declining reelection as President General.

[1] This letter is not in the Washington Papers nor in the Archives of the Cincinnati.

From Major-General HENRY KNOX.

New York 19 March 1787

My dear Sir

I have the satisfaction of acknowledging the receipt of your favor of the 8th[1] which I received on the 17th instant. . . .

I have never written to you concerning Your intention of declining to accept again the presidency of the Cincinnati—I can only say that the idea afflicts me exceedingly—

That the Society was formed with pure motives you well know—In the only instance in which it has had the least political operation, the effects have been truly noble. I mean in Massachusetts where the officers are still unpaid and extremely depressed in their private circumstances, but notwithstanding which the moment the government was in danger, they unanimously pledged themselves for its Support—While the few wretched officers who were against government were not of the Cincinnati. The clamor and prejudice which existed against it, are no more—The men who have been most against it Say, that the Society is the only bar to lawless ambition and dreadful anarchy to which the imbecillity of government, renders us so liable, and the same men express their apprehensions of your resignation.

Could I have the happiness of a private conversation with you, I think I could offer you such reasons, as to induce you to suspend your decision for another period of three years. Suffer me then my dear Sir, to entreat that you would come to Philadelphia one week earlier, than you would be in order to attend the convention, and to chear the hearts of your old military friends with your presence—This would rivet their affections and entirely remove your embarrassment in this respect of attending the convention

God who knows my heart, knows that I would not solicit this step, were I of opinion that your reputation would suffer the least injury by it—I fully beleive that it would not—But I believe that should you attend the convention and not meet the

[1] See page 294.

Cincinnati, that it would sorely wound your sincere friends and please those who dare not avow themselves your enemies

With affectionate respects to Mrs Washington I am my dear Sir etc.

[*Washington Papers*]

General Washington's former military secretary writes him that he is likely to be reelected President General at the General Meeting of May 1787, whether he wishes it or not. That is what happened.

From Lieutenant-Colonel DAVID HUMPHREYS.

New Haven March 24th. 1787

My dear General

I have but just had the pleasure to receive your two favours of the 18th. of Feby. and 8th instant. . . .[1]

Notwithstanding your circular letter to the Cincinnati, I think it probable the General Meeting will re-elect you President—I hope they will—for matters, I am confident, will in some way or another work right before all is over. . . .

[*Washington Papers*]

General Washington at length agrees to be one of Virginia's delegates to the Constitutional Convention, and writes the Governor that he will likewise attend the General Meeting of the Society of the Cincinnati.

To Governor EDMUND [JENNINGS] RANDOLPH.

Mount Vernon, 28 March, 1787

Dear Sir,

Your favor of the 11th[2] did not come to my hand till the 24th, and since then till now I have been too much indisposed to acknowledge the receipt of it.

[1] Neither letter can be found.

[2] This letter, in the Historical Society of Pennsylvania, refers to General Washington's refusal of the appointment because of conflict with other arrangements.

To what cause to ascribe the detention of the letter I know not as I never omit sending once and often twice a week to the post office in Alexandria. It was the decided intention of the letter I had the honor of writing to your Excellency the 21st of December[1] last to inform you, that it was not convenient for me to attend he convention proposed to be holden at Philadelphia in May next; and I had entertained hopes, that another had been, or soon would be appointed in my place, inasmuch as it is not only inconvenient for me to leave home, but because there will be, I apprehend, too much cause to arraign my conduct with inconsistency in again appearing on a public theatre, after a public declaration to the contrary, and because it will, I fear, have a tendency to sweep me back into the tide of public affairs, when retirement and ease is so essentially necessary for and is so much desired by me.

However, as my friends, with a degree of solicitude which is unusual, seem to wish for my attendance on this occasion, have come to a resolution to go, if my health will permit, provided from the lapse of time between the date of your Excellency's letter and this reply the executive may not (the reverse of which would be highly pleasing to me) have turned their thoughts to some other character; for, independently of all other considerations, I have of late been much afflicted with a rheumatic complaint in my shoulder that at times I am hardly able to raise my hand to my head, or turn myself in bed. This consequently might prevent my attendance, and eventually a representation of the State, which would afflict me sensibly that the disorder that occasioned it.

If, after the expression of these sentiments, the executive should consider me as one of the delegates, I would thank your Excellency for the earliest advice of it; because, if I am able and should go to Philadelphia, I shall have some previous arrangement to make, and would set off for that place the 1st or 2d of May, that I might be there in time to account personally for my conduct to the general meeting of the Cincinnati, which is to convene the first Monday of that month. My feelings would be much hurt, if that body should otherwise ascribe my

[1] This letter, in the Washington Papers, urges General Washington to be a delegate to the Constitutional Convention.

attending the one and not the other occasion to a disrespectful inattention to the Society, when the fact is, that I shall ever retain the most lively and affectionate regard for the members of which it is composed, on account of their attachment to me and uniform support of many trying occasions, as well as on account of their public virtues, patriotism, and sufferings.

I hope your Excellency will be found among the *attending* delegates. I should be glad to be informed who the others are; and cannot without once more and in emphatical terms praying, that, if there is not a *decided* representation in *prospect* without me, another may be chosen in my room without ceremony and without delay, for the reason already assigned. For it would be unfortunate, indeed, if the State, which was the mover of this convention, should be unrepresented in it.

With great respect, I have the honor to be your Excellency's most obedient servant,

G°. Washington

[*Washington's Letter Books*]

General Washington, having accepted the office of a delegate to the Constitutional Convention, 1787, writes the Secretary General that he will likewise be present at the General Meeting of the Cincinnati.

To Major-General HENRY KNOX.

Mount Vernon, 2d April 1787

My dear Sir,

. . . If I should attend the Convention, I will be in Philadelphia previous to the meeting of the Cincinnati, where I shall hope and expect to meet you, and some others of my particular friends, the day before, in order that I may have a free and unreserved conference with you on the subject of it; for I assure you this is, in my estimation, a business of delicate nature.

That the design of the Institution was pure, I have not a particle of doubt; and it may be so still, is perhaps equally unquestionable; but *quære,* Are not the substance of the jealousies of it to be ascribed to the modification which took place at the last General Meeting? Are not these rejected *in toto* by some of the State societies, and partially acceeded to by others? Has any State so far overcome its prejudices as to grant a charter? Will the modifications and alterations be insisted on or given up in the next meeting? If the first, will it not occasion warmths and divisions? If the latter, and I should remain at the head of this Order, in what light would my signature appear in contradictory recommendations? In what light would the versitility appear to foreign members, who perhaps are acting agreeably to the recommendations of the last General Meeting?

These, and other matters which may be agitated, will, I fear, place me in a disagreeable prediciment if I should preside, and were among the causes which induced me to decline the honor of it, previously to the meeting. . . .[1]

[*Archives of the Massachusetts Cincinnati*]

The Assistant Secretary General, fearing that General Washington would not alter his decision to decline reelection as President General, hastens to send him diplomas for his signature while yet in office. Some of these diplomas, signed in blank by General Washington, were used after his death.

From Major GEORGE TURNER.

New York, April 5th. 1787

Sir,

At the Request of the Cincinnati of South-Carolina, I have the honour to forward herewith, for the Favour of your Excellency's Signature, an Hundred and two Diplomas. The Box containing them, encloses, also, a Return of the Members for whom they are intended: The additional Diplomas are meant for those who may chuse to have Duplicates; excepting one,

[1] The text in Washington's Letter Books is somewhat different. General Knox replied on 9 April 1787, see page 302.

which is designed for Lieutenant-Colonel Langborn, now abroad.

As the Society of that State have expressed an anxious Desire to be honoured with your Name, Sir, as their President, I feel equally anxious to lay these Diplomas before your Excellency in due Time to obtain it.

May I request to have them returned to me here by some safe Conveyance, addressed to *George Turner in New York* (and, lest I may be absent) *To the Care of the honorable William Grayson in Congress.*[1]

With the greatest Respect, Sir, I have the honour to be etc.

P. S. The Box goes to the Care of Doctor [James] Craig at Alexandria[2]

[*Washington Papers*]

From Lieutenant-Colonel DAVID HUMPHREYS.

(Private)

Fairfield [Conn.] April 9th 1787.

My dear General.

Since I did myself the honor to address you on the 24th Ulto.[3] I have been in New York, & find such a variety of opinions prevailing with respect to the Convention, that I think it expedient to write to you again on the subject.

General Knox has shewn to me, in confidence, his last letter to you. tho' I cannot concur in Sentiments altogether, yet I think with him, should you decide to be present at the Convention, it will be indispensable to arrive in Philadelphia the preceding week, in order to attend the Genl Meeting of the Cincinnati. This may palliate, perhaps, obviate one of my former objections. . . .

[1] Colonel William Grayson, original member of the Virginia Cincinnati, was a member of the Continental Congress at this time. He was one of the first two Senators from Virginia under the Constitution.

[2] General Washington replied on 26 April 1787, see page 304.

[3] See page 297.

I imagine there will be no representation for this State at the Genl Meeting of the Cincinnati unless I attend myself.[1] Should I be disengaged from military affairs in season, I shall probably come on, & may pass the summer at Mt. Vernon. But every thing depends upon contingencies. . . .

[*Washington Papers*]

From Major-General HENRY KNOX.

New York 9 April 1787.

My dear Sir

I thank your for your kind favor of the second instant[2] which I received by the last post. . . .

Your ideas respecting the proceedings of some of the State Societies of the Cincinnati are but too just—I will most chearfully meet you in Philadelphia, at any time previous to the meeting that you may think proper, in order to discuss and fully consider this subject

The French packet has just arrived, by which I have a letter from the Marquis de la Fayette of the 7th of February

The Count de Vergennes is dead, and will probably be succeeded by the Duke de Vauguyon

The Marquis looks forward to military imployment in this Country for the reduction of the Western posts, and Canada

But one might venture to predict that no such operations will be undertaken, un[till][3] the government shall be radically amen[ded][3] At present we are all imbecility—I am my dear sir etc.

[*Washington Papers*]

---

[1] Colonel Humphreys was the only delegate of the Connecticut Cincinnati present at the opening of the General Meeting of 1787. Major-General Samuel Holden Parsons arrived in time to attend the later sessions. The other three Connecticut delegates, Colonel Jeremiah Wadsworth, Lieutenant Ralph Pomeroy and Dr. Ezra Stiles (President of Yale College) were absent.

[2] See page 300.

[3] The portions inserted in square brackets are supplied by the transcriber, because the ends of these lines are clipped short.

To Governor EDMUND [JENNINGS] RANDOLPH.

Mount Vernon, April 9th, 1787.

My dear Sir,

In reply to your favor of the 2d [1] I have to request that you will not be at the trouble of forwarding any money to me from the treasury.

If I should attend the Service, it will suit me as well to receive it from you in Philadelphia as at this place. If I should not, I have no business with it at all.

It gives me pleasure to find by your letter that there will be so full a representation from this State—If the case had been otherwise I would in emphatical terms have urged again that, rather than depend upon my going, another might be chosen in my place; for as a friend, and in confidence, I declare to you that my assent is given contrary to my judgment, because the act will, I apprehend, be considered as inconsistent with my public declaration dilivered in a solemn manner at an interesting era in my life, never more to intermeddle in public matters.—This declaration not only stands on the files of Congress, but is I believe registered in almost all the gazettes and magazines that are published—and what adds to the embarrassment is, I had previous to my appointment informed by circular letter the several State Societies of the Cincinnati of my intention to decline the Presidency of that order & excuse myself from attending the next General meeting at Philadelphia on the first Monday in May assigning reasons for so doing which apply as well in the one case as the other. Add to these, I very much fear that all the States will not appear in Convention, and that some of them will come fettered so as to impede rather than accelerate the great object of their convening; which, under the peculiar circumstances of my case, would place me in a more disagreeable situation than any other member would stand in.—As I have yielded [2] however to what

[1] This letter concerns the Constitutional Convention, and does not refer to the Cincinnati.

[2] Chief Justice John Marshall's comments on General Washington's attendance of the Constitutional Convention and the General Meeting of 1787 of the Cincinnati are: "By giving the proposed meeting a constitutional sanction, and

appeared to be the earnest wishes of my friends, I will hope for the best; and can assure you of the sincere and

Affect regard with which
I am D Sir
Yr Obed Servant
G. Washington.

[*Washington's Letter Books*]

Extract from GENERAL WASHINGTON'S Diary.

Thursday, 26th April, 1787—. . . Receiving an Express between 4 and 5 Oclock this afternoon informing me of the extreme illness of my Mother and Sister Lewis,[1] I resolved to set out for Fredericksburgh by daylight in the Morning, and spent the evening in writing some letters on business respecting the Meeting of the Cincinnati, to the Secretary General of the Society, Genl. Knox.

A Captn. McCannon[2] came here in the evening and got 40 Diplomas signed for the Delaware line.

To Major GEORGE TURNER.

Mount Vernon, April 26, 1787.

Sir:

Your letter of the 5th. inst,[3] and the box containing the diplomas for the officers of the State of So Carolina, came duly

by postponing it to a day subsequent to that on which the Cincinnati were to assemble, it also removed one impediment, and diminished another, to the attendance of General Washington as a member. He persuaded himself that by repairing to Philadelphia previous to the second Monday in May, in order to attend the general meeting of the Cincinnati, he should efface any impressions unfavorable to the attachment he felt to his military friends, which might otherwise be excited in their bosoms by his appearing in a public character after declining the presidency of their society." (Marshall's *Life of Washington,* iv, 235.)

[1] Elizabeth (Betty), wife of Brigadier-General Fielding Lewis of *Kenmore,* Fredericksburg, Virginia.

[2] Captain William McCammon of the Delaware Regiment.

[3] See page 300.

to hand. I have signe[d] the diplomas and sent the box to Doctr. Craik[1] in Alexandria to be forwarded by a safe conveyance and have directed it to the care of Colo. [William] Grayson as you requested—The enclosed list I have returned agree[a]ble to your desire. I am, etc.

[*Washington's Letter Books*]

General Washington notifies the Secretary General of the Cincinnati that he will attend the General Meeting after all.

To Major-General HENRY KNOX.

Mount Vernon, April 27, 1787.

My dear Sir,

After every consideration my Judgment was able to give the subject, I had determined to yield to the wishes of many of my friends who seemed anxious for my attending the Convention which is proposed to be holden in Philadelphia the 2d Monday of May and though so much afflicted with a Rheumatick complaint (of which I have not been entirely free for six months) as to be under the necessity of carrying my arm in a Sling for the last ten days, I had fixed on Monday next for my departure, and had made every necessary arrangement for the purpose when (within this hour) I am called by an express, who assures me not a moment is to be lost, to see a mother and *only* sister (who are supposed to be in the agonies of Death) expire; and I am hastening to obey this Melancholy call after having just buried a brother[2] who was the intimate companion of my youth, and the friend of my ripened age.—This Journey of mine then, 100 miles in the disordered frame of my body, will, I am persuaded, unfit me for the intended trip to Philadelphia, and assuredly prevent my offering that

[1] Dr. James Craik of Alexandria, Virginia, was Chief Physician and Surgeon of the Continental Army and became an original member of the Maryland Cincinnati. He attended General Washington in his last illness.

[2] This was Colonel John Augustine Washington, who died in January 1787.

tribute to respect to my compatriots in Arms which results from Affection and gratitude for their attachment to, and support of me, upon so many trying occasions.

For this purpose it was, as I had (tho' with a good deal of Reluctance) consented, from the conviction that our affairs were verging fast to ruin, to depart from the resolution I had taken of never more stepping out of the walks of private life, that I determined to shew my respect to the General meeting of the Society by coming there the week before.—As the latter is prevented, and the other, it is probable, will not take place, I send such papers as have occasionally come to my hands, & may require the inspection, and the consideration of the Cincinnati. An apology for the order in which they are sent is highly necessary, and my present situation is the best I can offer—To morrow I had set apart for the Inspection and arrangement of them, that such only, as were fitting, might be laid before the Society; for unless I had time to go over them again with a person who understand the French language, I am not even certain that all of what I send may relate to the affairs of the Cincinnati, and certain I am, that some are too personal—the sending of which will not, I hope be ascribed to improper motives, when the *only* one I had (as I am in the moment of my departure from home & uncertain of returning to it) is that nothing which has been refered to me, may be with held.

In the jumbled order you will receive them, I send them by Doctr. [James] Craik in Alexandria to be forwarded by a safe hand in the Stage to Philadelphia

I make a tender of my affectionate regard to the members who may Constitute the General Meeting of the Society and with sentiments of the highest esteem, etc.

[*Washington's Letter Books*]

Mr. Lee writes General Washington, just as had Colonel Humphreys on 24 March 1787 (see page 297), that the Cincinnati are going to reelect him President General, despite his letter saying that he did not wish it (see letter of 31 October 1786, page 264).

From Mr. ARTHUR LEE.

New York May 13. 1787

Dear Sir

I have received private information, that it is the intention of the meeting of the Cincinnati to re-elect you as their President, notwithstanding your letter. They think you are so plegd to them, by some of your letters that you cannot refuse the Presidency. . . .

[*Washington Papers*]

Extract from GENERAL WASHINGTON'S Diary.

Tuesday, 15th May, 1787[1]—Repaired, at the hour appointed to the State Ho., but no more States being represented than were yesterday (tho' several more members had come in (viz. No. Carolina and Delaware as also Jersey)), we agreed to meet again tomorrow. Govr. Randolph from Virginia came in today.

Dined with the Members, to the Genl. Meeting of the Society of the Cincinnati.

General Meeting of 1787.
General WASHINGTON reelected President General.

Friday, May 18th [1787] P. M.

. . . Proceeded to ballot for officers of the General Society. The following were elected:

General Washington, president-general

Major-General Thomas Mifflin, vice-president-general (*vice* General Gates)

Major-General Henry Knox, secretary-general.

[1] This entry was made in Philadelphia where General Washington was attending the Constitutional Convention which met at the same time as the General Meeting of the Society of the Cincinnati. See the General's letter about attending the one and not the other, 31 October 1786, page 264.

Major George Turner, assistant secretary-general (*vice* General Otho H. Williams).

Resolved, That a committee of three be appointed to wait on His Excellency, General Washington, to inform him that the General Society have unanimously re-elected him their president.

The members chosen were General [Henry] Knox, Colonel [Alexander] Hamilton, and Mr. [Elias] Boudinot.

[*Minutes of the General Meeting of 1787*]

The Assistant Secretary General sends a copy of the Minutes of the General Meeting of 1787 to the President General.

From Major GEORGE TURNER.

Philadelphia 22d. May [17]87

Sir

I have the Honour to enclose an Extract from the Minutes of the late General Meeting,—which immediately concerns the Office of President-Genl.—Whenever the whole of the Minutes can be fairly transcribed the Copy will be forwarded to your Excellency by, Sir, Your etc.

[*Washington Papers*]

General Washington asked his former military secretary to draft an answer to Mr. Jeffeson's letter of criticism of the Cincinnati.

From Lieutenant-Colonel DAVID HUMPHREYS.

New Haven, May 28, 1787

My Dear General,

I intended fully, when I left Philadelphia, to have written you from New York, but on my arrival there my servant (who was a German) ran away, and I was so occupied in procuring another that I have not been able to take up the pen until the present moment.

Recollecting imperfectly, as I do the purport of Mr. Jefferson's letter as well as of the Extract from the Encyclopedie, I have found myself enbarrassed in attempting to say anything on so delicate a subject especially considering it a subject on whose merits Posterity is to judge, & concerning which every word that may be drawn from you, will probably hereafter be brought into question & scrutinized.

Under this view I have thought the less that could, with decency be said the better.

With sentiments of respect, friendship & consideration I have the honour to be, My dear General, your most Obed & Hble Servt.

D. Humphreys

Gen. Washington.

[Enclosure]

Sketch in Answer to Mr. Jefferson's Letter[1]

I scarcely know what to say respecting that part of your communication which concerns the Cincinnati. It is a delicate, it is a perplexing subject. Not having the extract from the Encyclopedia before me, I cannot now undertake to enter into the merits of the publication. It may, therefore, perhaps be as much as will be expected of me, to observe that the Author appears in general to have detailed very candidly & ingeniusly the motives & inducements which gave birth to the Society. Some of the subsequent facts which I cannot however, from memory pretend to discuss with precision, are thought by gentlemen who have seen the publication to be misstated; in so much that it is commonly said truth & falsehood are so intimately blended, that it will become very difficult to sever them. For myself I only recollect two or three circumstances in the narration of which palpable mistakes seem to have insinuated themselves. Major L'Enfant did not arrive & bring the Eagles during the session of the General Meeting, but

[1] See page 270.

some time before the Convention. The Legislature of Rhode Island never passed any Act whatever on the subject notwithstanding what Mirabeau & others had previously advanced. Nothing can be more ridiculous than the supposition of the author that the Society was instituted partly because the Country could not pay the Army except the assertion that the United States have not made full & compleat provision for paying, not only the arrearages, due the Officers, but the half pay or commutation at their option. From whence the author deduces an argument for its dissolution. Tho' I conceive this never had anything to do with the Institution, yet the Officers, in most of the States who never have, nor, I believe, ever expect to receive, one farthing of the principal or interest on their final settlement securities would doubtless be much obliged to the author to convince them how & when they received a compensation for their services. No foreigner, nor American, who has been absent some time, will easily comprehend how tender those concerned are on this point, I am sorry to say a great many of the Officers consider me as having in a degree committed myself, by inducing them to trust too much in the justice of their country. They heartily wish no settlement had been made, because it has rendered them obnoxious to their fellow citizens, without affording the least emolument.

For reasons I first mentioned I cannot think it expedient for me to go into an investigation of the Writer's deductions. I shall accordingly content myself with giving you some idea of the part I have acted, posterior to the first formation of the Association. When I found that you & many of the most respectable characters in the country would entirely acquiesce with the Institution as altered & amended in the first General Meeting of 1784 and that the objections against the hereditary & other obnoxious parts were wholly done away I was prevailed upon to accept the Presidency. Happily finding (so far as I could learn by assiduous enquity) that all the clamour & jealousies which had been excited against the original association had ceased, I judged it a proper time in the last autumn to withdraw myself from any farther agency in the business, and, to make my retirement compleat, agreeably to my original plan, I wrote circular letters to all the State Societies announcing my wishes, informing them that I did not propose to be at Philadelphia at the triennial Meeting & requesting not to be reelected President. This was the last step of a public nature I expected ever to have taken. But having since been appointed by my native State to attend he National Convention, & having been pressed to a compliance in a manner which it hardly becomes me to describe; I have in a measure been obliged to sacrifice my own Sentiments & to be present in Philadelphia at the very time of the General Meeting of the Cincinnati. After which I was not at liberty to decline the Presidency without placing myself in an extremely disagreeable situation with relation to that brave and faithful class of Men whose persevering friendship I have experienced on so many trying occasions.

[*U. S. Archives, State Dept., quoted by F. L. Humphreys, Life of David Humphreys, I, 415-418.*]

To Mr. THOMAS JEFFERSON.

Philadelphia, 30 May, 1787.

Dear Sir;

. . . I come now to the other part of your letter, which concerns the Cincinnati, on which indeed I scarcely know what to say. It is a delicate, it is a perplexing subject. Not having the extract from the *Encyclopedia*[1] before me, I cannot now undertake to enter into the merits of the publication. It may therefore be as much as will be expected from me to observe, that the author appears in general to have detailed very candidly and ingenuously the motives and the inducements, which give

[1] In this letter it is interesting to note how closely General Washington follows the answer to Jefferson's criticisms of the Cincinnati, prepared by Humphreys and inclosed in Humphreys' letter of May 28, 1787, page 309. Jefferson had sent an extract from an article in the *Encyclopédie*, being an account of the Society of the Cincinnati, and General Washington sent it to Knox, on 27 April 1787, see page 305. See also footnote, page 270.

birth to the Society. Some of the subsequent facts, which I cannot, however, from memory pretend to discuss with precision, are thought by gentlemen, who have seen the publication, to be misstated; insomuch that it is commonly said, truth and falsehood are so intimately blended, that it will become very difficult to sever them.

For myself, I only recollect two or three circumstances, in the narration of which palpable mistakes seem to have insinuated themselves. Monsieur L'Enfant did not arrive and bring the eagles during the session of the general meeting, but some time before that convention. The legislature of Rhode Island never passed any act whatever on the subject, (that ever came to my knowledge), notwithstanding what Mirabeau and others had previously advanced. Nothing can be more rediculous that the supposition of the author, that the Society was instituted partly because the country could not then pay the army, except the assertion that the United States have now made full and complete provision for paying, not only the arrearages due to the officers, but the half-pay of commutation at their option; from when the author deduces an argument for its dissolution. I conceive this never had any thing to do with the institution, yet the officers in most of the States, who never have nor I believe expect to receive one farthing of the principal or interest on their final settlement securities, would be much obliged to the author to convince them how and when they received a compensation for their services. No foreigner, or American, who has been absent some time, will easily comprehend how tender those concerned are on this point. I am sorry to say, a great many of the officers consider me as having in a degree committed myself by inducing them to trust too much in the justice of their country. They heartily wish no settlement had been made, because it has rendered them obnoxious to their fellow citizens, without affording them the least emolument.

For the reason I first mentioned, I cannot think it expedient for me to go into an investigation of the writer's deductions. I shall accordingly content myself with giving you some idea of the part I have acted, posterior to the first formation of the association.

When I found that you and many of the most respectable characters in the country would entirely acquiesce with the institution, as altered and amended in the first general meeting of 1784, and that the objections against the hereditary and other obnoxious parts were wholly done away, I was prevailed upon to accept the presidency. Happy in finding, (so far as I could learn by assiduous inquiry), that all the clamors and jealousies, which had been excited against the original association, had ceased, I judged it a proper time in the last autumn to withdraw myself from any farther agency in the business, and to make my retirement complete, agreeably to my original plan. I wrote circular letters to all the State Societies announcing my wishes informing I did not propose to be at the general meeting, and requested not to be reelected president. This was the last step of a public nature I expected ever to have taken. But, having since been appointed by my native State to attend the national convention, and having been pressed to a compliance in a manner, which it hardly becomes me to describe, I have, in a measure, been obliged to sacrifice my own sentiments, and to be present in Philadelphia at the very time of the general meeting of the Cincinnati. After which I was not at liberty to decline the presidency, without placing myself in an extremely disagreeable situation with relation to that brave and faithful class of men, whose persevering patriotism and friendship I had experienced on so many trying occasions. . . .

[*Washington's Letter Books*]

To the President of the French Cincinnati.

Philadelphia June 1st 1787

The enclosed resolution of the General Meeting of the Society of the Cincinnati, which I have the honor to transmit to Your Excellency is the best apology I can make for the trouble I am now about to give you.

Persuaded I am that Your Excellency will derive as much pleasure from offering to, and investing the Marquis de Bouillé with the Order of the Cincinnati, as it gives me to communicate for these purposes the sentiments of the Society.

With the greatest consideration and respect, I have the honor to be Your Excellency's Most Obed^{t} and most h^{ble} serv^{t}

G^{o}. Washington

His Excellency the Presdt & senior officer of the Society of the Cincinnati in France [1]

[*Fac simile, Contenson, La Société des Cincinnati en France, 257*]

From the Chevalier JEAN-JOSEPH DE GIMAT.

La Rochelle le 2 Juin 1787.

on me mande de paris, Monsieur, que Mr. Le Mis. de Lafayette, y est malade, et qui ne pourru peutetre pas de quelque tems, m'envoyer La Lettre de recommandation que Je lui ai demandé pour les Etats unis de L'amerique. Je vous envoye toujours mon Memoire, avec deux Lettres de ce General, et deux Certificats. Je vous prie, de vouloir bien presenter le tout, à M.M. Les Membres Supperieurs de La Societé de Cincinnatus, Je vous aurai toutes les obligations possibles, Monsieur, Si Je puis obtenir Cette Grace par vos Sollicitations, Si en revanche Je puis vous étre de quelque utilité Disposéz Je vous prie, de celui qui à l'honneur d'étre avec des Sentimens d'estimé et de consideration. etc.[2]

[*Washington Papers*]

[1] The only President of the French Cincinnati prior to its dispersion by the Terror, was the Count d'Estaing.

[2] Enclosed were two letters to Gimat from the Marquis de LaFayette, dated Paris, 16 January and 30 January 1787.

[Translation by Edgar Erskine Hume]

La Rochelle, 2 June 1787

I have heard from Paris, Sir, that the Marquis de LaFayette is ill there and could not for some time send me the letter of recommendation which I asked of him for the United States of America. I send you my memorandum, with two letters of the general and two certificates. I ask you to be so good as to present them all to the officers of the Society of Cincinnatus. I would be under all possible obligation, Sir, if I might obtain this favor through your recommendation. If, in return, I may be of any service to you, I beg you make use of one who has the honor to be, with sentiments of esteem and consideration, etc.

The Assistant Secretary General sends more diplomas to the President General for signature.

From Major GEORGE TURNER.

Lombard Street, [Philadelphia?] Saturday
[June 23, 1787?]

Sir,

The seventy two Diplomas left herewith, are part of those intended for the Gentlemen in France. The Remainder will be ready in a few Days.

The General-Meeting directed me to obtain the President's Signature to each—and I have now the Honor to lay them before your Excellency for that—Purpose.

With perfect Respect, Sir, I have the honour to be etc.

[*Washington Papers*]

From Major GEORGE TURNER.

Lombard Street [Philadelphia?] Saturday June 27th. [1787]

Sir,

The Bearer will deliver your Excellency an Addition of seventy eight Parchment Diplomas, and five on Paper, for Framing. If the others are signed the Bearer will receive them for me.

With great Respect I have the honour to be etc.

[*Washington Papers*]

Extract from General WASHINGTON'S Diary.

Wednesday, 4th July, 1787 [1]—Visited Doctr. Shovat's Anatomical figures, and (the Convention having adjourned for the purpose) went to hear (at the Calvanist Church) an Oration on the anniversary of Independence delivered by a Mr. Mitchell, a student of Law. After which I dined with the State Society of Cincinnati at Epple's Tavern, and drank Tea at Mr. Powell's.

From Colonel DE MAUDUIT DUPLESSIS.

Paris, 20. Juillet 1787.

Mon cher General,

. . . . Je vous envoye, Mon cher General, quelqu'uns de Ribans de Cincinnatus, Parce que je me suis aperçu qu'on n'en lenvoie pas en amerique—

Je vous prie de m'adresser ma Commission de Cincinnatus, Signé de vous, par la premiere occasion, je l'attends avec impatience; je ne l'ai pas encore reçu. nous en portons tous, en france, la decoration, avec plaisir, et nous vous en faisons honneur— . . .

[*Washington Papers*]

[1] This entry is made in Philadelphia where General Washington was still in attendance at the Constitutional Convention. Doctr. Shovat was Dr. Abraham Chovet or Chavet, who was located in Race Street between Second and Third Streets. Epplees Tavern was at No. 117 Race Street. Mr. Powell was Samuel Powell of Philadelphia (Fitzpatrick).

[Contemporary translation]

Paris 20th. July 1787.

My dear General,

. . . I send you, my dear General, some Ribband for the Cincinnati, because I observed it was scarce in America.

I beg that you would be so good as to address to me a diploma of the order of the Cincinnati, signed by yourself, as I have not received one. We all wear the decoration in France & look upon it as very honorary. . . .[1]

[*Washington Papers*]

To Commodore JOHN PAUL JONES.

Philadelphia, September 2, 1787.

Sir,

Should this letter reach you in time, the purport of it is, to beg your care of the enclosed to the Marqs. de la Fayette; and to inform you that all the letters, Memorials, and Papers of every kind which had been transmitted to me as President General of the Society of the Cincinnati, were forwarded (not expecting to attend it myself) to the last General meeting holden in this city but how they were acted upon is not in my power to inform you, not being at it. . . .[2]

[*Washington's Letter Books*]

From Major WILLIAM JACKSON.

[September 17, 1787]

Major Jackson presents his most respectful compliments to General Washington—

He begs leave to request his signature to forty Diplomas intended for the Rhode Island Society of the Cincinnati.

[1] See General Washington's reply, 8 January 1788, page 323.

[2] General Washington attended only a few of the sessions of the General Meeting of 1787.

Major Jackson, after burning all the loose scraps of paper which belong to the Convention.[1] will this evening wait upon the General with the Journals and other papers which their vote directs to be delivered to His Excellency
Monday Evening.

[*Washington Papers*]

To Major-General HENRY KNOX.

Mount Vernon, Oct. 15th, 1787

My dear Sir:

Your favor of the 3d instant came duly to hand.

The fourth day after leaving Phila I arrived at home & found Mrs. Washington a bed she having been tolerably sick, but the fruits of the earth almost completely destroyed by one of the severest droughts (in this neighborhood) that ever was experienced—The crops generally below the mountains are injured but not to the degrees that some of my neighbors are here.

The Constitution is now before the judgement seat. It has as was expected, its adversaries and its supporters, which will preponderate is yet to be decided. The former it is probable will the most active because the major part of them it is to be feared will be governed by sinister and self important considerations. Considerations in which no argument will work conviction—The opposition from another class of them (if they are men of reflection, information and candour) may perhaps subside on the solution of the following three last, but important questions.

1. Is the Constitution which is submitted by the Convention preferable to the government (if it can be called one) under which we now live?

2. It is probable that more confidence will, at this time, be placed in another convention (should the experiment be tried) than was given to the last? and it is likely there would be a better agreement in it? Is there not a constitutional door

[1] Constitutional Convention.

open for alteration or amendment? it is not probable that real defects will be as readily discovered after as before trial?—and will not posterity be as ready to apply the remedy as ourselves, if there is occasion for it when the mode is provided? To think otherwise will, in my judgement, be ascribing more of the Amor patria—more wisdom—and more foreign to ourselves, than I conceive we are entitled to.

It is highly probable that the refusal of our Gov. and Col. Mason to subscribe to the proceedings of the convention will have a bad effect in this state; for as you will observe, they *must* put only assigned reasons for the justification & explanations of their conduct probably these reasons will appear in terrific array with a view to alarm the people—Some things are already addresed to their fears and will have their effect. As far however as the sense of *this* part of the country has been taken it is thoroughly in favor of the proposed Constitution—further I cannot speak with precision—If a powerful opposition is given to it the weight thereof will, I apprehend, come from the southland, of James River & from the western counties.

Mrs. Washington and the family join me in every good wish for you and Mrs. Knox and with great and sincere regard I am my dear Sir

Yrs. affect.

Geo. Washington [1]

The Honble.

Gen. Knox

[Endorsed]: From His Excellency General Washington. Official No. 27.

[*Collection of the General Society, Anderson House*]

---

[1] This letter is included because it is the property of the Society of the Cincinnati, having been presented in 1941 by Dr. Montgomery Blair, member of the Virginia Cincinnati. The letter was given by General Knox's grandson, Rear-Admiral Henry Knox Thatcher, U. S. Navy, to Hon. Gustavus Vasa Fox, Assistant Secretary of the Navy. It is framed in wood from the *U. S. S. Constitution*, presented to Mr. Fox, 1869, by Edward Hartt, U. S. Naval Constructor. The framed letter was inherited by Mrs. Fox's grandnephew, Dr. Blair. It is on display at Anderson House, Washington, Headquarters of the Society.

From COUNT DE LA LUZERNE.[1]

Au Port au Prince Le 12. 9bre. 1787.

Monsieur.

L'assemblée qui devoit avoir lieu en france pour Statuer Sur le nombre et la qualité des officiers françois, qui ayant Servi dans la derniere guerre en amerique, pourroyent être agrégés à la Respectable Société du Cincinatus, n'ayant point encore été convoquée, je Suis Sollicité par Monsieur de Saqui des Tourés Capitaine de Vaisseau, que je connois particulierement et que je desire beaucoup d'obliger, de lui faire avoir la permission d'en porter la marque. Je doute que la branche francoise de la Société S'assemble jamais et je crois devoir vous consulter Sur les espérances et les desirs de monsieur de Saqui.

Cet officier embarqué en qualité de Lieutenant Sur le Vaisseau le Languedoc, ayant fait la campagne de Monsieur le Comte d'Estaing et y ayant été griévement blésse, fut obligé de repasser en France. Parmi les graces qui furent à cette epoque Sa recompense, il ne fut point a portée de Solliciter cette decoration accordée à d'autres a bien moins de titre. Il en étoit Susceptible, à cause de Sa blessure, ainsi que plusieurs autres officiers qui n'y avoient absolument aucun autre droit. Il est plus éligible que jamais depuis qu'il est Capitaine de Vaisseau, il la reclame et désireroit qu'elle constatat qu'il a été un des premiers françois qui ont porté les armes pour la défense de la Liberté de l'Amerique.

Je Prie Votre Excellence de me Faire connoître Si elle pense qu'il Seroit permis à cet officier, d'ont le mérite m'est connu, de porter le Signe au quel Sont reconnus ceux qui composent cette respectable Société. En mon particulier je Souhaiterois que ma recommandation Lui obtint la Faveur qu'il desire & dont je puis vous assurer qu'il est digne.

Je connois tout l'attachement de mon Frere pour vous, et je Sais l'amitié dont vous L'honorés. Je suis persuadé qu'il Se joindroit volontiers à moi en Faveur de monsieur de Saqui, S'il étoit à portée de la faire.

[1] Originally enclosed in: The letter of the Marquis de Barbé-Marbois to General Washington, dated 30 November 1787. See page 322.

Je Suis bien aise Monsieur que cette circonstance me mette à même de vous renouveller les assurances de mon Sincere attachement & la haute consideration avec la quelle j'ai L'honneur d'être etc.

[*Archives of the General Society*]

[Contemporary translation]

Port au Prince 12th Novr. 1787—

Sire,

The assembly which ought to have been held in France in order to particularize the number & quality of French officers, who, having served the last war in America, could be admitted into the respectable Society of the Cincinnati having not been yet convened; I am solicited by Monsieur de Saqui des Toures, Commander of a Ship, with whom I am particularly acquainted and very desireous of obliging, to obtain, for him, permission to wear the Insignia of the Order—I am doubtful whether the French branch of this Society will ever convene, and I thought it right to consult you upon the hopes & wishes of Monsr de Saqui.

This officer embarked on board the Languedoc in quality of Lieutenant, having served a cruize with the Count d'Estaing and being badly wounded was obliged to return to France.—Among the favors with which he was recompensed at that time. he was not at hand to solicit this decoration which was granted to others less deserving of it. He was entitled to it on account of his wounds, as well as many other officers who had absolutely no other recommendation for it.—He is more eligible than ever since he has become Commander of a Ship.—He claims it as having been one of the first Frenchmen who bore arms in defence of American Liberty.—

I beg your Excellency to inform me if you think this officer, whose merits are known to me, will be permitted to carry the Insignia by which this respectable society are distinguished.—For my own part, I should wish that my recommendation may obtain the favour which he desires, and of which I can assure you he is worthy.

I know the attachment which my Brother has to you, & I also know the friendship with which you honor him.—I am persuaded that he would willingly join me in favor of Monsr. de Saqui, if he was at hand.—

I am glad, Sir, that this circumstance has given me an occasion of renewing the assurances of my sincere attachment, and the high consideration with which I have the honor to be etc.

[*Washington Papers*]

From the MARQUIS DE BARBÉ MARBOIS.

Port au Prince, November the 30th. 1787.

Sir.

I have so many times experienced your Excellency's favour that I hope you'll forgive me for an application which I could not refuse to a brave officer who at the same time is a friend of mine. you will see by a letter of Count de la Luzerne which accompagnies this [1] that he takes a particular interest in knowing whether Mr. de Saqui des Tourets [2] can or not wear the insignia of the Cincinnati. I heartily wish your opinion may be in his favor & I shall regard it as one conferred on myself If I am ennabled to tell him he is thougt by you, Sir, a fit Subject for that Society. I know you cannot positively determine the question: but your opinion would considerably assist us in forming one. . . .[3]

[*Washington Papers*]

---

[1] La Luzerne's letter to General Washington, 12 November 1787, see page 320.

[2] Louis-Charles-Hilarion Chevalier de Saqui des Tourès was an honorary member of the French Cincinnati and therefore has the same right to wear the Eagle as any other member.

[3] General Washington replied on 4 April 1788, see page 326.

To Brigadier-General GEORGE WEEDON.

Dear Sir,

I have received your letter of the 25th. Ult^{o}. enclosing the proceedings of the Cincinnati of this State, which I am much obliged to you for forwarding to me.

I will, agreeably to your request, send some cuttings of the golden willow to Alexandria to be forwarded to you, but I imagine this is an improper season to put them out, for as they are to be propagated from the slip the spring seems to be the most suitable time for setting them; should these fail I will send you more in the spring if you will remind me of it.

I am D^{r}. Sir
Y^{r}. Most Obed^{t}. H^{ble}. Servant
G. Washington

Mount Vernon
December 3^{d}. 1787

[*Washington's Letter Books*]

To Colonel DE MAUDUIT DUPLESSIS.

Mount Vernon, January 8, 1788.

Sir:

I have to acknowledge the reception of your three letters, viz of the 12th. of Feby. the 26th. of March and the 20th July.—. . .[1]

When I was in Philadelphia last summer I signed a number of Diplomas for the foreign officers, members of the Cincinnati, which were sent by the Secretary General to the Counts De Estaing and Rochambeau this, I presume, will supercede the necessity of my sending one to you as you desired. I have the Honor, etc.

[*Washington's Letter Books*]

[1] See page 316. The letter of 26 March does not concern the Cincinnati. It mentions Duplessis's return to France.

From Count Auguste de Grasse.

Mon Général

La juste douleur que m'a occasionné La mort de mon Père, ne m'a pas permis d'avoir L'honneur d'En faire part à votre Excelence, dans les premiers momens de cet affreux Evénement. L'amitié qu'il vous avoit voué, mon Général, Etoit fondée sur L'Estime Et j'aime a me flatter que celle que vous d'aigniés lui accorder, avoit une baze aussi solide. C'Est par vous que mon père a obtenu les recompenses flatteuses des services qu'il avoit eu le bonheur de rendre à L'Amérique, conjointement avec Votre Excelence. C'Est à Vous, Mon Général, que je dois les quatres pièces de canon prisés à York Town, les temoignages Glorieux de votre Suffrage et de celui des Etats. C'est un trophee precieux pour moi. il décore au jourd'hui mes armes. Et il perpétura Eternellement dans ma famille La reconnoissance que vous a toujour conservé mon père. il seroit bien flatteu pour sa mémoire Et bien agréable pour moi de pouvoir conserver à son nom une autre preuve de la satisfaction du Congrès. L'Aigle de Cincinnatus avoit Eté originairement Etablis pour perpetuer d'age en age Le Souvenir De L'indépendance américaine. Daignés, Mon Général, m'obtenir des Etats la permission de porter celui dont ils avoient decoré mon père. C'Est une Grace que je demande avec instances a Votre Excelence, et je la Supplie d'Etre d'avance bien sure de ma reconnoissance.

Je suis avec Respect De Votre Excelence, Mon Général,

Le très humble
et très obeissant Serviteur

Paris ce 11 mars 1788 — Le Cte Auguste De Grasse

[*Washington Papers*]

[Translation by Edgar Erskine Hume]

General:

The natural sorrow occasioned by the loss of my father prevented my having the honor of informing Your Excellency of it in the first moments of this terrible blow. The friendship which he had vowed to you, General, was founded on esteem, and I like to flatter myself that that which you deigned to accord him had an equally solid foundation. It was through you that my father obtained flattering recompenses for the services which he had the good fortune to render America, together with Your Excellency. It is from you, General, that I have the four pieces of artillery taken at Yorktown, the glorious tokens of your tribute and that of the States. It is a precious trophy for me. It decorates my arms today. And it will perpetuate forever in my family the appreciation which you always had of my father. It will serve to honor his memory and it is most agreeable for me to be able to conserve for his name another proof of the satisfaction of the Congress. The Eagle of Cincinnatus was established originally to perpetuate from age to age the memory of American Independence. Deign, General, to obtain for me the permission of the States to wear the one with which they decorated my father. It is a favor that I earnestly ask of Your Excellency and I beg to offer you my gratitude in advance.

I am with respect for Your Excellency, General,

Your Most humble and obedient servant

Paris 11 March 1788 Count August de Grasse [1]

To Major-General HENRY KNOX.

Mount Vernon, April 4, 1788

Dear Sir,

The enclosed,[2] Mr. de Marbois has been informed, will be submitted to the General Meeting of the Society of the Cincin-

[1] General Washington replied on 18 August 1788, see page 333.

[2] This letter enclosed the following:

The Chevalier de La Luzerne to General Washington, 12 September 1787 (see page 320).

Monsieur de Marbois to General Washington, 30 November 1787 (see page 322).

nati—and for that purpose would be transmitted to the Secretary General.

With great esteem and regard I am, etc.

[*Archives of the General Society*]

To the MARQUIS DE BARBÉ MARBOIS.

Mount Vernon, April 4, 1788.

Sir,

I have regularly received the letter you did me the honor to write to me on the 30th. of November last,[1] accompanied by one from the Count de la Luzerne, respecting the claim of M. de Saqui des Tourets to be admitted a member of the Society of the Cincinnati.

I should certainly find myself extremely happy in an opportunity of gratifying the wishes of so meritorious an officer as M. des Tourets; if I thought myself at liberty to take any part whatever in the premises.—Recommended strongly as he is by the Count de la Luzerne and yourself I cannot have a doubt that he would be an acquisition and a credit to the Institution: nor can I have an hesitatation [sic] in beleiving that his pretentions are as good as those of some who have found admission into the Society. Yet as I have (amidst the almost innumerable applications that have been made to me) scrupulously avoided giving any decision and only referred the Documents I had received to the General Meeting I flatter myself that I shall be considered as having done every thing that was properly within my sphere, by making a similar referrence in the present instance.—

You will be sensible, I perceive Sir, that, from the Constitution of our Society, it would not have been right in me to have given a positive determination of the Question. It would now be less proper than ever for me to take that upon myself. For, having by a circular letter to the several State Societies requested that I might not be re-elected President on account of

[1] See page 322.

my numerous avocations: the last Genl. Meeting was pleased so far to indulge me, as to make it a condition for inducing my acceptance, that I should be absolutely excused from all trouble and application incident to the office; and the whole business should desolve on the Vice President, viz, General Mifflin. As I shall not be present at the next General Meeting, I will transmit the application of M. des Tourets to Genl. Knox, the Secretary of the General Society.

The appointment of the Count de la Luzerne to the office of Minister of Marine and his *consequent removal to Europe,* will, I presume, supersede the expediency of my addressing him on this subject. Had that not been the case, I should have seized with eagerness the occasion of paying the tribute of my homage to his acknowledged talents and virtues. I am truly rejoiced to hear of the felicity of Madame de Marbois and yourself and hope you will be made still more happy *in the growing cement* of the two nations to which you allude. I am, etc.

[*Washington's Letter Books*]

Poor Major L'Enfant was still trying to collect his debt for the Eagles!

From Major PIERRE-CHARLES L'ENFANT.

New York April the 15 1788

Sir

Having already taken the liberty of troubling your Excellency with the particular of my circumstances owing to the Cincinnati affaire—and finding that their resolutions of the last general meeting in consequences of my application on the subject has been of no relief to me it is become incumbent on me that I should once more sollicite your Excellency patronage on the occasion therefore I take the liberty to enclose here in an adresse to the Honable the General assembly of the Society which I am inform is to be held in philadelphie in may next & I beg you will Sir do me the favour of laying it before them. your Excellency will see by its content that I have only received

229 dollrs as part of the money which they voted in my favor in may 1787. also that I have not been reimbursed of any part of the two other sums the payment of which had been recommanded to the Road Island and So Carolina societies and Consequently that I have been forced to go from my words which I had engaged under the assurances that had been given me, of receiving some money in september last. which circumstances deprived me of the facility which I hoped I should otherwaise have obtained and more over so much roused those people whom had trusted my words that they are now determine to prosecut me without mercy.

On an other part Marquis de la fayette to whom I had sent at the time a copy of the last resolutions of the Cincinnati respecting to this affaire and on whose support I much depended to make those people easy—appear to have himself misunderstood the matter and belive that the money voted for has been paid to me at the time appointed which mistake as I am informe by some of my friend in paris has made him exclaim much against me for not having sent that money to the people to whom it belong—and your Excellency will doubtless be sorry to ear that the Marquis himself positively opposed my interest in france on that account, a circumstance which made me fel in an attempt I had lately made to obtain from the Court some favour that had been promised me long befor and on which I now depended considering the good disposition of severals of the present ministry toward me. not only this Sir but I am at this instant Summonded to discharge the whole of the capital own on my former engagements and also the interest there on for three year a circumstance most chagrining considering that the sum of the interest was not considered at the last general meeting of the Society and that it is to be feared it will not be easely obtained at present When every thing demonstrate the backwardness with which the Several Society comply with the last requisition for the money voted in may 1787. indeed should they refuse to Exerte themselves on this new occasion and on the other saide should the people persist in demanding both the principal with the interest of thier money I must be utterly ruined.

your Excellency well known how little Sparfull I have been

of my personal means trough all the transaction of the Cincinnati affairs and what has been my wish to conceal the causes of my Embarassment—but Sir ietherto I could depend upon the generous assistance of a parent whose frindship for me Supply'd all my want but unfortunatly and in this juncture of affairs I am deprived of the best of father and With him I may say of all most all my fortune because the largest portion of this incom he derived it from the King favor and consequently I can have no raite to it after his death.

from this your Excellency may easely conceive what my Embarassment must be, and you will no doubt also perceive the necessity there is that the Cincinnati endeavour at this next meeting to paid me the 3014 dollar which they had voted in may last and also that they will take charge of the 886 dollar now own by the Road Island and So Carolina Society which will bring the principal they shall have to pay to 3671 dollars deduction being made of the 229 doll already paid as is said above.

as with what relate to the interest money should the Society be out of power to facilitate in the payment thereof I should wish they would then enter into some resolution such as may serve me to obtain from the people concerned the termes which I may propose them.

I beg your Excellency will excuse the liberty I take and I am With great respect etc.[1]

[*Archives of the General Society*]

Major L'Enfant's claim for reimbursement for his expenses in connection with procuring the Eagles of the Cincinnati in Paris, also the plate for the Diploma, was long before the Society. General Washington, while sympathetic, always took the position that L'Enfant had exceeded his instructions (see page 30). Moreover the General had been promised, on accepting the President Generalcy, that he would be spared having to attend to the details of the Society's business.

[1] Enclosed with this letter were a copy in French, and one in English (both by L'Enfant) of his petition to the General Assembly of the Cincinnati, 15 April 1788. For General Washington's reply, 28 April 1788, see page 330.

To Major PIERRE-CHARLES L'ENFANT.

Mount Vernon, April 28, 1788.

Sir:

I have been duly favoured with your letter of the 15 Instt.,[1] enclosing a Memorial to the General Meeting of the Cincinnati; and, agreeably to your request, shall transmit the Enclosure to the Secretary, to be laid before the meeting.

As your embarrassments have been a source of long and severe inquietude, I should be truly happy in knowing that they were removed. But, as it was the express condition of my accepting the Presidency of the Society, " that I should be exempted from all applications and cares respecting it: I trust when this stipulation shall be generally known that all addresses will be made to the Vice-President or Secretary. . . .

[*Hayes Memorial Library, Fremont, Ohio*]

To Major-General HENRY KNOX.

Mount Vernon, April 28, 1788

My dear Sir

Enclosed is a letter [2] and a Memorial from Major L'Enfant which he is informed shall be transmitted to you, to be laid before the General Meeting of the Society of the Cincinnati, about to be held in Philadelphia

With sentiments of great esteem and friendship I am etc.

[*Archives of the General Society*]

---

[1] See page 327.
[2] L'Enfant letter of 15 April 1788, see page 327.

To the COUNT DE ROCHAMBEAU.

Mount Vernon, April 28, 1788.

My dear Count:

I have just received the letter which you did me the honor to write to me on the 18th of January; [1] and am sorry to learn that the Count de Grasse, our gallant coadjutor in the capture of Cornwallis, is not more. . . . the Cincinnati in some of the States have gone into mourning for him. . . . [2]

[*Washington's Letter Books*]

The Society of the Cincinnati held an extra General Meeting in Philadelphia, 6-7 May 1788: Major-General Mifflin, the Vice-President General, presided. Though the extra General Meeting had been called by the regular General Meeting of 1788, there was no quorum. The only State Societies which sent delegates were those of Massachusetts, Rhode Island, New Jersey, Pennsylvania and Delaware. General Mifflin reports to the President General.

From Major-General THOMAS MIFFLIN.

Philadelphia, May 8, 1788.

Sir,

I have the honour to transmit to your Excellency the Copy of a Circular Letter [3] to the State-Societies of the Cincinnati from the Gentlemen who have attended here in consequence of the Recommendation of the General Meeting in May last.

The Members present not making a Quorum, no other Business could be entered upon.

I am, etc.

[*Washington Papers*]

---

[1] This letter announcing the death of de Grasse, does not mention the Cincinnati.

[2] The Count de Grasse died in Paris in 1788 at the age of sixty-six.

[3] The Circular letter, a copy of which appears in the Minutes of the meeting, concerns Major L'Enfant's account against the Society for Eagles, etc., of which so much is recorded.

From Major George Turner.

Philadelphia, May 11, 1788.

Sir,

I must apologize for not forwarding to your Excellency with General Mifflin's Letter of the 8th. Instant [1] (which was committed to my Care) the Copy of the Circular Letter it was intended to enclose. It was an omission occasioned through Hurry, and which I did not recollect till this moment. I have now the honour to send it herewith, and of being, with the highest esteem, etc.

[*Washington Papers*]

From Major-General John Sullivan.

Durham, July 7th 1788.

Sir.

I am directed by the Society of the Cincinnati in New Hampshire to convey their congratulations to your Excellency, and to the Society in General, on the ratification of New Hampshire by a sufficient number of States, not only to establish it as a national form of government, but thereby to fix upon a permanent basis, those liberties, for which, under the direction and order of your Excellency they have so cheerfully contended. They now view with inexpressible pleasure the arrival of that happy period, when by that establishment of a truly republican, energetic and efficient national government, they and their posterity may enjoy those blessings, which as freemen, they esteem an reward for all the toils and dangers, which they experienced in the course of a long and perilous war.

[1] See page 331.

I have the honor to be, with most exalted sentiments of esteem and respect.[1]

Your Excellency's

Most Obedient Servant

Jno Sullivan

By order of the Society

Jeh. Fogg,

Secy.

[*Archives of the New Hampshire Cincinnati*]

General Washington writes to the son of the Count de Grasse, who has recently died.

To AUGUSTE, COUNT DE GRASSE.

Mount Vernon, August 18, 1788

Sir:

The letter which you did me the honor to write on the 11th. of March[2] last is before me, and affords an occasion of testifying the sincerity of my regrets for the distressing event announced in it. Be persuaded, Sir, I should do injustice to my feelings, if my disinterested friendship did not sympathize with your filial duty, in expressions of the most genuine grief, for the death of your father. Indeed the merits of the Count de Grasse and the services which he had the happiness of rendering to this country, have given a singular poignancy to the melancholly, which United America feels for his loss. You need not doubt but those merits and those services will be as long held in remembrance here, as the honorable testimony of this Nations gratitude for them shall be preserved in your family.

After these pointed assurances and expressions of real esteem for your father; the son of my gallant friend and successful associate in arms will not find it difficult to comprehend

[1] General Washington replied on 1 September 1788, see page 334.

[2] See page 324.

the interest I take in whatever concerns his reputation and glory. But it rests not with me to grant permission for anyone to bear the Insignia of the Cincinnati. All I can do will be to refer your request and pretensions to the Genl. meeting of that Society, who alone are competent to gratify your wishes. The General Meetings are Triennial. The next will not be untill a year from the next May: Although I am the President, I do not expect to attend, because it is stipulated and understood that I shall be exempted from the trouble of the Office. For this reason, I will forward a transcript of your Letter to Genl. Knox, who is the Secretary, with a request that it may be laid before the General meeting and that the result may be made known to you.

With sentiments of the highest regard and consideration, I am, etc.

[*Washington's Letter Books*]

To Major-General John Sullivan.

Mount Vernon, Sept. 1st, 1788.

Sir:

It is with great personal satisfaction, I receive the congratulations of the Society of the Cincinnati in New Hampshire, on the present state of our public affairs.[1]

I shall take care to convey the instrument expressive of their sentiments to the Secretary of the General Meeting, that, being deposited in the archives, the purport may be made known accordingly.

The prevalence of so good dispositions from one extremity of the continent to the other (with few exceptions) seems indeed to afford a subject of mutual felicitations, to all who delight in their country's prosperity. But the idea, that my former gallant associates in the field are now about to receive, in a good national government, some compensation for the toils and dangers which they have experienced in the course of a long and perilous war, is particularly consolatory to me.

[1] See General Sullivan's letter of 7 July 1788, page 333.

I entreat that the members of your State Society will believe that I interest myself much in their prosperity, and that you will accept the professions of sincere regard and esteem, with which

I have the honor to be
Sir

Yr. Most Obed't
Most Humble Serv't
G. Washington

The Hon'ble Gen. Sullivan,
President of the State Society of the Cincinnati
in New Hampshire.

[*Archives of the New Hampshire Cincinnati*]

From Captain DENIS-NICHOLAS COTTINEAU DE KERLOGUEN.

Port au Prince, September 4, 1788.

Honourable Sir!

Ever Since the Glorious Peace which fixt the American Independence, have I wished for a favourable Opportunity to address Your Excellency, which I have at last obtained through my good Friend Mr. J[ohn] C[onrad] Zolliekoffer who has the Honour of presenting this Letter.

So conspicious a part, as Your Excellency has had in this perilous affair, in Conducting the same Under so many Difficuties, will be handed down to after ages by History, But Whilst all the World admires Your Disinterested ness.

Your So Generously remembering those brave officers who fought Under Your Banners; in instituting the Order of the Cincinnatus as a token of their Bravery inspires even Foreigners who have a Share in the American Contest with a Noble Ardour to become Members of Such a Patriotic and Heroic Order.

It is this which occasions this address to Your Excellency, I being own of those Foreigners by Birth a Natif of France, who early in the War became animated with those Principles of Liberty even before the Alliance with France, fitted out the

Pallas a Stout, well armed and Manned Frigatte of 24 Guns, and laden with Warlike Stores, which early in the Spring 1778, brought in to North Carolina, where I entered Imediately in the Servise with my Good Friend Mr. Zolliekoffer, building with my Own Sailors Fort Hancok, on point Lookout as bygoing Commission from the State of North Carolina certifies.

But the Pallas having taken her Cargo on Board, I entered likwise the service of the United States in Naval Department, and Sailing for France fall in with the British Frigatte La Brune, which I engaged and would have taken her to a Certainty had not an other Fregatte come to her Relief, and which Action being reported to His Most Crist. Majesty Purchased the Pallas and again entrusted her to my Command and Confirming my Commission from Congress with Order to join the famous Paul Jones on a Cruise.

How we Sailled and fell in with the Briti[s]h Fregatte Seraphis of 44 Guns, and the Fregatte Scarborough and took them both, as facts so memorable, as they well authenticated, the Seraphis Fregatte was taken by Paul Jones, and the Scarborough by me, this induced His Most Crist. Majesty to refer [sic] on Paul Jones the Military Order of Merite, and Nominated me an Officer of His Royal Marine Nevertheless continuing me in the servise of the United States, and I am this Moment Under Orders if any War should brackout Between France or Great Britain to Join Immediately either the French or the American Navy.

Thus Circumstanced I approach Your Excellency as Great Master of the Order of Cincinatus in flattering hopes if my Servises come within the prescribed Rules and Limits of this Noble Order I may be admitted and Incorporated therein. Any of the Usual Expences will be Defray'd By my Friend Mr. Zolliekoffer who will Transmit to me the Diploma. He has long be[en] wishing for the same admission but as he is on the Spot he can pleade his own cause before Your Excellency.[1]

In this happy Expectation, I have the Honour to remain, etc.

[*Archives of the General Society*]

[1] Captain Cottineau de Kerloguen was elected an honorary member of the Pennsylvania Cincinnati in 1795. General Washington replied to this letter on

General Washington writes to an original member of the New Jersey Cincinnati of the unreasoning criticism of the Cincinnati, and even of its President General. Therefore, though the General is interested in heraldry, he feels that it may be a dangerous topic politically.

To Colonel WILLIAM BARTON.

Mount Vernon, September 7, 1788

Sir:

At the same time I announce to you the the receipt of your obliging letter of he 28th of last month,[1] which covered an ingenious essay on *Heraldry,* I have to acknowledge my obligations for the sentiments your partiality has been indulgent enough to form of me, and my thanks for the terms in which your urbanity has been pleased to express them.

Imperfectly acquainted with the subject, as I profess myself to be, and persuaded of your skill as I am, it is far from my design to intimate an opinion, that heraldry, coat-armour, &c., might not be rendered conducive to public and private uses with us; or that they can have and tendence unfriendly to the purest spirit of republicanism. On the contrary, a different conclusion is deducible from the practice of Congress and the States; all of which have been established some kind of *Armorial Devices* to authenticate their official instruments. But Sir, you must be sensible, that political sentiments are very various among the people of the several States, and that a formidable opposition to what appears to be the prevailing sense of the Union is but just declining into peaceable acquiescence. While, therefore, the minds of a certain portion of the community (possibly from turbulent or sinister views) are, or affect to be, haunted with the very spectre of innovation; while they are indefatigably striving to make the credulity of the lessinformed part of the citizens subservient to their schemes, in believing that the proposed general government is pregnant with the seeds of discrimina-

21 February 1789, see page 344. See also the letters exchanged between him and the French Consul in Baltimore, the Chevalier d'Annemours on this subject, pages 340 and 342.

[1] This letter is in the Washington Papers. It contains no reference to the Cincinnati.

tion, oligarchy, and despotism; while they are clamorously endeavouring to propagate an idea, that those, whom they wish individuosly to designate by the name of the "well-born" are meditating in the first instance to distinguish themselves from their compatriots, and to wrest the dearest privileges from the bulk of the people; and while the apprehensions of some, who have demonstrated themselves the sincere, but too jealous, friends of liberty, are feeling alive to the effects of the actual revolution, and too much inclined to coincide with the prejudices above described; it might not, perhaps, be advisable to stir any question that would tend to reanimate the dying embers of faction, or blow the dormant spark of jealousy into an inextinguishable flame. I need not say, that the deplorable consequences would be the same, allowing there should be no real foundation for jealousy, in the judgment of sober reason, as if there were demonstrable, even palpable, causes for it.

I make these observations with the greater freedom, because I have once been a witness to what I conceived to have been a most unreasonable prejudice against an innocent institution, I mean the Society of the Cincinnati. I was conscious that my own proceedings on that subject were immaculate. I was also convinced, that the members, actuated by motives of sensibility, charity, and patriotism, were doing a laudable thing, in erecting that memorial of their common services, sufferings, and friendships; and I had not the most remote suspicion, that our conduct therein would have been unprofitable, or unpleasing, to our countrymen. Yet we have been virulently traduced, as to our designs; and I have not even escaped being represented as short-sighted in not forseeing the consequences, or wanting in patriotism for not discouraging an establishment calculated to create distinctions in society, and subvert the principles of a republican government. Indeed, the phantom seems now to be pretty well laid; except on certain occasions, when it is conjured up by designing men, to work their own purposes upon terrified imaginations. You will recollect there have not been wanting, in the late political discussions, those, who were hardy enough to assert, that the proposed general government was the wicked and traitorous fabrication of the Cincinnati.

At this moment of general agitation and earnest solicitude,

I should not be surprised to hear a violent outcry raised, by those who are hostile to the new constitution, that the proposition contained in your paper had verified their suspicions, and proved the design of establishing unjustified descriminations.

I remain with great esteem, etc.

[*Toner Transcripts, Library of Congress*]

To Major-General HENRY KNOX.

Mt. Vernon, Sept. 10, 1788.

Sir.

For the purpose of laying them before the next General Meeting of the Society of the Cincinnati, I enclose you the congratulation address of the State Society of New Hampshire,[1] on the ratification of the new constitution, by a sufficient number of States to give efficacy thereto &c—and an extract of a letter from the Count Augustus de Grasse,[2] son to the Admiral of that name, our compatriot in arms. With sentiments of the highest esteem and regard,

I have the honor to be
Sir
Your most obed and
Most Humble Serv.
G. Washington.

The Honble
Maj. Gen. Knox

[*Archives of the New Hampshire Cincinnati*]

---

[1] See General Sullivan's letter of 7 July 1788, page 332.

[2] See General Washington's letter of 18 August 1788 to the younger Count de Grasse on his father's death, page 333.

From Brigadier-General GEORGE WEEDON.

Fredericksburg, Decr. 2^{d}. 1788

Dear Sir

I have the honor of transmiting you a copy of the proceeding of the last meeting of the Virginia Society of cincinnati held in Richmond the 13th & 14th of Novr. 1788.[1]

A very severe fit of the gout which crippled me for three months has deprived me the pleasure of visiting you at Mount Vernon this fall agreeable to promise.

With very great esteem and respect
I am my dear Genl.

Your ob^{t}. Servt.

G. Weedon

From

General Weedon
2^{d}. Decr. 1788
[Enclosure]

[*Washington Papers*]

The French Consul in Baltimore transmits to the President General, the request of a French officer for admission to the Cincinnati.

From the CHEVALIER D'ANNEMOURS.

Baltimore, February 15, 1789.

Sir,

I take the liberty of applying to your excelency on a Subject in which the merit and the Sentiments of the parti concerned will, I hope plead an appology for the trouble it may give you; and it is also the only one I can offer for the intrusion of this letter: Give me leave to lay it under you Excelency's Eyes.

Monsr. contineau de Kerloquin,[2] had, in the year 1779, the

[1] See E. E. Hume, *Papers of the Society of the Cincinnati in the State of Virginia, 1783-1824* (1938), 174-176, for copy of these Minutes.

[2] See Captain Cottineau de Kerloguen's letter of 4 September 1788, page 335.

honour of being promoted to the ranck of a captain in the continental navy. in that quality, he took, by order of the then minister plenipotentiary of Congress at Versailles, the Command of the continental frigate *Pallas,* fitted out at l'orient, in france, under the superior command of capn. Paul Jones. during the celebrate engagement of that distinguished american officer with his Britannick majesty's Ship *Seraphis,* capn. Cotineau engaged and took the British frigate the Scarborough. the honour that capture did him in his Sovereign's, as well as in the publick oppinion; together with the approbation of the american minister procured him a respectable rank in the royal navy of his Country, with the Singular favour of retaining, Still, his Commission in the Service of the United States. he continued to Serve, in this double capacity, the two countries from which he had received Such flattering marks of consideration; till peace having put a period to the war, and Sealed the independence of America, rendered also his active Service less urgent. he then went over to the island of hispaniola, where his fortune, which he had neglected for military Glory, required his immediate presence; and with a furlow that continued him in the french Service, leaving him Still at liberty to Consider himself as an american officer.

from Port au Prince, Where he resides now, I have, Sir, received a letter from that gentleman, who is an intimate acquaintance of mine, in which he desires me to apply to your Exelency in order to obtain admission in the Society of cincinatus. the fervour of this sollicitation Shows that he is perfectly sensible how greatly that admission would honour him. I have, in Consequence of his request, laid before you a Statement of that part of his military Service Which appear'd to me more Susceptible of grounding his pretensions; for I might, also, have mentioned that previous to the epocha at which he enterred in the navy of the united States, he had allready been advantageously employ'd by the State of north Carolina. but on this point, as well as on any further Elucidation, I take the liberty to refer your Exelency to M. Zolliekoffer; a Gentleman to Whom he has also wrote for the Same purpose; and who will have the honour to deliver you this.

Will you Exelency permit me to intreat you to take his

application under you immediate protection, and yourself in behalf of his demand? I can answer for him, that the favour will exite in his breast Such Sentiments of Gratitude, as Can be equalled by none, exept those of the particular respect with which I have the honour to be, etc.[1]

[*Archives of the General Society*]

To the CHEVALIER D'ANNEMOURS.

Mount Vernon, February 20, 1789

Sir:

The letter which you did me the honor of writing to me on the 15th[2] came to my hands at George Town the 16th. at a time when it was not in my power to give it an answer: but by sentiments on the purport of it were fully delivered to Captn. Zollickoffer[3] to whom I beg lieve to refer you. Briefly they were, that Major Cottineau de Kerloguin[4] was either a member, of right to the Society of the Cincinnati agreeably to the letter of the Institution, or his admission as an honorary one depended according to the Spirit of it, upon the merits of his particular case. If the first (for I have not the Institution by me to refer to; and therefore have referred Captn. Zollickoffer to the Secretary General, Genl. Knox, or to the Assistant Secretary, Genl. Williams for information) there remains nothing more for him to do than to comply with the Requisites and send his Diploma to be (first Countersigned by the Secretary Genl. Knox) for my signature. If the second, it rests not with me, but with the General meeting of the Society to be holden in Philadelphia the first Monday of May 1790 to decide on his case, at which meeting it is not expected I shall attend because

[1] General Washington replied on 20 February 1789, see next letter.

[2] See page 340.

[3] John Conrad Zollickoffer served as a Captain of North Carolina Militia, 1778-1780. He died in 1796.

[4] Captain Denis Nicholas Cottineau de Kerloguin (or Kerloguen), French Navy. See his letter of 4 September 1788, page 335, and General Washington's reply, 21 February 1789, page 344.

49

Mount Vernon 21 February 1789

My dear Sir,

I have the honor to enclose a letter from Mons.r Cottineau de Kerloguin requesting an admission into the Society of the Cincinnati — and one from the Chevalier D'Annmours setting forth the services of that Gentleman and his pretensions to admission. Both of which I must beg you to lay before the Society at their next General Meeting that they may take the necessary steps thereon; unless it shall appear, by the Institution, that he is a member of right

I am, my dear Sir,
very affectionately
Yr most Obedt &
Hble Servt

Go Washington

General Knox —

President General Washington to Secretary General Knox regarding a French officer's application for admission to the Society of the Cincinnati.

[*Archives of the General Society*]

it was agreed at the last Genl. Meeting that I should be leased of the duty of the President which were to be executed by the Vice President now Governor Mifflin. To whom, [or] to the Secretary General, I will transmit your letter with that of Major Cottineau de Kerloguion in order that the merits of his pretensions (if they do not give him a *legal* claim from the tenor of his Commission and length of Service) may be taken into consideration at the first General Meeting of the Society.

I have the honor etc.

[*Washington's Letter Books*]

To Captain Denis Nicholas Cottineau de Kerloguen.

Mount Vernon, February 21, 1789

Sir:

I have had the honor to receive your letter of the 4th. September 1788 [1] which was handed to me by your friend Captn. Zollickoffer, to whom I fully delivered my sentiments upon the purport of your letter, and who will undoubtedly take every necessary step towards your *legal* or *honorary* admission into the Society of the Cincinnati.

It is not in my power to say anything decidedly upon the propriety of your claim, as I was at the last General Meeting of the Society, exonorated from the duties of the Presidency, have not the Institution by me, and it will not be expected that I shall attend the next General Meeting, which will take place on the first Monday in May 1790 in the City of Philadelphia, nor perhaps any future meeting of the Society. I have therefore transmitted your letter to the Secretary Genl. Knox to be laid before the next Genl. Meeting where the merits of your pretensions will claim that attention which they deserve.

I have the honor etc.[2]

[*Washington's Letter Books*]

[1] See page 335.

[2] On 21 February 1789, General Washington sent the letters of d'Annemours and Cottineau de Kerloguen to General Knox, Secretary General, with a brief note. All three letters are in the Archives of the General Society, (see pages 343 and 345.

To Major-General HENRY KNOX.

Mount Vernon, February 21, 1789.

My dear Sir,

I have the honor to enclose a letter from Monsr. Cottineau de Kerloquin [1] requesting an admission into the Society of the Cincinnati—and one from the Chevalier D'Anmours [1] setting forth the services of that Gentleman and his pretensions to admission.—Both of which I must beg you to lay before the Society at their next General Meeting that they may take the necessary steps thereon; unless it shall appear (by the Institution) that he is a member *of right.*—

I am, etc.

[*Archives of the General Society*]

From the BARON DE MONTLEZUN DE LA BARTHETTE.

A Bordeaux le 25 février 1789.

Mon Général,

Au moment de traverser les mers pour avoir l'honneur de vous offrir mon respectueux hommage, et dans l'espoir de votre puissante protection pour me faire obtenir la grace que j'ambitionne, au moment dis-je de venir la Solliciter moi même, une maladie cruelle me met hors d'état de m'embarquer et me Contraint d'autant plus, qu'à l'époque où ma Santé me permettrait peut-être d'entreprendre le voyage, il ne resterait pas a ma disposition le temps Suffisant pour l'effectuer, puis qu'au 1er. de juin je Suis forcé d'être de retour à mon régiment. la bonté de ma cause m'empêche néanmoins de désespérer du Succès et m'enage a vous faire part, Mon Général, et de ce que je Sollicite et des raisons que je puis donner en ma faveur. j'ai été assez heureux pour Commencer ma Carrière militaire et faire mes premières armes, pendant la guerre Célèbre Soutenue pour la Cause de la liberté. j'ai eu Surtout l'avantage, mon général, de me trouver Sous vos ordres au Siège d'York, où je marchai avec le détachement des chasseurs du régiment de touraine, qui mit

[1] See pages 335 and 340.

le feu aux abattis de la redoute de gauche. mais Ce que je crois encore plus favorable à ma cause, et ce qui pourrait me faire espérer d'obtenir pour un cas particulier une grace particulière, C'est que mon père a fait cette même guerre en qualité de Lt. Colonel du régiment de touraine, qu'entr'autres il a eu l'honneur, mon Général, de Commander Sous vos ordres la tranchée de Gauche pendant tout le Siege d'York, et qu'enfin, à la Suite des blessures qu'il a reçus pendant le cours de cette guerre, j'ai eu le malheur de le perdre: moment cruel qui me Laissa Sans appuy, et me priva de ce que j'avais de plus cher au monde! que puis-je dire de plus? ah! Si C'était un droit à vos bontés, et Si de mon côté je n'ai jamais démerité, Si j'ai le Suffrage de Ceux avec qui j'ai passé ma vie dans la Scrupuleuse observation des lois de l'honneur, dois-je désespérer que les américains veuillent bien m'honorer d'une marque flatteuse de Consolation. cette grace Serait de m'admettre á la Société de *Cincinnatus.*

permettez moi, mon Général, de vous adresser avec les papiers et certificats que j'ai cru nécessaires, un mémoire que je vous Supplie de faire lire á l'assemblée des membres de Cincinnatus, les priant au cas qu'ils veuillent bien me faire l'honneur de m'admettre, de vouloir bien aussi m'en donner avis, à ma Garnison à *perpignan en roussillon.* je pourrais observer que Ce ne Serait pas donner lieu aux réclamations des autres officiers, puis que je Suis le Seul qui Servit avec Son père.

me pardonnerez vous, mon Général, d'avoir osé prendre Sur un temps aussi prétieux que le vôtre pour vous faire part de mes intérêts. Si quelque chose peut me rassurer, C'est que je ne puis Craindre de vous offenser, en vous donnant l'occasion d'accorder une Grace.

je Suis avec respect Mon Général etc.[1]

[*Archives of the General Society*]

[1] Enclosed were the following documents:

1. Letter from the Count de Fléchin to Montlezun, 14 February 1782.
2. Letter from Montlezun to the Society, undated.
3. Order of the King, 15 May 1785, appointing Montlezun First Lieutenant in the Touraine Regiment. (See page 111 *seq.* for *fac simile*).
4. Certification from the *Juge d'Armes,* 8 September 1770, as to the nobility of Montlezun's family. (See page 375 for *fac simile*).

[Translation by Edgar Erskine Hume]

Bordeaux, 25 February 1789

General,

At the moment when I was about to cross the seas to offer you my respectful homage, and in the hope of your powerful assistance to help me achieve my ambition, at that moment, I say, when I was about to ask it myself, a cruel illness made it impossible for me to embark and constrained me, instead, to await the time when my health would permit me to undertake the voyage, by which time the leave at my disposal was insufficient to permit it, since by the first of June I had to return to my regiment. The justice of my cause nevertheless makes me hope for success, and to ask for your help, General, for what I ask, in view of the reasons that I give in my own behalf. I was happy, in beginning my military career, of first bearing arms in the celebrated war waged for the cause of Liberty. I had above all, General, the advantage of finding myself under your orders at the siege of York, where, General, I participated with a detachment of *chasseurs* of the Tourraine Regiment, which set fire to the *abattis* of the left redoute. But that which I feel most favorable for my cause, and that which makes me hope the more that my particular case may receive special grace, is that my father took part in this same war as a Lieutenant-Colonel of the Tourraine Regiment, which he had the honor, General, to command under your orders at the left trenches during the siege of York, and that on account of the wounds he received in that war, I had the misfortune to lose him. A cruel blow which struck without warning, and which deprived me of what I held most dear in the world! What more can I say? Ah, if it might be through your goodness, and if on my side I have never been unworthy, if I have the suffrage of those with whom I have passed my life in scrupulous observation of the laws of honor, may I not hope that the Americans will do me the honor of such a flattering mark of consolation? This favor would be to admit me into the Society of *Cincinnatus.*

Permit me, General, to forward you the papers and certificates that I have thought necessary, and with them a memorandum which I beg you to read to the assembly of the members of Cincinnatus, asking them in case they wish me to have the honor of admission, to be so good as to give me notice thereof at my garrison of Perpignan en Roussillon. I may observe that this would not give rise to objections on the part of other officers, for I am the only one who served with his father.

Pardon me, General, for having presumed to take your precious time in order to ask you to help with my interests. If anything might reassure me, it would be that I do not fear to offend you, in giving you this opportunity to grant a favor.

I am with respect, General, etc [1]

When General Washington was elected President of the United States several of the State Societies of the Cincinnati as well as the General Society, sent him congratulatory addresses. He replied formally to each.

ADDRESS BY THE PENNSYLVANIA CINCINNATI.

Address to GEORGE WASHINGTON, President and Commander in Chief of the Army and Navy of the United States of America &c &c.

Sir:

The Standing Committee of the Pennsylvania State Society of the Cincinnati, embrace this early opportunity of waiting on your Excellency with their congratulations on your unanimous appointment, by the People, to the office of First Magistrate of this great empire; it being the strongest evidence of *your* unrivalled merit, and of *their* exalted wisdom. Permit us to express our peculiar joy and pride upon the occasion, that *our* beloved General, and the President General of *our* Society, has received the free sufferage of each of our fellow-citizens of these States. We have now the most perfect assurance, that th inestimable rights and liberties of human nature, for which

[1] See original letter for note as to the inclosures.

we have toiled, fought and bled, under your command, will be preserved inviolate; and we felicitate our country, that their national safety and dignity are secure, and that they have the best grounded prospects of all that happiness, which a good Constitution, under a wise and virtuous administration, can afford. As we have the fullest confidence that our Society, whose basis is friendship and charity, will, equally with others, enjoy those blessings, and partake of your regard, so we beg leave to assure you, that we shall never be wanting in our endeavours to contribute all in our power to your personal comfort and honour, and the prosperity and glory of your government.[1]

Signed by order of the Committee

Thomas M'Kean, Vice-President

Philadelphia, April 20, 1789.

[*Washington Papers*]

REPLY TO THE PENNSYLVANIA CINCINNATI.

To the State Society of the Cincinnati of Pennsylvania

Gentlemen,

The congratulations of my fellow-soldiers and faithful followers in the military line of this State, on my election to the Chief Magistracy of the Union, cannot but be exceedingly flattering and pleasing to me; for my mind has been so deeply

[1] General Washington reached Philadelphia on 20 April 1789, about 1 p. m., and at 3 p. m. he was entertained at a public banquet at the City Tavern. He lodged at the house of Robert Morris and the next morning, April 21, left for Trenton. Previous to his departure he received (the order in which these were delivered is not known) complimentary addresses from the president and executive council of Pennsylvania; the judges of the Supreme Court; the mayor, recorder, aldermen, and common council of Philadelphia; the president and faculty of the University of Pennsylvania; the Pennsylvania State Society of the Cincinnati; and the ministers, church wardens, and vestrymen of the German Lutheran congregation in and near Philadelphia. All of these addresses and his answers are in the Washington Papers, Library of Congress (Fitzpatrick's *The Writings of George Washington,* xxx, 289 n.).

affected with a grateful sense of the attachment and aid I have experienced from them, during the course of our arduous struggle for liberty, that the impression will never be effaced.

Heaven alone can foretell whether any, or what advantages are to be derived by my countrymen from my holding the office, which they have done me the honor of conferring upon me, not only without my solicitations, but even contrary to my inclinations.

I promise nothing but an unremitted attention to the duties of the office. If by that attention I may be so fortunate as still to continue to possess the affectionate regard of my fellow-citizens, and particularly of that body of which you are the representatives, it will be no small addition to my happiness. The support which they and you have promised cannot fail, under the smiles of Providence, to contribute largely to the accomplishment of my wishes by promoting the prosperity of our common country. In the meantime I thank you, Gentlemen, for the interest you so kindly take in my personal comfort and honor, as well as in the prosperity and glory of the general government.

G. Washington.

[*Washington's Letter Books*]

From the Baron de La Vallière.

Cap le 26e. May 1789.

Votre Excellence, Monsieur, a Eté instruite dans les tems d'hostilité Et de guérre des services qu'avec inclination Et empressements j'ay rendus Comme Commandant pour le Roy au Mole et ses dependances a Messieurs Les Commandts de Batiments Et negotiants des Etats unis; j'ai l'honneur d'adresser a Votre Excellence En divers tems plusieurs officiers Et jeunes gens français a qui Vous avés Bien Voulu donner des Emplois Et m'en avés accusé Reception En m'en temoignant Votre satisfaction.

j'ay Eté assés heureux que d'être util aux Respectables Etats unis En protegeant Leur Batiments Et En Empechant Les Corsairs Ennemis de s'en Emparer, j'ay Reçu des temoignages de satisfaction Des Capitns. de Votre Nation—

on me flatte, Monsieur, d'une marque de Contentement qui me fera Le plus grand plaisir, C'est de L'admission dans l'honorable Societé de Cincinnatus ainsy que La Eté Mr. De Lilencourt Brigadier des armées du Roy Et autres qui n'ont Eté a l'amerique.

j'ose Esperer Cette même faveur Et prie Votre Excellence d'en acheminer L'effet a La premiere assemblée de la Societé.

je suis avec Le plus Respectueux attachement de Votre Excellence Monsieur, etc.

[*Archives of the General Society*]

[Translation by Edgar Erskine Hume]

Cap 26 May 1789

Your Excellency, Sir, has known, during the time of hostilities and war, of the services with inclination and eagerness I have rendered, as Commandant for the King at the Mole, to the commanders of ships and merchants of the United States. I have had the honor to send Your Excellency at various times a number of officers and young Frenchmen to whom you have been good enough to give employment. And you have acknowledged this to me in evidence of your satisfaction.

I have been fortunate enough to be of use to the honorable United States in protecting their ships and in preventing enemy corsairs from capturing them, and have received evidences of the gratitude of the captains of your nation.

I would be flattered, Sir, by a mark of your satisfaction, which would give me the greatest pleasure. This is admission into the honorable Society of Cincinnatus, as have been M. de Lilencourt, Brigadier of the Armies of the King, and others who have been in America.

I dare hope for this same favor and beg Your Excellency to put this into effect at the first assembly of the Society.

I am with the most respectful attachment to your Excellency, Sir, etc.

From the COUNT D'ESTAING.

a Paris le 8 Juin 1789.

Monsieur,

Le Pere de la Patrie l'est aussi de toux ceux qui ont fait des efforts pour lui être utile. Votre Excellence la prouvé aux Marins françoix en obtenant de la société de Cincinnatus qu'ils Seraient traittes comme les officiers de l'armée de terre. il m'a fallu resister au désir de ceux des deux services qui ont été particulièrement mes Camarades. J'ai Voullu m'adresser qu'une listte pour chaque service, affin de moins importuner la Société et S. E. le Général Knox.—il m'a paru convenable que la marine fut traittée comme l'armée de terre et j'ai cru ne pas pouvoir envoyer une Liste avant l'autre—l'activité de notre marine a rendu longues les diverses decisions du Roy par lesquelles Sa Majeste d'après les grades et les preuves des services distingués, accompagnés d'actions éclatantes, et de blessures, m'a ordonné d'autoriser, enconséquence des Resolves de la Société, et succéssivement, ceux des officiers de sa Marine qu'elle en a jugé digne, a porter L'aigle Americaine.

Des marins qui font le tour du Monde avec Mr. Le Comte de la Pérouse n'ont pu même encore prouver leurs droits, et les faire Valloir, mais il m'est impossible de me refuser d'avantage a la Juste impatience que les officiers déja décores des marques de la Société ou d'en recevoir les Diplômes.

Votre Excellence a démontré a l'univers, a la postérité, et particulierement a mon Cœur, que les plus grandes affaires, dans les circonstances même les plus impératives, ne l'empeschoint jamais de S'occuper de ce qui est juste, et de ses amis. Je ne crains donc par de la suplier de s'interesser a l'éxpédition des Diplosmes dont Jai l'honneur de lui envoyer les Listes—Les familles dont les parents ont porté avant de mourir Les marques de la société Souhaittent d'obtenir des diplosmes qui seront pour elles un titre d'honneur consolant—les noms de Baptême n'ont pu être mis ainsi que cela m'avoit été prescrit avant tous les noms de famille. L'eloignement de beaucoup d'officiers la rendu impossible, mais leurs Lettres et leurs grades empêcheront les méprises, et Je pense que les Diplosmes du service de terre devroient être addressés directement a Mr. Le

Comte de Puy segur Ministre de la Guerre, ainsi que tous les Diplosmes du Service de la Marine a Mr. Le Comte de La Luzerne Ministre de ce département. J'ai l'honneur d'en écrire a Mr. Le Comte de Moustier par qui ce paquet vous parviendra. . . .[1]

[*Archives of the General Society*]

[Translation by Edgar Erskine Hume]

Paris, 8 June 1789

Sir,

The Father of his Country is such also to all those who have made efforts to be useful to him. Your Excellency has proved this to the officers of the French Navy in obtaining from the Society of Cincinnatus the right of being considered, just as are officers of the land forces. I cannot resist the desires of those of the two services who have been my comrades. I have thought to send a list for each service, at least to ask the Society and His Excellency General Knox, but it seems more convenient that the navy be treated as the land forces and I do not want to send in one list in advance of the other. The activity of our navy has required some time for the decisions of the King by which His Majesty, according to rank, proofs of distinguished service, accompanied by acts of gallantry and wounds, has ordered me to authorize, in consequence of the resolves of the Society, certain of the officers of his Navy, whom he has judged worthy of the honor, to wear the American Eagle.

The sailors who made the voyage around the world with the Count de la Pérouse, have not yet been able to prove their rights to have it, but it is impossible for me to refuse this in view of their just impatience since the officers have already received the decorations and diplomas of the Society.

Your Excellency has demonstrated to the universe, to posterity and particularly to my heart that even the most important affairs, even amid most imperative circumstances, never pre-

[1] General Washington replied on 13 October 1789, see page 358.

vent you from occupying yourself with what is just, and for his friends. I do not fear, then, to ask your interest in the sending of diplomas of which I have the honor to send you the list. Families whose members have borne before their deaths the badges of the Society hope to obtain the diplomas which will become for them valued titles of honor. The baptismal names might be added as well as the family names. The distance of many of the officers makes it impossible, but their grades may be given. I think that the Diplomas for the Army might be addressed directly to the Count de Puy Ségur, Minister of War, while those for the Navy to the Count de La Luzerne,[1] Minister of that Department. I have had the honor to write to the Count de Moustier, by whom this package is sent you.

From the CHEVALIER DESNOYERS.

Basse terre Guadeloupe le 12 Juin 1789.

Monsieur,

On ne scait lequel on doit le plus admirer du sage discernement des Etats unis en vous Confiant Leur administration Générale, où du Sacrifice Généreux que Vous avéz fait de Votre Goût pour la vie privée, En acceptant la Place de Président de la Convention. je Saisis avec le plus vif empressement Cette Circonstance pour vous rendre des hommages qui Vous sont dus à Tant de Titres, et pour Suplier Votre Excellence de Prendre En Consideration le Mémoire que j'ai L'honneur de Vous adresser Ci Joint qui Servira à Vous Convaincre Combien Je Suis Jaloux d'obtenir une marque de faveur et de Protection de la part d'une Nation pour la quelle J'ai eu La Gloire de Verser mon Sang.

Je Dois, Monsieur, avoir l'honneur d'observer a Votre Excellence que J'ai adressé plusieurs mémoires au Géneral Lincoln le dernier à la Datte du 20 Juillet dernier. Son Silence Me fait Croire qu'aucun de Ces mémoires ne lui est parvenu, J'éspére

[1] César-Henri, Count de La Luzerne, Minister of Marine of France 1789-1790, was the younger brother of the Chevalier (later Marquis) Anne-César de La Luzerne, Minister of France to the United States and who was made a member of the Cincinnati by the terms of the Institution itself.

que Celui ci aura un meilleur Sort et que Vous d'aigueréz L'appuyer de toute Votre protection. je ne Connais d'autre moyen de Vous prouver ma Reconnaissance qu'en Vous assurant que J'inspirerai à Mes fils les Sentimens de Zèle et d'attachement dont Je Suis penetré pour votre nation.

Je Suis avec Respect, Monsieur, etc.[1]

[*Archives of the General Society*]

[Translation by Edgar Erskine Hume]

Basse Terre, Guadeloupe, 12 June 1789

Sir,

One does not know which most to admire, the sage discernment of the United States in confiding their administration to you, or the general sacrifice you have made of your desire for private life, in accepting the office of President of the Convention [i. e. President of the United States]. I seize with the greatest satisfaction this opportunity to render you the hommage which is due you for so many reasons, and to beg Your Excellency to take into consideration the memorandum [1] which I have the honor to address you herewith, which will serve to convince you how desirous I am of obtaining a favor from a nation for which I have had the glory of shedding my blood.

I should, Sir, inform Your Excellency that I have sent several memoranda to General Lincoln, the last of them of date 20 July last. His silence makes me think that none of these memoranda has reached him. I hope this one will have better fortune and that you will give it your support. I know of no better means of proving to you my gratitude than of assuring you that I inspire my sons with the sentiments of zeal and attachment with which I am filled for your nation.

I am with respect, Sir, etc.

---

[1] Enclosed in this letter was a petition by Desnoyers, dated, 13 June 1789 and addressed to the Committee of the Society, asking that he be admitted to membership.

From the CHEVALIER BONNIER DE ST. COSME.

Basse terre Guadeloupe le 24 Juin 1789

Monsieur

Je crois ne pouvoir mieux faire que de M'adresser a vous pour Solliciter La faveur d'etre admis dans L'ordre de Cincinnatus dont Votre Excelence est le createur et le Veritable Soutien j'ai ete Blessé au siege de Savannah d'un Coup de fusil au travers de La poitrine a Le tete du Detachement de quatre cens hommes du Regt. D'armagnac. les incomodites que me sont Restés de cette terrible Blessure me rapellent bien souvent que jai versé mon Sang pour La Liberté que votre Excelence a si bien Soutenue et accomplie et il seroit flateur pour moy et mes enfants de porter cette decoration La devoir a mes Services et a La Justice de Votre Excelence qui fait Ladmiration de toute L'Europe

Je Suis avec Respect etc.[1]

[*Archives of the General Society*]

[Translation by Edgar Erskine Hume]

Basse terre, Guadeloupe, 24 June 1789

Sir,

I know of no better way to address you to solicit the favor of being admitted into the Order of Cincinnatus, of which Your Excellency is the creator and the true support, than that I was wounded at the siege of Savannah by a gunshot which pierced my breast, while at the head of a detachment of four hundred men of the Regiment d'Armagnac. The disability which remains from this terrible wound, recalls ever that I have shed my blood for that Liberty which Your Excellency has so well supported and achieved, and it would be flattering for me and my children to wear this decoration in recognition of my services, and the justice of Your Excellency which has the admiration of all Europe.[1]

[1] In this letter as enclosures are two copies of a petition by St. Cosme, dated, 25 June 1789 and addressed to the Committee of the Society, asking that he be admitted to membership.

ADDRESS BY THE RHODE ISLAND CINCINNATI.

ADDRESS of the Society of the CINCINNATI in the State of Rhode Island, to the PRESIDENT of the UNITED STATES.

Sir,

Expressions of respect and attachment are a tribute which the citizens of America owe to your prudence, your patriotism, and valor; to the successful display of which, they are already endebted for their freedom; and from a continuance of the exercise of those qualities they may anticipate the highest state of political happiness. Under these impressions, Sir, we the Society of the Cincinnati of the State of Rhode Island, most sincerely congratulate you upon your appointment to the Chief Magistracy of the Union, by the unanimous sufferage of more than three millions of free citizens; and appointment rendered the more dignified by the manner in which it was conferred, and the more pleasing to your fellow-citizens from a conviction that they could no where place the sacred deposit, for which they have so long and arduously contended, with equal safety to themselves, and honor to their country. We cannot help expressing at the same time the strong obligations we feel for the sacrifice of domestic ease and retirement, to which we are sensible the love of your country alone could have prompted you. And although we are not admitted to a participation of the good effects of the government over which you so deservedly preside, yet we fondly flatter ourselves that the period is not far distant, when the mistaken zeal which has lately prevailed in this State will give way to a more enlightened policy. We can only add, Sir, our ardent wishes for your health and happiness. Long, long may the United States be blessed with a life to which they are so highly endebted, and may the close of your days be as peaceful and happy to yourself, as the meridian of them has been useful and glorious to your country.

Isaac Senter, President
Robert Rogers, Secretary

Rhode Island, September 3, 1789.

[*Washington Papers*]

Reply to the Rhode Island Cincinnati.

To the *President* and *Members* of the *Rhode Island State Society* of the *Cincinnati.*

Gentlemen,

In returning my grateful thanks for the flattering and effectionate sentiments expressed in your address of the 3d instant, I beg you will do justice to the sincerity of my regard, which reciprocates, with great pleasure, the warmest wishes for your happiness, political and personal.

Under a persuasion of the candor and support of my fellow-citizens, I yielded obedience to the voice of my country; and, impressed with a sense of duty, I forsook the pleasures of domestic retirement, to promote (if my best exertions can have such tendency) the object of a dearer interest. Those expressions of support have been amply fulfilled, and my fondest hope of their candour has been gratified by a kind and partial country.

I am much pleased, Gentlemen, with the hope which you entertain, that mistaken zeal will give way to enlightened policy; and I desire to repeat to your society, assurances of the most affectionate esteem.

G. Washington

United States, September 14, 1789.

[*Washington's Letter Books*]

To the Count d'Estaing.

New York, October 13, 1789

Dear General:

I have been honored with the receipt of your letter of the 8th of June,[1] enclosing a list of Officers who wish to receive diplomas from the society of the Cincinnati.

[1] See page 352.

General Knox will forward to your Excellency, by the Count de Moustier, who is so oblidging as to favor this letter with his care, Diplomas for the first forty five names on your list, he has sent to the Commandant of the Squadron, now at Boston, Diplomas for the Vicomte de Pontever Gien,[1] Marquis de la Galisoniere,[2] Monsieur de Burand de Braije,[3] and the Marquis de Traversay,[4] and he hopes to obtain of sufficiency of Diplomas to complete your list, which he will transmit to you by the next Packet for France. . . .

With sentiments of respectful Affection and esteem, I have the honor, etc[5]

[*Washington's Letter Books*]

ADDRESS BY THE MASSACHUSETTS CINCINNATI.

ADDRESS of the MEMBERS of the SOCIETY of the CINCINNATI in the Commonwealth of MASSACHUSETTS, to the PRESIDENT of the UNITED STATES.

Sir,

Amidst, the various gratulations which your arrival in this metropolis has occasioned, permit us, the Members of the Society of the Cincinnati in this Commonwealth, most respectfully to assure you of that ardor of esteem and affection which you have so indelibly fixed in our hearts as our glorious leader in war, and illustrious example in peace.

After the solemn and endearing farewell on the banks of the Hudson, which our anxiety presaged as final, most peculiarly pleasing is the present unexpected meeting. On this occasion we cannot avoid the recollection of the various scenes of toil and danger through which you conducted us; and while we contemplate the trying periods of the war, and triumphs

[1] Henri-Jean-Baptiste, Vicomte de Pontevès-Giens.
[2] Athanase-Scipion-Barrin, Marquis de La Galissonnière.
[3] Jean-Baptiste-Alexandre Durand de Braye.
[4] Jean-Baptiste Prévost de Sensac, Marquis de Traversay.
[5] The Count d'Estaing replied on 20 March 1790, see page 366.

of peace, we rejoice to behold you, induced by the unanimous voice of your country, entering upon other trials and other services alike important, and, in some points of view, equally hazardous. For the completion of the great purposes which a grateful country has assigned you, long very long, may your invaluable life be preserved. And as an admiring world, while considering you as a soldier have long wanted a comparison may your virtues and talents as a statesman leave them again without a parallel.

It is act in words to express an attachment founded like ours. We can only say, that when soldiers, our greatest pride was a promptitude of obedience to your orders—as citizens, our supreme ambition is to maintain the character of firm supporters of that noble fabric of Federal Government, over which you preside.

As Members of the Society of the Cincinnati, it will be our endeavour to cherish those sacred principles of charity and fraternal attachment which our institution inculcates. And while our conduct is that regulated, we can never want the patronage of the first of patriots and the best of men.

William Eustis, Vice-President

Boston, October 27, 1789.

[*Washington Papers*]

Reply to the Massachusetts Cincinnati.

To the Members of the Society of the Cincinnati, in the Commonwealth of Massachusetts.

Gentlemen,

In reciprocating with gratitude and sincerity the multiplied and affecting gratulations of my fellow-citizens of this Commonwealth, they will all of them with justice allow me to say that none can be dearer to me than the affectionate assurances which you have expressed. Dear indeed is the occasion which restores an intercourse with my faithful associates in prosperous and adverse fortune; and enhanced are the triumphs of peace, participated with those whose virtue and valor so largely contributed to procure them. To that virtue and valor your country has confessed her obligations. Be mine the grateful task to add the testimony of a conviction, which it was my pride to own in the field, and it is now my happiness to acknowledge in the enjoyments of peace and freedom.

Regulating your conduct by these principles which have heretofore governed your actions as men, soldiers and citizens, you will repeat the obligations conferred on your country, and you will transmit to posterity an example which must command their admiration, and obtain their grateful praise. Long may you continue to enjoy the endearments of fraternal attachment, and the heart-felt happiness of reflecting that you have faithfully done your duty.

While I am permitted to possess the consciousness of that worth which has long bound me to you by every tie of affection and esteem, I will continue to be your sincere and faithful friend.

G. Washington

Boston, October 27, 1789.

[*Washington's Letter Books*]

Extract from General Washington's Diary.

Tuesday, 27th October, 1789[1]—At 10 o'clock in the Morning received the visits of the Clergy of the Town. All went to an Oratorio—and between that and 3 o'clock rec'd the Address of the Governor and Council—of the Town of Boston—of the President, etca. of Harvard College, and of the Cincinnati of the State; after wch. at 3 o'clock, I dined in a large and elegant Dinner at Fanuiel Hall, given by the Gov'r and Council, and spent the evening in my lodgings. . . .

---

[1] The entry was made in Boston. The Oratorio was in King's Chapel. The invitation to the concert of sacred music, signed by Thomas Bulfinch and Shrimpton Hutchinson, dated 18 October 1789, is in the Washington Papers, Library of Congress. The several addresses to General Washington are also in the Washington Papers.

Even at late as 1789, though the French branch of the Society of the Cincinnati was well established in Paris, applications were occasionally received by General Washington from French officers seeking membership.

From Lieutenant-Colonel DE TOURVILLE.

Calais, 16 November 1789.

Your Excellency,

The officers of the Regiment of Royal Auvergne, formerly Gâtinois, penetrated with admiration and esteem for His Excellency, General Washington, take the liberty of addressing themselves directly to him, to request of his equity and through his intercession with the illustrious members of the Assembly, the flattering decoration which has only been conferred upon generals and colonels, whilst all the other French officers, who have co-operated in the success of the siege of Yorktown and of the capture of the enemy's army, have been denied this distinction—a privation which has been felt most keenly by all the officers and notably by those of the Grenadiers and Chasseurs who participated in the assault on the great redoubt and carried it with such spirit as to merit the applause of Your Excellency, who besides was so satisfied with the manner in which the regiment behaved on that occasion and during the siege, that Your Excellency presented it with a mortar taken in the redoubt, a mortar which the Regiment of Royal Auvergne preciously preserves as a flattering testimonial of the esteem of Your Excellency for the Regiment.

All the officers present at the siege of Yorktown, and in whose names I have the honor to address Your Excellency, jealous of sharing in the remembrance and glory of this ever memorable event, earnestly pray Your Excellency to obtain from the illustrious members of the Assembly in the United States a diploma of the Society of the Cincinnati, with authority to be decorated with the Order.

The satisfaction, as well as gratitude, which these officers will experience in obtaining this favor, which they believe they have merited, will be extreme. This request is common to nine regiments and to the engineer officers who have had the advantage of serving under the orders of Your Excellency.

Those of the regiment of Royal Auvergne, formerly Gâtinois, charge me to offer further their thanks to Your Excellency, as well as their profound respect and the highest esteem for your person and your talents, so useful to your country.

I am, with respect, Your Excellency's most obedient and very humble servant.

de Tourville[1]

Lieutenant-Colonel of the Regiment
Major of the same at the Siege of Yorktown, and First Major of Brigade

[*Archives of the General Society*]

ADDRESS BY THE SOUTH CAROLINA CINCINNATI.

ADDRESS of the SOCIETY of the CINCINNATI in the STATE of SOUTH CAROLINA, to GEORGE WASHINGTON PRESIDENT of the UNITED STATES.

Sir,

Possessed of every feeling that can act on grateful hearts, the Society of the Cincinnati established in the State of South Carolina, beg leave to congratulate you on the happy occasion which has once again placed you in a situation of rendering general good to their country.

Retired from the busy scenes of life, to reap the rewards of your virtuous acts, and to enjoy the glory you had already obtained, your fellow-citizens receive you with exulting happiness; they saw in you the patriot-hero the friend and saviour of their country; and with hearts filled with gratitude and affection, they invoked the All-wise Disposer of human events to render that retirement happy.

The period, however, arrived when the abilities of the virtuous patriot were again to be called forth to assume a public character. A general political government was formed,

[1] Tourville became an honorary member of the French Cincinnati.

by which the happiness of the country for whose liberty you had fought, was now to be established. To preside at the head of this new government, to establish it with permanency, the people sought, in the Great Washington, the virtues on which they could rely with safety, and from which they might expect to receive every benefit without allay. They had experienced his abilities, they had experienced his integrity, and his inviolable love for his country. Nor did they seek in vain. The same noble spirit which actuated you at the beginning of our late contest with Great Britain, now operated. You received and obeyed the summons; and although you should make a sacrifice, yet you nobly determined, it was the voice of your country, in whose service every inferior consideration of ease and retirement must give place.

As citizens, we congratulate you, Sir, on this additional proof of your country's confidence. As soldiers who partook with you in many of the dangers and hardships which attended the general army under your command, we beg leave to express our warmest attachment to your person, and sincerest wish for your happiness and honor; and that we may, under your rule, supported by your amiable virtues, happily experience and long enjoy the fruits of a government which has for its basis the good of the people of America.

By Order of the Society
William Moultrie, President.

[*Washington Papers*]

REPLY TO THE SOUTH CAROLINA CINCINNATI.

To the State Society of the CINCINNATI in SOUTH CAROLINA.

Gentlemen,

From a conviction that the dispositions of the Society of the Cincinnati established in the State of South Carolina are peculiarly friendly to me, I cannot receive their congratulations on the occasion which gave birth to their Address, without emotions of peculiar satisfaction.

The interest that my fellow-citizens so kindly took in the

happiness which they saw me enjoy in my retirement after the war, is rather to be attributed to their great partiality in my favor, than to say singular title I had so their gratitude and effection.

Notwithstanding that I was conscious that my abilities had been too highly appreciated; yet I felt, that, whatever they were, my country had a just claim upon me, whenever the exercise of them should be deemed conducive to its welfare. With such feelings, I could not refuse to obey that voice which I had always been accustomed to respect, nor hesitate to forego a resolution which I had formed of passing the remainder of my days in retirement. And so far am I from having reason to repent of the decided measure I took, in the crisis of organizing a new general government, that I ought rather, perhaps, to felicitate myself upon having met the wisest, and experienced the assistance of a patriotic and enlightened people, in my arduous undertaking.

Always satisfied that I should be supported in the administration of my office, by the friends of good government in general, I counted upon the favorable sentiment and conduct of the officers of the late army in particular. Nor has my expectation been deceived. As they were formerly distinguished by their eminent fortitude and patriotism in the military service, during the most trying occasions, so are the same men now, mingled in the mass of citizens, conspicuous for a disinterested love of order, and a jealous attachment to the preservation of the rights of mankind. Nor is it conceivable that any members of the community should be more worthy of the enjoyment of liberty, or more zealous to perpetuate its duration, than those who have so nobly and so successfully defended its standard in the new world.

I sincerely thank you, Gentlemen, for your expression of attachment to my person, and wish for my happiness and honor. On my part, I can only dare to engage, it shall be my incessant study, that you may happily experience as long and and enjoy the fruits of a government, which has for its basis the good of the American people.

G. Washington

[*Washington's Letter Books*]

From the COUNT D'ESTAING.

Sir:

The letter with which you have had the goodness to honr me dated October 13th,[1] has been transmitted to me by M. le Comte de Moustier, as well as the diplomas with which he was charged. I have transmitted them to the officers to whom they were destined. Deign to accept, I beseach you, with that indulgent goodness which is your characteristic, the homage of my thanks. Those which each one of my comrades have charged me to tender to you vary in expression, but unite in sentiment. Some envy the good fortune of the Squadron which was at Boston—others desire to be so happy as to show their duty to you; and none fail to signify the satisfaction which they feel in proposing so honorable a title and to transmit it to their families. The signature of M. George Washington is placed above those of the greatest Sovereigns that ever existed; they show it with a kind of religious veneration; for when liberty is rightly understood it becomes the divinity of the human race—and you, Sir, ought not to be surprised that you are the Messiah of it.

Those officers who have not received their diplomas express the greatest desire to obtain that benefit—they have charged me to solicit it—deign, I pray you, to speak of it to His Excellency, General Knox. All my friends threaten to quarrel with me if they have not this signature which is superior to all titles,—and the Emperors of Germany decorate themselves with it to this day. Cæsar enslaved his country, you have liberated yours. How much more worthy are you, than he, to this homage! Your fellow citizens and posterity have decreed that the name of Washington shall not be lessened by any qualification [titles]. The United States owe to you peace and political energy—the two bases of all good government, which cannot exist and be durable longer than while the executive authority enjoys all its powers within the immutable bounds of liberty.

As an American citizen I partake of this good fortune by my attachement to my new country and I take the more lively

[1] See page 358.

and sincere interest in the glory which you have procured for it; I do not fear to add, as a French citizen, that I not only expect the moment in which I can say as much of this country but that I think and hope it is not far distant.

I am with Respect, Sir, Your most Obedient and most Humble Servant,

Estaing

Paris, 20th March, 1790

To M. George Washington,
President of the United States of America

[*Washington Papers*]

Noailles, LaFayette's brother-in-law, was becoming enthused with republican ideals. Here he asks General Washington to extend the entrance requirements of the Cincinnati to include all officers who had served in the American War of Independence. Soon after this letter was written, Noailles took his seat in the Assembly. He escaped to the United States during the Terror.

From the VISCOUNT DE NOAILLES.

Paris, April 24th, 1790.

Dear General,

I have, though remote, incessantly borne you that share of admiration you have filled every Frenchman's breast with who has marched under your colors. It is not only now with a spirit replete with freedom that I durst address you, but partaking of all the rights nature has reserved to mankind and America had reaped the first benefits of. In the French Revolution which portends the greatest blessings, almost all those who have beheld the foundation of liberty in the United Provinces, have brought from thence of American spirit, and have displayed it with undaunted courage, as they have had a hand in preparing the Revolution, so are they doomed in firmly supporting its establishment. Such a brotherhood has been of the utmost help, and will be our greatest prop. It is in your power to contribute to its indissolubility by a deed both equitable and useful. The national dignities are the only badges we set value on, and are willing to preserve. The Cross of St. Louis, the sign of military service, is going to be conferred throughout all ranks of the army. Condescend in granting the same favor on all the officers who have been under your orders, and who have contributed as well as we to the salvation of the commonwealth. Condescend to obtain for them the right of bearing the Order of Cincinnatus which we shall hold the dearer when we behold our brethren dignified with it. Fill up their vow and our own. It is in the name of the small army you had some esteem for I durst petition the favour. In granting us a second reward, at having our fellows at arms honoured as well as we with a benefaction that evinces that liberty has been labored for. Such a bounty were less pleasing, and were perhaps impossible in experiencing its influence, if you were not so generous as to diffuse it over all those who are entitled to it.

The deliberation to be held on this request is that the officers of the French army who were in America at the time M. de Rochambeau left the continent to repair to the Leeward Islands, as also those of the legion of Lauzun be indulged with the leave of bearing the Order of Cincinnatus, provided they give an unexceptionable testimony of their service, and obtain a certificate of their corps, revised and signed by General Rochambeau.

Numbers of French officers have brought from the American war but scars. They will receive an healthy remedy when they have an additional proof of their service.

I have the honour to be with respect, dear General,

your most humble and obedient servant,

Noailles
A member of the National Assembly

[*Archives of the General Society*]

GENERAL MEETING OF 1790.

General WASHINGTON reelected President General

Tuesday, May 4th, 1790

. . . The general meeting then proceeded to the election of officers for the Society for the ensuing three years, and, upon counting the votes, it appeared that the following persons were unanimously chosen, viz.:

His Excellency George Washington, Esq. (late commander-in-chief of the armies of the United States), president-general.
Major-General Thomas Mifflin, vice-president-general.
Major-General Henry Knox, secretary-general.
Major William Macpherson, assistant secretary-general. . . .

[*Minutes of the General Meeting of 1790*]

GENERAL MEETING OF 1790.

Address to the President of the United States from the Delegates of the State Societies of the Cincinnati.

Philadelphia, May 4, 1790

To the President of the United States of America

Sir,

We the Delegates of the State Societies of the Cincinnati, assembled at our triennial general meeting congratulate you on being unanimously elected the Head of our rising republic.

As a part of the community we felicitate our countrymen on this happy event, and we embrace the first opportunity of expressing our sentiments with no less zeal than sincerity.

When we say we love and revere you as a Father we not only speak the language of our own hearts, but we speak the language of all, who have fought, suffered, and conquered under your command. Were poverty and consciousness of duty our only recompense still should we glory in the part we have acted For our motives, as they regarded our country, will afford us satisfaction as well through the vicissitudes of life, as in the moment of dissolution—As members of our Institution, on a former occasion, we appealed to Heaven and our own hearts for the purity of our intentions—Our fellow-citizens will witness that the conduct of the Officers and Soldiers of the late American Armies has not been less patriotic in peace than it was glorious in war.

A good constitution was the object for which we risked our lives and experienced unparalleled difficulties—We are happy in the conviction that our views are answered in the present government of the United States—While we applaud the wisdom of our countrymen in placing you at the head of it, we pledge ourselves to support its administration with the remnants of lives long since devoted to the public service.

We need not enumerate your titles to the gratitude of your Country; or echo in the suffrages of our particular Constitutents the public sentiment But we may say that we see with exultation our Countrymen beginning to reap the fruits of independence under the auspices of the Person, who was more instrumental than any other in its establishment. May you as a reward for your services enjoy length of days and every temporal blessing, and may such blessings be a prelude to everlasting felicity!

Signed in behalf of the general meeting

T. Mifflin
Vice President General.

Attest. H. Knox. Secretary General.[1]

[*Washington Papers*]

---

[1] The Minutes of the General Meeting of 1790, quoting this address in full, add:

"*Resolved*, That the foregoing address be presented to the President of the United States by a committee of nine, to wit:

General Knox
Colonel Hawkins
General Clarkson
General Matthews
Captain Dayton
Colonel Wadsworth
Colonel Gunn
Colonel Smith
Colonel Humphreys

Resolved, That the same committee inform the president-general of his election for the ensuing three years."

Reply to the General Meeting.

To the Delegates of the State Societies of the Cincinnati assembled at their triennial Meeting.

Gentlemen

Although it is easier for you to conceive, than for me to explain the pleasing sensations which have been excited in my breast by your congratulations on my appointment to the head of this rising Republic: yet I must take the liberty to thank you sincerely for the polite manner in which you felicitate our Countrymen, and testify your regard to me on this occasion.—

In addition to that reward for your sufferings & Services which arises from the consciousness of having done your duty; you have erected monuments more expressive of your merits than even the universal applause of your Country, in the establishment of its Independence and Sovereignty. Nor should any possible circumstances of poverty or adversity compel you to give up that sweet satisfaction for the part you have acted, which ought to attend you as well through the vicissitudes of life as in the moment of dissolution

The candour of your fellow-citizens acknowledges the patriotism of your conduct in peace, as their gratitude has declared their obligations for your fortitude and perseverance in war.—A knowledge that they now do justice to the purity of your intentions ought to be your highest consolation, as the fact is demonstrative of your greatest glory.—

The object for which your gallantry encountered every danger, and your virtue sustained unparalleled difficulties, has happily been attained.—A Government, promising protection and prosperity to the People of the United States, is established; and its operations hitherto have been such as to justify the most sanguine expectations of further success.—It was naturally to be expected, that lives which had long since been devoted on the Altar of Freedom, could never be offered at the Shrines of Anarchy or Despotism.—And the offer which you make of the residue of those lives to support the Administration of this Government is not less a proof of its excellence, than an encouragement for those concerned in its execution to use their best endeavours to make it a source of extensive and permanent blessings to their Country.—

Whatever titles my military services may have given me to the regard of my Country, they are principally corroborated by the firm support of my brave and faithful Associates in the field: and, if any consideration is to be attributed to the successful exercise of my civil duties, it proceeds, in a great measure, from the wisdom of the Laws, and the facility which the Disposition of my fellow-citizens has given to their Administration.

To the most affectionate wishes for your temporal happiness, I add a fervent prayer for your eternal felicity.

[*Archives of the General Society; printed in the Minutes of the General Meeting of 1790*]

Extract from General Washington's Diary.

Saturday, 8th May, 1790—Exercised in the Coach with Mrs. Washington and the Children in the forenoon.[1]

Received from Genl. Knox, Secretary Genl. of the triennial Genl. Meeting of the Cincinnati held at Philadelphia the first Monday of this Month, the Copy of an Address from that body to me to which I was to return an answer on ——— next.[2]

The wife of Marshal the Count de Rochambeau uses her influence with General Washington to assist a French officer seeking the Eagle of the Cincinnati.

From the COUNTESS DE ROCHAMBEAU.

Paris the 18th November, 1790

Sir:

I hope that your Excellency will give me the leave to beg a favor of your justice. I think it just to intercede for the Baron

[1] The children above mentioned were Mrs. Washington's grandchildren: George Washington Parke Custis and Eleanor Parke Custis.

[2] See pages 369 and 371.

de Closen who was an aide-de-camp to Mr. Rochambeau during the American war. He longs with the desire to be a member of the association of the Cincinnati. The officers who were employed in the French army and younger than him in the military service have been decorated with this emblem of liberty, and such a reward given by your Excellency's hand shall increase its value.

I flatter myself that you will receive the assurances of the respect and veneration I have for your talents and your virtue, well known in the whole world.[1]

I have, [etc].

La Comtesse de Rochambeau

Extract from General Washington's Diary.

Wednesday, 4th May, 1791[2]—Dined with the Members of the Cincinnati, and in the evening went to a very elegant dancing Assembly at the Exchange, at which were 256 elegantly dressed and handsome ladies.

In the forenoon (indeed before breakfast today) I visited and examined the lines of attack and defense of the City and

[1] [J. J. Jusserand's *Brothers in Arms*, page 119.] The name of Closen is not found in the list of members. Jusserand (p. 131) mentions that Closen was a colonel and knight of Saint-Louis and as aide-de-camp to his old chief, Rochambeau, once more, he served in defense of the northern frontier at the beginning of the French Revolution. A footnote is:

"A lithographed portrait mentions the later-day titles and dignities of: 'I. C. Louis, Baron de Closen Maréchal de Camp, chambellan et chevalier des ordres français pour le Mérite et de la Légion d'Honneur, ainsi que de celui de Cincinnatus des États-Unis de l'Amérique Septrionale.' Reproduced by C. W. Bowen, who first drew attention to this journal, *Century Magazine*, February 1907. Closen died in 1830, aged seventy-five."

For General Washington's reply, 20 July 1791, see page 373.

[2] General Washington was in Charleston, South Carolina, at this time. The dinner was, says Henderson (p. 176) at McCrady's Tavern. The scene of battle visited by the General in the forenoon was, of course, that of the defense of Charleston against the combined forces of Sir Henry Clinton and Vice-Admiral Marriot Arbuthnot in 1780. Washington evidently thought it a mistake to allow the troops to be shut up in the town by a superior land and sea force. Rather Charleston should have been given up, as New York had been in 1776. Thus, while the British would have taken the town, the American Army would have been saved further fighting.

was satisfied that the defense was noble and honorable altho' the measure was undertaken upon wrong principles and impolitic.

Extract from General Washington's Diary.

Monday, 9th May, 1791 [1]—At six o'clock I recommenced my journey for Savanna; attended by a Corps of the Cininnati and most of the prinipal Getlemen of the City as far as the bridge over Ashley River, where we breakfasted, and proceeded to Colo. W. Washington's at Sandy-hill with a select party of particular friends—distant from Charleston 28 miles.

Extract from General Washington's Diary.

Friday, 13th May, 1791 [2]—Dined with the Members of the Cincinnati at a public dinner given at the same place, and in the evening went to dancing Assembly, at which there was about 100 well dressed and handsome ladies.

ADDRESS BY THE GEORGIA CINCINNATI.

THE ADDRESS OF THE SOCIETY of the CINCINNATI of the STATE of GEORGIA

To George Washington

President of the United States and President General of the Society of the Cincinnati

Sir,

We the Members of the Society of the Cincinnati of the State of Georgia beg leave to offer our most sincere congratulations on your safe arrival in this state,

[1] General Washington was in Charleston, South Carolina, at this time. Colonel Washington was Colonel William Washington who had served in the War as Lieutenant-Colonel, Third Regiment of Continental Dragoons and was an original member of the Society of the Cincinnati of the State of South Carolina.

[2] This entry was made at Savannah, Georgia. The place of the dinner was the Coffee Room of Brown's Coffee House. The "Assembly" attended by the General is described in a contemporary account by Henderson (p. 219).

Nous Antoine-Marie d'Hozier-de Sérigny, Chevalier; Juge d'Armes de la Noblesse de France, et en cette qualité Commissaire du Roy pour certifier à Sa Majesté la Noblesse des Elèves de l'Ecole Royale Militaire et du Collège Royal de la Flèche, Chevalier Grand-Croix-Honoraire de l'Ordre Royal de St. Maurice de Sardaigne.

Certifions au Roi que Barthélemy-Sernin du Moulin-de-Montlezun-de la Barthette, né le huit de Décembre mil sept cent soixante-deux, fils de Jean-François du Moulin-de Montlezun-de la Barthette Capitaine au Régiment d'Auvergne Infanterie, Chevalier de l'Ordre Royal et Militaire de St. Louis, et de Dame Marie du Burguet-de Fonpeyre sa femme, a la Noblesse nécessaire pour être admis au nombre des Gentilshommes que Sa Majesté fait élever dans le Collège Royal de la Flèche. En foi de quoi Nous avons signé ce présent Certificat, l'avons fait contresigner par notre Secrétaire, et y avons fait apposer le Sceau de nos Armes. A Paris le huitième jour du mois de Septembre de l'an mil sept cent soixante-dix.

d'Hozier-de Sérigny

Pour Duplicata.

Par Monsieur le Juge d'Armes de la Noblesse de France,

Duplessis

The Chevalier de Montlezun de La Barthette's nobility of birth is attested by this certificate from the famous Hozier, King of Arms of France. This document was attached to the Chevalier's application to General Washington for the Eagle of the Cincinnati. See page 345.

[*Archives of the General Society*]

It is more easy for you to imagine than for us to describe the mingled emotions of gratitude, of respect, and affection, your presence inspires. Whether we look back to the interesting scenes of the late war, when three millions of people committed their dear treasure—their liberties, to your protection—or to the present time, when the same people, become an independent empire, have called on you with one voice to be the Guardian of their Government and Laws—in either view we shall find equal motives of admiration for the wisdom of your conduct, and of reverence for your virtues.

In these sentiments we are conscious that we do but express the feelings of every American citizen; yet we flatter ourselves we may justly be suppposed to have a more lively degree of sensibility in our affection from the relation in which we stand, as Officers who had the honor to serve under you during the late war, and as President General of our Society—a relation in which it is our highest pride to be considered.

This is perhaps the last opportunity we may have of tendering you in person the sincere professions of attachment: be pleased to accept them, Sir, as the genuine effusions of our hearts; and suffer us, at the same time, to assure you, that it shall be our constant endeavour to pursue the same conduct towards our country that formerly procured us the honor of your esteem and regard.

That you may long—very long live to enjoy the grateful applause of mankind—the noblest reward of virtue, and make your fellow citizens happy, is our ardent wish, and shall be our constant prayer.

By Order

ANTHONY WAYNE, President.

REPLY TO THE GEORGIA CINCINNATI.

To the MEMBERS of the SOCIETY of the CINCINNATI of the STATE of GEORGIA

Gentlemen,

Your congratulations on my arrival in this state are received with grateful sensibility—your esteem and attachment are replied to with truth and affection.

Could the praise of an individual confer distinction on men whose merits are recorded in the independence and sovereignty of their country, I would add, with grateful pride, and tribute of my testimony to the public acknowledgement—I would say how much you had achieved, how much you had endured in the cause of freedom—Nor should my applause be confined to the military virtues of your character—with the enduring epithet of gallant brother-soldiers, your civic worth has connected the respectable title of deserving fellow-citizens.

Your conduct in war has commanded my esteem, your behaviour in peace exacts my approbation.

My opinions will ever do justice to your merits—my heart will reciprocate your affection—and my best wishes implore your happiness.[1]

Go. Washington

[*Georgia Gazette No. 434, 19 May 1791*]

To the COUNTESS DE ROCHAMBEAU.

Philadelphia, July 20, 1791

Madam:

It is but a short time since I had the honor to receive your letter of the 18 of November,[2] in which you interest yourself in behalf of Baron Closen that he may be admitted a Member of the Society of the Cincinnati.

You must be sensible, Madam, of the great pleasure it would give me to comply with any request which might come from the Countess de Rochambeau, if it was in my power to do it. But I regret that in this instance I cannot please myself my gratifying you, for at a general meeting of the Society of the Cincinnati, it was resolved to refer all claims and applications from Gentlemen of the French Nation, for admission into the Society to the Counts Rochambeau and D'Estaing, and the Marquis de la Fayette, as it was justly presumed they were

[1] The address was delivered to General Washington on the occasion of his visit to Savannah, 14 May 1791.

[2] See page 372.

better acquainted with the claims and merits of their Countrymen than the Americans could be, and, since that resolution all applications of this description which have been made to the Society here, have been referred to these Gentlemen. This being the case I flatter myself you will be persuaded Madam that my declining an interference in this instance will not be imputed to a disinclination to oblige you, but to a necessary adherence to impartiality and propriety.

With the highest respect, I have the honor, etc.

[*Washington Papers*]

Even Spanish officers sought membership in the Cincinnati.

From SEÑOR ESTEVAN JOSEPH MARTINEZ.

Havana [Cuba], April 14, 1792.

Ex[celentisi]mo S[eñ]or

Entendido en que V E. sera sabedor de los beneficios, que rendi a la Expedición Bostonesa, que mandabá el Capitán Juan Kendrick altiempo que Yo era Comandante en Jefe de otra, sobre la Costa del Norueste de América, me atrebo a molestar a V E. afin de que interponiendo sus respectos con los señores del Congreso, me distingan con la or[de]n del Sensenatus, delo que quedarè agradecido a V E.

Yo salgo de esta Plaza para Madrid afin del corriente, lo participo a V E. para que me imponga sus preceptos, que obedecerè gustoso.

Dios gu[ard]e a Vd. m[uchos] a[ños].

[*Archives of the General Society*]

[Translation in Jefferson's handwriting]

From STEPHEN JOSEPH MARTINEZ.

Havana [Cuba], April 14, 1792.

Most excellent Sir

Supposing that Y. E. is acquainted with the services which I rendered to the Bostonian expedition commanded by Capt.

John Kendrick at the time when I was commander in chief of another on the North West coast of America, I take the liberty of troubling Y. E. to the end that interposing your influence with Congress, they may distinguish me with the order of Cincinnatus, for which I shall be very thankful to your Excellency.

I leave this place for Madrid the end of the present month. I mention it to Y. E. that you may lay me your commands which I shall obey with pleasure.

God preserve you etc.

[*Archives of the General Society*]

To Governor BEHAGUE of the French Winward Islands.

Philadelphia, June 3, 1792

Sir:

I have received the duplicate of the polite letter which you did me the honor of writing to me on the 28th. of may 1791.[1] The first has not reached my hands.

The obliging manner in which you express your wishes to prove the sincerity of your attachment to the United States by keeping up and encouraging the treaty of amity which unites France and America, merits all acknowledgements of good citizens of this Country, as well as the protection which you mention to have given to the American Vessels on the coasts of the Isle of Belle Isle, where you commanded in the late war.

The Constitution of the Society of the Cincinnati does not permit the President to decide on the qualifications for admission into the Society. He can only grant diplomas to such as may have been admitted in conformity to the general Institution, And in order to be better informed of the pretensions of foreign Officers for admission, power was given to Count de Rochambeau, the Marquis de la Fayette and the Count d'Estaing to admit such as should appear to have well-grounded pretensions, to wear the Insignia of the Order; and the Certificate of those

[1] This letter cannot be found.

Gentlemen being transmitted to the Secretary of the Society (which office is now filled by General Knox) will entitle the person to whom it is granted to a Diploma.

With sentiments of due consideration, I have the honor, etc.[1]

[*Historical Society of Pennsylvania*]

General Washington's Secretary forwards a letter of application for the Cincinnati to the Secretary General.

Mr. TOBIAS LEAR to Major-General HENRY KNOX.

[Philadelphia, Pennsylvania], July 10, [1792].

Dear Sir,

The enclosed letter[2] applying for an admission into the Society of the Cincinnati is sent to you by the President' Order—

With truth & sincerity I am etc.

[*Archives of the General Society*]

General Washington's Secretary transmits to the Secretary General of the Cincinnati another French officer's request for admission as a member.

From Mr. TOBIAS LEAR to Major-General HENRY KNOX.

[Philadelphia, Pa.], April 27th: 1793

Dear Sir,

The President directs me to transmit to you the enclosed letters praying for the admission of a M. Fled into the Society of the Cincinnati,—that you may do with them what is right—

[1] On 25 April 1784, General Washington addressed letters to the Governor of Barbados and other of the West Indies, introducing "the bearer, Major George Augustine Washington, a Nephew of mine" who had been advised by his physicians to take a trip to the West Indies on account of his bad health. This Major Washington, son of the General's brother Charles, was an original member of the Society of the Cincinnati in the State of Virginia.

[2] Letter from Estevan J[ose]ph Martinez to General Washington, 14 April 1792. See page 378.

& if you should think it necessary to give an answer thereto the President wishes you to do it.

I am Dear Sir etc.[1]

[*Archives of the General Society*]

From Monsieur de Flad.[2]

Cayenne le 16 fevrier 1793.

Monsieur

J'ai L'honneur de vous prier de bien vouloir mettre sous les yeux du congrès Le memoire cy joint; il contient la demande de La décoration de L'ordre de Cincynatus, L'usage à jusqu'a ce jour consacré que ceux qui auroient eû L'avantage de servir La cause de votre liberté, jouiraient de ce precieux don de L'instant qu'ils seroient promu au grade de Colonel.

Je me trouve dans cette position, et éloigné de France, et de Monsieur de Rochambeau qui, au nom des etats unis de L'amerique en est le distributeur; je m'adresse au congrès, attachant un bien plus grand prix a cette glorieuse recompense, en la tenant directement de L'illustre assemblée que vous presidé.

Daignez Monsieur L'assurer des vœux que je forme pour La prosperité, et celle de votre republique, je serai toujours attaché par Le Sentiment comun à tous Les amis de La liberté, et particulierement pour Le Souvenir honorable que je me retrace souvent d'avoir pû combattre pour son indépendance.

Daignez Monsieur Le Président agréer L'assurance de ces sentimens, ils sont inseparable de La haute vénération et du profond respect etc.

[*Archives of the General Society*]

[1] Enclosed in this letter was that of Flad of 16 February 1793 to Washington (*q. v.*).

[2] Enclosed in this letter is a "Memoire" by de Flad, setting forth his qualifications for membership in the Society, addressed to "Le Congrès" and bearing an attestation dated 15 February 1793. This letter, with its enclosure, was enclosed in Lear's letter of 27 April 1793, to Knox.

[Translation by Edgar Erskine Hume]

Cayenne, 16 February 1793

Sir,

I have the honor to beg you to have the kindness to place the inclosed memorandum before Congress. It contains my request for the decoration of the Order of the Cincynatus, which has been reserved to those who had the advantage of serving the cause of your liberty, achieving this precious gift at the time that they attain the grade of Colonel.

I am stationed here and far from France, and M. de Rochambeau, who, in the name of the United States is the distributor. I address myself to Congress, attaching a greater value to this glorious recompense, in obtaining it directly from the illustrious assembly over which you preside.

Deign, Sir, to be assured of the good wishes that I have for the prosperity of your republic. I shall ever be attached by that sentiment common to all friends of Liberty, and particularly by the honorable service that I well recall of having fought for its independence.

Deign, Mr. President, to receive the assurance of these sentiments; they are inseparable with the high veneration and profound respect, etc.[1]

General Meeting of 1793.

General Washington reelected President General

May 7th [1793]

. . . The meeting duly proceeded to the choice of the officers to serve the next ensuing three years, when the following persons were duly elected, to wit:

George Washington, president-general
Thomas Mifflin, vice-president-general
Henry Knox, secretary-general.
William MacPherson, assistant secretary-general. . . .

[*Minutes of the General Meeting of 1793*]

[1] See original letter for note as to inclosures.

From Mr. ELIAS BOUDINOT.

Elizabeth Town [N. J.] Novr. 12th 1793

Dear Sir

The troubling you to read the enclosed oration[1] may perhaps need an Apology, undoubtedly the liberty I have taken, to address it to you, without your express permission, renders one absolutely necessary.

A number of concurring Circumstances, added to the subject & design prompted me to it, and a dependance on your known Candor & Friendship makes me hope, it will not give Offence—

Mrs. Boudinot joins me in the most respectful & affectionate Compliments to Mrs. Washington

I have the honor to be with every Sentiment of Duty & Respect etc.[2]

[*Washington Papers*]

To Mr. ELIAS BOUDINOT.

Philadelphia, November 27, 1793.

Dear Sir,

I have been duly favoured with your letter of the 12. Instt., and the Pamphlet[3] which accompanyed it. I am sensible of the honor you have done me in the address, and am grateful for the flattering expression of it.—I shall peruse the Sentiments which you have breathed in the Pamphlet with pleasure as soon as my leizure will allow me to read it.—At present I am

[1] Boudinot's oration before the Society of the Cincinnati, 1793, was published with the following title: "An oration delivered at Elizabeth-town, New-Jersey, agreeably to a resolution of the state Society of Cincinnati, on the Fourth of July, M.DCC.XCIII, Being the seventeenth anniversary of the independence of America. By Elias Boudinot. Elizabeth-town, Printed by Shepard Kollock, 1793." Pages 32. For Boudinot's letter transmitting the pamphlet, see above.

[2] General Washington replied on 27 November 1793, see page below.

occupied in collecting and arranging the materials for my communications to Congress.

With best wishes for the health and happiness of Mrs. Boudinot and yourself, and, with every great esteem and regard, I am etc.

[*Washington's Letter Books*]

The following letter from Jefferson to Madison is quoted as having a bearing on Jefferson's efforts to induce General Washington to abandon the Cincinnati.

Mr. THOMAS JEFFERSON to Mr. JAMES MADISON.

Monticello, Dec. 28, 1794.

Dear Sir,

. . . The denunciation of the democratic societies is one of the extraordinary acts of boldness of which we have seen so many from the fraction of monocrats. It is wonderful indeed, that the President should have permitted himself to be the organ of such an attack on the freedom of discussion, the freedom of writing, printing & publishing. It must be a matter of rare curiosity to get at the modifications of these rights proposed by them, and to see what line their ingenuity would draw between democratical societies, whose avowed object is the nourishment of the republican principles of our constitution, and the society of the Cincinnati, a *self-created* one, carving out for itself hereditary distinctions, lowering over our Constitution eternally, meeting together in all parts of the Union, periodically, with closed doors, accumulating a capital in their separate treasury, corresponding secretly & regularly, & of which society the very persons denouncing the democrats are themselves the fathers, founders, & high officers. Their sight must be perfectly dazzled by the glittering of crowns & coronets, not to see the extravagance of the proposition to suppress the friends of general freedom, while those who wish to confine that freedom to the few, are permitted to go on in their principles & practices. I here put out the sight of persons whose misbehaviour has been taken advantage of to slander the friends of popular rights; and I am happy to observe that as far as the circle of my observation & information extends, everybody has lost sight of them, and views the abstract attempt on their natural & constitutional rights in all its nakedness. I have never heard, or heard of, a single expression of opinion which did not condemn it as an inexcusable aggression.

[*Ford's Writings of Jefferson, vi, 516*]

ADDRESS BY THE PENNSYLVANIA CINCINNATI.

Address by the Pennsylvania Cincinnati—(and of the Members from the other State Societies at present in Philadelphia)

To George Washington—President of the United States.

Sir,

Upon this auspicious day[1] and in contemplation of an approaching public event, the most affecting, which can ever occur to us, either as men, as Citizens, or as your former fellow Soldiers, we desire to congratulate, and address you.

As Men we offer to you the homage of a pure and heartfelt affection—as citizens we express to you the gratitude, which results from a just sense of the highest obligations—and as fellow-Soldiers we declare the respectful and inviolable attachment, which we feel to a beloved and venerated Chief.

The moment, in which America is to lose the public services of her most illustrious Citizens, would indeed be inconsolable, did not the review of his wise, firm, and virtuous administration, as Chief Magistrate, present a series of conduct, which it will be the pride and happiness of his Successors to emulate and attain.—

With this consolatory reflection, we naturally associate the proud sentiment, that, in the instance of your dignified retirement from office, our country will exhibit to the world the rare

[1] The day was, of course, General Washington's sixty-fifth birthday.

and interesting spectacle that official station and authority are not required to obtain and to continue the utmost distinction among mankind, or to command the highest degree of their admiration and applause.

To that gracious Providence, whose goodness has heretofore preserved you a prime Agent of human happiness, we prefer our fervent supplications for your present and future felicity.

Signed by order and on behalf of the Society—February 22, 1797.

Tho[mas] Mifflin

[*Washington Papers*]

Reply to the Pennsylvania Cincinnati.

To the Members of the Pennsylvania society of the Cincinnati, & the Members of the other State Societies of the Cincinnati at present in Philada.

United States, February 22, 1797

Gentlemen,

Your congratulations, & the expression of your attachment & approbation of my public services, are received with gratitude & reciprocated with sincerity.

Endeared to me by every consideration of public & private worth, I shall carry into that retirement, which you are pleased to mention in terms so flattering, an invariable affection & esteem towards the faithful comrades of my military career; & my best prayers will be offered for their present and future happiness.

[*Washington Papers*]

Address by the Rhode Island Cincinnati.

The Rhode Island State Society of the Cincinnati
to
George Washington President of the United States

Sir.

In looking forward to the period which is intended to terminate the career of your public life, our feelings will not permit us to suspend the deep acknowledgments of that debt of gratitude which is your due from a Country to whose Independence and Happiness you have so essentially contributed. The interesting scene of your intended retirement revives in the minds of our fellow Citizens in general the many proofs of eminent wisdom and unshaken patriotism displayed in the field, the glory of which can be eclipsed only by the innumerable evidences of your firm, enlightened and uniform attachment to republican and constitutional principles displayed in your political transactions.

While the testimonies of respectful affection and grateful attachment are arising to you from every part of the union, a similar attention from a Society of Citizens who have "laid down in peace Arms assumed for public defence," cannot be unacceptable on this occasion.

By this address we do not think of adding anything to the lustre of a Character composed of an assemblage of the eminent public and private virtues, a Character, which like bodies highly polished, may attract, but as readily eludes the envenomed shafts of envy; and which the virtuous can only admire.

We do but attempt to express the honest feelings of every member of the Society, in whose behalf we address you, when we say that we extremely regret the occasion of a retirement dictated by reasons which must silence every objection to the measure. In that retirement may you meet all that tranquility and happiness you so ardently desire, and enjoy all the blessings of private and domestic life. There may you still live to receive the rich harvest of your labors and services in the peace and prosperity of your Country, in the fervent affection of your fellow Citizens, the applauses of an admiring World, and the higher Pleasures of an approving conscience. May your lengthening days still extend your usefulness and your setting sun shine with undiminished lustre till a reward more than Man can give shall be yours.

Impressed with these sentiments, and actuated by the pleasing sensibility of personal affection and gratitude, Respected Sir, we bid you Adieu.

Providence February 25th 1797.

Enos Hitchcock
Jere.h Olney
Jno S. Dexter
William Allen
Ephraim Bowen Junr — Committee
Thomas Smart
Dan.l S. Dexter
Saml Snow [1]

[*Washington Papers*]

REPLY TO THE RHODE ISLAND CINCINNATI.

To the Rhode Island State Society of the Cincinnati.

Gentlemen

For your affectionate address on my retireing from public life, I beg you to accept my grateful acknowledgements;—And be assured, that no circumstances can tend more to sweeten the few remaining years of my life, than the pleasing remembrance of my services having been approved by those who have par-

[1] These members of the Rhode Island Cincinnati were: Brigade Chaplain Enos Hitchcock; Lieutenant-Colonel Jeremiah Olney, Vice-President of the Society; Major John Singer Dexter, sometime Secretary and later President of the Society; Captain William Allen, sometime Treasurer and later Secretary of the Society; Major Ephraim Bowen, Jr., Treasurer; Captain Thomas Smart; Captain Daniel Singer Dexter; and Captain Samuel Snow.

ticipated in the arduous struggle to establish our Independence, or to regulate the important Era of our civil affairs.—

In bidding you adieu, I pray that the best of Heavens blessings may rest upon you.

Philadelphia 6th March
1797

G Washington

[*Archives of the Rhode Island Cincinnati*]

ADDRESS FROM THE SOUTH CAROLINA CINCINNATI.

To The President General of the Society of the Cincinnati

Sir,

At a late meeting of the Cincinnati of this State convened for the purpose of addressing the President of the United States on the critical situation of this Country it was resolved that a Committee be appointed to write to the General Society requesting that they wou'd at their next meeting take into consideration the propriety of altering the Ribbon to which the badge of the Society was directed to be appendant, as indicative of the Union between the United States and France,—It was thought that such a distinction was no longer applicable to the relative situation of the two Countries, and that it became incumbent upon us at such a moment to renounce every Military badge or appearance of connections with a nation whose Civil and Political Union by treaty had been declared void and no longer binding upon us. We therefore in obedience to the resolve above mentioned communicate to you the wish of our State Society and request you will lay the same before the General Society at their next meeting for the consideration of the members thereof.

We are with great esteem & Respect, Sir, Your Obedient Servants,

[Lieutenant-Colonel]
J[ohn] F[aucheraud] Grimké
[Major] Thomas Pinckney
[Ensign] Adam Gilchrist
} the Committee

Charleston, August 30th, 1798.

[*Contemporary Copy in the Archives of the Virginia Cincinnati*]

Reply to the South Carolina Cincinnati.

(Under date of 14 January 1799, the South Carolina Society recorded)—

1799 January 14th., A letter received from the President General of the Society in answer to the letter wrote by the Committee on the subject of altering the Ribbon to which the badge is appendant was handed by Col°. Grimké the Chairman of that Committee and is as follows—

Mount Vernon 20th October 1798

Gentlemen,

I have been honored with your favor of the 30th of August communicating the Resolve of the Cincinnati of the State of South Carlina respecting the propriety of altering the Ribbon to which the badge of the Society was directed by the Constitution to be apendant, as indicative of the Union between the United States and France, and have transmitted it to the Secretary General, to be laid before the Society at the next meeting of its Delegates.

With great esteem and regard I have the honor to be, Gentlemen, Your most Ob^{dt} H^{ble} Servant

G°. Washington

Lt. Col°. J. F. Grimké
Major Thomas Pinckney Committee of the Cincinnati State S° Carolina.
[Ensign] Adam Gilchrist

Whereupon: Resolved that Official copies of the Resolution of this Society relative to the proposed alteration in the Ribbon to which the Badge is appendant be furnished the several State Societies of the Cincinnati, accompanied with the letter written by the Committee to the President General, and his answer thereto, attested by the Secretary.

Attest: G. Reid, Secy

[*Contemporary Copy in the Archives of the Virginia Cincinnati Original in Washington Papers*]

(The inclosed resolution is):

1798 August 22d: Resolved that this Society do write to the Parent Society requesting them to consent to an alteration of the Ribbon worn by the Society to which the badge is appendant as the blue and white which were indicative of the Union between the United States and France is no longer applicable to the relative situations of the two Countries.

Resolved that Colo Grimké Major Pinckney and Capt Gilchrist be a Committee to write to the President of the General Society on the above subject

1798 October 8th: Colo Grimké as Chairman of the Committee appointed to write to the President of the General Society reported the following Letter which was read and approved.

COPY: To the President General

This is the last letter, as far as the records show, written by General Washington to the Society of the Cincinnati. It was sent less than fourteen months prior to his death.

To Major-General HENRY KNOX

Mount Vernon, October 23, 1798

My dear Sir

The enclosed,[1] although of old date, is just come to hand. And believing you are still the Secretary General of the Society of the Cincinnati, I transmit it to you; to be laid before the next General Meeting of its Delegates; as there is no probability that I shall be at it myself. . . .

[*Washington's Letter Books*]

Here is the last reference to General Washington in the Minutes of the Cincinnati. He died less than six months later, on 14 December 1799 at Mount Vernon.

GENERAL MEETING OF 1799.

General WASHINGTON Reelected President General.

Wednesday, May 8th [1799]

. . . The members present then proceeded to the election of officers for the ensuing three years, when it appeared from the ballots that the following gentelmen were duly elected:

General George Washington, president-general
Major-General Alexander Hamilton, vice-president-general
Major William Jackson, secretary-general
Brigadier General William Macpherson, treasurer-general
Dr. Nathan Dorsey, assistant secretary-general. . . .

[*Minutes of the General Meeting of 1799*]

The widow of General Washington sends, through the letter of the General's faithful Secretary, her thanks to Major John Singer Dexter, sometime Secretary of the Rhode Island Cincinnati, for a copy of a publication sent her.

[1] There is no copy of the mentioned inclosure.

Mr. Tobias Lear to Mr. John Dexter.

Mount Vernon May 6th 1800

Sir,

Mrs. Washington requests I will communicate to you her best thanks for your polite letter to her of the 15th of April, inclosing, agreeably to the direction of the Standing Committee of the Society of the Cincinnati in the State of Rhode Island, a Copy of Doctor Hitchocks [1] excellent Discourse on an Event deeply afflicting to herself and regreted by all;—and she begs you will assure the Committee of the Sensibility with which she receives this mark of respect and veneration for the memory of her late beloved Partner.—

With great consideration
I have the honor to be,
Sir,
Your most obedt. Servt.

Tobias Lear.—

John Dexter Esq.

[*Archives of the Rhode Island Cincinnati*]

Resolutions of the Virginia Society upon the Death of General Washington.

At the meeting of the State Society of Cincinnati of Virginia convened at the Capitol in the City of Richmond on the 18th day of December 1799. . . .

It was moved by Mr. Matthews and seconded by

that,—in consequence of the melancholy information received of the death of General George Washington, who

[1] The title of the pamphlet is: "A discourse on the causes of national prosperity, illustrated by ancient and modern history, exemplified in the late American revolution. Addressed to the Society of the Cincinnati, in the state of Rhode-Island, at their annual meeting at East-Greenwich, July 4, 1786. By Enos Hitchcock. Providence: Printed by Bennett Wheeler, 1786." 28 pages.

being no less esteemed and venerated for his great virtues and eminent talents as a Statesman and fellow Citizen, than he was justly beloved and admired for his Courage and Conduct, as a brother Soldier; and it being the wish of this meeting to Manifest to the present, and future times, the Sincerity with which they Commemorate that Courage and Conduct, and those talents and Virtues, as well as the deep affliction which they now feel at his loss—the meeting come to the following Resolution.

Resolved that this meeting will wear a black Crape on the left Arm for three months—And that they cannot suppress their expectations that the same Mark of Sorrow and Respect will be shown to every other member of the Society in Virginia.

And on the question that the said Resolution be adopted, it was Unanimously agreed to, and the meeting adjourned.

[*Archives of the Virginia Cincinnati*]

Resolutions of the New York Society on the Death of General Washington.

1799,

On December 21, a Special Meeting was convened in consequence of the intelligence of the death of General *Washington*, when it was

Resolved, that the members of this Society will wear full mourning as for a Father, for six months, during which time they will also wear the badge of the Society covered with black crape. A committee was appointed to act in conjunction with committees from the Corporation of the City of New York, and other bodies, to agree upon the best manner of paying suitable honors to the memory of the illustrious deceased.

Subsequently, Congress having recommended that the 22d of February be set apart for the purpose of testifying the public grief on this event, the Society requested the *Rev. Dr.* William Linn[1] to deliver a discourse adapted to the mournful

[1] The Eulogy of the Rev. Dr. Linn was published under the title: "A Funeral Eulogy, occasioned by the Death of General Washington. Delivered February 22d 1800, before the New-York State Society of the Cincinnati, by William Linn, D. D., New-York: Printed by Isaac Collins, no 189, Pearl-Street, 1800" (pp. 44).

occasion. The solemnities were observed in the new Dutch Church in Nassau street, and were opened with a solemn dirge on the organ, followed by a prayer by the *Rev. Dr.* Rodgers, an anthem was sung, and the eulogy delivered by the *Rev. Dr.* Linn. There was a voluntary upon the organ at the conclusion.

[*Archives of the New York Cincinnati*]

Action of the Massachusetts Cincinnati on General Washington's Death.

1800, January 15—At a special meeting it was ordered "that the members of the Society continue to wear a black crape cockade in the hat till after the 5th day of July next, as a badge of mourning for their deceased President-general, *George Washington*"; and "that the Standing Committee appoint some member of the Society to deliver an oration at the annual meeting on the fourth of July next, commemorative of the American Revolution, and of the virtues and talents which distinguished the eventful life of the illustrious Washington"

[It does not appear that an oration was delivered in accordance with this vote; that before the town authorities, 4th July, was delivered by Joseph Hall, Esq.].

[*Memorials of the Massachusetts Society, 1873, 64*]

Resolutions of the New Jersey Society on the Death of General Washington.

Upon the most profound impression of veneration and affection, the Society of the Cincinnati, at a general meeting, are called upon to express the mournful tribute of their sorrow, at that awful dispensation of Providence, which has recently removed from their councils, their much revered and lamented President General.

The arduous, tho' successful struggle which terminated in establishing the liberties of our country, and in which they fought under his banners, and shared with him the dangers and toils of the field, attached him to the Societies by ties of the most intimate and endearing nature. His valor and prudence seemed to control the events of war, led the American armies to victory, and achieved the independence of their country. Whilst mingling their tears with those of their fellow citizens, they are naturally impelled to pour out the effusions of a deeper regret, for the irreparable loss which they have sustained.

But it is not only in their relationship to this illustrious character, as soldiers, that the Society of the Cincinnati have cause to deplore his loss.

When the storm had ceased to rage, and the blessings of peace had been restored, their country was suffering under the weakness of a confederation, which threatened the existence of that Union, which their joint efforts in arms had so essentially contributed to establish.

With his auspicious co-operation, a Constitution was formed, calculated by its wisdom and energy to redeem us from that prostrate state, to which we had been reduced, and to restore that representation which our country had lost, from the imbicility of the old system. The administration of the government was committed to his care, and his country will ever hold in grateful remembrance the inflexible virtue and fortitude, with which he conducted its affairs and saved from the effects of domestic faction and foreign intrigue.

After a second retirement from the scenes of public life in which his merits as a Statesman, rivalled his fame as a soldier; his country at the approach of danger, again required his services. The crisis was important and the situation delicate; a nation which had mingled it blood with ours in the defense of our liberties, had now assumed a hostile appearance. A war from this unexpected quarter threatened the peace of our country.

Washington who never hesitated when urged by a sense of duty, obeyed the call of the government. He again abandoned his beloved retirement, hazarded a reputation, consummate in every point of view, and assumed the command of the armies. His military companions who had frequently witnessed the magniminity of his conduct in seasons of adversity as well as of triumph, felt the full force of their country's appeal to arms, whilst *Washington* was their leader.

In this momentous crisis in our affairs, by the inscrutable decrees of Heaven, he was snatched from America and the world.

Under this pressure of calamity which more peculiarly operates upon the sensibilities of this Society, their only consolation is derived from the animating reflection, that although he is summoned to the enjoyment of the happy destinies of a future state, the bright example of his virtues and talents will still survive, and the inheritance of his name, prove a future incentive to heroes and legislators who will strive to emulate his fame, and merit the glory he has acquired.

[*Archives of the New Jersey Cincinnati*]

Inventory of General Washington's Estate.

Eagles of the Cincinnati

After General Washington's death sworn appraisers made, in accordance with Virginia law, an inventory of the articles of his personal estate, listing them and giving the value of each.

The Inventory, a part of the records of Fairfax County, gives the articles found in: " The New Room, the Little Parlor, the Front Parlor, the Dining Room, the Bed Room, the Passage, the Closet under the stair-case, the Piazza, from the foot of the Stair-case to the second Stairs, the Passage on the second floor, the Front room on the second Floor, the Third Room, the Fourth Room, the Small Room, the Room which Mrs. Washington now keeps, Mrs. Washington's Old Room, the Study, the Iron Chest, Plate belonging to Mount Vernon, and Plated Ware."

The valuables in the " Iron Chest " are:

In the Iron Chest

Stock of the U. S.	6 per cent. 3746 Dr. Deferred, 1873 3 per cent. 2946	3746 2500	$ 6,246.00
25	Shares Stock of the Bank of Alexandria		5,000.00
24	do. do. Potomac, (at 100 st'g)		10,666.00
	Cash		254.70
1	Sett of Shoe and Knee Buckless, Paste, in Gold		250.00
1	Pair of Shoe and Knee Buckless, Silver		5.00
[1] 2	Gold Cincinnati Eagles		30.00
[1] 1	Diamond do		387.00
1	Gold Watch, Chain, two Seals, and a Key		175.00
1	Compass in Brass Case		.50
1	Gold Box, Presented by the Corp. of New York		100.00
5	Shares of James River Stock at $100		500.00
170	Shares of Columbia Stock at $40		6,800.00
1	Large Gold Medal of General Washington		150.00
1	Gold Medal of St. Patrick's Society		8.00
1	Ancient Medal (another Metal)		2.00
11	Medals in a Case		50.00
1	Large Medal of Paul Jones		4.00
3	Other Metal Medals		1.00
1	Brass Engraving of the Arms of the United States		10.00
1	Pocket Compass		5.00
1	Case of Instruments, Parallel Rule, &c.		17.50
1	Pocket Book		5.00

[*Court Records of Fairfax County, Virginia*]

---

[1] The value placed on the Eagles in 1799 by the appraisers is interesting in the light of modern prices. The gold Eagles made in Paris under L'Enfant's supervision sell today at auction for about $1500 each. The value of the Diamond Eagle is beyond price. It is probably the most important relic of General Washington, except the estate of Mt. Vernon itself. Added to its Washington interest, it has been worn by all of Washington's twelve successors, Presidents General of the Cincinnati.

Resolutions on the Death of General Washington.

General Meeting of 1800

Wednesday, May 7th [1800]

. . . Mr. Bingham, from the committee appointed for that purpose, reported the following testimonial of respect to the memory of General Washington, which was twice read, unanimously agreed to and ordered to be entered on the records of the Society as the first act of the present meeting after its organization:

"Under the most profound impression of veneration and affection, the Society of the Cincinnati, at a general meeting, are called upon to express the mournful tribute of their sorrow, at their awful dispensation of Providence, which has recently removed from their councils, their much revered and lamented president-general.

"The arduous, though successful struggle which terminated in establishing the liberties of our country, and in which they fought under his banners, and shared with him the dangers and toils of the field, attached him to this Society, by ties of the most intimate and endearing nature. His valor and prudence seemed to control the events of war, led the American armies to victory, and achieved the independence of their country. Whilst mingling their tears with those of their fellow-citizens, they are naturally impelled to pour out the effusions of a deeper regret, for the irreparable loss which they have sustained.

"But it is not only in their relationship to this illustrious character, as soldiers, that the Society of the Cincinnati have cause to deplore his loss.

"When the storm of war had ceased to rage, and the blessings of peace had been restored, their country was suffering under the weakness of a confederation, which threatenend the existence of that union, which their joint efforts in arms had so essentially contributed to establish.

"With his auspicious co-operation, a constitution was formed, calculated, by its wisdom and energy, to redeem us from that prostrate state to which we had been reduced, and to restore that reputation which our country had lost, from the imbecility of the old system. The administration of the government was committed to his care, and his country will ever hold in grateful remembrance the inflexible virtue and fortitude with which he conducted its affairs, and saved it from the effects of faction and foreign intrigue.

"After a second retirement from the active scenes of publice life, in which his merits as a statesman rivaled his fame as a soldier, his country, at the approach of danger, again required his services. The crisis was important, and the situation delicate; a nation which had mingled its blood with ours in the defence of liberties, had now assumed a hostile appearance; a way from this unexpected quarter threatened the peace of our country.[1]

"Washington, who never hesitated when urged by a sense of duty, obeyed the call of the government. He again abandoned his beloved retirement, hazarded a reputation, consummate in every point of view, and assumed command of the armies. His military companions, who had frequently witnessed the magnanimity of his conduct in seasons of adversarity, as well as of triumph, felt the full force of their country's appeal to arms, whilst Washington was their leader.

"In this momentous crisis of our affairs, by the inscrutable decrees of Heaven, he was snatched from America and the world.

"Under this pressure of calamity, which more peculiarly operates upon the sensibilities of this Society, their only consolation is derived from the animating reflection that although he is summonded to the enjoyment of the happy destinies of a future state, the bright example of his virtues and talents will still survive, and the inheritance of his name prove a future incentive to heroes and legislators, who still strive to emulate his fame and merit the glory he has acquired."

[*Minutes of the General Meeting of 1800*]

---

[1] Note the similarity in wording to the New Jersey resolutions, page 395.

Mrs. Washington died at Mount Vernon on 22 May 1802. She was born Martha Dandridge, being the widow of Daniel Parke Custis at the time of her marriage to General Washington in 1759.

Extracts from the Will of Mrs. Washington.

In the name of God amen. I Martha Washington of Mount Vernon in the county of Fairfax being of sound mind and capable of disposing of my worldly estate do make ordain and declare this to be my last will and testament hereby revoking all other wills and testaments by me heretofore made. . . .

Item I give and bequeath to my grandson George Washington Parke Custis all the silver plate of every kind of which I shall die possessed, together with the two large plated coolers, the four small plated coolers with the bottle castors, and a pipe of wine if therebe one in the house at the time of my death—also the set of Cincinnati china [1] and Table china, the bowl that has a ship, in it, the fine old china jars which usually stand on the chimney piece in the new room . . .

[*Will dated 4 March 1802, Fairfax County, Virginia*]

---

[1] "The Cincinnati china, much of which was destroyed when the Union troops took over Arlington at the commencement of the Civil War, may be described roughly, as the porcelain known as Chinese Loewstoft. It was made in Canton, according to the design of Major Samuel Shaw, or at least according to Chinese interpretation of his idea, which was a heavy, floriated border of Canton blue, with a trumpeting winged figure in flight (supposedly Fame) in the center of each piece. She holds suspended in her left hand the Cincinnati eagle emblem. Two of the plates are at Mount Vernon, in which the winged figure is in full color; but so delicately tinted that the contrast between it and the deep blue border is disturbing. The china was purchased for the General in the summer of 1786 by Colonel Henry Lee, in New York, for about 150 dollars, Washington's accounts showing that on August 23 he sent Lee, by the hand of Colonel Humphreys, £45: 5: 0 for that purpose. A letter of acknowledgment to Lee, in October, stated that the china had reached Mount Vernon, with very little damage" (J. C. Fitzpatrick, *The Last Will and Testament of George Washington*, 1939, 57, 64).

SUPPLEMENT

Brief Biographies of those with whom General Washington corresponded concerning the Society of the Cincinnati

SUPPLEMENT

Lieutenant-Colonel John Allison.

Major, First Virginia State Regiment, 3 March, 1777; Lieutenant-Colonel, 1 February 1778 and served as such until February 1781. He was an original member of the Society of the Cincinnati in the State of Virginia.

The Chevalier d'Annemours.

Chevalier Charles-François-Adrien Le Paulinier d'Annemours was born in Normandy in 1742. At the age of twelve, with a patrimony of 600 livres, he embarked for America to seek his fortune. Later he worked for several years for shipping companies at Marseilles. He was captured by the British during the Seven Years War, and was held in England as a prisoner of war for eighteen months. After the close of the war he resided for two years in England and there perfected his knowledge of English. He removed to Martinique in 1768 and later lived in the British colonies. In 1773 he returned to France. In 1777 he came to America in order to volunteer in the Continental Army, but failed to gain a commission. He followed Congress for some two years, reporting to the Count de Vergennes, Minister of Foreign Affairs of France. In 1779 he was appointed Consul General of France in Baltimore, with jurisdiction over Maryland and the States to the southward. His name is variously spelled, by himself and others, d'Anmours, Danmours, d'Anemours, and d'Annemours.

Armand, see La Rouërie.

Lieutenant-Colonel Henry Babcock.

Born at Westerly, Rhode Island, 1736; graduated at Yale College at the head of his class when but sixteen; Captain of a Company of Rhode Island Militia, 1754; served in the field against the French, 1756; promoted Major, 1757; Lieutenant-Colonel, 1758; commanded five hundred men at Ticonderoga. During the Seven Years (French and Indian) War, made five campaigns; thereafter resided in London for a year; appointed commander at Newport, 1776, by the Rhode Island Legislature; drove off *H. M. S. Rose* with an eighteen pounder; died in 1800. He was ineligible to membership in the Society of the Cincinnati under the terms of the Institution.

The Marquis de Barbé-Marbois.

François Marbois, later Count and Marquis de Barbé-Marbois, a member of the French diplomatic service, was born at Metz, 1745. He was Consul General of France in the early days of the American Revolution, having come to America as secretary to the Chevalier de La Luzerne, 1779, when that officer succeeded Gérard as Minister Plenipotentiary of the King of France. As Consul General and Chargé d'Affaires, Barbé-Marbois remained in the United States until 1785; He was Intendant at Santo Domingo, 1785-1790. He was deported to Guyana 18 Fructidor of the Year 5, but managed to be transferred to the island of Oléron, and in the Year 8 returned to Paris. He was created Grand Officer of the Legion of Honor, 1803, and later received the title of Count and the Grand Cordon of the Order of Saint Hubert of Bavaria. He was charged with the duty of selling Louisiana to the United States for fifty million francs, but was able to obtain eighty millions of which twenty were applicable to indemnities. Napoleon granted him 192,000 francs. He was President of the Court of *Comptes,* 1807-1834; Senator, 1813; Peer of France, 1814. He was the author of numerous works. He died 12 February 1837. His classic *Histoire de la Louisiane* was published in Paris in 1829.

The Count de Barras.

Jacques-Melchoir, Count de Barras-Saint-Laurent, was born in Provence. He was commissioned *Garde de la Marine*, 1734; *Lieutenant de Vaisseau*, 1754; *Capitaine de Vaisseau,* 1762; *Chef d'Escadre*, 1778; Lieutenant-General, 1782; Vice-Admiral, 1792. He commanded the *Zèle* in the squadron of the Count d'Estaing in Rhode Island waters and at Savannah, 1779. He returned to France in the *Concorde* in May, 1781 in order to take command of a French squadron destined for service in the United States. Though senior to de Grasse he served loyally under him with his eight ships of the line, and four frigates, September, 1781, in order to assure naval superiority at the siege of Yorktown, to which place he transported the artillery of the allied armies. He returned to France in 1782 and was created a Knight Grand Cross of the Royal and Military Order of Saint-Louis, 1784. Original member of the Cincinnati by the terms of the *Institution* itself.

Barthette, see Montlezun de La Barthette.

Colonel William Barton.

Born at Warren, Rhode Island, 1748; Adjutant of Richmond's Rhode Island Regiment, 1775; Captain, 1775; Brigade-Major of Rhode Island Troops, 1776; Major of Rhode Island State Troops, 1776; Lieutenant-Colonel, 1777; Colonel, 1777 and served as such to the close of the War. On 4 July 1777 he, with a party of forty-one volunteers, succeeded in landing in Rhode Island, then occupied by the British, and captured Major-General Prescott and his A. D. C. Major William Barrington. He received a vote of thanks from the Rhode Island Assembly and the Thanks of Congress and "an elegant sword provided by the Commissary-General of Military Stores." He was wounded in the British retreat from Warren, 1777. In 1787 when Rhode Island declined to send a delegation to the Federal Convention, he joined with others in pledging support to the Convention. Member of the State Convention of 1790 which adopted the Federal Constitution. Having refused to pay a judgment on land that had been granted him, he was held as a prisoner for fourteen years and was visited by LaFayette in 1824. He died in Providence, 1831. Original member of the Rhode Island Cincinnati.

Bonnier, see Saint-Cosme.

The Count de Behague.

Jean-Pierre-Antoine, Count de Behague, entered the French cavalry in 1744; Commandant-en-chef of Guyana, 1764, then distraught by mutineers; Brigadier, 1762; Lieutenant-General, 20 May 1792; Governor of Martinique, 1792; an endorsement on General Washington's letter to him, dated 3 June 1792 is: "Count Behague, Governor Genl. of the French Winward Islands." There is a notation on this letter: "This letter from Genl. Washington was transmitted to me confidentially during the civil Commotions then existing in the French Winward Islands. The govr. Genl. (Behagues) had been driven by the Revolutionists from the Island of Martinique. this letter is therefore retained by F. Skipwith." It is further endorsed as being sent by Mr. James Caustic from Washington, D. C., to Robert Gilmore in 1832. He went to reside in England in 1797, and died in London in the first years of the nineteenth century. He was a Chevalier of the Royal and Military Order of Saint-Louis.

Mr. Pieter Johan van Berckel.

Pieter Johan van Berckel, born 1725, Burgomaster of Rotterdam, was Netherlands Minister to the United States, 1783-1786, being the first of all diplomatic representatives accredited to the new country. He sailed for Philadelphia, 23 June 1783, the very day of the ratification of the treaty between the United States and The Netherlands. He was forced to make the voyage on a Netherlands warship because, though the other belligerents had signed preliminary treaties of peace with Great Britain, that country and The Netherlands had not yet been able to agree on terms. He was received by Congress, 31 October 1783, as Minister Plenipotentiary. He spoke at Princeton, 1783, on the occasion of the signing of the Peace Treaty between the United States and Britain. In 1785 he removed his offices from Philadelphia to New York. In 1786 he was succeeded by his son who had been his secretary. He spent his last years in Newark, New Jersey, where his tombstone in the churchyard of Christ Church is inscribed: " In memory of Hon. Van Bercken of Rotterdam, minister Plenipotentiary from The State of Holland to the United States of America. He departed this life Dec. 24, 1800, in the . . . year of his age." He was the brother of Englebert François van Berckel, Pensionary of Amsterdam, who had drawn up a preliminary draft of a treaty with William Lee (brother of Arthur), to take effect as soon as Britain should recognize the independence of the United States.

The Marquis du Bouchet.

Denis-Jean-Florimond Langlois de Montheville, Marquis du Bouchet, was born at Clermont-Ferrand, 1752; cadet in the Royal Corps of Artillery, 1767; Aspirant, 1768, in which capacity he served in Austria; Sub-lieutenant in the Regiment de la Marche, 1770, participating in the Corsican campaign. In 1777 he reached Philadelphia and was commissioned Captain; promoted Major, he served on the staff of Major-General Gates at Saratoga; in the same year his health became impaired and he resigned his commission and returned to France. In 1780 he returned to America as Aide-de-Camp to the Count de Rochambeau, with whom he served to the end of the war. In 1783 he was promoted Lieutenant-Colonel of Infantry and created Chevalier of the Royal and Military Order of Saint-Louis; Colonel and Adjutant General, 1791; he joined the force of Condé and in 1802 returned to France; *Maréchal de Camp*, 1814; Lieutenant-General, 1816; died at Paris, 1826. Original member of the French Cincinnati.

Mr. Elias Boudinot.

Born at Philadelphia, 1740; counsellor-at-law, 1760; serjeant-at-law, 1770; Trustee of the College of New Jersey (now Princeton University), 1772; member of the Committee of Correspondence for Essex County, New Jersey, 1774; was instrumental in having the New

Jersey Assembly approve proceedings for a Continental Congress; member of the New Jersey Provincial Congress, 1775; Commissary General of Prisoners, Continental Army, 1775, with pay of a colonel; delegate to the Continental Congress, 1777; reelected until 1784; President of the Continental Congress, 1782; acting Secretary of Foreign Affairs, 1783; served on more than thirty committees, usually as chairman; signed the treaties of Peace with Great Britain and of Alliance with France; helped ratify the Constitution in New Jersey and accompanied Washington into New York for his inauguration as first President of the United States; Director of the United States Mint, 1795; Doctor of Laws of Yale College, 1790; died at Burlington, New Jersey, 1821. He was elected an honorary member of the New Jersey Cincinnati, 1783.

The Count de Bougainville.

Louis-Antoine, Count de Bougainville, was born in Paris, 1729; established a reputation as a savant by his *Treatise on Integral Calculus,* Part I of which appeared in 1754-1756. He was admitted to practice as an advocate, but in 1753 accepted a commission as Aide-Major in the Picardy Battalion. Aide-de-Camp to Secretary Chevert of the French Embassy in London, he was elected to Fellowship in the Royal Society. As a captain of Dragoons he distinguished himself under Montcalm in the Canadian campaign, being wounded and promoted colonel, 1758. In 1763 he was commissioned *Capitaine de Vaisseau* in the French Navy and in 1766 set out on his voyage around the world, which was made famous by his publication in 1771 of an account of his experiences. He command the *Guerrier*, 1778, later the *Languedoc* as *Capitaine de Pavillon* under d'Estaing in Rhode Island and at Savannah. Under the command of de Grasse he commanded the *Auguste* of 80 guns in the Chesapeake, 1781, and at the battle of Les Saintes, 1782. Promoted Vice-Admiral, 1792, he was a member of the Royal Academy of Sciences, the Royal Academy of the Marine and the Institut de France. He was given the rank of *Maréchal de Camp* in the land forces, 1780, and decorated with the Royal Military Order of Saint-Louis. Napoleon made him a Senator of the Empire and a Grand Officer of the Legion of Honor. His son, Rear-Admiral Baron de Bougainville (born at Brest, 1781) succeeded him as hereditary member of the Cincinnati, with permission of King Louis XVIII, in 1820. The flower *bougainvillea* was named in honor of the Count de Bougainville, who died in 1811. Original member of the French Cincinnati.

The Marquis de Bouillé.

François-Claude-Amour de Bouillé du Chariol, Marquis de Bouillé, was born at the Château de Cluzel, Auvergne, 1739; cadet in the Regiment of the Prince de Rohan-Rochefort, 1754; Captain of the Dragoons de la Ferronnays, 1756; Colonel of the Regiment du Vexin and Brigadier-General of Infantry, 1770; Maréchal de Camp, 1778; Lieutenant-General, 1782; Commandant of the *Trois-Evêchés,* 1787; in Alsace, Lorraine and the Franche-Comté, 1790; General-in-Chief of the Army of the Meuse, Sarre and Moselle, 1790; Chevalier of the Order of the Holy Ghost and Governor of Guadeloupe, 1767, later in Martinique; Commandant General of the Winward Islands, 1777; served in Dominica, 1778; in Tobago, 1781; in Saint-Eustache, 1781; and Saint Christopher, 1782, as well as in Nevis and Montserrat in concert with the Count de Grasse. In 1790 he took part in the Nancy insurrection and refused the baton of a Marshall of France offered him by the King. He opposed the arrest of the King at Varennes, 1791, and emigrated to Germany, later going to London where he died, 1800. His *Mémoires sur la Révolution* and other memoirs have been published. Elected an Honorary Member of the French Cincinnati at its foundation.

Bretonnière, see La Bretonnière.

The Marquis de Castellane-Majastre.

Henri-César, Marquis de Castellane-Majastre, was born in Provence, 1733; *Garde* in the Navy, 1749; Lieutenant, 1762; *Capitaine de Vaisseau*, 1777; *Chef d'Escadre*, 1784; in command of the *Flore* he brought four prises into Toulon, 1778; commanded the *Marseillais* of 74 guns in the fleet of the Count de Grasse, 1781-1782, taking part in the battles of the Chesapeake and Les Saintes; Knight of the Royal and Military Order of Saint-Louis; Chevalier of Honor and Devotion of the Sovereign Military Order of Saint John of Jerusalem (Order of Malta); Governor of the isles of Sainte-Marguerite. He was an original member of the French Cincinnati.

The Chevalier (Marquis) de Chastellux.

François-Jean, Chevalier (later Marquis) de Chastellux, was born in Paris, 1734, of a noble Burgundian house. Entered the Army at the age of twelve as lieutenant in the Auvergne Regiment of infantry, 1750; Knight of the Royal and Military Order of Saint-Louis, 1750; Colonel of the Regiment de la Marche, 1762, taking part in the campaigns of the Seven Years War; Brigadier, 1769; *Maréchal de Camp*, 1780; Major-General in the Army commanded by the Count de Rochambeau during the war for American Independence; Inspector of Cavalry and Infantry, 1787. For his important part in the capture of Yorktown was cited by General Washington, thereafter returning to France in the *Emeraude* with Rochambeau. He was the grandson of the Chancellor d'Aguesseau, at whose house he met d'Alembert and Helvétius with whom he engaged in the work of the philosophers and encyclopedists. Among other writings he published *De la félicité publique*, 1772, as a result of which he was elected to the French Academy, 1774. Member of the American Academy of Arts and Sciences of Boston and of the American Philosophical Society of Philadelphia. His *Voyages dans l'Amérique septentrionale*, describing his experiences 1780-1782, appeared in two volumes in 1786, wherein he described the customs of the United States which he greatly admired. He died in Paris, 1788. He was a knight of the Order of Saint-Lazare and of Notre Dame du Mont-Carmel. Original member of the French Cincinnati.

Major-General George Clinton.

Born at Little Britain, New York, 1739; served for a short time in the privateer *Defiance* sailing from New York, 1758; subaltern in the regiment of his father Charles Clinton, and was a member of the expedition under Colonel John Bradstreet against Fort Frontenac on Lake Ontario; studied law and practiced for a short time; member of the Provincial Assembly of New York, 1768; member of the Committee of Correspondence appointed by the Assembly, 1775; Brigadier-General of Militia, 1775; voted for the separation of the Colonies from Britain, but was absent on military duties when the Declaration of Independence was signed, 1776; Brigadier-General, Continental Army, 1777; elected to the officers of both Governor and Lieutenant-Governor of New York, 1777; served as Governor for six terms; commanded American forces at Forts Clinton and Montgomery, 1777; Brevet Major-General, 1783; elected Vice-President of the United States, 1808, and held the office for two terms; died in office, 1812. His elder brother was Major-General James Clinton (1733-1812) and his younger brother DeWitt Clinton (1769-1828), the statesman and savant. All three were original members of the New York Cincinnati.

Colonel Ethis de Corny.

Louis-Dominique Ethis de Corny was born at Metz, 1736; Subdelegate of the Intendance of Franche-Comté, 1762; Provincial Commissary of War in Britainy and Normandy; sailed for America in the *Hermione*, 1780 with LaFayette; arrived in Boston, 1780; had the duty to make advance arrangements for the arrival of Rochambeau's army; Lieutenant-Colonel of Cavalry, 1780; Colonel, 1780; returned to France in the *Alliance* in the uniform of an American colonel; appointed Commissary in Chief by the King, 1781; resigned from the American Army, 1782; War Commissary of the Swiss Guard, 1784; Procureur-Général du Roi and of the City of Paris, 1785; Knight of the Royal and Military of Saint-Louis, 1787; member of the Academy of Besançon; he was first a member of the Society of the Cincinnati in the State of Virginia but transferred to the French Society, 1788.

Captain Cottineau de Kerloguen.

Denis-Nicholas Cottineau de Kerloguen's name is generally misspelled and not infrequently given as "K/loguen," the sign "/" representing the not unusual Breton abbreviation for "er." A Breton naval officer who commanded the *Pallas* 24 in the action under Commodore John Paul Jones off Scarborough Head, 23 September 1779. Some details of his service are given in the letter of the French consul in Baltimore, the Chevalier d'Annemours, 15 February 1789, *q. v.* As he served under a French letter of marque and claimed French nationality, he was ineligible to membership in the Cincinnati under the rule limiting French members to a rank not below Colonel, or its equivalent in the French Navy. He was elected an honorary member of the Pennsylvania Cincinnati, 1795, and later, on his removal to Georgia, affiliated with the Cincinnati of that State. He was born at Nantes about 1745 and became a planter in Santo Domingo, whence he was driven to the United States by the insurrections of 1791-1792. He settled in Philadelphia and for a season was a shareholder and settler on the Susquehanna at the French Royalist Colony of Azilum. Later removed to Savannah, Georgia, where he died 29 November 1808. He was a Knight of the Royal and Military Order of Saint-Louis, a fact noted on his gravestone in the Colonial Cemetary, Savannah, also that he was a *Lieutenant de Vaisseau*, French Navy. His widow, sister of the Marquis de Montalet, later returned to France, "where she graced the court of Louis XVIII."'

Brigadier-General Elias Dayton.

Born at Elizabeth-Town (now Elizabeth), New Jersey, 1737; early apprenticed as a mechanic; Lieutenant of militia, 1756; Captain 1760, serving under Wolfe at Quebec and against Pontiac near Detroit; later opened a general store; chosen Alderman just before the Revolution; member of the local Committee of Thirty-One, 1774; Muster-Master for Essex County, New Jersey, 1775; Colonel Third New Jersey Regiment, Continental Line, 1776; in January of that year led seventy-seven volunteers in three shallops to capture the British supply-ship *Blue Mountain Valley*; his son Jonathan served under him first as a paymaster and then as a captain; his regiment was at Albany, May 1776, and built Fort Schuyler and also Fort Dayton (at Herkimer), and warded off Indian raids from Johnstown and German Flats, returning to Morristown, March 1777; served at Bound Brook, Staten Island and Brandywine; spent the winter of 1777-1778 at Valley Forge; had horses shot from under him at Germantown, Springfield, and Crosswicks; declined election to Congress; for his service at Morristown General Washington commented "Colonel Dayton merits particular thanks"; transferred to the Second New Jersey Regiment, Continental Line, 1781; Brigadier-General, Continental Army, 1783, on General Washington's recommendation; after the war was Major-General of Militia; trustee of the Presbyterian Church; Recorder of Elizabeth, 1789; Member of the New Jersey Assembly, 1791-1792 and 1794-1796. He was the first President of the New Jersey Cincinnati, of which his son, Captain Jonathan Dayton was also an original member, and for whom the city of Dayton, Ohio, is named.

The Chevalier Desnoyers.

It would appear from the memorandum accompanying his letter to General Washington, that he was a lieutenant of the Regiment of Guadeloupe, of which he commanded a corps of four hundred men at the siege of Savannah, where he was wounded. At the time of his letter to General Washington, 12 June 1789, applying for admission to the Order of the Cincinnati, he was a lieutenant colonel of infantry at Basse-Terre, Guadeloupe. His claim was disallowed, presumably because he was only a lieutenant at the time of his service in the American War. He was a Chevalier of the Royal and Military Order of Saint-Louis.

Destouches, see Touches.

Major John Singer Dexter.

Lieutenant, First Rhode Island Regiment, Continental Line, 1775; First Lieutenant and Adjutant, Ninth Continental Infantry, 1776; Captain, First Rhode Island Regiment, Continental Line, 1777; Assistant to the Adjutant General, 1779; retained in Olney's Rhode Island Battalion, 1781; Major, 1781, and served to 1783. He was an original member of the Rhode Island Cincinnati, being its Secretary, 1784, Vice-President, 1812, and President, 1814.

BRIGADIER JEAN-BAPTISTE VIGNOURNIN DUPLESSIS.

COLONEL THOMAS-ANTOINE DE MAUDUIT DUPLESSIS.

Jean-Baptiste Vignournin Duplessis, *Brigadier des armées du Roy,* was Governor of the Islands of Saint Vincent. He was elected an honorary member of the Georgia Cincinnati, 1786; Chevalier of the Royal and Military Order of Saint-Louis. He is nearly always confused with Colonel Thomas-Antoine de Mauduit Duplessis (1753-1791) who served under Continental Commission and received the brevet of Lieutenant-Colonel for service at the battles of Brandywine, Germantown and Fort Mercer. He returned to France in 1779 and did not revisit America. He was an original member of the French Cincinnati. In 1787 he commanded a regiment at Port au Prince, Haiti, where he was murdered by his own men.

LIEUTENANT-GENERAL DUPORTAIL.

Louis Lebègue de Presles Duportail was born at Pithiviers, 1743. After training at the Engineer School of Mézières, he was commissioned second lieutenant, 1 January, 1762; promoted Engineer, 1765; Captain, 1773 and as such was authorized to proceed to the United States, where Congress appointed him Lieutenant-Colonel, 1777; Colonel, 1777; Brigadier-General Commandant of Engineers, 1777, and had charge of the miners and sappers, and was director of fortifications; Major-General, 1781. He was present at the battles of Brandywine, Germantown, and Monmouth, and was charged by Washington with many important military missions. He was chief engineer of the defenses of Charleston, at the capitulation of which he was taken prisoner, 1780, being exchanged a few months later. He was the chief engineer at the siege of Yorktown. At the end of the War he was honorably discharged from the service of the United States. In the meantime in France he had been made Lieutenant-Colonel, attached to the infantry, 1780; Knight of the Royal and Military Order of Saint-Louis, 1782; Brigadier of Infantry, 1783 and given a pension of 2300 *livres.* In 1787 he was authorized to serve as instructor of the Neapolitan Army. In the same year he was appointed *Aide Maréchal Général des Logis* in the General Staff Corps; promoted *Maréchal de Camp,* 1788, and was employed in the departments of Seine-Inférieur and Eure, 1790; Minister and Secretary of State for War, 1790; Lieutenant-General, 1792; emigrated at the Terror and returned to the United States. Died at sea on his journey back to France, 1802. Original member of the French Cincinnati.

THE COUNT D'ESTAING.

Charles-Hector, Count d'Estaing, was born at the Château de Ravel, in Auvergne in 1729. He entered the army as a colonel of infantry under Lally Tollendal, Commandant General of the French Establishments in the East Indies, and served in the campaign in India, being severely wounded and captured at the siege of Madras, 1759. On being released, he armed two ships and served once more in the war and for a second time was taken prisoner. Commissioned *Chef d'Escadre,* 1762, and promoted Lieutenant-General of the Sea Forces, 1767, in which year he was created a Knight of the Holy Ghost, highest French decoration; Vice-Admiral, 1777, and as such commanded the first squadron which sailed from Toulon, 12 April 1778, for America, arriving three months later. His campaign in Rhode Island waters was unsuccessful, the British fleet slipping through his hands during a storm. He was victorious in the Antilles, at Saint Lucia, Saint Vincent and Grenada. Returning to the United States he was present at the siege of Savannah, 1779, thereafter returning to France. He commanded the Franco-Spanish fleet and convoyed a commercial fleet to the Antilles. He was elected the first President of the Society of the Cincinnati in France, being the senior French officer who had served in the American War. Governor General of Touraine, 1785; Member of the Assembly of Notables at Versailles, 1787, and in 1789 commanded the National Guards there stationed. He embraced the principles of the Revolution and was made Admiral in 1792. He was arrested during the Reign of Terror and on 24 April 1794 perished on the guillotine. He was a Grandee of Spain of the First Class.

ETHIS DE CORNY, see CORNY.

MONSIEUR DE FLAD.

This is presumably that Captain-Commandant de Flad of the Regiment Royal Deux-Ponts, which served in the Auxiliary Army under the Count de Rochambeau. He was not admitted a member of the Cincinnati, probably because he did not hold a sufficiently senior military rank.

THE BARON DE FOCK.

Johan Henric, Baron von Fock, a Swedish nobleman, was born 1753; served first as an officer in the Swedish Army; Captain of Schomberg's Dragoons in France, 1779; came to America as Adjutant of the

Duke de Lauzun, who commanded the vanguard of the French expedition, 1781; present at the siege of Yorktown, and returned to France with Lauzun, bearing the news of the victory, to the King; the Swedish Ambassador in Paris, Count Gustav Filip de Creutz, wrote to His Swedish Majesty on 25 November 1781, " [Lauzun] has great praise for Monsieur de Fock. . . . In a cavalry attack where Lauzun's hussars repulsed a furious charge by the English dragoons, Fock exhibited an extraordinary valor and intelligence. He [Lauzun] has asked me to solicit from Your Majesty the Cross of the Order of the Sword for Messrs. Fersen and Fock. Monsieur de Rochambeau will demand the same kind of favor from them here." The King accordingly created Fock a Knight of the Sword. The Baron de Fock was ineligible for admission to the Order of the Cincinnati having not attained the rank of Colonel. He spent his last years in England, where he lived under a changed name. He died there in 1817.

Major Jean-Daniel de Gambs.

Born at Strasbourg, 1741; Major of the Regiment de Bourbonnais; pensioned 5 December 1781 for good conduct at Yorktown. He was not admitted a member of the Society of the Cincinnati because his rank was below that of Colonel, a requisite grade for eligibility on the part of officers of the French forces.

Vice-Admiral Arnaud le Gardeur de Tilly.

Arnaud le Gardeur de Tilly, born 1733, became a *Garde* in the Navy, 1750; *Lieutenant de Vaisseau,* 1763; Lieutenant-Colonel, 1777; *Capitaine de Vaisseau,* 1778; *Chef de Division,* 1786; Rear-Admiral, 1792; Vice-Admiral, 1792; Commanded the frigate *Concorde* 26 which defeated the *Minerva* 32 after a brilliant combat off Cape François, Santo Domingo, 1778, a victory recorded in a painting ordered by the Minister of War; wounded in combat, 1779. Commanded the *Eveille* 79 in Rhode Island waters, and took part under des Touches in the battle of the Chesapeake, 1781; served under Vaudreuil at Yorktown. Imprisoned during the Terror but liberated on the 9th Thermodor. Chevalier of the Royal and Military Order of Saint-Louis. His younger brother, the Chevalier le Gardeur de Tilly, was *Lieutenant de Vaisseau,* 1771, and was killed, 1778, while serving under his brother during the battle between the *Minerva* and the *Concorde.*

DON DIEGO DE GARDOQUI.

Became Chargé d'Affaires of Spain in the United States, 1785. During the American Revolution he had acted as agent through whom funds passed from Spain to the United States. He was a member of the firm of Gardoqui and Son, of Bilbao. John Jay, then American diplomatic agent in Madrid, had many conversations with Gardoqui. On 3 September 1780 Gardoqui hinted to Jay that there be an equivalent for the Spanish loans, in the form of a recognition of Spanish monopoly of the navigation of the Mississippi, ship-timber, vessels, tobacco, etc. Jay claimed that he made no promises to Gardoqui (Wharton, iv, 64). The "Spanish Conspiracy," which has been the subject to much study, though it is a confused chapter of American history, was said to have been devised by Gardoqui. For this reason his memory is cordially hated in Kentucky and other States that would have been affected by a successful conspiracy.

MAJOR-GENERAL HORATIO GATES.

Born at Maldon, Essex, England, 1728/9; Lieutenant, British Army, under General Cornwallis, serving in Nova Scotia, 1749-1750; Captain of an independent company of foot, New York, 1754; severely wounded at Braddock's Defeat, 1755; served under General Monckton in the Martinique Expedition, 1761; Major, Forty-fifth Regiment of Foot, British Army, 1762; took up land granted him for military services, Berkeley County, Virginia, 1772; Lieutenant-Colonel of Virginia Militia, Lord Dunmore's War, 1774; Adjutant General with the rank of Brigadier-General, Continental Army, 1775; Major-General, Continental Army, 1776; in command of the Northern Army, 1777; awarded a Gold Medal and the Thanks of Congress for victory over General Burgoyne at the battle of Saratoga, 1777; succeeded General Weedon as President of the Society of the Cincinnati in the State of Virginia, 1783; chosen Vice-President General at the first General Meeting of the Cincinnati, 1784; transferred his membership to the New York Cincinnati; Member of the New York Legislature, 1800-1801; died at *Rose Hill*, New York City, 1806.

LIEUTENANT DE GENEVY DE PUSIGNAN, see PUSIGNAN.

THE CHEVALIER DE GÉRARD.

Conrad-Alexandre, Chevalier de Gérard, was born at Massevaux in Alsace, 1729. After having been employed in diplomatic duty at the court of the Elector Palatine and at the Court of Austria, he was appointed to the Ministry of Foreign Affairs by Choiseul in 1766. He was Secretary of the Council of State under the Count de Vergennes, being specially charged with American affairs, and dealing directly with Silas Deane, the American representative in Paris. He signed the Treaty of Amity and Commerce between France and the United States, 1778, and was then appointed Minister of France to the United States. He reached America with the fleet of the Count d'Estaing 1778. He rendred valuable services in reorganizing American finances and brought about a good understanding between the two countries. His health having been impaired, 1779, he was succeeded as Minister by the Chevalier de La Luzerne. By order of Congress his portrait was painted by Charles W. Peale and hung in Independence Hall in Philadelphia, and a medal was struck in his honor. He was voted the Thanks of Congress and was received in special session, 1778. He was a member of the Assembly of Notables, convoked at Versailles, 1787. Died, 1790. Though he held no military rank, he was made an original member of the Society of the Cincinnati in the terms of the Institution itself.

The Chevalier Jean-Joseph de Gimat.

As Lieutenant in the Regiment de Viennois, 1776, he was authorized to serve in America. Major, Continental Army, 1776; served as Aide-de-Camp to Major-General the Marquis de LaFayette; promoted Lieutenant-Colonel, 1777; present at the battle of Brandywine, 1777, and the operations at Whitemarsh, the battle of Monmouth, the siege of Newport and the battle of Rhode Island; in command of a battalion of infantry he served under LaFayette at Yorktown where he was wounded in the capture of Redoute No. 10; returned to France, 1782; captain of grenadiers in the Regiment de Viennois, 1778; major, 1779; colonel of the Regiment of Martinique, 1782; Governor of St. Lucia from 1789 to 1792 when he resigned from the service. He was an original member of the French Cincinnati.

The Count de Grasse, Marquis de Tilly.

Lieutenant-General François-Joseph-Paul de Grasse-Tilly, Count de Grasse and Marquis de Tilly, was born at Bar in Provence, 1722; *Garde de la Marine,* in the service of the Sovereign Military Order of Malta, 1734; served in the Levant in the *Eole*, 1738; served in the *Ferme*, *Diamant*, *Castor* and *Syrène*, French Navy, 1740-1746; served in the *Emeraude*; captured off Cape Finisterre, 1747; remained a prisoner of war on parole in England until the Peace of Aix-la-Chapelle; *Lieutenant de Vaisseau*, 1754; served in the *Ambiteuse*, *Amphion* and *Tonnant*; present at the capture of Minorca; served in the West Indies; commanded the *Zéphir* in the exploration of the coast of Guinea; *Capitaine de Vaisseau*, 1762; commanded the *Protée* in the West Indies, 1762-1765; commanded the *Heroine* against the Saletin pirates, 1765; commanded the *Amphitrite* in Santo Domingo under the Count d'Estaing, 1775; commanded the *Intrépide* under the Count Duchassault, 1776; commanded the *Robuste* in the action of Ushant, 1778; *Chef d'Escadre*, 1779; participated in the capture of Grenada and the siege of Savannah, 1779; Lieutenant-General of French Naval Forces in the West Indies, 1781; successfully engaged the fleet of Rear-Admiral Sir Samuel Hood, Royal Navy, off Martinique, 1781; successfully engaged the fleet of Rear-Admiral Thomas Graves, Royal Navy off the Capes of the Chesapeake, 1781; cooperated with the American and French land forces at the siege of Yorktown, 1781; received the Thanks of Congress, 1781; engaged the fleet of Sir Samuel Hood, Royal Navy, in the West Indies, 1781; defeated and captured in action with Vice-Admiral Sir George Brydges Rodney, Royal Navy, near Dominica, 1782; transported to England as a prisoner of war and released on parole; tried by court martial for his defeat, but was acquitted; Knight Commander of the Royal and Military Order of Saint-Louis, and a Knight of Honor and Devotion of the Sovereign Military Order of Malta. Died in Paris, 1788. Original member of the French Cincinnati. His descendants were present at the Centennial of the Yorktown victory, 1881 and the Sesquicentennial, 1931 as guests of the United States Government.

AUGUSTE, COUNT DE GRASSE.

Alexandre-François-Auguste de Grasse-Rouville, Count de Grasse, Marquis de Tilly, Seigneur de Flins, Mondreville, le Chambrier, Saint-Kaurent les Jonchères, de Laval, le Boulaye, Présonnet, and la Geneste, was the only son of Admiral the Count de Grasse, the French Naval commander during the War of American Independence, original member of the Cincinnati. The younger de Grasse was born at Versailles, 1765, entered the military service as a sublieutenant in the Regiment du Roi, 1781 and in 1784 became a captain in the Regiment Pologne Royal. In 1788 he was appointed a captain in the Royal Guienne regiment of cavalry and served in Santo Domingo. In 1794 he entered the United States Army, under Paul Hyacinthe Perrault as a Temporary Engineer, charged with the construction of fortifications on the coasts of South

Carolina and Georgia. Admitted an hereditary member of the Society of the Cincinnati in the State of Georgia, 1796. On his return to France, he was commissioned a major of cavalry, 1802. At the Restoration he served in 1814 in the Household of Louis XVIII, and later in the Army in Belgium under H. R. H. the Duke de Berri. He corresponded frequently with General Washington and in a letter of 1795 asked him for his portrait. He died at Versailles, 1845 leaving four daughters. His descendants live in the United States.

Major-General Nathaniel Greene.

Born at Potowomut, Rhode Island, 1742; worked in his father's iron foundry till 1770 when he moved to Coventry to take charge of the family forge there; Freeman of Warwick, 1765; Deputy to the General Assembly, 1770-1772 and 1775; was "put from under the care" of the Friends meeting, 1773, because he had attended a military parade; helped to organize the Kentish Guards, a militia regiment, 1774; appointed by Rhode Island on the committee to consult with Connecticut, 1775; Brigadier-General, Continental Army, 1775; in command of the army of occupation in Boston after the British departed; after battle of Harlem, was given command of troops in New Jersey, 1776; Major-General, 1776; played an important part at the battle of Trenton, 1776; present at battles of Brandywine and Germantown, 1777; spent the winter at Valley Forge; Quartermaster General of the Continental Army, 1778; for his "wise, decisive and magnanimous conduct at Eutaw Springs, S. C." received the Thanks of Congress and was presented with a stand of captured British colors, 1781; again received the Thanks of Congress, 1783, and was presented with two captured British field pieces, 1783; became President, at its formation, of the Society of the Cincinnati in the State of Rhode Island and Providence Plantations, 1783; spent much of the last years of his life in Savannah, where he died, 1786.

The Count de Grouchet.

Pierre-Philippe, Count de Grouchet de Soquence, was a native of Normandy. In his memorial to the General Meeting of the Cincinnati, which accompanied his letter of 20 October 1786 (duplicate of that of 20 October 1785) to General Washington, he gave his age as fifty (1785) and said he was "at present lieutenant of the Marshal of France (1785) and that he served in the "campaign of Savannah and pensacola." Nothing about him found in print. He was probably of insufficient rank for admission to the Cincinnati.

LIEUTENANT ALEXANDRE DE GUBIAN.

Lieutenant Alexandre de Gubian held the rank of *Lieutenant de Frigatte* and signed himself "*ancien lieutenant de frigatte de marseille*" in his letter of 13 June 1784 to General Washington. He was not of sufficiently senior grade to be eligible to the Ordre de Cincinnatus, as he called it. General Washington calls him G*a*bian.

MAJOR-GENERAL ALEXANDER HAMILTON.

Born in the island of Nevis, British West Indies, 1757; sent to New York for his education; graduated at King's College (now Columbia University), 1773; in 1774 began writing and speaking against British measures; Captain, Provincial Company, New York Artillery, 1776; selected by General Washington as his principal Aide-de-Camp, with rank of Lieutenant-Colonel, 1777. Served as such to the end of the War. Member of the Continental Congress 1782; member of the New York Legislature, 1787; member of the Constitutional Convention; Member of the Continental Congress, 1788; first Secretary of the Treasury of the United States, by General Washington's appointment; took part in the expedition under General Henry Lee to suppress the Whisky Rebellion in Pennsylvania, 1794. Major-General, and Inspector-General, United States Army, 1798; honorably discharged, 1800. Killed in a duel with Aaron Burr, 1804. Vice-President of the New York Cincinnati, 1788. Elected Vice-President General of the Society of the Cincinnati, 1799, and upon General Washington's death succeeded him as President General and retained the office to the end of his life. Married the daughter of Major-General Philip Schuyler of New York, a fellow member of the Cincinnati. Fort Hamilton, New York, bears his name.

COLONEL BENJAMIN HAWKINS.

Born in Granville (now Warren) County, North Carolina, 1754; member of the senior class at the College of New Jersey (now Princeton University) at the outbreak of the American Revolution; appointed interpreter on General Washington's staff, because of his knowledge of French; later one of General Washington's Aides-de-Camp; member of the North Carolina House of Commons, 1778, 1779 and 1784; chosen by the North Carolina Legislature, 1780, to procure arms and munitions for the State's defense; Member of the Continental Congress, 1781-1784, 1786, and 1787; appointed by Congress to negotiate treaties with the Cherokee and Creek Indians, 1785; delegate to the North Carolina

Convention which ratified the Federal Constitution, 1789; elected United States Senator, 1789 and served to 1795; appointed Indian agent for all tribes south of the Ohio River, by President Washington, 1796, and held office until his death in Crawford County, Georgia, 1816. He was an original member of the North Carolina Cincinnati.

Colonel William Heth.

Born near Pittsburgh (then considered Virginia territory), 1750; Lieutenant of Morgan's Company of Virginia Riflemen, Lord Dunmore's War, 1774; Clerk of Frederick County, Virginia, Committee of Safety, 1774; Taken prisoner at Quebec, 1775; Major, Eleventh Virginia Regiment, Continental Line, 1776; Lieutenant-Colonel, Third Virginia Regiment, Continental Line, 1777; Colonel, 1778; Taken prisoner at the fall of Charleston, 1780; on parole to the end of the War; Member of the Virginia Council, 1787; Commissioner to settle Virginia Claims in Northwest Territory, 1788; Member of the Virginia Constitutional Convention, 1788; Collector of the Ports of Richmond and Bermuda Hundred from General Washington's first term as President, until 1802; died at Richmond, Virginia, 1807; buried at Curle's Neck, Virginia; Treasurer of the Virginia Cincinnati from 1784 until his death. To his care and wisdom in managing the fund the greatest credit is due. His brothers, Henry and John, were also original members of the Virginia Cincinnati.

The Baron de Holtzendorff.

Louis-Casimir, Baron de Holtzendorff, was born in Berlin, 1728, being the son of a Privy Councillor of the King of Prussia; was living in Paris at the outbreak of the American War of Independence; commissioned Major, 1776; Lieutenant-Colonel, Continental Army, 1776; present at the battles of Brandywine and Germantown; resigned, 1778; in France was appointed Captain of infantry, 1779, and attached to the Anhalt (later Salm Salm) Regiment; Aide-de-Camp to the Count de Witgenstein, 1781; Captain, 1784; in the service of The Netherlands, 1785; received a pension. He is said to have been well thought of by Saint-Germain, and was recommended by Silas Deane as a "first class man," but after his return to Paris became a thorn in the flesh to Franklin. He was the author of *Essai Général sur la Tactique prussiene*, and other works, being a good writer.

LIEUTENANT-COLONEL DAVID HUMPHREYS.

Born at Derby, Connecticut, 1752; graduated at Yale, 1771; M. A., 1774; volunteered as Adjutant of the Second Regiment of Connecticut Militia, 1776; Wrote his verses " Adieu thou Yale, Hear ye the din of battle? Clang of Arms? " at this time; Captain, Sixth Connecticut Regiment, Continental Line, 1777; transferred to the Fourth Connecticut, 1781; transferred to the Second Connecticut, 1783; Brigade Major to General Parsons, 1777; Major and Aide-de-Camp to General Putnam, 1778; Aide-de-Camp to General Greene, 1780; Lieutenant-Colonel and Aide-de-Camp to General Washington, 1780; resigned, 1783; presented with a sword by Act of the Continental Congress, 1781, as a testimony of his fidelity and ability; he celebrated Washington in verse and was a frequent guest at Mount Vernon; Secretary to the Commission for Negotiating Treaties of Commerce with Foreign Powers, 1784; member of the Connecticut Assembly, 1786; Commandant of a Regiment, created " for operations should these become necessary," 1786; Special Secret Agent to obtain information for the American Government in London, Lisbon and Madrid, 1790, when war between Spain and Britain was threatened; Commissioner of Algerine Affairs, 1793; Fellow of the Royal Society, London; his best known poem is that " On the Future Glory of the United States "; died in Connecticut, 1818. Original member of the Connecticut Cincinnati.

MAJOR-GENERAL JEDEDIAH HUNTINGTON.

Jedediah Huntington was born at Norwich, Connecticut, 1743; graduated at Harvard College, 1763, and settled in Norwich becoming his father's associate in business—the West India trade. Became an active Son of Liberty at the approach of the Revolution. Appointed Ensign of the First Norwich Company of militia, 1769; Lieutenant, 1771; Captain 1774; in the same year he was made a Colonel of militia; as such served in the Lexington Alarm, 1775. Commissioned Colonel of the Eighth Connecticut Regiment, Continental Line, 1775; Colonel, 17th Continental Infantry, 1776; Colonel, First Connecticut Regiment, Continental Line, 1777; Brigadier-General, Continental Army, 1777 and served as such to the close of the War, receiving the brevet of Major-General in 1783. His service in the field was valuable. In 1777 he cooperated with Arnold and later joined Putnam at Peekskill. He was a member of the Court Martial that tried General Charles Lee. After retirement from the Army he held several civic offices, such as sheriff of New London County, Treasurer of Connecticut, and

Delegate to the Constitutional Convention. President Washington appointed him Collector of Customs for the Port of New London, 1789, which office he retained until his death, 1818. He was the first President of the Society of the Cincinnati in the State of Connecticut.

MAJOR WILLIAM JACKSON.

Born in Cumberland, England, 9 March 1759; left an orphan in his youth he was brought up in South Carolina; Second Lieutenant, First South Carolina Regiment, Continental Line, 1776; First Lieutenant, 1777; participated in the expedition against St. Augustine, Florida, 1778; Major and Aide-de-Camp to General Lincoln, 1780; taken prisoner at the capture of Charleston, 1780, and was a prisoner on parole to 1783; accompanied John Laurens to France, 1781, as secretary of the mission; entrusted with the shipment of the supplies acquired by Laurens, to the Continental Army; assistant Secretary of War under General Lincoln, the first holder of the office of Secretary, 1782, and served as such for two years; helped settle the mutinous outbreak of Pennsylvania troops, 1783; secretary of the Constitutional Convention, upon Washington appointment, 1787; at the close of the Convention the records were burned by its order, except the journal of the proceedings and the aye and nay votes. These in Jackson's handwriting are the only written records of the Convention; member of the Pennsylvania bar, 1788; in the next year was unsuccessful as candidate for the office of Secretary of the United States Senate; Washington then appointed him one of his personal secretaries; declined Washington's offer of appointment as Adjutant General of the Army, 1791; United States Surveyor of Customs for Philadelphia, by Washington's appointment, this being one of the President's last official acts. In 1818-1819 he was delegated by the surviving officers of the Continental Army to obtain for them an equitable adjustment of their promised half pay. Papers concerning this are in the archives of the Society of the Cincinnati in the State of Virginia; died in Philadelphia, 18 December 1828. An original member of the Pennsylvania Cincinnati, he was its Secretary, 1785-1787. In 1796 he was elected Treasurer General as successor to General McDougall, first holder of that office. He was elected Secretary General, 1799, succeeding General Knox, the first of the Society's eight Secretaries General.

MR. THOMAS JEFFERSON.

Born at Old Shadwell, Virginia, 1743; attended preparatory school under the Rev. Mr. Maury; graduated at the College of William and

Mary, 1762; studied law, was admitted to the bar and began practice, 1767; Member of the Virginia House of Burgesses, 1769-1774; prominent in pre-Revolutionary movements; Member of the Continental Congress, 1775 and 1776; Chairman of the Committee that drew up the Declaration of Independence; made and presented the first draft of the Declaration that was submitted to Congress, 2 July 1776; signed the Declaration of Independence, 4 July 1776; Governor of Virginia, 1779-1781; member of the Virginia House of Delegates, 1782; Member of the Continental Congress, 1783-1785; Minister Plenipotentiary to France, 1784, and then sole Minister to the King of France, 1785, for three years; Secretary of State of the United States in President Washington's Cabinet, 1789 to 1793; Vice-President of the United States, 1797-1801; President of the United States, 1801-1809; active in founding the University of Virginia; died at Montecello, Albermarle County, Virginia, 1826. Mr. Jefferson was the most bitter and most influential of the enemies of the Society of the Cincinnati and attacked it on every occasion. This did not prevent his asking the President of the Virginia Society, Judge Taliaferro, to have the Virginia Society's fund donated to his brain-child, the University of Virginia! The request was refused, and in a letter Judge Taliaferro gave the reasons therefor in plain words.

COLONEL FRANCIS JOHNSTON.

Lieutenant-Colonel, Fourth Pennsylvania Battalion, 4 January 1776; Colonel, Fifth Pennsylvania Regiment, Continental Line, 27 September 1776; served as such until retired 17 January 1781; an original member of the State Society of the Cincinnati of Pennsylvania, he was elected its first Assistant Treasurer, 1783 and in 1785 became its Treasurer. He was succeeded by his son, Alexander Washington Johnston at his death on 22 February 1815, and the son was, in 1825, elected the first of the Society's Assistant Treasurers General. He was a member of the Standing Committee of the Pennsylvania Cincinnati, 1787-1798.

COMMODORE JOHN PAUL JONES.

Born in Kirkudbrightshire, Scotland, 1747; known as John Paul until 1773, when he took the name Jones in honor of a friend; his first voyage in the *Friendship* took him to Fredericksburg, Virginia, where his elder brother, William, lived; at age of nineteen he became mate on the *Two Friends*, 1766; in 1769 commanded the *John*, merchantman of Dumfries and made two voyages to the West Indies; master of the *Betsey of London*, 1773; in his attempt to put down a mutiny on board, he killed the leader of the mutineers; went to Virginia to avoid trial; commissioned Lieutenant in the Continental Navy, 1775; being the senior officer from the Colonies south of Pennsylvania; his professional successes were immediate and he established a great reputation before the end of the year; Captain, Continental Navy, 1776; in command of the sloop *Ranger*, 1777 in this ship he raided the British coast and captured the British sloop, *Drake*; King Louis XVI of France placed the old *Duras* under Jones's command, who renamed it *Bonhomme Richard* as a compliment to Benjamin Franklin. Jones was given command of a combined American and French fleet of five ships, 1779; was victorious in the action with the British *Serapis* and other ships, 1779; the Masonic Lodge of the Nine Sisters in Paris, had his bust done by Houdon; the King presented him with a gold-hilted sword and made him a Knight of the Order of Military Merit, probably the first decoration conferred on an American and perhaps the only one during the Revolution; in command of the French ship *Ariel* he captured the British *Triumph*, 1781; received the Thanks of Congress, 1781; awarded a Gold Medal by Congress, 1787; made a Rear-Admiral in the Imperial Russian Navy by the Empress Catherine, and served against the Turks, 1788; received the Order of Sainte Anne from the Empress; appointed Commissioner to treat with Algiers by President Jefferson, 1792, but he died in Paris in that year before receiving notice of this; his remains brought back to America, 1905, by an American squadron to which a French cruiser was attached, and buried in the chapel of the Naval Academy, Annapolis. A national monument in his memory was erected in Potomac Park, Washington, 1912. Original member of the Pennsylvania Cincinnati.

Lieutenant the Baron de Kalb.

Frédéric, Baron de Kalb, was born in Paris, 1765, being the eldest son of Major-General Jean, Baron de Kalb, the Bavarian volunteer in the French service who came to America in the same ship as LaFayette in 1777, and who was mortally wounded at the battle of Camden, 1780. The eldest son of that officer, who was killed in the service, was of course, eligible to hereditary membership in the Society of the Cincinnati, in terms of the Institution. Young de Kalb was one of the first foreign hereditary members. He served in the French Army until the Revolution, when he was condemned by the military tribunal and perished on the guillotine, 1793. Being without male issue, the right to membership passed to his younger brother, Elie, Baron de Kalb, who served in the forces of Condé during the emigration, and later in the

Austrian Army. He returned to France in 1892, where his descendants now live.

THE COUNT DE KERGARIOU-LOCMARIA.

Théobald-René, Count de Kergariou-Locmaria, was born at the Château de Coëtilliau, 1739; *Garde*, Royal Navy, 1755; *Lieutenant de Vaisseau,* 1770; Chevalier of the Royal and Military Order of Saint-Louis, 1775; *Capitain de Vaisseau*, 1779; *Chef de Division*, 1786. He commanded the frigate *Serin,* 1774; capturing a number of British vessels which had violated the treaty concerning the transportation of slaves. Succeeded to the command of the *Belle-Poule*, 1778, and to the command of the *Junon*, 1780. As commander of the *Sibylle*, he transported in 1782, two million *livres* for the use of the French Expeditionary Force. While in command of sixteen sail en route to America, he was engaged by the British fleet and was severely wounded, 1783. At the time of his emigration during the French Revolution, he had made nine campaigns in America, three voyages around the Cape of Good Hope among others. He was several times severely wounded during his command of nine ships. He participated in the expedition to Quiberon Bay where he was made prisoner and shot in 1795. He was an original member of the Society of the Cincinnati of France, as was also his brother, Pierre-Joseph, Marquis de Kergariou, Rear-Admiral in the Royal Navy.

KERLOGUEN, see COTTINEAU DE KERLOGUEN.

MAJOR-GENERAL HENRY KNOX.

Born in Boston, Massachusetts, 1750; Lieutenant, Boston Grenadier Corps, 1768; volunteer at the battle of Bunker Hill, 1775; Colonel, Continental Regiment of Artillery, 1775; Brigadier-General and Chief of Artillery, Continental Army, 1776; present at the siege of Yorktown, 1781; Major-General, Continental Army, 1782; Secretary General of the Society of the Cincinnati at its establishment, 1783, having been the first to suggest the creation of the Society; Commander-in-Chief, Continental Army, 1783-1784; Secretary of War, 1785-1794; United States Commissioner for settling the Eastern Boundary on the Saintroix River, 1796; Master of Arts, Dartmouth College, 1793; Vice-President General, Society of the Cincinnati, 1805; Fellow of the American Academy of Arts and Sciences, 1805; Died at *Montpelier* near Thomaston, Maine, 1806. Fort Knox, Kentucky, bears his name.

LA BARTHETTE, see MONTLEZUN DE LA BARTHETTE.

THE COUNT DE LA BRETONNIÈRE.

Louis-Bon-Jean de la Couldre, Count de La Bretonnière, was born at Marchésieux, Manche, 1741; appointed *Garde* in the Royal Navy, 1755; *Lieutenant de Vaisseau*, 1772; captain, 1780; commandant de la Marine at Cherbourg, 1784; *Chef de Division*, 1786; He commanded *l'Aigrette* 32 and later *l'Aréthuse* 28, which was destroyed on the rocks at Molène, 1779; thereafter he commanded *La Tourterelle*, charged with convoying merchant vessels. As Apprentice Engineer he had charge of the construction of the fortifications at Cherbourg and other places. He was retired, 1792 and after being arrested at the outbreak of the French Revolution, was set at liberty; appointed by General Bonaparte to a post in the Ministry of Marine; died at Paris, 1809. He was a Chevalier of the Royal and Military Order of Saint-Louis and of the Legion of Honor. Original member of the French Cincinnati.

THE MARQUIS DE LA FAYETTE.

Marie-Jean-Paul-Yves-Roche-Gilbert du Motier, Marquis de LaFayette, was born at the Château de Chavaniac, Cantal, 1757, son of the Marquis de La Fayette who was killed at the battle of Minden, 1759; musketeer, 1771; sub-lieutenant in the Regiment de Noailles dragoons, 1773; Captain of the same, 1775; with great enthusiasm for the American cause he fitted the *Victoire* at his own expense and sailed to America, April 1777, having engaged to enter the American Army as a volunteer; commissioned Major-General by the Continental Congress, 1777; wounded at the battle of Brandywine, 1777; spent the following winter at Valley Forge; present at the battles of Barren Hill, Monmouth and the siege of Newport; received the Thanks of Congress, 1779; returned to France to work for the American cause; appointed *Mestre de Camp* by King Louis XVI and given command of the dragoon Regiment du Roi; voted a sword of honor by Congress, which was presented by Benjamin Franklin, Minister of the United States in Paris, 1780; given permission by the King to return to America, 1780; received with honors by Congress and given command of a division; participated in the Jersey campaign, 1780; took an important part at the siege of Yorktown, 1781, commanding one of the three American divisions holding the right of the Army; retired from the American service, 1783; orginal member of the Society of the Cincinnati in France and given the duty by the General Meeting of passing on the claims of French officers who had served under American commissions; returned to America, 1784; Member of the Assembly of Notables,

1787; Deputy of the Nobility of Riom to the States General, 1789; commander of the National Guards, Paris, 1789; Lieutenant-General, 1791; General-in-Chief of the Army of Flanders, 1792; proscribed by the Jacobins and ordered arrested, 1792; escaped across the frontier but was captured by the Austrians and imprisoned in the fortress of Olmütz for five years, being released at the treaty of Campo Formio, 1797; declined honors offered him by Napoleon under the Consulate and the Empire; appointed Deputy during the Hundred Days and during the Restoration; made a journey to the United States, 1824, as the guest of the Nation, being then the last surviving Major-General of the War for American Independence; visited each of the twenty-four States; received by the Cincinnati in each of the States where branches existed; Commander-in-Chief of the National Guards of France, 1830; died in Paris, 1834 and buried in the Picpus Cemetary in earth brought from America, so that though buried in France he sleeps in American soil. To his descendants the Cincinnati have given a privilege not shared by any other person. *All* of his male descendants are eligible for membership, not merely the eldest under the law of primogeniture. (For his connection with the Cincinnati, see E. E. Hume, *LaFayette and the Society of the Cincinnati,* Johns Hopkins Press, 1934.)

THE CHEVALIER (later Marquis) DE LA LUZERNE.

Anne-César de La Luzerne de Beuzeville, Chevalier de La Luzerne, later Marquis de La Luzerne, was born at Paris, 1741. Entered the Regiment of the Guard, 1754; Captain in the Burgundian Cavalry Regiment, 1771 and in the same year Colonel of French Granadiers, and of the Provincial Regiment of Caen; brigadier, 1780; promoted *Maréchal de Camp*, 1781, in the recognition of his services in America. Envoy Extraordinary to Maximillian-Joseph, Elector of Bavaria, 1777-1778; Minister Plenipotentiary to the United States, 1779-1784, in which year he succeeded Gérard as Ambassador to Great Britain. Served as such until his death at Southampton, 1791. Contributed a good part of his fortune to the American cause and received the Thanks of Congress and of General Washington. By the terms of the Institution of the Society of the Cincinnati he was made a member. Knight of the Royal and Military Order of Saint-Louis, 1785, in which year he was created a Marquis. Pennsylvania named a county in his honor, his name being also given to a lake in the Adirondacks, New York. His lengthy correspondence with General Washington is preserved in the French Foreign Office and in the Library of Congress. He was a Knight of Honor and Devotion of the Sovereign Military Order of Saint John of Jerusalem (Order of Malta).

He had two distinguished brothers. César-Henri, Count de La Luzerne, Lieutenant-General, was Minister of Marine, 1789-1790. On 12 November he wrote from Port au Prince to General Washington, mentioning his brother's friendship for the General. The third brother, César-Guillaume, Count de La Luzerne, Cardinal, Bishop of Langres, Peer of France under the Restoration, was a famous religious writer.

Count Charles de Lameth.

Charles-Malo-François, Count Charles de Lameth, was born in Paris, 1757 was the brother of Count Alexandre-Théodore-Victor de Lameth and the father of Count Alexandre-Théodore-Victor de Lameth, all three original members of the Society of the Cincinnati in France. He was Captain in the de la Rochefoucauld Regiment of Dragoons and as such accompanied the Count de Rochambeau to Rhode Island in 1778 as his Aide-de-Camp. He became the first *Aide-Maréchal des Logis* in the French Auxiliary Army in America and participated in the expedition commanded by the Chevalier des Touches into the Chesapeake, being present at the naval action there on 16 March 1781. At Yorktown he led the attack on Redoute No. 9, on 14 October 1781, being the first to scale the parapet, where he was severely wounded by two bullets, one of which fractured his arm. His physical condition made his return to France necessary, where he received a pension and was appointed *Mestre de Camp* and *Lieutenant en second* in the Orléans Regiment of Dragoons, 1782, later being commissioned commandant of the Regiment of *Cuirassiers du Roi*, cavalry. He was a Deputy of the noblesse to the States General, 1789; President of the Assembly, 1791. He directed with Barnave, Duport and his brothers, the popular party, but in spite of his advanced ideas he was deposed. Promoted *Maréchal de Camp*, 1792, and served as such in the Army of the North until 10 August, when he was arrested and imprisoned, later being released. He emigrated, but returned to France in 1801 and was appointed General of Brigade, and made Governor of the Grand Duchy of Würzburg, 1809; Envoy to Spain, 1812; Lieutenant General, 1814; Deputy of the Arrondissement of Pontoise, 1829; died at Paris, 1832. Details of his life are to be found in the two volumes, *Mémoires* and *Souvenirs* of his brother Théodore.

Colonel Charles Armand-Tuffin, Marquis de La Rouërie.

Charles Armand-Tuffin, Marquis de La Rouërie, one of the most brilliant cavalrymen of the American War, was born at Fougères in Brittany, 1750. Served in the American Army under the name " Colonel

Armand." Sublieutenant in the Regiment of the French Guard, 1776. In a duel with the Count de Bourbon-Busset over an affair with Mlle, Beaumesnil of the Opéra, he wounded his adversary seriously and fled to America to escape punishment, having received the necessary permission. He reached the United States in 1777 three months before LaFayette and was commissioned Colonel-Commandant of the first battalion of the Partisan Legion, composed of infantry and dragoons, raised by voluntary enlistment. He took an important part in the several campaigns of the War of Independence, being present at the engagements at Elk River, Brandywine, Whitemarsh, Monmouth, the campaigns in New Jersey and Connecticut, and at Tarrytown. On the death of Brigadier-General Count Pułaski at Savannah he was given command of the whole Partisan Legion. For his conduct at the battle of Camden he received the Thanks of Congress. Brigadier-General, Continental Army, in 1783 he became chief of cavalry. In 1780 he received six months leave and visited France where the King created him a Knight of the Royal Military Order of Saint-Louis. Returning to America he served to the close of the war, being honorably discharged, 18 May 1784. He returned to his estates in Britainy; was present in the Assembly of Notables, 1788 representing his province. At first attracted to the principles of the French Revolution, he was dismayed at the excesses of the fanatics and emigrated. Hunted by the agents of the police, he died of a fever at the château of la Guyomarais, near Lamballe, 1793. His correspondence with General Washington was extensive. He was one of the first French officers to become a member of the Cincinnati.

THE BARON DE LA VALLIÈRE.

L—— -F——, Baron de La Vallière, was Governor of Santo Domingo, 1775-1777, and possibly is the Baron de La Vallière who was Governor of Martinique. He was, as he says in his letter to General Washington, 26 May 1789, Commandant under the King's orders for the Mole Saint Nicholas, Haiti, and dependencies, during the American Revolution.

MR. TOBIAS LEAR.

Born at Portsmouth, New Hampshire, 1762, son of Colonel Tobias Lear, a prosperous shipmaster; graduated at Harvard College, 1783; traveled and studied thereafter in Europe; engaged by General Washington as his private secretary after his retirement, 1785; was Washington's secretary for seven years, residing at Mount Vernon, where he endeared himself to all the Washington household; published " Observations on the River Potomack, the Country Adjacent, and the City of Washington," 1793, the earliest separate monograph on the District of Columbia; settled in Alexandria, Virginia, 1794; President of the Potomac Canal Company, 1795; married Frances Basset Washington, niece of Mrs. Washington and widow of Major George Augustine Washington, General Washington's nephew and an original member of the Virginia Cincinnati; General Washington appointed him his Military Secretary with the rank of Colonel, 1798, when war threatened; according to tradition he was the last person to whom General Washington spoke, being at his bedside when the end came; appointed Consul at Santo Domingo by President Jefferson, 1801, a most difficult post for the fierce revolution was in progress there; appointed Consul General at Algiers, 1802; assisted in making treaties with Algiers and with Morocco between 1803 and 1805; was expelled from Algiers at the outset of the War of 1812 when the Dey expected Britain to win; appointed accountant in the War Department, 1812; died in Washington by his own hand, 1816.

Mr. Arthur Lee.

Born at *Stratford*, Westmoreland County, Virginia, 1740, the mansion where General Robert Edward Lee was born in 1807; educated at Eton College and the University of Edinburgh, where he studied literature, general science and medicine; M. D., 1764; elected Fellow of the Royal Society, 1766; began the practice of medicine at Williamsburg but forsook it for the law; returned to London and studied at Lincoln's Inn and the Middle Temple, 1768; admitted to the bar, 1775; wrote extensively in the defense of the rights of the American Colonists; appointed one of the three commissioners (the others were Franklin and Deane) to negotiate a treaty with France and secure aid, the result being the Treaty of Commerce and Amity, 1778; returned to America, 1780, and was elected to the Virginia House of Delegates, 1781; then to the Continental Congress, where he served until 1784; Commissioner to negotiate the Indian treaties of Fort Stanwix, 1784 and Fort McIntosh, 1785; died unmarried at *Landsdowne*, Middlesex County, Virginia, 1792. He was a brother of Francis Lightfoot Lee and Richard Henry Lee, both Signers of the Declaration of Independence, and a cousin of "Lighthorse Harry" Lee, Original Member of the Virginia Cincinnati, and father of General Robert Edward Lee.

Major-General Henry Lee ("Lighthorse Harry").

Born at *Leesylvania*, Prince William County, Virginia, 1756; A. B., College of New Jersey (now Princeton University), 1773; Captain in

Colonel Theodoric Bland's Regiment of Virginia Light Dragoons, 1776, later the First Continental Dragoons, 1777; Major-Commandant, 1778, and Lieutenant-Colonel, 1780, commanding *Lee's Partisan Corps*, to the end of the war; awarded a Gold Medal and the Thanks of Congress for "bravery displayed in the attack at Paulus Hook," 1779; Member of the Virginia House of Delegates, 1785; Member of the Continental Congress, 1785-1788; Member of the Virginia Constitutional Convention, 1788; Lee County, Virginia, named in his honor, 1792; Governor of Virginia, 1791-1794; Commanded the United States forces sent to suppress the Whisky Rebellion in Pennsylvania, 1794; Major-General, United States Army, 1798-1800. Member of the Sixth Congress of the United States, 1799-1801; in a eulogy pronounced, at their request, before both houses of Congress after Washington's death, he pronounced the often-quoted words, "He was first in war, first in peace, and the first in the hearts of his fellow citizens." Died at Cumberland Island, Georgia, 1818. He was the father of General Robert Edward Lee, Confederate States Army. He was one of the Delegates of the Virginia Society at the Triennial General Meeting, Philadelphia, 1784.

MAJOR PIERRE-CHARLES L'ENFANT.

Born at Paris, 1754; Lieutenant, French Colonial Forces, 1776, with permission to serve in America; First Lieutenant, Corps of Engineers, Continental Army, 1776; Captain, 1778, serving at his own expense; wounded at the siege of Savannah, 1779; captured at the fall of Charleston, 1780; exchanged for a Hessian officer, 1782; Major, 1783, be special resolution of Congress at General Washington's recommendation; presented drawings of the Eagle for the approval of members at the first meeting of the Society of the Cincinnati, 1783; returned to France to have the Eagles made, as directed by General Washington, 1783; commissioned Captain, Provisional Forces of France and granted a pension of 300 *livres* by H. M. King Louis XVI, 1783; returned to America, 1784, bringing the diploma plate and the Eagles for distribution at the first Triennial Meeting of the Society in Philadelphia; was only partly reimbursed for the sums he had expended; honorably retired from the Continental Army, 1784; converted the old City Hall of New York City into Federal Hall, and there General Washington was inaugurated as first President of the United States, 1789; designed the city of Washington and was architect of several of the public buildings, 1791; temporary Engineer, constructing the defenses of Fort Mifflin, 1794; laid out the town of Paterson, New Jersey; appointed Professor of Civil and Military Engineering, United States Military

Academy, West Point, 1812, by President Madison, but declined; died in Prince George County, Maryland, 1825, and was there buried, having become an American citizen; reinterred in the National Cemetary, Arlington, Virginia, 1909, with appropriate ceremonies in which the American and French Governments and the Society of the Cincinnati participated.

CAPTAIN NICHOLAS-GEORGES LE ROY.

Ensign, Second Pennsylvania Regiment, Continental Line, 1779; Lieutenant, 1781; transferred to the First Pennsylvania Regiment, 1783; Brevet Captain, 1784 and served until 20 June 1784. He participated in the New Jersey campaign and served later under the orders of Major-General Wayne and Major-General de LaFayette, being present at the siege of Yorktown. He was an original member of the State Society of the Cincinnati of Pennsylvania, transferring in 1784 to the Society of the Cincinnati in France.

THE COUNT DE LILANCOURT.

Jean-Baptiste, Count de Lilancourt-Taste, was Colonel Commandant *en Second* in the northern part of Santo Domingo, 1775; brigadier of colonial troups and Governor of the Colony, 1776-1783. In his capacity of commandant in chief of the troups of Santo Domingo he received from the Count de Grasse information that it was the plan of Generals Washington and Rochambeau to attack either Sir Henry Clinton in New York or Earl Cornwallis at Yorktown. De Grasse asked Lilancourt's cooperation, and he, on his own responsibility, detached a division from his command, and placed it under the orders of the Marquis de Saint-Simon. The troups were embarked in the fleet of de Grasse and in a number of merchant vessels and took part in the siege of Yorktown. Upon Rochambeau's recommendation Lilancourt was admitted an original member of the Cincinnati. In 1784 he was made Brigadier of Infantry and later in the same year, commander-in-chief at Santo Domingo. He was retired in 1785 and created Chevalier of the Royal and Military Order of Saint-Louis. Original member of the French Cincinnati.

MAJOR-GENERAL BENJAMIN LINCOLN.

Born at Hingham, Massachusetts, 24 January 1733; elected town clerk, 1757, and Justice of the Peace, 1762; member of the Massachusetts Legislature, 1772 and 1773 and during the next two years sat in the Provincial Congress, being elected secretary of that body; for a time during the absence of Joseph Warren, 1775, he acted as its president. Adjutant of the Third Regiment of Suffolk County, 1755; Major, 1763; Lieutenant-Colonel, 1772. Appointed Brigadier-General by the Council, 1776; Major-General, of Militia, 1776, and given command of the troops stationed near Boston; Major-General, Continental Army, 1777; wounded at the battle of Saratoga, 1777, where he succeeded against Burgoyne's flank, breaking the enemy's communications with Canada; Received the Thanks of Congress, 1777, for his conduct at Saratoga; captured by General Clinton in South Carolina, 1779, and paroled; joined the Continental forces at Yorktown and continued in service to the end of the war; appointed Secretary of War by Congress, 1781, being the first holder of that office; appointed to lead the Massachusetts Troops engaged in suppressing Shay's Rebellion, 1787; made his famous night march to Petersham, capturing the remnant of Shay's band; member of the Constitutional Convention, 1788; Lieutenant-Governor of Massachusetts, 1788; Collector of the Port of Boston, 1789; Federal Commissioner to treat with the Creek Indians, 1789 and on a similar mission in Ohio, 1794; Lincoln County, Virginia, one of the three original counties of what is now Kentucky, named in his honor, 1792; died at Boston, 9 May 1810. He was the first President of the Massachusetts Cincinnati.

LUZERNE, see LA LUZERNE.

BREVET MAJOR-GENERAL LACHLAN MCINTOSH.

Born at Raits, Badenoch, Scotland, 1725; brought to Georgia by his parents, Highland Jacobite refugees, 1736; member of the Georgia Provincial Congress, 1775; Colonel, First Georgia Regiment, Continental Line, 1776; Brigadier-General, Continental Army, 1776; wounded in a duel with Governor Button Gwinett of Georgia, 1777; taken prisoner by the British on the fall of Charleston, 1780; exchanged in the same year for General O'Hara (who was destined to make the formal surrender at Yorktown); Brevet Major-General, 1783; elected a delegate to Congress, 1784; was twice Commissioner to adjust boundary disputes between Georgia and South Carolina; one of the four Congressional Commissioners to treat with the Indians, 1785-1786; died at Savannah, 1806. He was the first President of the Georgia Cincinnati.

COLONEL THOMAS MCKEAN.

Born in Chester County, Pennsylvania, 1734; studied law and became Deputy Prothonotary and Recorder for the Probate of Wills,

New Castle County, Delaware, 1752; had extensive legal practice in Delaware and New Jersey; Deputy Attorney General, 1756; Clerk of the Delaware Assembly, 1757-1759; member of the Assembly, 1762-1779; assisted in compiling the provincial laws and was a leader in opposing the Stamp Act, 1765, ordering, as Justice of the Court of Common Pleas, for business to proceed as usual on unstamped paper; Collector of the Port of New Castle, 1771; Speaker of the Assembly, 1772-1773; represented Delaware in the Continental Congress, serving on five standing committees; Signer of the Declaration of Independence, 1776; Speaker of the Delaware Assembly, 1776; Acting President of Delaware, 1777; Chief Justice of Pennsylvania, 1777; at the same time was congressman, assemblyman and acting president of one State and chief justice of another; President of Congress, 1781; Governor of Pennsylvania; 1799; died in Philadelphia, 1817. He was elected an Honorary Member of the Pennsylvania Cincinnati in 1783, and was elected its Vice-President in 1785.

Mr. James Madison.

Born at Port Conway, King George County, Virginia, 1751; studied under private tutors and graduated at the College of New Jersey (now Princeton University), 1771; studied law there for one year and then was admitted to the Virginia bar; Member of the Committee of Safety from Orange County, Virginia, 1774; Delegate to the Williamsburg Convention, 1776; member of the First General Assembly of Virginia, 1776; unanimously elected a member of the Executive Council, 1778; Member of the Continental Congress, 1780-1783 and 1786-1788; prominent delegate in the Federal Constitutional Convention in Philadelphia, 1787, and often known as the "Father of the Constitution of the United States"; elected to the First, Second, Third, and Fourth Congresses of the United States; declined appointment by President Washington of a mission to France, 1794; declined General Washington's offer of appointment as Secretary of State in the same year; Member of the Virginia Assembly from Orange County, 1799; Presidential Elector on the Republican (now Democratic) ticket, 1800; appointed Secretary of State in President Jefferson's Cabinet, 1801; served to 1809; President of the United States, 1809-1817; Delegate to the Virginia Constitutional Convention, 1829; Rector of the University of Virginia and Visitor of the College of William and Mary; died at *Montpelier*, his estate in Orange County, Virginia, 1836.

JOSEPH MANDRILLON.

Born at Bourg in Bresse, 1743 at an early age entered commerce; made a voyage to America and opened an office in Amsterdam. He took part in the political troubles which upset Holland at this period, and published a number of tracts against the Stadtholder. At the beginning of the French Revolution he went to Paris where he alligned himself with the constitutional party. He was accused of having engaged in treasonable correspondence with the Duke of Berwick, and was condemned to death. He was guillotined on 7 January 1794. He published, *Le Voyageur américain, ou Observations sur les colonies britanniques* (Amsterdam, 1783), and also a translation from the English, *Le Spectateur américain, or Remarques générales sur l'Amérique septentrionale* (Amsterdam, 1784; Bruxelles, 1785 and 1795). He was a persistant petitioner for membership in the Cincinnati because of his interest in the United States. In his letter of 24 January 1787 to General Washington, he signed himself " Member of the Academies of Science of Holland, Bresse and Philadelphia."

MARBOIS, see BARBÉ-MARBOIS.

CAPTAIN ANTOINE-CLAUDE DE MARCELLIN.

Commissioned Ensign, Second Pennsylvania Regiment, Continental Line, 1779; Lieutenant, 1781; transferred to the Third Pennsylvania Regiment, 1783; retained in the Pennsylvania Battalion, 1783; brevet Captain, 1784 and served until 20 June, 1784; original member of the State Society of the Cincinnati of Pennsylvania.

SEÑOR ESTEVÁN JOSEPH MARTINEZ.

This Spanish officer has not been identified. He was probably a junior officer ineligible for membership in the Cincinnati. Only his own statements, in his letter to General Washington, 14 April 1792, are found as to his service.

LIEUTENANT-COLONEL FRANCIS MENTGES.

Commissioned Adjutant of Atlee's Pennsylvania Musket Battalion, 22 March 1776; First Lieutenant, 9 August 1776; Major Eleventh Pennsylvania Regiment, Continental Line, 27 September 1776 (or 25 October 1776 according to *Pennsylvania Archives*) ; transferred to the Seventh Pennsylvania Regiment, Continental Line, 1 July 1778; Lieutenant-Colonel Fifth Pennsylvania Regiment, Continental Line, 9

October 1778; retired 1 January 1783. He was an original member of the State Society of the Cincinnati of Pennsylvania, and a member of the Standing Committee, 1786-1800.

JUDGE JAMES MERCER.

Born at *Marlborough,* Stafford County, Virginia, 1736; educated at the College of William and Mary; Captain, French and Indian (Seven Years) War, being for a time stationed at Fort Loudoun at Winchester, Virginia; studied law and was admitted to the bar; represented Hampshire County, Virginia (now West Virginia) in the House of Burgesses, 1762-1776; member of the Virginia Conventions of 1774, 1775 and 1776; member of the first Committee of Safety of Virginia, 1776; Member of the Continental Congress, 1779-1780; Judge of the General Court of Virginia, 1779-1789; Trustee and President of the Fredericksburg Academy, 1786-1790; Judge of the first Virginia Court of Appeals, 1789 until his death in Richmond, Virginia, 1793. He was a brother of Lieutenant-Colonel John Francis Mercer, also a member of Congress.

COLONEL WUIBERT DE MÉZIÈRES.

Antoine-Félix Wuibert de Mézières came to the United States as a volunteer, and was commissioned Engineer, 26 June 1776, and stationed first at New York; promoted Lieutenant-Colonel, and took part in the defense of Fort Washington, where he was taken prisoner by the enemy on 16 December 1776; sent to England he was exchanged in 1778. He was invited by Captain John Paul Jones to embark in his *Bonhomme Richard* 40, took part in the famous engagement with *H. M. S. Serapis.* He was made prisoner for a second time in the Antilles and soon exchanged. For the third time he was captured by the British while en route back to the United States in a commercial vessel. He was exchanged, 3 September, 1781 and on reaching Philadelphia was appointed Colonel and Chief Engineer, 1783. He served as such to the end of the war and became an original member of the State Society of the Cincinnati of Pennsylvania; transferred to the French Cincinnati, July, 1784.

MAJOR-GENERAL THOMAS MIFFLIN.

Born in Philadelphia, 1744; graduated at the College of Philadelphia (now the University of Pennsylvania), 1760; entered business in Philadelphia, after travel in Europe; member of the Pennsylvania

Provincial Assembly, 1772 and for four successive years; member of the First Continental Congress and helped to draft the Association of 1774; elected to the Second Continental Congress, but sought military service after the battle of Lexington; commissioned Major, 1775, and appointed Aide-de-Camp to General Washington; Major and Quartermaster-General, Continental Army, 1775; with rank of Colonel also 1775; Brigadier-General, 1776 and relieved as Quartermaster-General; present at the battles of Trenton and Princeton; Major-General, Continental Army, 1777; assisted in the defenses of Philadelphia: Member of the Board of War, 1777; resigned, 1779 but continued to hold the grade of Major-General without pay; member of the Pennsylvania Assembly, 1779; Member of the Continental Congress, 1782-1784; member of the Federal Convention, 1787; member of the Supreme Executive Council of Pennsylvania, 1788, being its President until 1790; Governor of Pennsylvania, 1790-1799; died Lancaster, Pennsylvania, 1800. He was the second President of the Pennsylvania Cincinnati, elected in 1789, succeeding Major-General St. Clair when the latter became Governor of the Northwest Territory. In 1787 he was elected Vice-President General as successor to General Gates.

The Chevalier de Montlezun de La Barthette.

Jean-François du Moulin de La Barthette, Chevalier de Montlezun, was born at Aire (Guyene), 14 June, 1729; he was known in the Army as the Chevalier de Montlezun. Lieutenant in the Regiment of Auvergne, 1745; Captain, 1755; Captain of Grenadiers, 1774; *Chef de Battalion*, 1775; Captain Commandant of the Regiment de Gâtenais, 1776; Lieutenant-Colonel of the Regiment de Touraine, 1779; took part in the campaigns of 1745-1748 in Germany and Flanders, and that of 1752-1762 in Germany. Served in America from 1778 to 1782; Attached to the Regiment of Touraine he left the Antilles in 1778 under the orders of the Marquis de Saint-Simon, being present at the siege of Yorktown. The same regiment, after a short stay in Martinique, reembarked, under the orders of the Count de Grasse and the Marquis de Bouillé, and took part in the capture of Brimstone Hill in the island of Saint Christopher, 1782: He was wounded in naval combat three days before the battle of Les Saintes, this being the third time he had been wounded in action—the first at the capture of the citadel of Antwerp, 1746, and the second at the action at Corbach, 1760. Chevalier of the Royal Order of Saint-Louis. Original member of the French Cincinnati.

Major-General William Moultrie.

Born in Charleston, South Carolina, 1730; member of the House of Commons, 1751; Captain in the Provincial Regiment in the Cherokee War; for some ten years a Member of the Assembly; Member of the First and Second Provincial Congresses, 1775-1780; Colonel, Second South Carolina Regiment, Continental Line, 1775; received the Thanks of Congress, 1776, for his gallant conduct in repulsing the British attack on South Carolina; Brigadier-General, Continental Army, 1776; defeated the enemy at Beaufort, 1778; was captured at the fall of Charleston, 1780; a prisoner on parole for two years at Haddrell's Point, opposite the city; exchanged, 1782; Major-General, Continental Army, 1782; member of the South Carolina House of Representatives, 1783; Lieutenant-Governor of South Carolina, 1784; Governor, 1785; member of the Senate, 1787; member of the South Carolina Convention which ratified the Federal Constitution, 1789; died in Charleston, 1805. First President of the South Carolina Cincinnati. Fort Moultrie, in Charleston Harbor, bears his name.

Brevet Lieutenant-Colonel Thomas Mullens.

A volunteer in the Regiment de Clare, Irish Brigade of the French Army, 1760; sublieutenant in the Berwick Regiment, 1770; received permission to go to America as a volunteer, 1776; Brigade-Major to Brigadier-General Prudhomme de Borre, 19 May to 14 September, 1777; received the brevet of Lieutenant-Colonel for his brilliant conduct at the battles of Germantown and Brandywine; Aide-de-Camp and Brigade-Major to Major-General Thomas Conway, 3 October 1777 to 28 April 1778; permitted to return to France, 1778; First Lieutenant in the Berwick Regiment, 1778; Captain, 1779, when he was appointed to a company of Guides destined for service with Rochambeau's army in the United States; served through the remainder of the War of Independence under Rochambeau being present at the siege of Yorktown, 1780; *Capitaine en second* in the Berwick Regiment, 1785; became Captain Commandant in the following year; retired from the French service, 1791; Chevalier of the Royal and Military Order of Saint-Louis; original member of the French Cincinnati.

The Viscount de Noailles.

Louis-Marie, Viscount de Noailles, was born in Paris, 1756, son of Maréchal de Mouchy, and brother-in-law of LaFayette. He commanded one of the assault divisions at the siege of Savannah, later commanding the *Régiment de Soissonais* to the end of the American War. He participated in the naval engagement in the Chesapeake and at the siege of Yorktown, where he presented the articles of capitulation. He was a deputy of the *Noblesse* to the States General, 1789, and proposed the abolition of the privileges of the nobility. He was president of the Constitutional Assembly, 1791. During the Reign of Terror he escaped to the United States, 1792, returning to France in 1803. He served in the expedition to Santo Domingo where he was gravely wounded, dying at Havana, 1804. During the Terror his wife, both parents, his paternal grand-parents, his maternal grandmother, and his mother-in-law, the Duchesse d'Ayen, perished on the guillotine. His descendant and representative in the French Cincinnati, Adrien-Maurice, Duke de Noailles, was one of the official guests of the United States at the Yorktown Centennial, 1931.

Mr. Thomas Paine.

Born in Thetford, England, 1737, son of a poor Quaker corset-maker; attended school until thirteen years of age and was then apprenticed to his father's trade; served on a privateer *King of Prussia* in the Seven Years War; was active in attempts to have Parliament raise the wages of excisemen and others; met Benjamin Franklin in London and, impressed by his ideas, secured letters of introduction from him and sailed for Philadelphia, 1774; in Philadelphia supported himself largely by contributing to Aitken's *Pennsylvania Magazine*; his pamphlet, *Common Sense*, published in 1776, urged immediate declaration of independence; 120,000 copies of this publication were sold in a few weeks, and probably half a million in all; in the same year he published *Crisis*, which began with the famous words, " These are times that try men's souls"; appointed Secretary of the Committee on Foreign Affairs, by the Continental Congress, 1777; in 1781 he accompanied John Laurens to France in search of financial aid for the Colonies; after the Peace, spent two years in England; to Paris, 1789 where, as in London, he acted as a self-appointed missionary of world revolution; in 1791 he published his famous *Rights of Man*, the work for which he is best known; was made a Citizen of France, 1792, at the same time that the honor was conferred on Washington, Hamilton, Madison and certain Europeans of republican principles; elected to the Convention, Paris, as a French citizen, 1792; as he could not speak French his friend Condorcet spoke for him; at the trial of King Louis XVI he urged moderation, suggesting that the King be imprisoned until after the war or banished for life; after the fall of the Gironde group he did not attend the Convention longer; deprived of his French citizenship and imprisoned, 1793, as an Englishman, though he was at the time outlawed in England; was never brought to trial; released at the request of Colonel James Monroe, American Minister, who claimed him as an American citizen; on his release from prison, 1795, he was restored to his seat in the Convention; lived in Paris until the Treaty of Amiens, 1802, after which he returned to America; in 1796 he wrote to General Washington accusing him of bad faith or at least indifference to his sufferings in France, a letter that did much to injure Paine's reputation in the United States; died at New Rochelle, New York, 1809. His influence during the American and French Revolution was very great, but it is difficult, even now, to arrive at a fair judgment of his acts and of his place in history.

Major William Pierce.

Born, 1740, probably, in Georgia, though he spoke of himself as a Virginian and serving the Revolution as a Virginia officer; Captain, First Continental Artillery, 1776; served as aide-de-camp to Generals Sullivan and Greene throughout the war; received the Thanks of Congress "in testimony of his particular activity and good conduct during the whole action at Eutaw Springs, S. C."; was also presented with a sword; Brevet-Major, 1783; member of the Georgia House of Representatives 1786; member of the Continental Congress from Georgia, 1786; member of the Federal Convention to frame the Constitution, 1787; died in Savannah, 1789. He was the Vice-President of the Georgia Cincinnati, being the second holder of that office.

Portail see Duportail.

Lieutenant de Genevy de Pusignan.

Alexandre-César de Genevy de Pusignan was born 4 April 1741 at Roanne (Forez). He was *Lieutenant en Second* in the Regiment of Auxonne. According to his letter, 16 October 1784, to General Washington, he was in temporary command of a company at the siege of Yorktown, and was promoted Captain on his return to France. His rank, of course, precluded his admission to the Cincinnati.

Brigadier-General Rufus Putnam.

Born at Sutton, Massachusetts, 1738; apprenticed to a millwright, 1754; and was educated unaided; served in the French and Indian War, 1757, in the region of Lake Champlain, where his practical training came into play in the construction of defensive works; thereafter practiced surveying; member of a committee to explore and survey the lands on the Mississippi that were claimed as bounties by the veterans of the French and Indian War, though the project failed; Lieutenant-Colonel of Brewer's Massachusetts Regiment, 1775; Lieutenant-Colonel 22nd Continental Infantry, 1775; Colonel Engineer, 1776; he sought to have Congress create a Corps of Engineers, and when they did not he resigned and accepted command of a Massachusetts Regiment, serving in that capacity in the campaign against Burgoyne, rebuilding the fortifications at West Point, and later at the engagements at Stonypoint and Verplanck Pont; Brigadier-General, Continental Army, 1783; appointed Surveyor of Western Lands, 1785 by Congress; a leader in the settlement of Revolutionary veterans in Ohio; Judge of the Northwest Territory, 1790; Brigadier-General, United States Army, 1792; as such made a treaty with the lower Wabash tribes at Vincennes, 1792; resigned from the Army, 1793; appointed Surveyor-General of the United States by President Washington, 1796; delegate to the Ohio Constitutional Convention, 1802; died 1824. Original member of the Massachusetts Cincinnati. He was a cousin of Major-General Israel Putnam of Connecticut.

GOVERNOR EDMUND [JENNINGS] RANDOLPH.

Born at *Tazewell Hall*, Williamsburg, Virginia, 1783; graduated at College of William and Mary, 1766; Deputy Mustermaster-General, Southern Department, Continental Army, 1776; Aide-de-Camp to General Washington; Member of the Virginia Convention, 1776; first Attorney General of Virginia, 1776-1786; Member of the Continental Congress, 1779-1782; Governor of Virginia, 1787-1788, refusing re-election; Member of the Virginia House of Delegates, 1788; first Attorney General of the United States (in President Washington's Cabinet), 1789; Secretary of State of the United States, 1794-1795; Grand Master of Masons in Virginia, 1786-1789; Member of the Constitutional Convention, 1787; Randolph County, Virginia, named in his honor, 1787; successfully defended Aaron Burr (member of the New York Cincinnati and former Vice-President of the United States) against a charge of high treason, 1807, the trial taking place in the hall of the House of Delegates in the Virginia Capitol; died at *Carter Hall*, Clarke County, Virginia, 1813. He was one of the Honorary Members of the Virginia Cincinnati elected in the year of its institution, not being eligible to original membership as he has not served the requisite three years.

THE COUNT DE ROCHAMBEAU.

Jean-Baptiste-Donatien de Vimeur, Count (later Marquis) de Rochambeau, Marshal of France, Commander of His Most Christian Majesty's Land Forces in America, 1778. Born at the Château de Rochambeau in Vendôme, 1725; Cadet Cavalry Regiment de Saint-Simon, 1741; served in the War of the Austrian Succession; Cornet, 1742; present at the capture of Ellenbogen and Caden, the relief of Braunau and the retreat to Eger; Captain, 1743, commanding a troop on the Rhine; present at the capture of Weissemburg, of Lautern and of Suffelsheim, the affair of Haguenau and the siege of Fribourg, 1744; present at the sieges of Mons, Charleroi and Namour, and the battle of Raucoux, 1745; Aide-de-Camp to the Count de Clermont-Tonnerre, 1746; Colonel of the Infantry Regiment de la Marche, 1747; commanded his regiment at the battle of Lawfeldt; twice severely wounded, 1747; present at the siege of Maestricht, 1748; Governor of Vendôme, in succession to his father, the Marquis de Rochambeau, 1755; participated in the Minorca expedition under Marshal the Duke de Richelieu, 1756; conducted the assault of Fort St. Philippe and for gallant conduct was promoted Brigadier of Infantry and decorated with the cross of the Royal and Military Order of Saint-Louis, 1756; captured the fort of Rawenstein from the Russians, 1757; present at the defeat of the Hanovarians at Hastenbeck, 1757; present at the battle of Crevelt, 1758; Colonel of the Regiment of Avergne, which he commanded at the battles of Minden and Warbourg, 1759; severely wounded at the battle of Clostercamp, 1760; *Maréchal de Camp* and Inspector General of Infantry, 1761; present at the battles of Grünberg and Filinghausen, 1761; promoted Commander of the Royal and Military Order of Saint-Louis, 1766; promoted Knght Grand Cross of the same, 1771; Governor of Ville-Franche, 1776; assigned command of the Army in Normandy destined for the contemplated invasion of Britain, 1778; Lieutenant-General and assigned command of the *Auxiliary Army* for service in America, 1780; commanded the French land forces in the capture of Yorktown, 1781; invested with the cordon and plaque of a Knight of the Order of the Holy Ghost, 1783; Chief Commander in Picardy, 1784; elected Vice-President of the Society of the Cincinnati in France, 1784; Governor of Alsace, 1789; Member of the Assembly of Notables, 1788; Marshal of France, 1791; Commander of the Army of the North in the Austrian War, 1792; imprisoned in the Conciergerie, tried and acquitted, 1793; appointed Grand Officer of the Legion of Honor by Napoleon, 1804; died at the Château de Rochambeau, 1807.

THE COUNTESS DE ROCHAMBEAU.

The wife of Lieutenant-General the Count de Rochambeau, later Marshal the Marquis de Rochambeau, was Jeanne-Thérèse d'Acosta, daughter of Emmanuel Tellez d'Acosta, *enterpreneur des vivres*, and Marie-Antionette Fizenne, his wife. Her father was very rich and claimed descent from a noble family originally of Trancoso, Portugal. At the time of her marriage to Rochambeau in Paris, 22 December, 1749, the Countess was nineteen years of age, " small of statute and of agreeable face." She brought her husband a *dot* of 316,443 *livres*. She survived her husband.

ROUËRIE, see LA ROUËRIE.

ROY, see LE ROY.

MAJOR-GENERAL ARTHUR ST. CLAIR.

Born at Thurso, Caithness, Scotland, 1736; studied medicine at the University of Edinburgh and was apprenticed to William Hunter, the great London anatomist; Ensign in Sixtieth Foot, British Army, 1757 and served with Lord Amherst in Canada; was with General Wolfe at Quebec, 1758; resigned from army with commission of Lieutenant, 1762; purchased an estate in Pennsylvania; appointed agent of the Colonial Government in western Pennsylvania by Governor Penn, 1771; Justice of the County Court of Westmoreland County at its foundation, 1773; Member of the Committee of Safety for Westmoreland County, 1775; Colonel of Pennsylvania Militia, 1775 and took part in the Canadian expedition; Colonel, Second Pennsylvania Batallion, Continental Line, 1776; Brigadier-General, Continental Army, 1776; Major-General, 1777 and served as such to the end of the war; was with Washington in the campaign and battles of Trenton and Princeton; at Ticonderoga, 1777, for surrender of which was tried by court martial, but exhonorated; Delegate from Pennsylvania to the Continental Congress, 1785-1787; President of the Continental Congress, 1787; Governor of the Northwest Territory, 1787-1802; while serving as such approved the changing of the name of the chief Ohio town from Losantiville to Cincinnati, in honor of the Society; Major-General, United States Army, 1791; defeated by the confederated Indian army at " St. Clair's Defeat," 1791; resigned from the army, 1792; died at his home the *Hermitage,* near Ligonier, Pennsylvania, 1818. First President of the Pennsylvania Cincinnati.

The Chevalier Bonnier de Saint-Cosme.

According to his memorial, he served as an officer of the French Expedition in the American Revolution and was wounded in the chest at the siege of Savannah, 9 October, 1779, at the head of a detachment of 400 men of the Regiment of Armagnac. His name is not found in Contenson's *La Société des Cincinnati et la Guerre Américaine d'Independence* or in Noailles, *Marins et soldats français en Amérique, 1778-1783.* His application for admission to the Order of the Cincinnati was not granted, probably because of his inferior rank.

The Marquis de Saint-Simon.

Claude-Anne de Rouvroy, Marquis de Saint-Simon-Montbléru, was born at the Château de la Faye, Charente, 1743; Cadet of artillery, 1754; Lieutenant of the Regiment of Auvergne, 1756; Lieutenant and Brigade Chief of the Bodyguard of the King of Poland, 1758; Brigadier, 1770, Colonel of Provincial Regiment of Poitiers, 1771; Colonel of the Regiment of Touraine, 1775; Brigadier in the army of the Marshal de Broglie and *Maréchal de Camp,* 1780; Commander of the Royal and Military Order of Saint Louis, 1781; Governor of Saint-Jean-Pied-de-Port, 1782; commanded the detachment of 3,400 men of the Regiments of Gâtinais, Agénois and Touraine with 100 artillerymen and 100 dragoons transported from Santo Domingo to Yorktown by the Count de Grasse, 1781; seriously wounded at the siege of Yorktown, and was highly commended by General Washington for his gallant conduct; Deputy of the Nobility in the States General, 1789; emigrated with the Princes of the Blood, 1792; Adjutant General of the Count d'Artois (later King Charles X), serving with him in Spain, 1793; formed in Spain the Royal Legion of the Pyranees (Saint Simon's Legion), at the head of which he was wounded at Arquinzun, 1794; Lieutenant-General in the Army of the King of Spain; formed the Bourbon Regiment, 1796 and with it served in the Balearic Islands; commanded the Spanish Division which cooperated with the French troops in the campaign against Portugal, 1801; served aganst the French Republic, 1808, and was condemned to death by a military commission; pardoned by Napoleon after confinement in the citadel of Besançon until 1813; Captain-General of Spain, 1814; General of the Waloon Guards and Grandee of Spain, First Class, 1803; Knight Grand Cross of the Royal and Military Order of Saint-Louis and Grand Cross of the Royal Order of Charles III of Spain; died at Madrid, 1819. Original member of the French Cincinnati. His younger brother, Claude de

Rouvroy, Baron de Saint-Simon and their cousin, Claude-Henri de Rouvroy, Count de Saint-Simon, were also members of the Society.

MAJOR WINTHROP SARGENT.

Born at Gloucester, Massachusetts, 1 May 1753; graduated at Harvard College, 1771; Lieutenant of Gridley's Regiment of Massachusetts Artillery, 1775; Captain-Lieutenant of Knox's Regiment of Continental Artillery, 1775; Captain, Third Continental Artillery, 1777; Aide-de-Camp to General Howe, 1780 to the close of the war; Brevet Major, 1783; surveyor on the Seven Ranges in Ohio, 1786; Secretary of the Ohio Company, 1787; took an active part in the settling of the colony at Marietta, 1788; appointed by Congress Secretary of the Northwest Territory of the Ohio, 1787 and was in charge during the frequent and prolonged absences of the Governor, General St. Clair (*q. v.*) ; Adjutant General of the Army in the field under General St. Clair, 1791 and was wounded in action with the Indians on the Maumee, 1791; wounded in the action at Fort Recovery in the same year; first Governor of Mississippi Territory, 1798; died on a steamboat northbound from New Orleans on the Mississippi River, 3 January 1820. He was a member of the American Philosophical Society and of the American Academy of Arts and Sciences. Original Member of the Massachusetts Cincinnati. The best account of what transpired at the first General Meeting of the Society of the Cincinnati, Philadelphia, 1784 is in his journal, which was published by his grandson, Winthrop Sargent, in the Publications of the Historical Society of Pennsylvania, 1858.

MAJOR-GENERAL PHILIP JOHN SCHUYLER.

Born at Albany, New York, 1733; commanded a company under General William Johnson in the expedition against Crown Point, 1755; served under Colonel John Bradstreet in the expedition of 1756; Major and Deputy Commissary under Lord Howe in Abercrombie's ill-fated expedition against Ticonderoga, 1758; Boundary Commissioner to settle line between New York and Massachusetts, 1764; Member of the New York Assembly, 1768; member of the New York Delegation to the Second Continental Congress, 1775; appointed one of the four Major-Generals under General Washington, 1775; tried by court martial but exhonorated for his failure at Ticonderoga, 1777; resigned 1779; member of the Board of Commissioners for Indian Affairs, 1779; Member of the Continental Congress, 1778-1781; New York State Senator, 1780-1784; United States Senator, 1789-1791; member of New York Senate, 1792-1797; United States Senator, 1797-1798, when he resigned on account of ill health. He became Vice-President of the New York Cincinnati in 1786. He died in Albany, 1804. He was the father-in-law of Major-General Alexander Hamilton, second President General of the Society of the Cincinnati. Fort Schuyler, New York, bears his name.

The Marquis de Ségur.

Philippe-Henri, Marquis de Ségur, was born at Paris, 1724; Colonel in the Ségur Regiment, 1745; *Maréchal de Camp*, 1749; Lieutenant-General, 1760; Governor of Franche-Comté, 1775; Minister of War, 1780; Marshal of France, 1783; Knight Commander of the Order of the Holy Ghost, 1767; distinguished himself during the War of the Austrian Succession, particularly at Raucoux, and at Laufeld, at both of which battles he was wounded; gravely wounded at the battle of Clostercamp during the Seven Years' War; succeeded the Prince de Montbarey as Minister of War and as such was actively in charge of preparations for the French Expeditionary Force in America under Rochambeau; remained Minister of War until 1787, playing an important part in army reorganization and helping service conditions for soldiers; abolished flogging in the French Army; created a General Staff; died at Paris 1801. His son, Louis-Philippe, Count de Ségur, *Maréchal de Camp*, was an original member of the French Cincinnati.

Major-General William Smallwood.

Born in Charles County, Maryland, 1732; was sent to school in England; served as a volunteer in the French and Indian War; member of the Maryland Assembly, representing Charles County, 1761 and became one of its leaders. Joined the Maryland Non-partisan Association, 1769; delegate to the Maryland Convention, 1775; in the same year joined the Association of Freemen of Maryland, which advocated " opposition by arms to British troops, employed to enforce obedience to the late acts and statutes of the British Parliament, for raising revenue in America." Colonel of the Maryland Regiment, 1776; wounded at the battle of White Plains, 1776; Brigadier-General, Continental Army, 1776; Major-General, 1780. The Act of Congress of 1780 resolved " That the Thanks of Congress be given Brigadiers Smallwood and Gist, and to the officers and soldiers in the Maryland and Delaware Lines . . . for their bravery and good conduct displayed in the action of the 16th of August last near Camden, in the State of South Carolina "; served to the close of the war. Elected Delegate to the Continental Congress, 1784, but declined to serve; Governor of Maryland, 1794 and reelected for three consecutive terms; as Governor, called the convention which ratified the Constitution of the United States, a movement which had his active support; died unmarried in Prince George's County, Maryland, 12 February 1792. He was the first President of the Maryland Cincinnati.

SOCHET, see TOUCHES.

THE BARON DE STEUBEN.

Frederick William Augustus Henry Ferdinand, Baron von Steuben, or de Steuben, as he called himself in America, was born at Magdeburg, Prussia, 1730; educated at the Jesuit colleges of Neisse and Breslau; present with his father at the siege of Prague, 1744; Cadet in the von Lestwitz Infantry Regiment of Prussian Guards, 1747, and served in the Seven Years War; Ensign, 1749; Lieutenant, 1753; wounded at the battle of Prague, 1757; present at the battle of Rossbach, 1757; Adjutant General of General von Mayer's Corps of Volunteers, 1758; Adjutant General of General von Hulsen's Army, 1759; wounded at the battle of Kunnersdorf, 1759; Adjutant General to General von Knobloch, 1761, and served in the Pommeranian campaign; present at the capture of Schweidnitz, 1761; captured by the Russians at the fall of Treptow, 1761, and sent a prisoner to St. Petersburg; released by the Tsar Peter III, 1762; Aide-de-Camp to H. M. Frederick the Great, King of Prussia, 1762; Grand Marshal of the Court of the Prince of Hohenzollern-Hechingen, 1764-1774; Colonel and Grand Marshal of the Court of the Margrave Karl Frederick of Baden, 1775; while on a visit to Paris became interested in American affairs through the Count de Saint-Germain, French Minister of War, and volunteered for service in the Colonies, to which he was transported at French expense, 1777; Major-General and Inspector General of the Continental Army, 1778; wrote *Regulation for the Order and Discipline of the Troops of the United States,* 1779, which was adopted by the Continental Congress as standard; in command of the District of Virginia, 1780; took part in the siege of Yorktown, 1781; presided at his Headquarters at the meeting of officers which adopted the Institution of the Society of the Cincinnati, and at which it was resolved to request General Washington to become President General, 1783; awarded a gold-hilted sword and given the Thanks of Congress and a pension of $2,400 by Act of Congress, 1784; Vice-President of the New York State Society of the Cincinnati, 1785; President, 1786; designed the flag of the New York Cincinnati, 1786, which in 1905 was adopted by the General Society of the Cincinnati; died at Steubenville, Ohio, 1794, having willed his property to his two Aides-de-Camp, Benjamin Walker and William

North (both members of the Cincinnati) to the exclusion of his Prussian relations. He was a Knight of the Order of Fidelity of Baden, the insignia of which he usually wore with his Eagle of the Cincinnati. His collateral descendants were present, as guests of the United States Government, at the Centennial, 1881, and Sesquicentennial, 1931, of the siege of Yorktown.

MR. THOMAS STONE.

Born at *Poynton Manor*, Charles County, Maryland, 1743; received an early classical education and studied law at Annapolis with Thomas Johnson (first Governor of the State of Maryland) ; practiced law at Frederick, Maryland; Member of the Continental Congress, 1775, 1779, 1784 and 1785; member of the Maryland Senate, 1779-1783; Signer of the Declaration of Independence, 1776; member of the Committee which framed the Articles of Confederation; Maryland Commissioner to confer with those of Virginia over the jurisdiction of the Chesapeake Bay; elected a delegate of Maryland to the Contitutional Convention, but declined to serve on account of the illness of his wife; died at Alexandria, Virginia, 1787.

DR. DAVID STUART.

Dr. David Stuart of Fairfax County, Virginia, a warm friend of General Washington, was appointed by him a member of the first Board of Commissioners for the District of Columbia. He had been appointed by General Washington a member of the Virginia Commission to lay out the Federal City. In 1783 he married Eleanor Calvert Custis, the widow of John Parke Custis, General Washington's stepson, and was often consulted by General Washington about the education of the Custis children. In his will, the General said "to Doctor David Stuart I give my large shaving & dressing Table, and my Telescope." The shaving and dressing table has been restored to Mount Vernon and the telescope is in the possession of the Armour Institute of Technology, Chicago. Fitzpatrick says that Dr. Stuart was the son of John Stuart, third Earl of Bute. This is not borne out by the Scots Peerage (Paul). Moore in his *Famly Life of George Washington* says that Dr. David Stuart was the son of the Rev. William S. Stuart, a graduate of the College of William and Mary, and son of the Rev. David Stuart, rector of St. Paul's Church, King George County, Virginia. Dr. Stuart died about 1815 at the approximate age of sixty-two.

Major-General John Sullivan.

Born at Sommersworth, New Hampshire, 1740; studied law and practiced for several years; Major of New Hampshire Militia, 1772; Delegate to the First Continental Congress, Philadelphia, 1774; member of the Second Continental Congress, 1775, by whom appointed a Brigadier-General, 1775; Major-General, 1776; served through the siege of Boston until the evacuation by the enemy, 1776; succeeded General John Thomas in command of the Northern Army, 1776; captured at the battle of Long Island, 1776 and was taken before Lord Howe, who sent him to Washington with peace overtures; when these failed he was exchanged for General Prescott, British Army; led an unsuccessful expedition against the British posts on Staten Island, 1777; suspended from command by the Continental Congress, for this failure, but was exhonorated; spent winter of 1777-1778 at Valley Forge, later assuming command in Rhode Island; led an expedition into western Pennsylvania, 1779, where he routed the Loyalist and Indian forces; received the Thanks of Congress for this victory; resigned, 1779; Member of the Continental Congress, 1780-1781; member of the New Hampshire Constitutional Convention, 1782; Attorney General of New Hampshire, 1782-1786; President (Governor) of New Hampshire, 1786; Chairman of the New Hampshire Convention of 1788 which ratified the Federal Constitution; Speaker of the New Hampshire Assembly, 1788; President of New Hampshire, 1789; United States District Judge of New Hampshire, 1789 until his death at Durham, New Hampshire, 1795. First President of the New Hampshire Cincinnati.

Brigadier-General Jethro Sumner.

Born in Nansemond County, Virginia, 1733; Lieutenant of Virginia Militia in the French and Indian War, 1755-1761; was in command of Fort Bedford, 1760; emigrated to North Carolina about 1764; Justice of the Peace, 1768; High Sheriff, 1772-1777; represented Bute County in the Revolutionary Provisionary Provincial Congress, 1775, which elected him Major of minute-men of Halifax District; Colonel, third Battalion, North Carolina Continental Line, 1776; present at the defense of Charlestown, 1776; and at Brandywine, Germantown and Valley Forge, 1778; commissioned Brigadier-General by the Continental Congress, 1779; present at battle of Stone Ferry, 1779; aided in the defense of North Carolina when invaded by Cornwallis, 1780; died at his home in Warren County, North Carolina, 1785. First President of the North Carolina Cincinnati.

LIEUTENANT-COLONEL TENCH TILGHMAN.

Born at *Fausley,* Talbot County, Maryland, 1744; graduated at the College of Philadelphia (now University of Pennsylvania), 1761; Secretary and Treasurer of the Continental Congress's Commissioners to the Six Nations, 1775; adopted by the Onondagas; Captain of an independent company of the Flying Camp, 1776; Military Secretary of General Washington, 1776; Lieutenant-Colonel and Aide-de-Camp to General Washington, 1777; presented with "a horse properly caparisoned and an elegant sword in testimony of their high opinion of his merit and ability" by the Continental Congress, 1781; selected by General Washington to carry to the Continental Congress the news of the surrender of Earl Cornwallis, 1781, the highest honor Washington could pay him; Original Member of the Maryland Cincinnati; General Washington presented him with an Eagle that is probably the best preserved of those given by the President General to his military family, and has been used as a model for the replicas now in use; died in Baltimore, 1786.

TILLY, see GARDEUR DE TILLY; and DE GRASSE-TILLY.

SURGEON-GENERAL JAMES TILTON.

Born in Kent County, Delaware, 1745; received degree of Bachelor of Medicine at the College of Philadelphia (now the University of Pennsylvania), 1768; after three years practice of medicine at Dover, Delaware, received the degree of Doctor of Medicine, 1771, from his *alma mater*; Lieutenant of Infantry in the Delaware Militia when the American Revolution began; Regimental Surgeon of the Delaware Regiment, Continental Line, 1776; with that regiment present at the battles of White Plains, Trenton, and Princeton, where the regiment was almost wiped out; Hospital Physician, Continental Army, 1777 by Act of Congress; in command of the hospital at Princeton after the retreat from the battle of Brandywine, 1777; later was in charge of the military hospitals at Morristown, Trenton, and New Windsor until 1780; conducted a hospital at Williamsburg during the siege of Yorktown, 1781, and was in charge of the hospitals in Yorktown after the surrender; continued in service to the end of the war; first President of the Delaware Cincinnati holding that office until 1795; resumed the practice of medicine at Dover after the war; appointed Physician and Surgeon General of the United States Army during the War of 1812; to him is due the credit for improvements in military sanitation and the introduction of the hut system of quartering troops, the forerunner of modern barracks construction; retired from the service in 1815 on account of a malignant tumor of the knee which necessitated the amputation of his leg, an operation which he withstood with fortitude and, of course, without anesthesia; made all the arrangements for the operation himself and directed the operating surgeon; member of the American Philosophical Society; died at Dover, Delaware, 1822. Tilton General Hospital, Fort Dix, New Jersey, bears his name.

REAR-ADMIRAL CHARLES-RENÉ-DOMINIQUE SOCHET DES TOUCHES.

Charles-René-Dominique Sochet des Touches was born at Luçon, Vendée, 1727. Entered the naval service as ensign, 1743; *Lieutenant de Vaisseau,* 1756; *Capitaine de Vaisseau,* 1772; Commander of the Royal and Military Order of Saint-Louis, 1782; *Chef d'Escadre,* 1784; Rear-Admiral, 1792. He was sent to Ouessant, 1778, in command of the *Neptune* in the fleet of the Chevalier de Ternay, charged with the duty of transporting the French Army under the Count de Rochambeau, 1780. After the death of Ternay he succeeded to the command of the fleet, 15 December 1780, holding the command until the arrival of the Count de Barras in May of 1781; participated in the indecisive battle in the Chesapeake with Admiral Arbuthnot, 16 March 1781; present at the siege of Yorktown, 1781; received the Thanks of Congress, 4 April, 1781, with a pension equivalent to 800 *livres.* After the close of the Yorktown campaign, he was sent to Saint-Christophers. He was arrested in March, 1793, in connection with the troubles of the Vendée, but was liberated by the *Vendéens* in the following May; served in their army and fell at Prinquian, Lower Loire, in 1794. Original Member of the French Cincinnati the *Institution* itself declaring him a member.

COLONEL DE TOURVILLE.

Charles-Bertin-Gaston Chapuy de Tourville, entered the French service in 1755; commissioned sublieutenant in the Regiment of Auvergne, 1756; major in the Gâtinais Regiment, 1776; served under the Count d'Estaing in Rhode Island, before Boston and at the siege of Savannah, where he was wounded. He was ordered from Santo Domingo to Yorktown under the orders of the Marquis de Saint-Simon, where he took over the duties of major-general of the detachment; promoted lieutenant Colonel in the Royal Auvergne (formerly Gâtinais) Regiment; later becoming Colonel of the same, which was known as the Eighteenth Regiment of Infantry in 1791. He was a Knight of the Royal and Military Order of Saint-Louis. Elected an Honorary Member of the French Cincinnati at its foundation.

Governor Jonathan Trumbull.

Born at Lebanon, Connecticut, 1710; graduated at Harvard, 1727; licensed as a minister by the Windham Association, and was considering a call when, 1731, his elder brother died and he entered business with his father. Member of the General Assembly, 1733; Speaker, 1739; member of the Council, 1754; Deputy Governor, 1766. As Chief Justice of Connecticut he was successful in turning aside applications of royal customs officers for writs of assistance, 1768-1769; Governor of Connecticut, 1769, and actively supported the Continental cause. " His relations with Washington became close, the commander writing him on an average of every ten days until 1778, thereafter less frequently." Said by some to have been the prototype of " Brother Jonathan." LL. D. of Yale and of Edinburgh. Died 1785. His son, also Jonathan Trumbull, was a Revolutionary soldier, Governor of Connecticut, and original member of the Connecticut Cincinnati.

Deputy Adjutant General Jonathan Trumbull, Jr.

Jonathan Trumbull, Jr., son of Governor Jonathan Trumbull, was born at Lebanon, Connecticut, 1740; entered Harvard College at the age of fifteen, graduating, 1759 as salutatorian of his class; M. A., 1762 when he delivered the commencement oration. Selectman of Lebanon, 1770; Member of the Connecticut Legislature, 1774, 1775, 1779, 1780, and 1788, in the last mentioned year he was elected Speaker of the House. Appointed by the Continental Congress, " Pay master of the forces for the New York department, 1775. He was the first Comptroller of the Treasury, to which office he was elected by Congress, 1778. In 1781 appointed Lieutenant-Colonel and Military Secretary to General Washington, Commander-in-Chief and continued as such to the end of the War. Member of the First, Second, and Third Congresses of the United States; Speaker of the House of Representatives, 1791. Member of the United States Senate, 1794; Deputy Governor of Connecticut, 1796; Governor, 1797. Died at Lebanon, 1809. He was the first Secretary of the Connecticut Cincinnati.

Major George Turner.

Second Lieutenant, First South Carolina Regiment, Continental Line, 17 June 1775; First Lieutenant, 16 May 1776; Captain 28 April 1777; In 1778 he was appointed Aide-de-Camp, with the rank of Major, to General Robert Howe, while retaining his commission in the line; taken prisoner at the fall of Charleston, 12 May 1780. He was paroled to

Philadelphia in 1781 and was appointed Commissary of Marine Prisoners; resided there until the peace, never resigning his commission in the line. In his absence from South Carolina he was deranged upon the reform of the Southern Army and so deprived of his right at that time to the brevet of major. Brevet Major, 30 September 1783; original member of the Society of the Cincinnati of the State of South Carolina. The Society's records of 1793 mentioned him as being in Marietta (Ohio?). In 1787 he was elected Assistant Secretary General of the Cincinnati, being succeeded at the Triennial of 1790 by William McPherson of Pennsylvania.

VALLIÈRE, see LA VALLIÈRE.

MR. SAMUEL VAUGHAN.

A London merchant, resident in Virginia, was born in 1720. He was a deep admirer of General Washington. His manuscript sketch of the serpentine road, west of the mansion at Mount Vernon, is preserved there. In February, 1785, he sent General Washington "a marble chimney piece," mentioned in the General's diary under date of 6 April, 1785. It consists of three panels, sculptured in high relief, celebrating agricultural life. It has never been removed from its original position and may be seen today at Mount Vernon. Vaughan visited Mount Vernon in 1787, at which time he made the "sketch plan." He returned to London soon after this. The portrait of General Washington by Gilbert Stuart, known as the "Vaughan type portrait," was ordered by Samuel Vaughan's son, John, a resident of Philadelphia, for his father. Samuel Vaughan died in 1802.

MONSIEUR DE VENIE.

The name "Venie" is almost unquestionably a misspelling, of which General Washington's Letter Books are full. There were three officers of the name *Vernier* in the Regiment of Metz, Auxiliary Army: Jean Vernier, *Lieutenant en troisième,* born 14 February 1737 at Blamont; Jean-Paul Vernier, also a *Lieutenant en troisième*; and "Vernier, aide major," about whom nothing further is stated. General Washington was probably writing to one of these officers, but there is no way of knowing which.

THE COUNT DE VERGENNES.

Charles Gravier, Count de Vergennes, was born at Dijon, 1717; Secretary of the Embassy in Portugal, 1740-1749, with his uncle, de Chavigny, whom he accompanied to Germany, 1744; Minister Plenipotentiary at Trèves, 1750; Ambassador at Constantinople, 1754; at Stockholm, 1771; appointed Minister of Foreign Affairs by King Louis XVI, 1774 in the ministry of Maurepas. He renewed the alliance with the Swiss Cantons by the Treaty of Soleure, 1777 and maintained peace in Europe against the Emperor Joseph II, by the Treaty of Teschen, 1779; best known for his preparations for French participation in America's War of Independence; died at Versailles, 1787.

The Marquis de Vienne.

Louis-Pierre, Marquis de Vienne, was born in Paris, 1746; Lieutenant *à la suite*, 1754, in the Regiment de Clermont, cavalry, commanded by his father, Lieutenant-General the Marquis de Vienne; Cornet, 1757; Captain of La Marche Cavalry Regiment, 1757; Major of Cavalry in the same regiment, 1757; by royal permission he came to America in 1778 as a volunteer; served in Rhode Island under the Count d'Estaing; *Maréchal des Logis* at St. Lucia, Grenada, and Savannah; returned to France, 1780; emigrated, 1791 and was employed at Treves in the service of the Princes; *Chasseur Noble à pied* in the Army of Condé at Nuremberg, 1800; Colonel, 1816; *Maréchal de Camp* (honorary), 1825; created a Chevalier of the Royal and Military Order of Saint-Louis, 1780. For service in America he received the brevet of Colonel (not Lieutenant-Colonel, as stated by Heitman, who calls him " de Vienna ").

The Baron de Vioménil.

Antoine-Charles du Houx, Baron de Vioménil was born at Fauconcourt, Lorraine, 1728. Commissioned in the Regiment de Limousin, 1740; Ensign, 1741; Captain, 1747; Chevalier of the Royal Military Order of Saint-Louis, 1758; Colonel of volunteers of Dauphiné, 1759; Brigadier of Infantry, 1762; Colonel of the Legion of Hainault (later the Legion of Lorraine), 1763; *Maréchal de Camp*, 1768; Royal Commissioner to Poland, 1771; Commander of the Royal and Military Order of Saint-Louis, 1771; Inspector General of Light Troops, 1772; commanded a brigade in the Lorraine Division, and as second in command to the Count de Rochambeau, served in America during the War for Independence. After Rochambeau's return to France, 1780, assumed command of the French Expeditionary Force; Governor of La Rochelle and Knight Grand Cross of the Royal and Military Order of Saint-Louis, 1781; Lieutenant-General, 1783; commander of the second division of Lorraine, 1788; retired 1790. He served in the campaigns of 1744 to 1748 in Flanders and was wounded at the siege of Berg op Zoom. Aide-de-Camp to Lieutenant-General Chevert in Germany, 1757, and served with the Austrian Army, 1758-1762 in Germany and 1768-1769 in Corsica. In 1771 with a group of French volunteers in Poland opposed the Confederation of Bar, taking part in the defense of the Castle of Krakow. In America he took part in all the principal operations of the French forces, particularly distinguishing himself against Benedict Arnold in Virginia. He was in the naval battle of 1781 on board the *Duc de Bourgogne.* At the siege of Yorktown he commanded one of the assault columns. Thereafter he returned to France but came again to America in 1782 in the *Hermione.* Was present on board the *Gloria* of 40 guns against the *Hector* of 74 guns. Took command of the French Army at Boston in December 1782 and received the Thanks of Congress and the personal congratulations of General Washington. Special commissioner to Coblenz, 1792. As a loyal defender of the Royal Family he was mortally wounded in the defense of the Tuileries, 1792. Through an oversight and possibly a misinterpretation of the Institution, he was not at first admitted to the Cincinnati as an original member, a mistake soon rectified by the Society. His younger brother, Charles-Joseph-Hyacinthe du Houx, Count (later Marquis) de Vioménil, was also an original member of the Cincinnati as was likewise Charles-Gabriel du Houx, Baron de Vioménil.

LIEUTENANT-COLONEL BENJAMIN WALKER.

Born in London, England, 1753; attended the Blue-coat School; emigrated to America and settled in New York City; Second Lieutenant, First New York Regiment, Continental Line, 1776; First Lieutenant, Webb's Continental Regiment, 1777; Captain, 1777; transferred to the Third Connecticut Regiment, Continental Line, 1781; Major and Aide-de-Camp to General Parsons, 1780; subsequently Aide-de-Camp to General Steuben, and later to General Washington; Naval Officer of Customs at the port of New York, 1791-1798; removed to Fort Schuyler, New York (now Utica), 1797; agent of the Earl of Bath for his estates in New York; Member of the Seventh Congress of the United States, 1801-1803, declining renomination; died in Utica, New York, 1818. General Steuben made him and Major North, his other Aide-de-Camp, his heirs at law. Their bas reliefs appear on the Steuben Statue in LaFayette Park, Washington. He was the first Secretary of the New York Cincinnati.

BRIGADIER-GENERAL GEORGE WEEDON.

Born in Westmoreland County, Virginia, *circa* 1730; Ensign, Virginia Militia, French and Indian War, 1755; Captain-Lieutenant, First

Virginia Regiment at Fort Loudon, 1758; Captain, Spotsylvania County, Virginia, Militia, 1764; Lieutenant-Colonel, Third Virginia Regiment, Continental Line, 1776; Colonel 1776; present at the battles of Brandywine and Germantown, 1777; Acting Adjutant General, Continental Army, 1777; Brigadier-General, Continental Army, 1777-1783; Commanded the Virginia Militia at the Siege of Yorktown, 1781; Postmaster at Fredericksburg, Virginia with office in the Rising Sun Tavern, until his death; First President of the Virginia Cincinnati; Representative of the Virginia Society on the Standing Committee of the General Society, 1783, until his death; died at Fredericksburg, 1793, unmarried. In the Rising Sun Tavern, built by General Washington's brother Charles, the Virginia Cincinnati first dined together, 1783. Their decendants there celebrated the sesquicentennial of the society a century and a half later.

Brigadier-General Otho Holland Williams.

Born in Prince Georges County, Maryland, 1749; family removed to the mouth of Conococheague Creek, then Frederick County, 1750; at this place General Williams in 1787 founded the town of Williamsport; family removed to Baltimore, 1767 where young Williams was employed as a clerk until 1774 when he returned to Frederick and embarked upon a commercial career. Commissioned First Lieutenant of Cresap's Company of Maryland Riflemen, 1775; served as such in the New England campaign and was present at the siege of Boston, being promoted Captain; when the rifle companies of Maryland and Virginia were consolidated, was made Major of Stephenson's Maryland and Virginia Rifle Regiment, 1776; taken prisoner at Fort Washington, 1776 where he was severely wounded; confined in New York where he shared a cell with Ethan Allen, exchanged, 1778; in meantime had been commissioned Colonel of the Sixth Maryland Regiment, Continental Line, 1776; rejoined the army and served in New Jersey, being present at the battle of Monmouth; was deputy adjutant-general under General Gates, 1780, was present at the battles of Camden and King's Mountain. Transferred to the First Maryland Regiment, Continental Line 1781; commanded the rear guard during Greene's retreat across North Carolina and took a distinguished part in the battles of Guilford Court House, Hobkirk Hill and Eutaw Springs; promoted Brigadier-General, Continental Army, 1782 and served as such to the end of the War; Naval Officer of the Baltimore district by election of the Maryland Legislature, 1783; appointed Collector of the Port of Baltimore by President Washington, 1789; on account of ill-health, declined the appointment as senior Brigadier-General commanding the

United States Army, 1792; died at Miller's Town, Virginia, 1794, and is buried at Williamsport, Maryland. He was the first Secretary of the Maryland Cincinnati, being elected its Vice-President in 1787, and President in 1792. He was elected the first Assistant Secretary General in 1784.

BRIGADIER-GENERAL JAMES WOOD.

Born on Frederick County, Virginia, 1741; member of the Virginia House of Burgesses from Frederick County, 1766-1775, being very active in Colonial affairs, particularly treaties with the Indians; member of the Constitutional Convention of 1776; member of the special committee to settle the affairs of Lord Dunmore, Governor of Virginia; Colonel of the Twelfth Virginia Regiment, Continental Line, 1776; this regiment designated the Eighth Virginia, 1778; served to the close of the War; Member of the Standing Committee of the Virginia Cincinnati elected at the time the Society was instituted, 1783. Represented the Virginia Society at the Triennial General Meeting of 1784. Brigadier-General of Virginia Militia, 1789; Vice-President of the Society of the Cincinnati in the State of Virginia, 1789; Member of the Executive Council of Virginia, 1784, and by seniority became Lieutenant-Governor; Governor of Virginia, 1796-1799; Clerk and Vestryman of Frederick Parish; Wood County, Virginia (now in West Virginia), named in his honor; President of the Society of the Cincinnati in the State of Virginia from 1802 until his death near Richmond, 1813. An active member of the "Virginia Society for Promoting the Abolition of Slavery and Protecting those Illegally Held in Bondage." In 1789 was one of the Presidential Electors who chose General Washington for President of the United States. Buried in the churchyard of St. John's Church, Richmond, where Patrick Henry made his famous oration.

WUIBERT, see MÉZIÈRES.

INDEX

INDEX

J

K

L

Q

R

Y

Z

PUBLICATIONS ABOUT THE SOCIETY OF THE CINCINNATI

BY

EDGAR ERSKINE HUME

BOOKS

1. Sesquicentennial History and Roster of the Society of the Cincinnati in the State of Virginia, 1783-1933, Richmond, published by the Virginia Cincinnati, 1933, 312 pages, 86 illustrations.
2. LaFayette and the Society of the Cincinnati. With introduction by the Duke de Broglie, Member of the French Academy, President of the Society of the Cincinnati in France, *Institut Français de Washington,* the Johns Hopkins Press, Baltimore, 1934, 63 pages.
3. Rules of Admission of the Society of the Cincinnati. Published by the Society under a resolution of 7 May 1932. General rules of admission and special rules of the thirteen State Societies and the Society in France (text of last in both French and English), Washington, 1934, 69 pages.
4. The Gift of the Fund of the Virginia Society of the Cincinnati to Washington College. With introduction by Dr. Francis Pendleton Gaines, President of Washington and Lee University, Richmond, 1935, 54 pages.
5. Brigadier-General Peter Johnston, Jr., Original Member of the Virginia Cincinnati. *Southern Sketches,* First Series, No. 4 Charlottesville, Virginia, 1935, 13 pages.
6. LaFayette in Kentucky. With introduction by His Excellency M. André de Laboulaye, Ambassador of France to the United States, published jointly by the Society of the Cincinnati in the State of Virginia and Transylvania University, Frankfort, Kentucky, 1937, 115 pages.
7. Minutes of the Standing Committee, Formerly known as the Committee on Rules and Ordnances, or the Standing Executive Committee of the Society of the Cincinnati, 1872-1932. Published by the Society of the Cincinnati, Inc., Washington, 1938, 100 pages.
8. Papers of the Society of the Cincinnati in the State of Virginia 1783-1825. Published by the Society of the Cincinnati in the State of Virginia, Inc., Richmond, 1938, 495 pages.
9. General Washington's Correspondence Concerning the Society of the Cincinnati, published by the Johns Hopkins Press, Baltimore, for the Society of the Cincinnati in the State of Virginia, Inc., Richmond, 1941, 516 pages, frontispiece and 7 *fac similia.*

ARTICLES IN JOURNALS

10. The Order of the Cincinnati in France and Original Members who were Légionnaires, *Légion d'Honneur,* New York, October, 1930, i, no. 2, 37-49. Reprinted with additions.
11. The Society of the Cincinnati [with account of the Society's connection with Washington and Lee University], *The Alumni Magazine,* Washington and Lee University, Lexington, Virginia, May, 1932, iii, no. 5, 9-10.
12. George Washington and the Society of the Cincinnati, *Literature Series, Publications of the United States George Washington Bicentennial Commission,* Washington, 1933, iii, 567-576. Reprinted by the Commission with additions and distributed as a Government document to all members of the Society, 34 pages.

13. The Society of the Cincinnati and the Corps of Engineers, United States Army, *The Military Engineer,* Washington, November-December, 1933, xxv, no. 144, 468-473. Reprinted with additions, 21 pages.

14. General George Washington's Eagle of the Society of the Cincinnati, *The Numismatist,* Baltimore, December, 1933, xlvi, no. 12, 749-759. Reprinted.

15. The Society of the Cincinnati in Philately, *The American Philatelist,* Cincinnati, Ohio, January, 1934, xlvii, no. 4, 203-207. Reprinted.

16. The Medals of the Society of the Cincinnati, *The Numismatist,* Baltimore, March, 1934, xlvii, no. 3, 149-158; April, 1934, xlvii, no. 4, 229-239. Reprinted.

17. The Attempt to Establish a State Society of the Cincinnati in Kentucky, *The Register,* Kentucky State Historical Society, Frankfort, July, 1934, xxxii, no. 100, 198-223. Reprinted.

18. Virginia's LaFayette. Address delivered in the old Hall of Delegates in the Capitol at Richmond on the Hundredth Anniversary of LaFayette's Death, 20 May 1934, the Governor of Virginia presiding. Broadcast over WRVA. *William and Mary College Quarterly,* Williamsburg, Virginia, July, 1934, Second Series, xiv, no. 3, 222-229. Reprinted.

19. LaFayette the Virginia Mason. Address delivered in open meeting of Washington-Alexandria Lodge of which Washington was Master and LaFayette a member, *Virginia Masonic Herald,* Highland Springs, Virginia, July, 1934, xxix, no. 6, 9-13. Reprinted.

20. The Virginia Society of the Cincinnati and the Grand Lodge of Virginia, *Virginia Masonic Herald,* Highland Springs, Virginia, November, 1934, xxix, no. 10, 13-16. Reprinted.

21. The Gift of the Fund of the Virginia Society of the Cincinnati to Washington College, *Virginia Magazine of History and Biography,* Richmond, April, 1934, xlii, no. 2, 103-115: July 1934, xlii, no. 3 198-210; October, 1934, xlii, no. 4, 304-316: January, 1935, xliii, no. 1, 47-56. (Later published in book form with additions.)

22. The Diplomas of the Society of the Cincinnati, *Americana,* New York, first quarter, 1935, xxix, no. 1, 7-47. Reprinted with 17 additional plates and a color reproduction, for the first time, of the Diamond Eagle of the Presidents General, 1935, 45 pages.

23. Orange County, Virginia, and the Society of the Cincinnati, *Tyler's Historical and Genealogical Magazine,* Richmond, January, 1935, xvi, no. 3, 175-182. Reprinted.

24. The Naming of the City of Cincinnati, *Ohio Archaeological and Historical Quarterly,* Columbus, January, 1935, xliv, no. 1, 81-91. Reprinted.

25. Steuben and the Society of the Cincinnati, *The American-German Review,* Philadelphia, March, 1935, i, no. 3, 17-59; 54. Reprinted.

26. Polska a Stowarzyszenie Cyncynnatów. Przetłumaczył Mieczysław Haiman [Poland and the Society of the Cincinnati. Translated into Polish by Miecislas Haiman], *Jaskółka* [The Swallow], Stevens Point, Wisconsin, June, 1935, viii, no. 6, 5-9; July, 1935, viii, no. 7, 27-31; August, 1925, viii, no. 8, 39-44. Reprinted.

27. Poland and the Society of the Cincinnati (same as No. 26, but in English), *The Polish-American Review,* Chicago, October, 1935, i, no. 10, 11-31. Reprinted, 1936, 26 pages.

28. LaFayette in Kentucky, *The Register,* published by the Kentucky State Historical Society, Frankfort, April, 1935, xxxiii, no. 103, 118-136; July, 1935, xxxiii, no. 104, 234-251; October, 1935, xxxiii, no. 105, 279-306; January, 1936, xxxiv, no. 106, 42-76; April, 1936, xxxiv, no. 107, 139-156. (Later published in book form with additions.)

29. " Lighthorse Harry " and his Friends of the Cincinnati, Address at the George Washington-Society of the Cincinnati Celebration, Washington and Lee University, 12 April 1935: also at the meeting of the Robert E. Lee Memorial Foundation, Stratford Hall, Virginia, 5 May, 1935, *William and Mary College Quarterly,* Williamsburg, Virginia, July, 1935, xv, no. 3, 271-281. Reprinted.
30. The Society of the Cincinnati and the Tammany Society, *The New York Genealogical and Biographical Record,* New York, January 1936, lxviii, no. 1, 45-50. Reprinted.
31. Admission to the Society of the Cincinnati in the State of Virginia. Questions and Answers for Applicants. Published by the Society, Richmond, 1936, 8 pages.
32. Early Opposition to the Society of the Cincinnati. Address delivered before the Society of the Cincinnati in the State of Rhode Island and Providence Plantations, 4 July 1936, at the Colonial House, Newport, Rhode Island, *Americana,* New York, October, 1936, xxx, no. 4, 597-638.
33. Membership in the Society of the Cincinnati. Address delivered before the National Genealogical Society, Washington, 20 March, 1937, *National Genealogical Quarterly,* Washington, March, 1937, xxv, no. 1, 1-7. Reprinted.
34. Dormant Rights to Membership in the Society of the Cincinnati in the State of Virginia, *William and Mary College Quarterly,* Williamsburg, Virginia, July, 1937, Second Series, xvii, no. 3, 363-370. Reprinted.
35. Same. *The Register,* Kentucky State Historical Society, Frankfort, July, 1937, xxxv, no. 112, 265-272. Reprinted.
36. Sketch of the late Captain Larz Anderson, sometime American Minister to Belgium and Ambassador to Japan. Reprinted from the *Minutes of the Society of the Cincinnati in the State of Virginia, Richmond,* 1937, 121-125, with additions.
37. The Society of the Cincinnati. Speech delivered in the House of Representatives of the United States by the Hon. Virginia E. Jenckes, Member of Congress from Indiana, 19 January, 1938, *Congressional Record,* Washington, 19 January, 1938, lxxxiii, no. 15, 1083-1085.
38. Kościuszko and the Society of the Cincinnati, Programme of *A Night in Poland,* Kościuszko Foundation, New York, 1938, 17-18.
39. The Rôle of the Society of the Cincinnati in the Birth of the Constitution of the United States. Address delivered on Constitution Day, 1937, at Reading, Pennsylvania, *Pennsylvania History,* University of Pennsylvania, Philadelphia, April, 1938, v. no. 2, 101-107. Reprinted.
40. The Society of the Cincinnati and Dickinson College, *Dickinson Alumnus,* Dickinson College, Carlisle, Pennsylvania, May, 1939, xvi, no. 4, 26-29.
41. Society of the Cincinnati, *Britannica Book of the Year,* Chicago, 1939, 163.
42. The Society of the Cincinnati in Fredericksburg Marks its Birthplace and Confers Honorary Membership on General Marshall, Chief of Staff of the United States Army, 30 March 1940. *Tyler's Quarterly Historical and Genealogical Magazine,* Richmond, Virginia, July, 1940, xxii, no. 1, 22-34. Reprinted.
43. Washington College and the Cincinnati, *Washington College Bulletin,* Chestertown, Maryland, July, 1940, xviii, no. 5, 22-24.
44. Rochambeau, Marshal of France: Friend of America. Address delivered 4 July 1940, at the dedication of the Rochambeau Monument, Newport, Rhode Island. Published by the city of Newport, 1940, and distributed at the close of the ceremonies, 15 pages.
45. The Society of the Cincinnati, *Encyclopædia Britannica,* London (new edition), in press.
46. The Society of the Cincinnati, *Americana* (Encyclopedia Americana), New York, new edition, in press.